NIETZSCHE
NOW!

First Warbler Press Edition 2024

ISBN 978-1-962572-41-5 (paperback)
ISBN 978-1-962572-42-2 (e-book)

Library of Congress Control Number 2024930968

warblerpress.com

NIETZSCHE
NOW!

THE GREAT IMMORALIST
ON THE
VITAL ISSUES OF OUR TIME

GLENN WALLIS

warbler press

Praise for *Nietzsche NOW!*
The Great Immoralist on the Vital Issues of Our Time
by Glenn Wallis

"Wallis considers Nietzsche's philosophy as it applies to everyday life. In these pages, the author, a professor, editor, and translator, aims to draw the reader into a kind of 'adventure' with his philosopher subject, Friedrich Nietzsche—it quickly becomes apparent that Wallis sees his project as an intensely modern, relevant discussion rather than an arid intellectual exercise...While offering a fast-paced and surprisingly comprehensive tour of the philosopher's life and works, Wallis attempts to demonstrate that Nietzsche was grappling with some of the same core issues that spark debates and headlines today, from nihilism and public catastrophism to questions of faith and civic responsibility...We need Nietzsche, Wallis insists, and we need him now, because he remains such an 'exceptionally *timely* thinker.' Those who've read Nietzsche and consider him to be a long-winded crank mostly operating on sedatives, sophistry, and syphilis will smile at Wallis's enthusiasm—and will likely be won over by it as well. At every turn, the author combines an encyclopedic knowledge of Nietzsche (his chapter outlining the philosopher's life, 'Reader, Nietzsche' is a tight little masterpiece in its own right) with an empathetic understanding of the man...A surprisingly engaging grafting of Nietzsche's philosophy onto the modern world."
—*Kirkus Reviews*

"Clearly written, relevant accounts are rare in the world of Nietzsche scholarship. *Nietzsche NOW!* is immensely readable. Our 'now' is as pessimistic as Nietzsche's 'now' but Wallis guides us, through Nietzsche's writings, towards coping with the same problems Nietzsche tackled, including truth, democracy, morality, and identity. The same problems but not the same. All now wear modern dress. Wallis's deep knowledge of Buddhism feeds into the transfigurative nature of the *Übermensch,* the radical figure who realizes the possibility for personal and social change, the figure whom we can all— why not?—strive to become."
—Sue Prideaux, author of *Edvard Munch: Behind the Scream,* Winner of the James Tait Black Prize for Biography; *Strindberg: A Life*, Winner of the Duff Cooper Prize; *I Am Dynamite!: A Life of Friedrich Nietzsche*, Winner of the Hawthornden Prize

"As an introduction to Nietzsche's life and thought, Glenn Wallis's book can be heartily recommended. He writes with brio, acumen, and good humour, covering an impressive range of topics, including Nietzsche on the nature of

truth and consciousness, on nihilism, and on values and virtues. He admirably probes his thoughts about democracy and identity, and best of all he shows that he is the thinker we have most to learn from today as we confront our individual and collective decadence. This is a lively and spirited introduction to a masterful stylist and our greatest educator."
—Keith Ansell-Pearson, Emeritus Professor of Philosophy, University of Warwick, England

"Glenn Wallis's *Nietzsche NOW!* is an exhilarating journey through the life and mind of Friedrich Nietzsche, brilliantly contextualizing his philosophy for our era. This vibrant book passionately navigates Nietzsche's time and his groundbreaking ideas, illuminating his influence on modern thought. Wallis masterfully connects Nietzsche's theories on morality, truth, identity, and democracy to today's crucial debates, including 'wokeness' and the iconic *Übermensch*. This work is not just an interpretation but a celebration of Nietzsche's enduring legacy, offering an indispensable, thrilling guide to understanding his philosophical impact in our time."
—Amir Eshel, Edward Clark Crossett Professor of Humanistic Studies, Stanford University

"Nietzsche uncannily predicted both the challenges and some of their solutions, both disastrous and promising, that we live through today. Populism, threats to democracy, the promise of equality, our appetite for destruction, and our willingness to let others think for ourselves—all of these topics are addressed in Glenn Wallis's extremely timely and remarkably accessible book on Nietzsche's legacy. Drawing on a deep knowledge of the academic scholarship but unencumbered by academic prose, as Nietzsche himself would have wanted, Wallis charts a surprisingly useful path through this extremely contemporary philosopher's work for our times."
—Eyal Peretz, Professor of Comparative Literature, Indiana University Bloomington

"At a time where Nietzsche is once again usurped by the far right, Glenn Wallis offers the perfect response. He walks us calmly and confidently through Nietzsche's dense forest of ideas, enabling us to *think with* his life and thought, to resist those who would usurp his thinking, to meditate and overcome along with him. Above all, he brilliantly conveys Nietzsche's sheer joy and living promise: as the philosopher with whom we can, time and again, grind new lenses, direct them, and open unexpected and vibrant new paths."
—Stefanos Geroulanos, New York University

To my grandson, Liam.
May you know *the great health!*

CONTENTS

PROLOGUE
WHY NIETZSCHE? WHY NOW?

LEARNING CHANGES US

THIS BOOK IS A GUIDE TO THINKING. IT TAKES AS FUEL FOR THOUGHT CERTAIN pressing contemporary issues. Our guide in this journey is the nineteenth-century German philosopher Friedrich Nietzsche (1844–1900). So the book is also an introduction to Nietzsche's thought. An important feature of *Nietzsche NOW!* is that it contains abundant passages directly from Nietzsche's writings. In so doing, I am honoring Nietzsche's fervent request, made toward the end of his sane life, that we do not mistake him for who he is not. This may seem obvious; but the history of reading Nietzsche is by and large the history of *mis*reading Nietzsche. So it is essential to read him carefully and thoroughly, like a cow chews her cud, as our guide puts it. Nietzsche has a reputation for being easy to read but hard to understand. He is "easy" (the scare quote is a major Nietzschean tripping warning—*take caution!*) because he is a masterful stylist. Nietzsche is a pleasure to read. He is, however, *difficult*.

Why Nietzsche? Nietzsche was a sworn enemy of the pat answer to a question. He was a devoted acolyte of perspectivism—of carefully considering a matter from multiple angles. His most cherished values were intellectual curiosity and existential courage. He was also scandalously irreverent and hilariously funny. And although he confessed that "*Nausea* toward people is my danger,"[1] his abiding passion was how to create a better world of, by, and for those very same *people*. Anticipating the spirit of "deep ecology" by a century, the better world that he envisioned included care for the earth and for animals. Prismatic, uncategorizable, and daring, Nietzsche is the perfect guide to our times.

---

1 *Ecce Homo*, "Why I Am A Destiny," 6. All translations are mine unless otherwise noted. I am translating from the *Digitale Kritische Gesamtausgabe von Nietzsches Werken und Briefen*: http://doc.nietzschesource.org/de/ekgwb. Wherever possible, however, I provide English titles for books and sections. Although these do, of course, vary from translation to translation, the reader should have no trouble locating the English source based on the information I provide in the notes. The opening epigraph is from *Beyond Good and Evil*, 231.

And how should we define these times? I'll mention three features that I feel are particularly salient to *Nietzsche NOW!* To begin, how about we define our times as *grimly divided*? Exacerbated by an internet culture that is accessible via our smartphones literally every minute day and night, we are at a loud, hostile, and very public impasse concerning vital questions of our shared social life. As the *Associated Press's* "Divided America" series puts it:

> It's no longer just Republican vs. Democrat, or liberal vs. conservative. It's the 1 percent vs. the 99 percent, rural vs. urban, white men against the world. Climate doubters clash with believers. Bathrooms have become battlefields, borders are battle lines. Sex and race, faith and ethnicity…the melting pot seems to be boiling over.[2]

But honestly, is this anything new? The terms of contention and the lines of division change from era to era, but, as any reader of history can tell you, contention and division remain constant. Might dissension simply be a necessary feature of a society? When people form into community—whether a family, a friend group, a workplace, or a nation—is a diversity of viewpoint avoidable? Is it even desirable? After all, what is the alternative—groupthink? Nietzsche does not believe that factionalism and friction necessarily entail discord. Or, expressed in more Nietzschean terms, what sounds discordant to our present ears may be transfigured into a *future music*. Still, given our present differences and what's at stake because of them, the question looms: how should we proceed? Nietzsche has many surprising suggestions; and *Nietzsche NOW!* will share these with the reader.

We have, however, a massive obstacle in our way. That obstacle represents the second defining feature of our times: a morality that is infused with "theologians' blood."[3] If we proceed with our current values in place, if we, consciously or not, insist on proceeding within the bounds of our shared sense of right and wrong, indeed of good and evil, we will remain stuck right where we are. And where are we? Nietzsche wants us to recognize that we are in a cultural-psychological space that "steams with the stench of slaughtered spirit."[4] We, ourselves, of course, are those slaughtered spirits, those diminished "last mortals" emitting the very stench. We have not,

---

2 *The Associated Press*, "Divided America," https://www.ap.org/media-center/press-releases/2016/divided-america-series-to-explore-tensions-underlying-campaign/. Accessed April 3, 2024. Ellipsis in original.
3 *The Antichrist*, 8.
4 *Thus Spoke Zarathustra*, "On Passing By."

however, become such people through mere chance. We have become what we are over two millennia of acquiescence to a quite particular moral code. Nietzsche argues that our morality is tainted by no less than the gargantuan institutional formation known as Christianity. Nietzsche wants us to observe that the influence of Christianity—on our very thinking, feeling, speaking, and acting—is not a benign matter. Quite the contrary, it is "the one great curse, the one great intrinsic depravity"[5] of our civilization. Our very conviction of what is *good, proper, and right*, and, conversely, what is *evil, improper, and wrong*, keeps us, furthermore, locked in the ruts of "modern ideology and the wishful thinking of the herd."[6] Nietzsche insists that the (Christianity-determined) values informing our "morality" must change, must be "transvalued," must be mutated into something more *noble*. Nietzsche is making severe demands on us here. Many readers will balk at these demands. *Nietzsche NOW!* aims to assist the reader in navigating the treacherous currents that follow.

This condition of contingency, of *having become* what we are, points to the third defining feature of our times: "we are experiments."[7] Hardly any matter is more empirically demonstrative than the fact that humanity has always been, is always, in a condition of becoming. This fact is demonstrative both diachronically and synchronically. That is, the long view of human history over time is brimming with evidence that cultures and people are in constant flux, changing their ways, their values, their self-understanding, and their very forms of life. And we can see the same fact playing out simultaneously, right now, over the broad expanse of the earth, with its four-thousand-some distinct cultures. While these changes appear to evolve in reaction to events, Nietzsche believes that we must intervene and proactively experiment with new forms of life. The fact, in Nietzsche's infamous proclamation, is that: "God is dead. God remains dead. And we have killed him."[8] We, *we moderns,* have emptied the universe of the certainties and securities of the past. In so doing, we have initiated an unprecedented cosmic-cultural-existential-psychological crisis that is equal parts liberating and terrifying. Nietzsche offers many high-octane passages about this crisis, and even a few about its resolution. *Nietzsche NOW!* aims to accompany the reader as they encounter the explosive force of his ideas.

Let's begin!

---

5 *The Antichrist*, 62.
6 *Beyond Good and Evil*, 44.
7 *Dawn*, 453.
8 *The Gay Science*, 125.

READER, NIETZSCHE

I WOULD LIKE TO INTRODUCE NIETZSCHE TO READERS UNFAMILIAR WITH HIS WORK.[1] My goal is to convey a *sense* of Nietzsche. Biographical facts are important, of course; but a *sense* of the person is even more so. I will, moreover, convey *my* sense of Nietzsche, as I feel him and understand him. I like Nietzsche. He has been my companion since the mid-1970s. That was when I discovered *Thus Spoke Zarathustra* and, along with my brother and a couple of friends, consulted the book for every pressing issue under a teenager's too-hot sun—becoming oneself, love and relationships, rejecting the herd, the evils of education, overcoming obstacles, and so much more. We felt personally and forcefully addressed by Zarathustra's admonishments: "I say to you: you must have chaos within to give birth to a dancing star."[2] Each of us *longed* to become an *Übermensch*. We were prepared to give whatever we had to follow Zarathustra's advice for *going under, crossing over,* and *rising up.* When, a few years later, I wrote my philosophy undergraduate thesis on his concept of the will to power, I came to know a side of Nietzsche's personality that was different from the, by turns, playful, mournful, silly, prophetic, occasionally adolescent Zarathustra. I was becoming acquainted with the Nietzsche who would soon feel compelled to explain, "I am no bogeyman,

---

1 If you would like to learn more, I recommend five biographies. If you only read one, I'd make it one of my first two suggestions. In Sue Prideaux, *I Am Dynamite!: A Life of Friedrich Nietzsche* (New York: Tim Duggan Books, 2018), Prideaux writes with a sensitivity to subtlety and nuance that would make Nietzsche blush—with pride *and* embarrassment. *I Am Dynamite!* won the prestigious Hawthornden Prize in 2019 and the *London Times* Biography of The Year for 2018. Leslie Chamberlain begins her *Nietzsche in Turin: And Intimate Biography* (New York: Picador Books, 1996) with the statement "This book is an attempt to befriend Nietzsche" and she succeeds. As the subtitle accurately indicates, the book is as deeply personal as it is insightful. It is also imaginative, in the best sense of the word. Curtis Cate's *Friedrich Nietzsche* (New York: The Overlook Press, 2005) is serious and densely detailed. Each of my final two recommendations is a "philosophical biography," the final one, frankly, more of the former than of the latter, though excellent treatments nonetheless: Julian Young, *Friedrich Nietzsche: A Philosophical Biography* (Cambridge: Cambridge University Press, 2010) and Rüdiger Safranski, *Nietzsche: A Philosophical Biography*, translated by Shelley Frisch (New York: W. W. Norton and Company, 2003).

2 *Thus Spoke Zarathustra*, Prologue, 5.

no moral monster.["3] Reading his works over several decades, I have come to have a deep appreciation of Nietzsche's "many colors," his "fifty yellows and browns and greens and reds," his world of richly complex "valuations, colors, accentuation, perspectives, scales, affirmations, and negations." So, here, I will try to do justice to his rich palette and to paint a portrait of our guide as I have come to see him.

Even readers who already know something of our Immoralist might be surprised to learn of the close connection between the person and the philosophy. The connection between the two is more than close; it is inextricable. Nietzsche is, in fact, (unintentionally?) explicit about this point.

> I have gradually come to realize what every great philosophy up to now has been: namely, the self-confession of its originator, and a type of inadvertent and unrecognized memoir; similarly, that the moral (or unmoral) intentions in every philosophy constitute the actual seed out of which the entire plant perpetually grows.[4]

Every thought, every word, every action, in short, every "intention," of a person, Nietzsche believes, seeds not only their philosophy: it contributes to the seeding of the entire "monster of energy"[5] that is our very world. Thinking, being, seeding the world with our intentions, is never the cold, abstract act of reason that philosophers make it out to be. Like mathematicians, philosophers habitually leave out the messy *lived* parts—the failures and wrong turns, the embarrassments and humiliations—and give us only their all-too-tidy, all-too-clever conclusions. Imagine a thinker whose finished product bears the marks of the motley jottings in his notebooks. Nietzsche can occasionally be like that. Next to ominous depictions of the rushing torrent of nihilism, we might read, "I have forgotten my umbrella," or even glimpse his shopping list: "toothpaste, buns, shoe polish."[6] Thinking is as necessary for him, and as personal, as toothpaste. And, speaking of

---

3 *Ecce Homo*, Preface, 2.

4 *Beyond Good and Evil*, 6. The term "up to now" *(bisher)* suggests that Nietzsche's has his *predecessors* in mind here, not himself or those "free spirits" to come. The subtitle to this book is, after all, *Prelude to a Philosophy of the Future*. Still, we would be hard-pressed to find a more self-referential oeuvre than Nietzsche's.

5 *NF*–1885, 38[12].

6 On the umbrella, see Jacques Derrida, *Spurs: Nietzsche's Styles,* translated by Barbara Harlow (Chicago: University of Chicago Press, 1979), 123; on the shopping list, see Bettany Hughes, *BBC Arts,* https://www.bbc.co.uk/programmes/articles/4CVpPWQkwbDzt4w2RjNHf2S/ forward-thinkers-how-marx-nietzsche-and-freud-shaped-the-lives-of-millions. Accessed July 6, 2022.

breakfast buns, Nietzsche learned firsthand that thinking and intending are, more often than we care to admit, an effect not of our exalted reason or intelligence but of the *gastric system*.[7] Your thinking about X or Y may well include traces of bad digestion or a pounding headache. Nietzsche certainly knew both of those painful realities in great intimacy. So let's begin our portrait of Nietzsche with his stomach.

One of Nietzsche's most popular bumper sticker sayings goes: "That which does not kill me makes me stronger."[8] Less well known is "A man should know the size of his stomach."[9] But the two are related. In getting a feeling for Nietzsche, we should know that he was prone to physical suffering, and to the mental desperation that follows in its wake. We should understand, too, that he neither romanticizes nor demonizes pain. As a feature, indeed an intimate feature, of *his* life, Nietzsche wants to learn how to transform inevitable pain into an ingredient of abundance. (What would be the alternative to such "transvaluation," of *not* making such an effort?)

Absolutely no local degeneration can be detected in me. No organically conditioned stomach pain, however severely I have suffered—as a consequence of complete exhaustion—the most profound weakness of the gastric system. The eye pain, too, which sometimes dangerously approached blindness, was only a consequence, not a cause: such that with every increase of vitality my ability to see also increased.—A long, all too long stretch of years means for me convalescence. It also means, unfortunately, relapse, decline, periodicity of a kind of *décadence*. After saying all of this, do I need to mention that I am *experienced* in questions of *décadence*? I have spelled it out frontwards and backwards. Even that delicate art of prehension, and of comprehension in general, that fine feeling for nuances, that psychology of seeing-around-the-corner, and for whatever else I have been capable, was first learned at that time, is indeed the actual gift from that time during which everything became more refined for me, the very ability to observe, as well as all of the organs of observation. To look through the lens of the sick toward *healthier* concepts and values, and again, the other way around, to look from the fullness and self-confidence of the *rich* life down into the secret work of the instinct for *décadence*—this has been

---

7 *Ecce Homo*, "Why I Am So Wise," 2.
8 *Twilight of the Idols*, "Epigrams and Arrows," 8. The full aphorism goes: "*From the military school of life*—What doesn't kill me makes me stronger."
9 *Ecce Homo*, "Why I Am So Clever," 1.

my longest training, my actual experience; if I am a master in anything, it is in this. I can now handle it, I have the hands for it: *reversing perspectives*. This is the first reason why for me alone perhaps a "reval-uation of values" is at all possible.[10]

One of Nietzsche's recurring images is that of "embodiment."[11] In this passage, I see him as an embodiment of his—and, more importantly, of our—culture. We are sick. We suffer serious gastric pain, but not for any inevitable, intrinsic, reason. Our pain is not a cause of our unhappiness. It is an *effect*. We improve here and there, and then lapse again into decline. As a society, we are *profoundly exhausted*. We feel as if we can't go on, that there is no way forward. Hence, we are intimately familiar with *"décadence."* Nietzsche uses this French word to describe not only our personal and col-lective *condition* of decay, decline, exhaustion but also our *attraction* to that which leads to such decline. We have become *too weak* even to resist those elements of culture, society, politics, entertainment, diet, social media, and technology that are destroying our vitality. In our enervating weakness, we have even come to *enjoy* these things.[12] Nietzsche's biography is very much a story of how we might confront and counter our personal and collective decadence. In this sense, his story has a certain *mythological* value for us—slaying the dragon of decadence, reversing the torrent of nihilism, overcom-ing the merely human, becoming an *Übermensch*. Drawn to the hero of our myth, we must emulate his "training." As the foregoing passage puts it, that means becoming adept in such matters as refining our organs of observa-tion, increasing our sensitivity to subtlety and nuance, acquiring the probing intuition of a psychologist. It means not losing sight of potentially healthy values, even while in the very throes of our sickness. And it means to remain vigilant, even in periods of joyous abundance, to the unconscious workings of our instinct for decadence. If we can emulate the hero of our myth and learn the arcane alchemy of *reversing perspectives*, we might just learn the coveted secret of transforming base metal into philosopher's gold—sickness

---

10 *Ecce Homo*, "Why I Am So Wise," 1.

11 The German word is *Einverleibung*.

12 Some readers may recall Neil Postman's 1985 book, *Amusing Ourselves to Death: Public Discourse in the Age of Show Business*. Postman (1931–2003) was a prominent American educator and culture critic. The basic idea in this book is very Nietzschean. Our danger, Postman argues, is depicted less in George Orwell's *1984* than it is in Aldous Huxley's *Brave New World*. That is, our oppression from state control is nothing to our oppression from addiction to amusement. We might say that, through our "instinct for *décadence*," in Nietzsche's words, we *auto-oppress*.

into health, our nihilistic hatred of life into *amor fati* (love of our fate), the decadent into the *Übermensch*. In the end, for Nietzsche the *magis*, it all comes down to the transubstantiation of values.

The more mundane aspects of Nietzsche's life might provide us with additional trainings, *in spirit*. So we will now turn to those.

CHILDHOOD AND YOUTH

I, the son of a Protestant country parson, was born on October 15, 1844 in the village of Röcken, near Merseburg. I lived here the first four years of my life. But when the untimely death of my father necessitated that we find a new home, my mother settled on Naumburg.[13]

Two delicious ironies in the life of Friedrich Wilhelm Nietzsche stand out at the beginning. The first is that Nietzsche was born on the birthday of the King of Prussia, Friedrich Wilhelm IV (1795–1861). Hence, his name. The younger Friedrich Wilhelm would become one of the fiercest despisers of the Prussian state, and, later, of the German Empire under heavy Prussian influence. Indeed, on the example of Prussia, "the state," in general, would become an object of Nietzsche's scorn. An even greater irony is that the self-proclaimed "Antichrist" who condemned Christianity as "the one great curse, the one great inherent depravity, the one great instinct of revenge for which no expedient is poisonous, underhanded, *low* enough—I proclaim it the one immortal stain of mankind,"[14] deeply admired his parson father and had loving lifelong memories of his parsonage home. The Antichrist, it turns out, came from a long line of Lutheran ministers. The six previous generations on his father's side had been Lutheran pastors. Nietzsche's maternal grand-father, too, had been a Lutheran pastor in the village of Pobles, not far from Röcken. Let's not, however, jump to the easy conclusion that Nietzsche's later execration of Christianity stemmed from religious abuses suffered as a child. The religion of his early years was relatively undogmatic and, it seems to me, mainly "cultural." He was, for instance, deeply affected by church music. After hearing the "Hallelujah" chorus from Handel's *Messiah*, Nietzsche wrote that he felt "as if I had to join in…the joyful singing of

---

13 Letter to Wilhelm Vischer. *BVN*–1869, 612. I am also consulting the Prideaux and Young biographies.
14 *The Antichrist*, 62.

angels, on whose billows of sound Jesus ascended to heaven."[15] As we will see, his eventual attack on Christianity was much deeper than anything that can be explained by negative exposure or even by the Oedipal complex ("I consider it a great privilege to have had such a father," he writes toward the end of his active life[16]).

As Nietzsche said, his family had to move out of the parsonage on the early death of his father. So five-year old Nietzsche, his younger sister Elizabeth, his mother, grandmother, two unmarried aunts, and a servant girl eventually moved to the considerably larger town of Naumburg. Nietzsche was surrounded by women in his youth. In a sentiment that would eventually lead him high into the mountains, Nietzsche expresses a feeling of claustrophobic estrangement from his surroundings:

> It was terrible for us to live in the city after we had been living in the country for so long. We avoided the gloomy streets and looked for the open spaces, like birds trying to escape from a cage…The huge churches and buildings of the marketplace, with its *Rathaus* [town administrative building] and fountain, the throngs of people, to which I was unaccustomed…I was astonished by the fact that typically these people did not even know one another. Among the most disturbing things to me were the long paved streets.[17]

From an early age, the precocious boy threw himself into his schoolwork. Falling into a pattern that would last his entire working life, Nietzsche studied until late at night and rose at five in the morning to continue. Because his lifelong health issues were already manifesting, this pattern was also one of "self-overcoming," a central concept in Nietzsche's philosophy. That is, applying himself to what was most valuable to him—in this case, study—*necessitated* an overcoming of the forces, internal and external, that worked against actualization of the value. His health was "devastatingly bad" at this time.

> Harrowing episodes of headaches with vomiting and extreme eye ache might last as long as a whole week during which he had to lie in a darkened room with the curtains drawn. The slightest light hurt his

---

15 Julian Young, *Friedrich Nietzsche: A Philosophical Biography* (Cambridge: Cambridge University Press, 2010), 4.

16 *Ecce Homo*, "Why I Am So Wise," 3.

17 Prideaux, *I Am Dynamite!*, 13.

eyes. Reading, writing and even sustained coherent thought were out of the question. Between Easter 1854 and Easter 1855, for example, he was absent from school for six weeks and five days.[18]

Nietzsche was striving—successfully, it turned out—to get into the renowned Schulpforta. Pforta, as it is known, was (and still is) a boarding school for intellectually gifted students. Founded in 1583 on the site of a twelfth-century Cistercian monastery, Pforta, in Nietzsche's day, retained many monastery-like features. Within its magnificent Gothic buildings, "surrounded by walls twelve foot high and two and a half foot thick,"[19] unfolded an education that was equal parts monastic and militaristic. The school day began at four in the morning and ended at nine at night. It was, using a recurring Nietzschean word, *hard*—extremely rigorous mentally, physically, and emotionally. But the type of education that Nietzsche received suited him very well. Based on the reforms of Wilhelm von Humboldt (1767–1835), Pforta emphasized ancient languages (students often conversed in Greek or Latin), literature (Nietzsche developed a lifelong love of Goethe), and history. The sciences and mathematics were also featured, though Nietzsche would always feel inadequately instructed in the former, and his disinterest in the latter nearly sunk him. Against the vocational orientation preferred by the Prussian state, Humboldt advocated for a deeply humanistic approach. In a letter to the king, he argues for his approach to education *(Bildung)* that forms *(bilden)* the whole person: "People obviously cannot be good craftworkers, merchants, soldiers or businessmen unless, regardless of their occupation, they are good, upstanding and—according to their condition—well-informed human beings and citizens."[20] As congenial as the curriculum was for Nietzsche, completion would take a determined application of his theory of perpetual self-overcoming:

---

18 Prideaux, *I Am Dynamite!*, 23.
19 Prideaux, *I Am Dynamite!*, 25.
20 Karl-Heinz Günther, "Profiles of Educators: Wilhelm von Humboldt (1767–1835)," *Prospects* Vol. 18, (1988), 127–136. https://doi.org/10.1007/BF02192965. Accessed July 15, 2022. Pforta has produced many eminent German figures, including, to name a few, the chancellor of the German Empire from 1909–1917, Theobald von Bethmann-Hollweg (1856–1921); the mathematician and descendant of Martin Luther, August Ferdinand Möbius (1790–1868); a founding philosopher of German Idealism, Johann Gottlieb Fichte (1762–1814); the founder of modern, documentation-driven history, Leopold von Ranke (1795–1886); and the classical philologist who would one day write a scathing take-down of Nietzsche's first book, *The Birth of Tragedy*, Ulrich von Wilamowitz-Moellendorff (1848–1931).

At Pforta they were treating Nietzsche's ghastly episodes of chronic illness, his blinding headaches, suppurating ears, "stomach catarrh," vomiting and nausea with humiliating remedies. He was put to bed in a darkened room with leeches fastened to his earlobes to suck blood from his head. Sometimes they were also applied to his neck. He hated the treatment. He felt it did him no good at all. Between 1859 and 1864 there are twenty entries in the sickness register lasting, on average, a week.[21]

Before moving on to his next life phase, the university, I'd like to share this portrait from Raimund Granier, a Pforta classmate:

In Schulpforta, Nietzsche was an excellent student, as is well known; but if I remember rightly mathematics was not his strong point. He did not stand out especially among his fellow students, but he immersed himself in his school assignments, especially ancient languages, and in his own particular studies…He did not join in the noisy games in the schoolyard, but as a fifth-year student, like we others, he liked to go to the nearby village Altenburg, where he drank not beer but, with great enjoyment, hot chocolate. Already at school he was extremely myopic, and his deep set eyes had a peculiar gleam. His voice could be very deep; generally it was as soft as his whole being. No one would then have suspected that someday he would attempt the revaluation of all values. His mustache, which later became so extraordinarily prom-inent, already began to appear in school…Nietzsche practiced music zealously already in Pforta and, since I can't play any instrument, he played for me, many a time—a lot of Chopin, if I remember rightly.[22]

UNIVERSITY

For his university studies, Nietzsche decided on Bonn. The dual attraction was Friedrich Ritschl (1806–1876) and philology. Ritschl was the fellow son of a poor country parson and, more importantly, the most renowned classical philologist of his time. (Ritschl is still considered the preeminent German classical scholar of the nineteenth century.) Just as importantly for someone

---

21 Prideaux, *I Am Dynamite!*, 36.
22 Sander L. Gilman, ed. *Conversations with Nietzsche: A Life in the Words of His Contemporaries*, translated by David G. Parent (Oxford: Oxford University Press, 1987), 9.

who, like Nietzsche, despised phony formality, Ritschl had a reputation for openness, warmth, humor, and liveliness—highly unusual public traits for a German professor at that time. The fact that dozens of his students went on to splendid careers attests to his fatherly concern and active support for them. Indeed, behind his back, Nietzsche affectionately referred to him as "Father Ritschl."[23] It is important to get a feel for Ritschl because in doing so we deepen our feeling for Nietzsche, who, during a formative period of his life so admired and emulated Ritschl. Here is a description from a student, Basil Gildersleeve (1831–1924), who would go on to become a preeminent American classical scholar and founder of the still-thriving *American Journal of Philology*.

Almost every one of the thousands who attended his courses faithfully could tell the same story. He radiated love and kindness…He stood when he lectured, his notes were there apparently for the fun of the thing, his gestures were animated, there was something almost French about his liveliness. His eyes, though shielded by spectacles, shone with excitement; his nose played a most important part in the drama, for he took snuff by the boxload, as it were, helping himself, at times, from the supply of a convenient student; his mouth went through the whole range of expression from rapt inspiration to bitter sarcasm. He was a thoroughly vivid personality, who stands before my mind as clearly today as in the spring months of more than thirty years since.[24]

Of course, there is always "another side." So, in the spirit of Nietzschean perspectivism, we should add that Ritschl was also "a pugnacious, high-tempered man, the old fighting blood of the [ancient Bohemians] was in his veins."[25] *All the more to recommend him!* Nietzsche must have thought. On his regular lunchtime visits to Ritschl's office, Nietzsche reports favorably that his professor, glass of red wine unfailingly at hand, "was free from all reserve; his anger with his friends, his dissatisfaction with existing conditions, the faults of the university, the quirks of the professors, it all poured

23 Julian Young, *Friedrich Nietzsche: A Philosophical Biography* (Cambridge: Cambridge University Press, 2010), 65.
24 Basil Gildersleeve, "Friedrich Ritschl," *The American Journal of Philology*, Vol. 5, No. 3 (1884): 340–341.
25 Gildersleeve, "Friedrich Ritschl," 340.

out of him such that he revealed himself to possess the opposite of a diplomatic nature. He also poked fun at himself."[26]

It was not, however, merely the man Ritschl who attracted Nietzsche to Bonn; it was also his love of philology. This love was inflamed at the classics-heavy Pforta. From his first book, *The Birth of Tragedy* to his last, *Ecce Homo*, Nietzsche reveals his deep, complex relationship to philology and to its practitioners, the philologists.

Philology is the study of an ancient culture using methods from literary analysis, textual criticism, linguistics, and history. It involves the slow, vigilant, rigorous, slow, slow reading of texts. The basic principle is that an ancient society's culture circulates vibrantly within its supposedly "dead" language, and the language courses through its texts. So, the culture is accessible to us through texts. A single word, as a microcosm of the culture, can, via the philological method, *slowly* be unraveled, thickened, and expanded, to reveal the macrocosm of the culture. For "philology" literally means love of the *word*, or, indeed, of the *syllable*, as William Cowper put it:

> philologists, who chase
> A panting syllable through time and space
> Start it at home, and hunt it in the dark,
> To Gaul, to Greece, and into Noah's ark.[27]

It is no accident that one of Nietzsche's lifelong mottos is *lento! lento! (slowly! slowly!)* Such a motto cannot *but* arise out of the rigors of philological training.[28]

---

26 Friedrich Nietzsche, "Rückblick auf meine zwei Leipziger Jahre" (A Look Back at My Two Years in Leipzig), n/p, *The Nietzsche Channel*, http://www.thenietzschechannel.com/works-unpub/youth/1868-rolg.htm. Accessed July 17, 2022.

27 From his 1779 poem, "Retirement," *Wikisource.* https://en.wikisource.org/wiki/Retirement_(Cowper). Accessed April 8, 2024.

28 I say this as someone who learned the philological method at the same university where Gildersleeve earned his Ph.D., namely, at Georg-August University in Göttingen, Germany. My focus was on Sanskrit. It was here that I first heard the name of Paul Deussen (1845–1919). Deussen was Nietzsche's friend and fellow classics stand-out at Pforta. The two of them journeyed together to Bonn to begin their university days. Deussen would eventually change his focus to the then-emerging fields of Sanskrit philology and Indology, within which the latter in particular he became a leading figure. Whenever I come across one of Nietzsche's many references to Brahmans, Chandalas, Vedanta, the laws of Manu, Hinduism, Indian epic literature, the caste system, various aspects of Buddhism, and more, I can't help but imagine him taking his old (if on-again, off-again) friend's books from the shelf, pressing his nose to the page, and scouring the text for what he might learn.

Philology in nineteenth-century Germany was not the obscure field that it is today. Rather, it was a kind of queen of the sciences, integral to understanding the classical languages and cultures that were, as the foundation of European humanities, essential to an intelligentsia. As a philological prodigy, Nietzsche was thus something of an elite among intellectual elites.

Yet, as promising as it began, of his time in Bonn Nietzsche says, "I have poorly squandered the year." He is furious mainly with himself. He made the "false step" of joining a fraternity devoted to drinking beer and chasing women. Worst of all, perhaps, was that he produced poor work; "I look scornfully at the work I completed in Bonn…Atrocious! The thought of that crap fills me with shame. Everything I produced in high school was better." Nonetheless, in a foreshadowing of his "weightiest thought"[29]—that of the eternal return of the same—and its corresponding *amor fati*, love of fate, Nietzsche has faith that a wider perspective will prove that "The bitter shell of the present, of reality, prevents me from enjoying the seed as yet. For, I hope that one day, from the standpoint of memory, I can joyously register this year, too, as a necessary part of my development."[30]

In fact, the good times with "Father Ritschl" that I mentioned actually did not fully develop until Ritschl's "fighting blood" necessitated his decampment to the University of Leipzig, with Nietzsche and other loyal students in tow. But before likewise following him to Leipzig, I think we should glance at a few consequential events from the wasted year in Bonn.

The first incident is one that "resounds down Nietzschean literature and legend."[31] It involves a visit he made one day to Cologne, a city some twenty miles up the Rhine River from Bonn. Cologne was also the city whose brothels Franconia, Nietzsche's fraternity, was known to frequent. Being shown the sights of the city by a carriage guide, Nietzsche asked to be taken to a restaurant. Instead, the guide brought him to a brothel. Did the guide mishear Nietzsche? That's hard to imagine since "restaurant" and "brothel" sound no more alike in German than they do in English. Did the carriage driver think that Nietzsche was giving him a knowing wink? Was "restaurant" code for "brothel" among young men of Nietzsche's age? In any case, Nietzsche ends up at a brothel. The following day he tells his friend Paul Deussen what happened:

---

29 *NF*–1884, 27[23].
30 All quotes in this paragraph are from a letter to Hermann Mushacke. *BVN*–1865, 478.
31 Prideaux, *I Am Dynamite!*, 42.

Suddenly, I found myself surrounded by a half-dozen creatures in tinsel and gauze, looking at me expectantly. I stood speechless for a while. Then I instinctively went to a piano as if to the only soul-endowed being in the place and struck a few chords. That dispersed my shock and I escaped to the street.

It is a humorous, somewhat slapstick, scene. Taking him at his word, we might wonder: why did Nietzsche run? Did he panic when, innocently believing himself to be entering a restaurant for a midday bite, he looks up to see six barely clad women staring "expectantly" at him? That would indeed be weird. Or did he simply lose his nerve? Did he (not so innocently) play at more than the piano? Deussen slyly suggests another motive:

According to this story and everything else I know about Nietzsche, I am inclined to believe that the words which Steinhart dictated to us in a Latin biography of Plato apply to him: *mulierem nunquam attingit* [he never touched a woman].[32]

The reason this incident so resounds through Nietzsche's life story is that it has sparked speculation about three related issues: his sexuality (was he asexual? heterosexual? bisexual? homosexual?); his cause of death (was it from the effects of syphilis? Of gonorrhea? Of some combination of sexually transmitted diseases?); and the origin of the former (an encounter with a woman in a brothel? With a man in a bathhouse or on the sandy beaches of Genoa?). Nietzsche scholars show virtually no interest in getting to the bottom of such matters, simply cannot do so, or perhaps they simply assume his heterosexuality. Hence, the perpetually distant "resounding" of such issues, all of which remain unsettled.

Speaking of scholarly conservatism, you might be surprised to learn that Nietzsche's years in Leipzig "were the happiest of his life." The suggestion challenges the "determined" effort in the scholarship to cast Nietzsche in the role of "the romantic stereotype of the misfit loner crippled by ill health."[33] Yes, that characterization has (some) merit *later* in his life. But, first, if just for a moment, *we must imagine Nietzsche happy.* He, at least, describes his student years in Leipzig as the "opposite" of the wasted Bonn ones: "Pleasant, dear friendships, unearned privileges from Ritschl, a number of like-minded student comrades, good tavern keepers, good concerts, etc., are

---

32 Gilman, *Conversations with Nietzsche*, 23–24.
33 Young, *Friedrich Nietzsche*, 64.

truly ample enough to make Leipzig a very dear city!"[34] He was excelling as a classical philologist. In fact, Ritschl found so much merit in a talk that Nietzsche gave to the student philological society that he recommended it for publication in the (still-thriving) renowned journal *Rheinisches Museum für Philologie*. Nietzsche was, Ritschl would later write, "the first from whom I have ever accepted any contribution at all while he was still a student."[35] Nietzsche says that he walked around in a daze on having his piece accepted for publication.[36]

Two additional exhilarating events in Leipzig would entail consequential lifelong influences on Nietzsche's person and work. The first was Nietzsche's discovery of the philosopher Arthur Schopenhauer (1788–1860), and the second was his meeting the composer Richard Wagner (1813–1883). Here's how Nietzsche encountered the "gloomy genius" who would disrupt his satisfaction with the narrow confines of philology and turn him toward the surging sea of philosophy.

One day, I found this book in old Rohn's antiquarian bookstore. Since it was completely unknown to me, I took the book in hand and started leafing through it. I don't know what demon whispered in my ear: "Take this book home with you." It happened in any case against my usual habit of not buying books too hastily. At home, I threw myself, together with my acquired treasure, into the corner of the sofa and allowed the energetic, gloomy genius to do his work on me. Here every sentence screamed renunciation, negation, resignation, here was a mirror in which I glimpsed world, life, and my own mind in terrible magnificence. Here, the whole indifferent solar eye of art gazed at me. Here I saw sickness and cure, exile and refuge, hell and heaven. The

34 Letter to Carl von Gersdorff. *BVN–1866*, 523. Young, *Friedrich Nietzsche*, 64–67, analyzes this passage in some detail.

35 In Walter Kaufmann, *The Portable Nietzsche* (London: Penguin Books, 1984 [1954]), 7. As far as I can tell, Nietzsche eventually had three articles published in the journal, including one in Latin, and also prepared an index for the years 1842–1869. See "Table of Contents, 1860–1869," *Rheinisches Museum für Philologie*, https://rhm.phil-fak.uni-koeln.de/en/inhaltsverzeichnisse/rhm-1860-1869. April 3, 2024. There is even an article on the subject: Thomas Brobjer, "Nietzsche's Forgotten Book: The Index to *Rheinisches Museum für Philologie*," *New Nietzsche Studies* 4, 2000, 157–161. The register must have been an extremely tedious and time-consuming task.

36 Friedrich Nietzsche, "Rückblick auf meine zwei Leipziger Jahre" (A Look Back at My Two Years in Leipzig), n/p, *The Nietzsche Channel*, http://www.thenietzschechannel.com/works-unpub/youth/1868-rolg.htm. Accessed July 17, 2022.

need for self-knowledge, indeed, for the self-dismantling, violently seized me.[37]

Over time, Nietzsche would come to reevaluate his valuing of Schopenhauer. He would come to see in him the very pessimism and exhaustion that so characterize our decadent age. But revaluation, we will see, is not the same as *repudiation*. Nietzsche's intellectual relationship with Schopenhauer was deep and complex, and he would return to the gloomy genius's thought throughout his life's work. As I have indicated, this multifaceted consideration of a thinker or an idea is one of the greatest lessons that Nietzsche can teach our rush-to-judgment age. Nietzsche's relationship with Wagner is a lesson in the same.

> All things considered, I could not have endured my youth without Wagnerian music. For, I was *condemned* to Germans. When one wants to be relieved of an unbearable pressure, hashish is necessary. Well, for me, Wagner was necessary. Wagner is the antidote par excellence for all things German.[38]

From the moment he heard Wagner's music, Nietzsche looked to it as nothing less than the key to Germany's cultural rebirth. Personally, too, the two men would form a highly complex, momentous friendship. Wagner, who was born the same year as Nietzsche's father, would play the part of master to Nietzsche's role as disciple. Cosima Wagner (1837–1930), the daughter of the Hungarian composer Franz Liszt and Wagner's second wife, would become (in Nietzsche's later decaying mind) Ariadne to Nietzsche's Dionysus. Nietzsche spent so much time at the Wagner's Swiss home in Tribschen that they gave him his own room. The only other person to enjoy such an intimate honor was Wagner's benefactor, King Ludwig II of Bavaria.

As the "antidote" metaphor suggests, Nietzsche was simultaneously healed *and* poisoned by Wagner. The German word for antidote is *Gegengift*, literally "counter-poison." So, when he says that Wagner is the antidote, the counter-poison, Nietzsche adds, "Poison, I do not deny it." Two of Nietzsche's late works would have Wagner as their focus: *The Case of*

---

37 Friedrich Nietzsche, "Rückblick auf meine zwei Leipziger Jahre" (A Look Back at My Two Years in Leipzig), n/p, *The Nietzsche Channel*, http://www.thenietzschechannel.com/works-unpub/youth/1868-rolg.htm. Accessed July 18, 2022.
38 *Ecce Homo*, "Why I Am So Clever," 6.

Wagner and *Nietzsche Contra Wagner*. As with virtually every person and idea that "violently seized" him during his life, Nietzsche poignantly acknowledges his love and admiration for Wagner in these works while also registering serious, often devastating, objections. A lesson for us?

PROFESSORSHIP

Nietzsche was not in Leipzig for long. His sheer brilliance as a student and a bit of luck combined to cast him abruptly "into the wide world, into a new and unfamiliar profession, into the heavy and oppressive atmosphere of duty and work."[39] In an event unheard of before or, as far as I can determine, since, in the German university world, Nietzsche was offered a professorship at the age of twenty-four. More astonishingly, he received this appointment before he had written a doctoral dissertation (he would never write it). We get a sense of what a "phenomenon" Nietzsche was from Ritschl's recommendation letter to the University of Basel.

> However many young talents I have seen develop under my eyes for thirty-nine years now, *never yet* have I known a young man, or tried to help one along in my field as best I could, who was so mature as early and as young as this Nietzsche [...] If—God grant—he lives long enough, I prophesy that he will one day stand in the front rank of German philology [...] He possesses the enviable gift of presenting ideas, talking freely, as calmly as he speaks skillfully and clearly. He is the idol and, without wishing it, the leader of the whole younger generation of philologists here in Leipzig who—and they are rather numerous—cannot wait to hear him as a lecturer. You will say, I describe a phenomenon. Well, that is just what he is—and at the same time pleasant and modest. Also a gifted musician, which is irrelevant here [...] What more am I to say? [...] He will simply be able to do anything he wants to do.[40]

Nietzsche and his family were understandably thrilled with his appointment. Elizabeth Nietzsche writes that one day an envelope was delivered.

---

39 Quoted in Young, *Friedrich Nietzsche*, 79.
40 Quoted in Walter Kaufmann, *The Portable Nietzsche* (London: Penguin Books, 1984 [1954]), 7–8.

It contained her brother's newly printed calling card: "Friedrich Nietzsche. Professor of Classical Philology at the University of Basel."

> Our dear mother's happiness and boundless surprise were beyond description. Then the marvelous news spread further and further. Everyone, even the newspapers, were astonished at this twenty-four-old professor. Praise, honor, and adulation resounded on all sides about our Fritz, so that it finally became too much for him and he once wrote with considerable annoyance: "What's so great about it? There's just one more professor on earth, that's all."[41]

Foreshadowing the deep ambivalence that was to come, Elizabeth adds that "From the very beginning, ever since he first got the appointment, my brother was not sheer delight and joy."

In the nineteenth century, "professor" carried extraordinary social prestige. Even with their low salaries, professors, indeed even secondary school teachers, typically "married the offspring 'of the most highly regarded families from within the civil service, the daughters of generals, of councilors of state, of provincial government presidents or directors.'"[42] The wife of a German professor, whatever her level of education, forever carried the enviable title of "Frau Doktor." The idolization of professors was particularly high for those teaching in the area of the classics, as was Nietzsche. So, in conventional terms at least, Nietzsche had arrived. We know, however, that Nietzsche was anything but conventional. There would be costs to pay.

The Swiss government required Nietzsche to give up his German citizenship. They did not want him to run off to what was widely considered, in this era of the aggressive Blood and Iron Chancellor, the inevitability of a Franco-German war. They also assumed that he would become a Swiss citizen. He never even applied. Nietzsche was thus stateless for the remainder of his life. In hindsight, this status was, of course, perfectly proper for a state-despising anti-nationalist "good European."

Nietzsche's teaching load cost him even more dearly. In addition to his university courses, he was also contracted to teach at the local *Pädagogium*. This was an elite secondary school, higher in status and difficulty than the common *Gymnasium*. To give an example of his onerous teaching load, in his first semester, Nietzsche taught four classes in the university and four in

---

41 Gilman, *Conversations with Nietzsche*, 30.
42 See Fritz K. Ringer, "Higher Education in Germany in the Nineteenth Century," *Journal of Contemporary History*, Vol. 2, No. 3, Education and Social Structure (1967): 123–138.

the *Pädagogium*.[43] As someone who taught two courses a semester, I find this load literally inconceivable. It is true that Nietzsche's university courses never attracted more than a handful of students, but that does not lessen preparation time or energy invested. On top of teaching, moreover, Nietzsche attended department meetings, university faculty council, committee duties, and office hours. He even served for a time as dean of humanities. He was known for generously filling in for colleagues who were unable to make a class. Finally, to support the university's goal of good relations with the people of Basel, Nietzsche offered public lectures.[44] After merely one year, at the age of twenty-five, Nietzsche was promoted to the exalted academic status of full professor. It is no wonder that Nietzsche would soon buckle under the pressures he faced.

How was Nietzsche as a teacher? I said that my goal in this biographical sketch is to convey a *sense* of the person Nietzsche. I believe that we can learn a great deal about a person from how they exercise their institution-ally-granted authority. By all accounts, Nietzsche's classroom was a place of seriousness and rigor combined with politeness and humor. He himself claimed that although he never once disciplined a student, "even the lazi-est pupils worked hard when they were in my classes." His secret for this outcome is remarkable. It has more in common with modern progressive education than with the severe, indeed often draconian, approaches typical of his milieu.

> Whenever a pupil failed to recite adequately…I publicly always blamed myself—I said for example that everyone had a right to demand of me further elucidation and commentary if what I said was too cursory or vague. A teacher has an obligation to make himself accessible to *every* level of intelligence.[45]

Nietzsche's pedagogical strategy did not go unnoticed by his students. From the accounts we have, they respected and admired him, and sometimes felt pity for him. Nietzsche's students offered the following recollections:[46]

[Professor Nietzsche] was not interested in a rote type of instruction.

43 *The Nietzsche Channel*, "Lectures," http://www.thenietzschechannel.com/lectures/lectures.htm. Accessed August 3, 2022.

44 See *The Nietzsche Channel*, "Lectures," http://www.thenietzschechannel.com/lectures/lectures.htm. Accessed August 3, 2022, and Young, *Friedrich Nietzsche*, 101–102.

45 Young, *Friedrich Nietzsche*, 102.

46 Gilman, *Conversations with Nietzsche*, "Professor at the University of Basel" section.

Most impressive was the man himself, the freedom and dignity of his whole behavior. Anything trivial was out of the question for him; everyone could feel this.

Even today I still esteem it highly to have had Nietzsche as a teacher. Without that my life would have been a bit poorer and more trivial. I am also grateful to him for the friendly attitude he had toward me.

Nietzsche was not a dry professional pedagogue, but an excellent teacher, who like [the historian] Ephorus from ancient Greece stepped with a leap across time and mores into the midst of his pupils, as if he were reporting of self-evident things he had seen with his own eyes.

His method of instruction was completely ruled by the spirit of aesthetic freedom. He was far from any rigid pedantry.

The inner freedom and superiority of his nature…resulted in the young professor's setting the boundaries of his school program unusually wide and expecting from us an independent treatment and mastery of the assigned work.

His strict sense of justice distinguished precisely between the limits of good will and of indolent negligence, and none of the favorite school tricks worked with him.

When Nietzsche was teaching, an exemplary discipline always prevailed in our class and it even carried over to the preceding and following intermission. Although we never heard a word of blame or ill-temper from our teacher, we had boundless respect for him.

Difficult hours as Nietzsche prepared for us, we felt it to be a distinction that he gave so much credit to our intelligence, and we had youth's fine sense for the violence which his high-flying spirit did itself for our sake.

[He had] a striking nobility of appearance and a captivating amiability of conduct.

[Having read his aggressive polemic in *Untimely Meditations*, I was] surprised by his kindliness, his inner seriousness, the absence of any sarcasm. He seemed intentionally to want to soften by his words the energy that his face expressed, the fire that flamed in his eyes. He gave an impression of eminent self-mastery. Strict toward himself, strict in matters of principle, he was, however, extremely benevolent in his judgment of other people.

Equipped with the strongest eyeglasses, he sat with his face almost touching his notebook on the lectern. Slowly and laboriously, the words struggled through his lips and often his speech was interrupted by pauses which caused one to worry that he might be unable to continue reading. In fact, sometimes he had to stop the class because the excruciating headaches that plagued him almost daily and deprived him of sleep at night became unbearable.

Nietzsche had a voice! Not the rounded tone of an orator, nor the sharply articulated but really ineffective modulation typical of the pathos of many a university professor. Nietzsche's speech, soft and natural as it struggled through his lips, had only one thing in its favor: it came from the soul!

Even today the enchantment of [Nietzsche's] voice continues to affect me!

He spoke slowly, often halting, not so much seeking an expression as checking the impression of his *dicta* to himself. If the thread of thought led him to something particularly extreme, then his voice also sank, as if hesitatingly, down to the softest *pianissimo*.

I can still see his big dark eyes, as they looked out with such humane warmth from under the bushy brows. I can still hear his soft gentle voice asking me various questions.

[From a student, though not Nietzsche's, who went for several walks with him:] During the whole conversation I did not know what I should admire more, the tremendous scope of his positive knowledge, the high flight of his lines of thought, or the brilliant, almost poetically beautiful language. That he bothered with me, a green, insignificant young man, who of course had absolutely nothing to offer him, and spoke with me in such an amiable, friendly manner, gave me the impression that at the bottom of his soul he must have been an unusually kind and loving person, and I was filled with deep gratitude toward him.[47]

Finally, an anecdote showing Nietzsche's humor. A student reports that Professor Nietzsche had assigned the reading of a passage describing, in Greek, Achilles's shield. At the beginning of class, Nietzsche asked a student if he had prepared. In an all-too-common classroom moment, the wholly unprepared student answered, "yes." "Good," said Nietzsche, "then describe the shield."

An embarrassing silence followed, as the pupil's excitement increased. For ten minutes Nietzsche, apparently listening, strode through the room with pensive steps, pretending to be listening to the fictive description. Finally, he said without any sharp emphasis: Now that N. N. has explained Achilles' shield to us, let us continue.[48]

INTERLUDE: WAR

In July 1870, France declared war on Germany. A mere three weeks later, Nietzsche wrote to the president of the university: "Given the present situation in Germany, you will not be surprised at my decision to fulfill my duty towards my Fatherland."[49] Though lasting only six months, by the end of the conflict half a million soldiers would be dead or wounded and over a quarter of a million civilian men, women, and children killed. Why would Nietzsche, who, we know, had deep animus toward nationalism, the state, and, indeed, toward Germany itself, volunteer for service? I think that Nietzsche's animus is in large part *because of* his war experience.

The university granted Nietzsche leave, but on the condition that he take a noncombatant position. So, in August 1870, he reported to the German army to begin training as a medical orderly accompanying a field ambulance. Shortly afterward, a train arrived in the hospital camp with dozens of wounded, dead, or dying civilian men, women, and children to attend

---

47 Gilman, *Conversations with Nietzsche*, 140.
48 Gilman, *Conversations with Nietzsche*, 37.
49 *BVN*–1870, 89.

to.[50] It only got worse from there. Just a few days later, Nietzsche writes to his mother that his unit marched eleven hours to the "horribly devastated" battlefield of Wörth, where he waded through "countless sad bodily remains laying strewn, and the powerful stench of corpses."[51] A few days later, he was given orders to the bring six wounded soldiers from Ars in France back to Germany. In a letter to Richard Wagner, Nietzsche writes:

> Being together with seriously wounded men for three days and nights, I was at the peak of my exertion. I had a miserable cattle car in which six suffering men lay, left alone at the time to care for them, bandage them, nurse them, and so on. All with shattered bones, several with four wounds; in addition, I diagnosed diphtheria in two of them. That I was able to bear it in this stew of pestilence, much less be able to sleep and to eat, seems to me now like the work of wizardry. But hardly had I delivered my transport to a hospital in Karlsruhe than signs of serious illness appeared in me.[52]

Nietzsche was diagnosed with severe dysentery and diphtheria. There is speculation that he may have even contracted syphilis in that cattle car. His treatment consisted in what, to contemporary ears, sounds like torture: silver nitrate, opium and tannic acid enemas, the wholly expected result of which was "to ruin the patient's intestines for life."[53]

On New Year's Day 1871, Nietzsche, suffering from "a kind of spiritual narcolepsy"[54] in addition to nausea and headaches, returned to Basel.

AN END AND A BEGINNING

It should not be surprising that Nietzsche returned to Basel a profoundly changed man. His already precarious health was forever shattered. He likely suffered from what we would today diagnose as post-traumatic stress syndrome: his letters suggest or directly mention recurring flashbacks of literally unspeakable images, incessant insomnia, prolonged bouts of depression, fragile nerves, the sudden descent of indescribable sadness. He writes to a

---

50 Prideaux, *I Am Dynamite!*, 80.
51 *BVN*–1870, 95.
52 *BVN*–1870, 100.
53 Prideaux, *I Am Dynamite!*, 81. On his treatment, see also *BVN*–1870, 103.
54 Prideaux, *I Am Dynamite!*, 85.

friend that night has fallen around him again, that he feels he is going to die unless something changes, something "I know not *what*." Most alarmingly, he says, "the barrel of a pistol is a source of relatively pleasant thoughts right now."[55] He is deeply grieved that sixteen of his brilliant, promising Pforta schoolmates were slaughtered on the battlefield. Witnessing the colossal brutality and stupidity of his nation's leaders, Nietzsche's hopes for a German cultural renaissance were forever dashed.

In a strangely overlooked facet of his biography, the war and its aftermath would leave Nietzsche drug-dependent for the rest of his life. One friend reports that Nietzsche told her that, surprised at the ease with which his "Dr. Nietzsche" calling card made it possible, he wrote his own prescriptions for the anti-anxiety sedative, chloral hydrate.[56] In a letter to another friend, he calculates that in only two months time he consumed 50 grams of pure chloral hydrate. This is an extreme overuse.[57] But it helped: "I have *never* slept so much without this drug. But I *have* been sleeping, fourteen nights in a row now—oh, what a relief!"[58] Even Elizabeth Nietzsche's 1895 biography *The Life of Nietzsche* contains numerous references to her brother's relationship to drugs. This is particularly remarkable given the effort she made—often involving deception, misrepresentation, and outright forgery—to present him in an almost hagiographical (and politically right wing) light. Yet even she diagnoses her brother's cause of death as "a brain exhausted by overstrain of the nerves of head and eye that could no longer resist taking drugs to excess, and thus became disabled."[59] The excessive taking of drugs is not denied, is indeed assumed as an obvious given, and merely provided an explanation. In a moving description, Nietzsche's friend Resa von Schirnhofer captures the pathos and prescience (and hallucination?) that characterizes this aspect of his life. Hearing that he had been suffering headaches, Schirnhofer went to see how he was doing.

> As I stood waiting by the table, the door to the adjacent room on the right opened, and Nietzsche appeared. With a distraught expression on his pale face, he leaned wearily against the post of the half-opened

---

55 *BVN*–1883, 373.

56 Resa von Schirnhofer, in Gilman, *Conversations with Nietzsche: A Life in the Words of His Contemporaries*, 161.

57 Today, the recommended dosage is 500 to 1000 mg once a day, and never for more than 2 weeks' use. https://www.drugs.com/dosage/chloral-hydrate.html. Accessed August 5, 2022.

58 *BVN*–1883, 372.

59 Elizabeth Förster-Nietzsche, *The Life of Nietzsche*, Vol. 2, translated by Paul V. Cohn (New York: Sturgis and Walton Company, 1915), 402.

door and immediately began to speak about the unbearableness of his ailment. He described to me how, when he closed his eyes, he saw an abundance of fantastic flowers, winding and intertwining, constantly growing and changing forms and colors in exotic luxuriance, sprouting one out of the other. "I never get any rest," he complained, words which were implanted in my mind. Then, with his large, dark eyes looking straight at me he asked in his weak voice with disquieting urgency: "Don't you believe that this condition is a symptom of incipient madness? My father died of a brain disease."[60]

I want to avoid reading too much into Nietzsche's drug use. After all, at this same time he is beginning to shape his explosive oeuvre. In the very letter that mentions the consolation of the pistol barrel, Nietzsche refers to a book that has just taken him a mere ten days to write. This book—it must have been the first part of *Thus Spoke Zarathustra*—he says, "appears to me now as a testament. It contains in the greatest sharpness an image of my being, as it is, once I had thrown off my entire burden."[61] Indeed, what did not kill Nietzsche, it turns out, made him stronger. The debilitating effects of the war on his body and mind, and his ability *somehow* to bounce back, endow such central Nietzschean ideas as *amor fati*, eternal recurrence, self-overcoming, rejection of the obedient "last mortal" with his pathological mediocrity and eviscerating morality, and embrace of the "*Übermensch*," with a deep, rich, authentic resonance. Nietzsche knew these things because he lived them.

In the depths of the defeat wrought by Nietzsche's war experience, a new life took root. Recall that in his letter of recommendation, Ritschl prophesied that his protege would "simply be able to do anything he wants to do." What Nietzsche wanted to do, it was becoming increasingly clear, was *philosophy*, not philology. In fact, in one of the great ironies in the history of academia, Nietzsche applied for a chair in the philosophy department at Basel only to be rejected as unqualified. In a highly unorthodox letter to the president of the university on his return from the war, Nietzsche illuminates the "strange conflict" that he finds himself in. After reminding the president of his recurring illnesses, which always suspiciously strike in the *middle* of the semester, Nietzsche, begs the president's "leniency, advice, and participation":

---

60 Resa von Schirnhofer, in Gilman, *Conversations with Nietzsche*, 164. Schirnhofer (1855–1948) was one of the first women to receive a doctorate in philosophy from the University of Zürich.
61 *BVN*–1883, 373.

I am living here in a strange conflict, and it is this that so exhausts me and wears me down even bodily. Intensely compelled by nature to think through a matter in terms of philosophical standards, and in long trains of thought to persist thinking through the problem continuously and undisturbed, I feel that I am constantly being buffeted here and there and knocked off course by the daily various tasks required by my position. I can hardly bear this simultaneous university and *Pädagogium* teaching in the long term because I feel that my actual task, to which, if necessary, I *must sacrifice every occupation*, my *philosophical* task, is suffering under this burden, indeed, is being reduced to a mere side activity. I believe that this account indicates in the sharpest terms what so wears me down here and prevents me from consistently experiencing joyful career fulfillment, and what, on the other hand, exhaust my body, increasing to my current sufferings: sufferings that, if they should continue to return, I will be forced, on purely physical grounds, to give up any philological profession.[62]

Nietzsche's unease in the role of professor of classical philology was matched only by his increasing unease in the role of *professor* in itself. He writes his benefactor, Ritschl, as if to reassure him, "I have now endured one year of my academic career. It's okay, it's okay! But [teaching] costs a lot of time and energy."[63] We don't have to read between the lines to sense Nietzsche's lack of enthusiasm here. In his "Schopenhauer as Educator," Nietzsche is more specific, if less direct, about what ails him about the university professor he has become. "To a great extent," he writes, "the scholar's task is mixed with finding certain 'truths,' but to do so in subordination to certain ruling people, classes, opinions, churches, and governments."[64] The university scholar is thus compelled, moreover, because "he feels that it is to his advantage to bring the 'truth' over to their side." This leads to a situation where "every generation of scholars has a spontaneous measure of *permitted* perspicuity; what goes beyond that limit is brought into question and used by the world of conventionality as almost grounds for suspicion." The reason that must have cut deepest—because most aligned to the work of a philologist—was

---

62 *BVN*–1871, 118.
63 *BVN*–1870, 68. On the same day, writing to his friend Erwin Rohde, he replaced "endured" *(ausgehalten)* the first year with "overcome" or even "survived" *(überwunden)* the first year. *BVN*–1870, 69.
64 *Untimely Meditations*, "Schopenhauer as Educator," 6; all quotes in this section.

the "sharp vision for what is near combined with profound myopia for what is distant and general."

> [The scholar's] field of vision is typically very narrow, and his eyes have to be kept close to the object of investigation. If the scholar wants to move his vision from one point of investigation to another one, he has to shift his entire viewing apparatus to the new point. He dissects an image into numerous pixels, like someone using opera glasses to see now the stage, now a head, now a piece of clothing—but never does the eye behold the whole. He never sees any single pixel connected to others, rather, he only infers their relationship; therefore, he generally has no strong impression of the whole. For example, because he is not able to gain an overview of it, he judges a text according to single parts or sentences or errors; he would be tempted to claim that an oil painting is a chaotic cluster of blots.

Everything about this depiction flies in the face of the broad humanistic education that Nietzsche received at Pforta. Indeed, according to the Humboldt-inspired pedagogy, such "myopia" violates education's very reason for being: cultivation of the whole person.

At this moment, Nietzsche was working on a book, *The Birth of Tragedy*, that would be a testament to his tension, indeed his constitutional incompatibility, with academia. Expectations for the book were high. Particularly given that he was spared the writing of a doctoral dissertation, much less the *Habilitation*,[65] much less several years in the academic trenches publishing tedious specialized articles, the academic world braced itself for what would surely be Nietzsche's explosive debut. And explode it did!

THE WANDERER

Nietzsche's first book, *The Birth of Tragedy Out of the Spirit of Music*, published in 1872, not quite two years after his return from the war, precipitated what I will characterize here as his period of wandering. From its theme—classical Athenian theater as the locus of the Greek's healthy confrontation with the interlocking instinctual, chaotic (Dionysian) and rational, orderly (Apollonian) aspects of life—the book would have struck the reader as

---

65 The *Habilitation* is the second dissertation, after the *Promotion*, or Ph.D., that German academics are required to produce in order to attain the rank of full professorship.

wholly conventional. However, the content and style of the book, indeed its very spirit, could hardly have been a clearer signal to the staid world of classical philology that the author was a brazen heretic. The typical philological monograph consists in a heavy apparatus of textual citations, often given in the original language as well as in translation; detailed etymologies and historical linguistic analyses; long, dense footnotes citing references and setting forth detailed elaborations; highly circumspect locutions in formulating arguments; labored, formal language, lacking the slightest trace of the author's personality, and so on. *The Birth of Tragedy* exhibits exactly *none* of these features. Imagine: not a single footnote, not a single Greek quotation! Aflame in the passion of its author, the academic world—you have probably already guessed—*hated* it.

Champion of traditional scholarship, rising academic, and fellow Pforta graduate, Ulrich von Wilamowitz-Moellendorff, captures (replete with aforementioned apparatus) the general consensus of the learned world regarding *The Birth of Tragedy* and its wayward author. "Wilamops,"[66] as Nietzsche would humorously come to refer to him privately, made it clear that his dual task in reviewing the book was both "criticizing and warning against it." So, reader—be warned![67]

> Mr. Nietzsche by no means presents himself as a scholarly researcher: insights achieved through intuition are presented partly in the style of the pulpit, partly through a journalistic reasoning…It is easy to prove here that dreamed of genius and impudence are directly proportionate to ignorance and lack of the love for truth…This work is the exact opposite of the way to research that the heroes of our science [of philology] have tread…Mr. N. reveals a truly childish ignorance the moment he deals with any archaeological issue.

66 The German noun *Mops* means "pug," as in the dog with the scrunched up sour-looking face. As Walter Kaufmann notes, it connotes "comic, stupid, coarse, unfriendly, and inelegant," and may be etymologically cognate with English "mope." The German adjective *mopsig* means "boring." See Walter Kaufmann, *Basic Writings of Nietzsche* (New York: The Modern Library, 2000 [1967], 7. In another letter, Nietzsche also refers to Wilamowitz as "Wilamo-Wisch" ("Wilamo-Bumph"; a bumph is extremely boring reading material that you must contend with, like an insurance form) and "Wilam Ohne Witz" ("Wilam Without Wit"). See *BVN*–1872, 242.

67 Quotes from Ulrich von Wilamowitz-Moellendorff, *Zukunftsphilologie! Eine Erwidrung auf Friedrich Nietzsches "Geburt der Tragödie"* (Berlin: Gebrüder Borntraeger, 1872), 6, 7, 8, 9. In a derisive play of Wagner's concept of *Zukunftsmusik* [Music of the Future], the title translates as *Philology of the Future! A Retort to Friedrich Nietzsche's "Birth of Tragedy."* This work is available in digitized form at https://www.google.com/books/edition/Zukunftsphilologie/wNFDAQAAMAAJ?hl=en&gbpv=0. Accessed August 7, 2022.

In a particularly low dig, Wilamowitz-Moellendorff writes "Since Plato, it is inscribed above the doors of philosophy: Aς μην μπει κανείς που είναι χωρίς γεωμετρία [Let no one enter this place without geometry]. I only wish they had adhered to this saying at Pforta, at least in the version: Aς μην φύγει κανείς από αυτό το μέρος [Let no one *leave* this place (without geometry)]," a reference to the fact that Nietzsche's poor performance in math almost prevented him from graduating Pforta.

The general consensus in the scholarship is that with the publication of his first book Nietzsche's academic career was dead in the water. Indeed, one highly influential scholar of the day proclaimed *The Birth of Tragedy* "sheer nonsense" and said that, academically, "Nietzsche is dead."[68] In the semester following the book's publication, no philology students, and only two students in total, enrolled in his university courses. Nietzsche himself would eventually come to recognize the limitations of his youthful book (recall that he was only twenty-seven when it was published). In "Attempt at Self-Criticism," a preface added to a later edition, he calls the book "questionable," and adds: "I now find this book impossible—I consider it poorly written, ponderous, embarrassing, image-obsessed and image-con-fused, sentimental, here and there saccharine." Yet, he also stood by it, and recognized its worth. He was right to do so. Two comments from eminent twentieth-century classics scholars bear this out. One called *The Birth of Tragedy* "a work of profound imaginative insight, which left the scholarship of a generation toiling in the rear"; and another, "a great book, by whatever standard one cares to measure it...It has cast a spell on almost everyone who has dealt with the subject since 1871."[69]

I am dwelling on this episode in Nietzsche's life because I think that we can see in it the contours of his place in the wider intellectual world. The academic guild of his day was as constitutionally incapable of recognizing his value as he was of conforming to its rules. The very thesis of *The Birth of Tragedy* grated against the received wisdom of the day—both scholarly and public—that the ancient Greeks were a cheerful, innocent, natural, almost childlike people. Such characteristics, moreover, made them worthy of emulation. In Bismarckian Germany, the admiration, bordering on obsession, for all things Greek, was becoming more thoroughly institutionalized via its explicit role in the curriculum and very spirit of the *Gymnasium* system.[70]

---

68 Quoted in Young, *Friedrich Nietzsche*, 154.
69 Quoted in Kaufmann, *Basic Writings*, 7–8.
70 See for instance, Suzanne L. Marchand, *Down from Olympus: Archaeology and Philhellenism in Germany, 1750–1970* (Princeton: Princeton University Press, 1996).

Nietzsche was as enthusiastic a philhellenist as anyone in Germany. But for the exact opposite reasons. For him, the ancient Greeks were a key to cultural renewal because of their willingness to confront *all* of life's realities, to hold the Apollonian and Dionysian in equilibrium. In other words, against child-like *innocence*, the Greeks, instructed by the tragic theater, dove headlong into the wild vicissitudes of visceral *experience*. And *this* is what made them exemplary human beings. At the very end of *The Birth of Tragedy*, Nietzsche presents a person who, through intuition or reverie, finds himself back in ancient Greece, "wandering beneath the lofty colonnades," beholding all around him "the incessant influx of beauty." Would not immersion in beauty compel the man to "raise his hand to Apollo and exclaim, 'blessed people of Hellas!'" Hearing this praise of Apollo, an old Athenian, intimately familiar with the demand for equilibrium, would reply, "But say this, too, you odd stranger: How much must this people have suffered to become so beauti-ful! Now, follow me to the tragedy, and sacrifice with me in the temple of both gods!"[71] The Greeks' cheerfulness, their naturalness, their capacity for saying *yes* to life, was worthy of emulation because it originated in a clear-eyed embrace of *all* of life—in the beautiful, the frightful, and everything in between. I view this point, crucial for an understanding of Nietzsche's thinking as a whole, as a thread woven into his entire life. We will return to it again and again in this text.

I said that the publication and aftermath of his first book precipitated a period of wandering for Nietzsche. He would write two more works—*Untimely Meditations* and *Human, All Too Human: A Book for Free Spirits*—in a decisively non-philological, indeed non-academic, style. Yet, ever the prognosticator, Nietzsche knew some major change was in the offing. He wrote a letter to his friend, Marie Baumgartner, from the spa town of Rosenlaui, where he was seeking relief from particularly severe and prolonged bouts of headaches and nausea. In the letter he speaks of "the *twilight* of my Basel existence" and adds revealing glimpses of what is to come, and why.

> I know it, feel it, that I have a higher destiny than the one granted by my very worthy position in Basel; also I am more than a philologist, as much as I might be able to use philology for my higher purpose. "I crave for myself"—that was actually the constant theme of the last ten years of my life. Now, when, after a year of being alone with myself (I

---

71 *The Birth of Tragedy*, section 25.

cannot express how rich, how joyfully creative I feel, in spite of all the pain, once people leave me alone) now, I will tell you in full awareness that I am not returning to Basel for good. How it will turn out, I do not know; but my freedom (oh, the external conditions for it must be as modest as possible) this freedom, I will conquer.[72]

Then, on May 2, 1879, he dictates a letter to the president of the university stating that, after a series of petitions over the years to take sick leave, he is now taking "the final step to request resignation from my current position as teacher at the university."[73] He gives as the reason his increasingly severe and frequent headaches and his deteriorating eyesight, "which permits me barely twenty minutes of reading and writing without pain." He reminds the president that he has made continual efforts to be rid of his recurrent ailments, but now "I have lost faith that I am able to resist my suffering any longer." A few days later, he wrote a friend, "I have resigned my professor-ship, and am going higher into the mountains—brought nearly to despera-tion and with little hope."[74]

The "wandering" that I referred to describes Nietzsche's living situation after resigning. The university granted him a small stipend. It was barely enough for a single person to live on. Fortunately, as we saw, Nietzsche determined that his freedom required only modest material circumstances. Eating little, renting small cheap rooms sometimes without heating, dressing in what eventually became threadbare clothing, Nietzsche lived itinerantly for the rest of his productive life. He wanders between St. Moritz and Sils Maria in Switzerland; Sorento, Genoa, Rome, and Turin in Italy; and Nice in France. If he had a home during this period, it was Sils Maria, "6000 feet above the sea and even higher above all human affairs!"[75] Sils Maria is a picturesque village in the Swiss alpine region known as the Engadine. In the 1880s, the population was just around 200 inhabitants. (Today it is around 700 in the off season.) Nietzsche loved the slow, quiet rhythms of the village, and he admired the simple, unpretentious people who lived there. He walked for six or more hours at a time on the dirt paths around the breathtaking lakes Silvaplana and Sils that border the village and on the stony ones that lead higher and higher into the awe-inspiring mountains.

---

72 *BVN*–1877, 661.
73 *BVN*–1879, 846.
74 *BVN*–1879, 847.
75 *NF*–1881, 11[141].

The wanderer in the mountains to himself. There are sure signs that you are going forward and higher: it is freer than before and the vista is wider, the air blows cooler yet milder on your face—you have of course disabused yourself of the foolishness that confuses mildness with warmth—your step has become livelier and more certain, courage and prudence have grown together. For all of these reasons, your way may now be lonelier and in any case more dangerous than before, though certainly not to the degree that those believe who watch you, the wanderer, stride the mountains from the misty valley.[76]

Ralph Waldo Emerson—a writer whom Nietzsche, incidentally, called his "*brother* soul"[77]—said that "great geniuses have the shortest biographies."[78] Nietzsche's period of wandering, between his university resignation in 1879 and his commitment to the mental asylum in 1889, was filled with the vibrant vicissitudes of life, from suicidal despair to ecstatic joy. And with Nietzsche more than any other thinker I know, it is crucial to take account of the life. He did, after all, consider philosophy to be at heart autobiography. Many events in Nietzsche's life are crucial to understanding his work. I will mention here only the following: his intense entanglement and wrenching, dramatic disentanglement with Richard and Cosima Wagner; his intense, hopeful, ultimately disappointing friendship with Lou Salomé; his troubling, emotionally erratic relationship to his mother and sister; his several intimate friendships, which, ultimately, could not save him from profound loneliness; his almost childlike enthusiasm for his work, particularly for *Zarathustra*, both the work and the figure, who was very much his alter ego; and his equally innocent-seeming bafflement at his near complete failure to sell books, much less to have the cultural impact he had intended. Given the scope of *Nietzsche NOW!*, we will have to be satisfied with Emerson's theory that "As a good chimney burns its smoke, so a philosopher converts the value of all his fortunes into his intellectual performances."[79] So, to conclude this biography of our Immoralist guide, I want to mention a plan that Nietzsche had in mind for his life immediately on resigning his professorship. Then, I will sketch his breakdown and final days.

---

76 *Human, All Too Human*, "Assorted Opinions and Sayings," 237.
77 *BVN*–1883, 477.
78 Ralph Waldo Emerson, *Representative Men*, "Plato; Or, The Philosopher," https://emersoncentral.com/texts/representative-men/plato-or-the-philosopher. Accessed August 9, 2022.
79 Emerson, *Representative Men*.

We might not even have "his intellectual performances" if Nietzsche's plan to become a *gardener*, like his hero Epicurus, while living in a *tower*, like his hero Hölderlin, had succeeded. On leaving the academic life, Nietzsche initially envisioned for himself the exact opposite of the wandering philosopher. The tower was located in his hometown of Naumburg. It was part of the medieval town wall. Writing to his mother—who had still not recovered from her deep disappointment and shame stemming from her son's resignation—just after having left Basel, Nietzsche begs her to secure the lease for him.

> My dear good mother…I must have the tower room. *Vegetable growing* completely matches my wishes and is in no way unworthy of a future "sage." You know that I am inclined towards a simple and natural way of life, I strengthen myself more and more in that way; for my health, too, there is no other cure. Real *work*, work that takes time and *effort* without straining the head, is necessary for me. Did not my father say that I would someday become a gardener? Admittedly, I am completely inexperienced, but otherwise not stupid.

Demonstrating his inexperience, Nietzsche adds that he will be able to commence his new life in the tower sometime around September and assures (?) his mother:

> How well that reconciles with the duties of gardening! What do you think? (What kind of *fruit* is there in the area around the wall?) For garden work, April and May to the middle of June, and again from the end of September to November—these seem to me to be the months for the *most important* work.[80]

Nietzsche seems sincerely to dream of such a life for himself. After the constant strain of Basel, it should not be surprising that he would long for the

---

80 *BVN*–1879, 867. Johann Wolfgang von Goethe, a person whom Nietzsche admired deeply, also lived in a garden cottage. Maybe Nietzsche's enthusiasm has something to do with Goethe's well-known contentment in his youthful Weimar days. Goethe reports: "I have a lovely garden beyond the town gates in a valley of beautiful meadows by the river. There is an old cottage which I'm having repaired. All is in bloom and the birds are singing…At night, in my garden, I will sleep here for the first time…It is a wonderful sensation to sit alone in the field and be at home. I hear the ticking of my clock and the sound of the wind and the millstream from afar." In John Armstrong, *Love, Life, Goethe: Lessons of the Imagination from the Great German Poet* (New York: Farrar, Straus and Giroux, 2006), 127.

quiet and solitude of his tower room. He says he found the very thought deeply soothing. So what happened? He explains in a touching letter to his close friend Franz Overbeck. Overbeck's wife Ida, who was very dear to Nietzsche, had sent him a gardening apron in a gesture of support for his new life. Somewhat chagrined, Nietzsche writes:

> Dear Friend, another word about the gardening apron. The tower and the area around it, both more picturesque and larger than I assumed, have nevertheless passed out of my hands and into someone else's. I recognized that my eyes are *much* too weak for gardening and that stooping down is wholly untenable for my head—considered close up, it turns out that vegetable farming is an impossibility, unfortunately, unfortunately! [...] The *best* thing about this whole episode is the expectation that I had; and to my happiness of hopeful gardening belongs, too, the hopeful gardening apron: for which I offer my heartfelt thanks to your wife.[81]

So, instead of tomatoes and apricots, we have *Beyond Good and Evil* and *The Antichrist*. Nietzsche's philosophy would thus be imbued not with the even earth of the garden but with the rugged peaks of the mountains. We will close out the productive period of Nietzsche's life with his own account of the "intellectual performances" that, in the end, matter more than anything to him.

> Whoever knows how to breathe the air of my writings, knows that it is the air of the heights, a *strong* air. One must be made for it, or else the danger of catching a cold is not small. The ice is near, the loneliness is terrible—but how calmly lie all things in the light! how freely one breathes! how much one feels *beneath* oneself!—Philosophy, as I have understood and lived it up to now, is the voluntary living in ice and high mountains—the seeking of all that is strange and questionable in existence, of all that which has hitherto been banned by morality. Out of the long experience that comes from wandering in that which is *forbidden*, I learned to consider the causes, out of which thus far have come moralizing and idealizing, to be very different from what may be desired: the *hidden* history of the philosophers, the psychology of their great names, came into the light for me.—How much truth can a

---

81 *BVN*–1879, 896.

spirit *bear*, how much truth can it *dare*? For me, that has increasingly become the actual measure of value. Error (belief in the ideal) is not blindness: error is *cowardice*…Every achievement, every step forward in knowledge, follows from courage, from hardness toward oneself, from cleanliness toward oneself…I do not refute ideals, I just put on gloves in their presence…*Nitimur in vetitum* [we advance toward that which is forbidden]: under this sign, my philosophy will one day triumph; for, thus far, one has, in principle, forbidden only the truth.[82]

BREAKDOWN AND DEATH

The story of Nietzsche's end is unspeakably sad. It unfolds over more than ten years, from the autumn of 1888 until his death in the summer of 1900. This long duration alone seems to give the lie to his doctors', and to history's, persistent diagnosis of neurosyphilitic infection, a condition that is fatal in the *short term*. A quite substantial body of medical literature exists that attempts to diagnose his illness using doctor reports, hospital records, accounts of symptoms, and descriptions by friends and relatives.[83] What concerns us here, recall, is getting *a sense* of the person, of Nietzsche, in the midst of his awful decline.

The canonical origin story of the collapse lies in a pathetic scene on the streets of Turin on January 3, 1889. Nietzsche was renting a room on the third floor of a house belonging to one Davide Fino and his family.[84] Fino had a newspaper shop on the ground floor of the house. In the story, Nietzsche,

---

82 *Ecce Homo*, Preface, 3. Along with dashes, Nietzsche regularly uses ellipses in his text as a device that has several functions: it affects timing, interrupts the flow, alerts the reader that a slight or abrupt shift is at hand, bends perspective. When I have omitted text, the ellipses is presented in brackets.

83 One study that takes all of these sources into account concludes: "Friedrich Nietzsche's disease consisted of migraine, psychiatric disturbances, cognitive decline with dementia, and stroke. Despite the prevalent opinion that neurosyphilis caused Nietzsche's illness, there is lack of evidence to support this diagnosis." See D. Hemelsoet, K. Hemelsoet, and D. Devreese, "The neurological illness of Friedrich Nietzsche," *Acta Neurologica Belgica*, Vol. 108, No. 1 (2008), 9–16, https://pubmed.ncbi.nlm.nih.gov/18575181. Accessed August 9, 2022. Several other articles are linked to on this page with such titles as: "The madness of Dionysus—six hypotheses on the illness of Nietzsche," "Friedrich Nietzsche's mental illness—general paralysis of the insane vs. frontotemporal dementia," and "Turin's breakdown: Nietzsche's pathographies and medical rationalities."

84 The house is at Via Carlo Alberto 6, across the street from the splendid Palazzo Carignano and around the corner from the grand National University Library. A plaque is affixed to the house stating that this was where he wrote his masterpiece *Ecce Homo*. It is also where he finished *The Antichrist*.

on a walk down the Via Po, sees a coachman mercilessly flogging a horse. The horse is whinnying, snorting, and groaning out of pain and sheer terror. Nietzsche rushes to the horse, throws his arms around her neck (it's always a "nag" in the story) in an attempt to protect and comfort her, bursts out crying, and finally collapses onto the ground, sobbing uncontrollably. Two policemen arrive. A crowd gathers. Davide Fino, perhaps being alerted that his tenant was in trouble, arrives on the scene and convinces the policemen to leave Nietzsche in his care. With this event, the process that leads to Nietzsche's commitment to a mental asylum begins.

Nietzsche scholars are divided on the veracity of the story. Apparently, it first appeared in an Italian daily some eleven years after the event, written up by an anonymous reporter who had interviewed self-identified witnesses as well as members of the Fino family. Still, I have not come across any reason to doubt the story. But like everything with Nietzsche, it is more complicated than meets the eye. Biographers point out that, if true, Nietzsche's sense of the tragic may lie behind this sad scene. For instance, in a letter to a friend, while discussing quite mundane matters—"spring has arrived...I have discovered *Turin*, an unknown city...nights are cool...did you receive the book I sent?"—Nietzsche, out of the blue, writes that he recently imagined a scene of "tearful morality": "Winter landscape. An old coachman with the expression of brutal cynicism, even harder than the surrounding winter, urinates on his own horse. The horse, poor ravaged creature, looks around gratefully, *very* gratefully."[85] Another possible (subconscious?) model for the scene on Via Po comes from Dostoyevsky, an author whom Nietzsche read and admired. In *Crime and Punishment*, the protagonist, Roskolnikov, dreams that a coachman brutally beats his horse to death. A young boy, "beside himself, made his way, screaming, through the crowd to the sorrel nag, put his arms round her bleeding dead head and kissed it, kissed the eyes and kissed the lips...'Father! Why did they kill the poor horse!' he sobbed, but his voice broke and the words came in shrieks from his panting chest."[86]

Back in his apartment, a doctor is called, the sedative Bromide is administered, and Nietzsche's closest friend, Franz Overbeck, is sent a postcard apprising him of his friend's deteriorating situation and requesting Overbeck to retrieve him. Overbeck shows up several days later, on January 7, 1889; and, ultimately, Nietzsche ends up in a mental asylum. I will come back to this point. First, I want to give a sense of what led to this moment.

---

85 *BVN*–1888, 1034.
86 Dostoevsky, *Crime and Punishment*, Chapter Five.

Reading through Nietzsche's letters, I feel it is safe to suggest that his slide into irreversible mental illness begins—or begins to *show*—in October, 1888. In an October 9 letter to Hans von Bülow, one of the nineteenth century's premier Romantic composers, conductors, and pianists—not to mention Cosima's husband when Nietzsche first met her at the Wagner house—Nietzsche writes:

> Honored sir, You have not answered my letter—You will once and for all be free of me, that I promise you. I think you must have a concept that the premier spirt of the age expressed a wish to you. Friedrich Nietzsche[87]

This haughty tone is highly uncharacteristic of the polite, respectful, patient, understanding, witty, and warm correspondent that Nietzsche almost invariably was. It also shows the megalomania that was beginning to set in. A couple of weeks later, he sends a perfectly uncalled for nasty letter to Malwida von Meysenbug, a considerably older, intelligent and cultured woman whom Nietzsche holds in the highest regard and has unfailingly shown the utmost respect: "I have gradually done away with virtually all of my human relationships. I have done so out of *disgust* that they take me for someone I am not. Now it is your turn."[88] He goes on to harangue her for various failings over the course of their friendship. In between such troubling letters, Nietzsche writes entirely "normal" ones. More worrisome is when Nietzsche starts interspersing coherent passages with ones that reveal the frightening signs of mental illness. For example, in a workaday letter to Heinrich Köselitz (Peter Gast), Nietzsche casually mentions: "From time to time now I look at my *hand* with mistrust because, it seems to me, I hold the fate of humanity 'in hand.'"[89] In another letter to Köselitz, he describes, almost in passing, something approaching a dissociative state: "Occasionally, I get extremely upset that I am incapable of speaking a single sincere, open word to anyone…I make so many dumb poses with myself and have such attacks of private buffoonery that I sometimes walk around the streets grinning—no other word fits—for thirty minutes straight." Once, when a funny thought had occurred to him, "It took four days to restore my face to a serious mien [...] I think that under such conditions one is ripe to

---

87 *BVN*–1888, 1129.
88 *BVN*–1888, 1135.
89 *BVN*–1888, 1137.

become the 'world-savior.'"[90] A couple of days later, he found himself "constantly grinning" after having attended a concert.[91] By January 1889 he signs himself almost exclusively, "The Antichrist," "Dionysus," "The Crucified," "The Immoralist," "a monstrous beast."

The Friedrich Nietzsche that Franz Overbeck discovered when he showed up on January 7, 1889, was, to put it bluntly, raving mad. He had kept the Fino children up several nights in a row, pounding on the family piano, singing at the top of his lungs, and dancing ecstatically (and naked) in his room. Overbeck sums it up: "I have never seen such a horrific picture of destruction."[92]

Nietzsche would slowly deteriorate, first in the asylum in Basel, then in the asylum in Jena, where he could be closer to his mother, then in his mother's house in Naumburg, and, finally, after the death of his mother, in Weimar, with his sister. As you might do with a toddler, Franziska Nietzsche kept a notebook with things her son said. It shows the horrible deterioration from a world-class mind of rare brilliance to that of an average three-year-old. One entry records Nietzsche saying:

I have translated much, I am accustomed. I lived in a good place in Naumburg and in a completely different place not Naumburg. I went up to the attic and awakened my sister. I lived in Naumburg a lot, because I was good. I swam in the Saale like a whale I was very fine and I played vocally in the cathedral. I was very fine because I live in a house. I write letters everyday to very good people and to His Majesty. I was very fine and give a house key to my mother every day…

[His mother, presumably:] What is that here?
[Nietzsche:] An ear.
—What is that here?
—A nose.
—What is that here?
—Hands I do not love.[93]

---

90 *BVN*–1888, 1157.
91 *BVN*–1888, 1168.
92 Cited in Young, *Friedrich Nietzsche*, 550.
93 Gilman, *Conversations with Nietzsche*, 234–235.

Before long, such simple utterances would devolve into mere moans and grunts. Although visitors report a dullness in Nietzsche's eyes,[94] apparently music still brightened him up. One visitor reports that whenever Nietzsche caught wind that a musical performance was to occur, "he was immediately ecstatic and emitted ugly, unarticulated sounds, a dull, horrible groaning. After the music began his whole face was transfigured and beamed indescribably. But this expression of excessive joy was, in its sickness, no less terrible than the animalistic behavior just before." And, in sickness as in health, "He grumbled with displeasure when strangers visited him."[95] All of this makes it all the more gruesome that Nietzsche's caregiver sister put him on display like a circus freak. One visitor to the Weimar residence, a Baron Friedrich von Schennis, reports the following. In celebration of Nietzsche's birthday, a grand dinner was held. At the end of the long table, decked out with the birthday feast, was a violet curtain. Toward the end of the dinner, the curtain parted. There sat the slumped, pale, hollow-eyed "sick man, dressed in a toga-like robe."[96]

Nietzsche died on August 25, 1900. As anyone close to him knew, he wanted a simple funeral, one completely devoid of the slightest trace of Christianity and pomp. For music, he wanted "Hymn to Life" *(Hymnus an das Leben)*, which was Lou Salomé's poem "Prayer to Life" *(Lebensgebet)* set to music by Nietzsche himself several years earlier.[97] His sister, who would inherit the rights to his soon-to-be profitable catalog, perverting it to ingratiate herself with the Nazis, arranged the funeral. It was a thoroughly Christian affair, and it was absurdly pompous. The music was that of a conservative composer, Giovanni Pierluigi da Palestrina, whose oeuvre

---

94 Graf Harry Kessler, who was a good friend of the family in later years, describes Nietzsche's look at this time as being "loyal and, at the same time, of not quite understanding, of a fruitless intellectual searching, such as you often see in a large, noble dog." In Prideaux, *I Am Dynamite!*, 366.

95 Gilman, *Conversations with Nietzsche*, 255–256.

96 This event is mentioned by Walter Benjamin in "Nietzsche und das Archiv Seiner Schwester. Kritiken Und Rezensionen: Walter Benjamin." Benjamin seems to doubt the validity of the account, saying that "it certainly can not be regarded as authenticated." He repeats it nonetheless because it "makes palpable the horror" that surrounded the Nietzsche-Archiv in its earliest days. See https://www.textlog.de/benjamin/kritik/nietzsche-archiv-schwester. Accessed October 13, 2023. Benjamin's understandable incredulity aside, some dozen accounts of Nietzsche being put on display are recorded in a chapter titled "On Display in Weimar," in Gilman, *Conversations with Nietzsche*, 237–262.

97 A version for piano and voice can be heard here: https://www.youtube.com/watch?v=aOfNaVnFmU8. Accessed April 3, 2024. Interestingly, Nietzsche writes to friend and fellow composer Peter Gast (Heinrich Köselitz) that he wants this piece to be performed publicly so that "people will be *seduced* to my philosophy." *BVN*–1882, 295. The question of the relationship between Nietzsche's music and his thought is quite interesting.

included one hundred and five church masses. Brahms was played as well. "Hymn to Life" was not. An arrogant, affected scholar of art history, one Kurt Breisig, stood to deliver a eulogy. One attendee, Fritz Schumacher, describes the "torment":

> In the little library room…the open coffin, covered with a veil, stood amid wreaths and flowers. It could not be avoided to step right close to it, and with a mixed feeling of reverence and shame one thus stood in closest proximity to the deceased. And now the Berlin cultural historian Kurt Breisig, leaning into the open window, began to give a eulogy. An obvious feeling commanded that the mood of the hour be captured in a few solemn, deeply felt words, in terms of both the internal and external situation of the moment. Instead, the speaker pulled out a thick manuscript and began to read. Since he had trouble holding his manuscript, a lecturing stand was improvised for him out of Frau Forster's sewing box, and now he mercilessly read to us a cultural-historical analysis of the phenomenon of Nietzsche. Seldom have I experienced grimmer moments. Scholarship pursued this man all the way to the grave under the guise of the culture against which he fought like no other. If he had revived he would long since have thrown the speaker out the window and chased us out of the temple—even us who were innocent of this outrage.[98]

Nietzsche wanted to die and, presumably, to be buried, in the one place on earth that he considered his "true home and breeding ground" for ideas, namely Sils Maria.[99] His sister instead arranged for him to be buried in Röcken, next to his parents (his mother had since died). As I mentioned earlier, Nietzsche expressed the "terrible fear that I will one day be pronounced holy…I do not want to be a holy man." So, keeping with the disregard and misunderstanding that plagued Nietzsche his entire life, in the final act before lowering his body forever into the earth, his closest friend, Peter Gast, pronounced him holy: "Peace be unto your ashes. Holy be your name to all future generations!"

---

98 Gilman, *Conversations with Nietzsche*, 248.
99 *BVN*–1883, 428; and *BVN*–1883, 427.

WE PERFECT READERS

When I imagine a perfect reader, they always turn out to be a monster of courage and curiosity, in addition something supple, cunning, cautious, a born adventurer and discoverer.[1]

THE AIM OF THIS BOOK IS TO COAX MY READER INTO THE KIND OF ADVENTURE that Nietzsche envisions for *his* perfect reader. And what an adventure that is! Why be coy—let me proclaim *right away* a result of this adventure. It is "a happiness that humanity has not known so far: the happiness of a god full of power and love, full of tears and laughter, a happiness that, like the sun in the evening, continually bestows its inexhaustible riches, pouring them into the sea, feeling richest, as the sun does only when even the poorest fisherman is still rowing with golden oars!"[2] All of this—from a self-proclaimed world-historical monster, immoralist, *antichrist*? Can it be—this from the man who announces *nihilism*, the "uncanniest of guests," lurking at our doorway? Who, proclaiming, "God is dead! and we have killed him!" inaugurates an epoch of "radical repudiation of value, meaning, and desirability"? Who "loves only that which is written in blood"? Who boasts of the "nobility" of the "blond beasts"? Who cautions, "You go to women? Don't forget the whip!"? Readers already exposed to Nietzsche's reputation as a brutish, humorless, über-macho, massively mustachioed Teutonic philosopher might be surprised at his endless talk of cheerfulness, health, love, and…humaneness. Yes. For the final sentence of that quote about our adventure's destination is "this godlike feeling would then be called—humaneness." Nietzsche wants us to embark on a journey to *becoming human…*and beyond.

We can say the same for themes addressed directly or indirectly in this book. What is the ideology of wokeness if not an attempt to uncover and thereby undermine *de-humanizing* practices of prejudice, discrimination, racism, sexism, and more? What is cancel culture if not a mechanism for

---

1 *Ecce Homo*, "Why I Write Such Good Books," 3.
2 *The Gay Science*, 337.

bringing to task public figures who have violated our shared moral standards? What is the struggle for LGBTQI+ and other identity-oriented rights if not a fight for *human* dignity, pure and simple? What is each of the themes addressed in this book if not a feature in the broader attempt to establish our *humaneness*? Indeed, what is animal liberation if not the acknowledgment that it is our *very humaneness* that demands that we cease all exploitation of nonhuman animals?

Given that our own culture seems thus to have the goods well in hand for establishing our humanity, our humaneness, against the brute forces of *inhumanity*, we must ask again: Why Nietzsche? Why Now? It is the very answering of this twofold question that comprises the book as a whole. So, it will come piece by piece, accumulating, I hope, into a satisfying answer. But stating the short, incomplete version of this answer at the outset will enhance our journey.

The German word that Nietzsche uses for "humaneness" in the above passage is *Menschlichkeit*. Some readers may glimpse here the Yiddish word *mensch* or *mentsch*. Where I live—on the east coast of the United States with a long tradition of Jewish immigration—this Yiddish word has entered into everyday discourse, denoting *a decent human being*. A *mensch* is a person who acts with integrity and honor. Using a term that is particularly important to Nietzsche, we might even say that a *mensch* is a *noble* person. If someone around here calls you a *mensch*, you should feel really good about yourself.

Yet, to be precise, the term just means *human*. So when someone says you are a *mensch*, they are simply acknowledging that you behave as a *human*. The deep assumption at work here is that the typical *homo sapiens* ape[3] has not necessarily attained the status of *human*. Similarly, the themes addressed in this book aim to bring us up to the status of *human*. That aim likewise assumes that, in persisting in our prejudices and discriminations, we are behaving as something less than a human. And this is where we can learn from Nietzsche.

Nietzsche wants us to become and then *overcome* the human. Hence, his (in)famous term, *Übermensch*, overhuman. As one of his book titles puts it, he would see in the exhortations of our current discourse on, say, equality, the *human, all too human*. What does this mean? His statement, "The Four Errors," explains.

---

3 Curious about this designation? See Beth Blaxland, "Humans are Apes—Great Apes," Australian Museum. https://australian.museum/learn/science/human-evolution/humans-are-apes-great-apes. Accessed April 7, 2024.

The Four Errors. Humans have been brought up by their errors: first, they saw themselves only incompletely; second, they conferred on themselves fantasized qualities; third, they felt themselves to be in a false ranking in relation to the animals and nature; fourth, they devised always new tablets of values, and accepted them for a time as eternal and unconditioned, so that now this, now that, human impulse or condition stood first, and was, as a consequence of the valuation, ennobled. When one has subtracted the effect of these four errors, one has also subtracted away humanity, humaneness, and "human dignity."[4]

So the short answer is that we need Nietzsche, and we need him *now*, because he is—I believe and hope to convince you—an exceptionally *timely* thinker for helping us (in the terms of the above quote): first, to see our blind spots; second, to distinguish between fabricated and integral human qualities; third, to show us our proper relation to animals and nature; and fourth, to inoculate us against the belief that our values are timeless and unconditioned. Such "errors" are, for Nietzsche, integral to our very humanity. Remove these features from your calculation of what constitutes the human, and you calculate away the very being that is "human." To err thus is, indeed, *human* through and through. So if "humaneness" is not, per se, the goal of our adventure, after all, what is?

I teach you the overhuman. The human is something to be overcome. What have you done to overcome the human?...I teach you the over-human. The overhuman is the meaning of the earth.[5]

Overcoming such errors leads to an overcoming of the (merely) human. That is the short version of our answer. If any further initial explanation of the notion is required, consider that the two passages following "The Four Errors" are titled "Herd Instinct" and "The Herd's Sting of Conscience." The adventure that Nietzsche prescribes is one ventured far from "the herd"—far away, that is, from our meaning-making, value-preserving community of conventionally like-minded people.

The reader may be getting the sense that our adventure is not a pleasure cruise to balmy climes. And the reader would be right. Nietzsche is inviting us to "descend into the netherworld of [our] soul."[6] He insists, after all, that

---

4 *The Gay Science*, 115.
5 *Thus Spoke Zarathustra*, Prologue, 3.
6 *Ecce Homo*, "Why I Write Such Great Books," 6.

"To make the individual uncomfortable. That is my task."[7] And why should we subject ourselves to such discomfort? Let's look further into the adventure in store for us.

The journey Nietzsche has in mind will lead you away not only from the herd, but also from the very *progenitors* of herd-like conscience; away, namely, from the smooth pathways of our current meaning-makers—our gurus, secular and religious; our confident life philosophers; our spiritual healers; our self-assured guides to culture, politics, and identity. None of the consolations proffered by such "'improvers' of humankind"[8] will be part of our Nietzschean adventure. No assurance that our precious opinions are necessarily close to anything like "right." No celebration of our values, our politics, even of our very sense of self. No gloriously preserved "hinterworld" awaiting us somewhere behind or beyond this troubled actual world. Certainly no protection by our chosen community. For Nietzsche, an insurmountable problem with such improvers of humankind is that they demand an affirmation, and hence, offer an "improvement" that is *too hasty* and *too easy*. These fashioners of our meaning-making communities require a kind of ideological fealty, an indiscriminate affirmation that is—and there is no polite way to put this—*ass-like*. "Always to bray *yea-yuh*—only the ass has learned *that*, and whoever is of its spirit."[9] Its spirit, of course, is one of a stubbornness and inflexibility that equates to the mental, emotional, and ideological intransigence that arguably defines our stuck, divided, gridlocked, hyper-partisan age.

Another reason to be "cautious," as Nietzsche advises his perfect reader, regarding the "improvement" wrought by humankind's improvers is that such improvement looks more like *ruination*.

> To call the taming of an animal its "improvement" sounds almost like a joke to our ears. Whoever knows what goes on in zoos doubts that the beasts are "improved" there. They are weakened, they are made less harmful, and through the depressive affect of fear, through pain, through wounds, and through hunger, they become sickly beasts.[10]

Nietzsche is attentive to animals throughout his life and work. Indeed, as we have seen, one of his last acts before being committed to a mental asylum

---

7 *We Philologists*, 192.
8 *Twilight of the Idols*, "The 'Improvers' of Humankind."
9 *Ecce Homo*, "Why I Write Such Great Books," 2.
10 *Twilight of the Idols*, "The 'Improvers' of Humankind," 2

may have been to embrace, in a fit of sobbing compassion, a carriage horse who was in the throes of a flogging. More importantly, as we will see in later chapters, Nietzsche does not accept a demarcation between "human" and "animal." His attentiveness to animals is concomitant with his attentiveness to humans. Why? Because humans *are* animals. In fact, a major problem, in Nietzsche's eyes, is the fact that humans have forgotten that they are animals. Again, more later. In this passage, Nietzsche is talking about the human animal using a reference to the nonhuman animal. Improvement of the human animal lies at the heart of each of the themes treated in this book. What Nietzsche is suggesting is that such "improvement" comes at the cost of *ruining* the person in quite decisive ways. We can take as an example one of the themes addressed in this book: equality. Nietzsche says that "Without the pathos of distance, the sort which grows out of the deeply rooted difference between the social classes"[11] no new world is possible—at least not the just and joyous world that I and, I imagine, my readers desire. Nietzsche wants to convince us that the concept of *equality* that we so virtuously invoke arises out of a specific context—nineteenth-century liberal democratic thought—and as such is a *hindrance* to our renewed world. This does not mean that he is advocating *inequality* as understood in that same context. But he *is* advocating for *something like it*, just *not* it. My point here is that Nietzsche is asking us to consider whether our contemporary notion of equality might have the same kind of "taming" effect that, say, hunger does on a zoo animal. He wants us to consider whether the individual, and indeed society as a whole, might likewise be *pained, wounded, depressed,* and *starved* by our culture's specific notion of equality. This may sound incredible, even distasteful to many readers. So I ask, can we, for now, follow Nietzsche's advice and not immediately "surrender to humanitarian illusions," since, after all, "truth is hard"?[12]

This point leads us to three crucial interrelated features of our adventure. One, it is full of surprises. Two, it is dangerous. Three, we must take our time. The surprise often lies in the danger, and the danger in the surprise. Hence, we must go slowly, *tarry*, even, at the very point of danger, and where we feel most surprised. Nietzsche can teach us short-attention-spanned, hyper-accelerated, quick-to-judge postmoderns something of great importance here. Learning his lesson of *lento! lento!* (slow! slow!) in the face of a suspicious-looking surprise is something we need *always* to learn, and *desperately* so in our age of memes, emojis, sound bites, texting

11 *Beyond Good and Evil*, 257.
12 *Beyond Good and Evil*, 257.

abbreviations, and 280 character tweets. Here is another thing Nietzsche can teach us: I imagine that most of my readers will agree that the increasing sensitivity—to slights and aggression, to slurs, bigotry, racism, misogyny, even to everyday small injustices—is a *good* thing. Nietzsche would agree. He believes, after all, that it is often the people with the most finely tuned sensitivities who become "the seed bearers of the future, the initiators of spiritual colonialization and the renewal of states and social communities."[13] The practice of *lento!* will help ensure that that same sensitivity, however, does not result in a premature reaction to dismiss, much less condemn, or *cancel* that which uncomfortably surprises us and reeks of unwanted danger. Contrary to a current truism, one's *feeling* is not always a reliable gauge to a situation.

Let's take as examples two of the more questionable assertions made earlier; namely, Nietzsche's caution, "You go to women? Don't forget the whip!" and his boast of the "nobility" of the "blond beasts." What was your response when you read those statements? Pretty brutal, aren't they? Surprising, I assume; and dangerous, obviously. The "whip" comment sounds inexcusably misogynistic and the "blond-beast" trope suggests collusion with proto-fascism. In fact, Nietzsche's persistent association with both of those noxious views can be traced largely to these two tropes. (And they are just the tip of the conceptual iceberg on our journey!) But deservedly so? So, here, we must *slow down.*

The whip. In many regards, Nietzsche was arguably what we would today label a *feminist.* Significant episodes from his life support this view. For example, as a professor, he was one of only four faculty members to vote for admission of women to Basel University. He was so perturbed when the motion failed, that he insisted on recording his dissenting view in the official record. Nietzsche, in fact, valued his many female friends for their high intelligence and deep knowledge. Malwida von Meysenbug (1816–1903), the author of *Memoirs of a Female Idealist*, recruited Nietzsche to join her "mission house for adults of both sexes to have a free development of the noblest spiritual life, so that they could then go forth into the world to sow the seeds of a new spiritualized culture." With Nietzsche involved, she further recounts, "I was convinced I could attract many women students… in order to develop them into the noblest representatives of the emancipation of women."[14] Nietzsche's respect extended to his younger sister, Elizabeth,

---

13 *The Gay Science,* 23.
14 C. P. Janz, *Friedrich Nietzsche: Biographie* (3 vols) (Munich and Vienna: Carl Hanser Verlag, 1978); quoted in Julian Young, "Nietzsche and Women," *The Oxford Handbook of*

as well. From the time she was a young girl, Nietzsche encouraged her to develop her intellectual capacities—to read, to think, to reason, to reach her potential, to assert herself in conversation, to take a stand, to *become* someone. Because he believed Elizabeth to be wholly capable, Nietzsche was perpetually frustrated when she invariably opted for the diminished role expected of a middle-class woman in Victorian-era Germany. In the 1897 biography of her brother "Fritz," Elisabeth Förster-Nietzsche comments on the very issue at hand:

> How did it come about that my brother is generally considered a misogynist? I believe it is due to a little remark from *Zarathustra*: "You are going to women? Do not forget the whip!" For that is the only thing which a hundred thousand women know about Nietzsche. They do not even bother to check up in *Zarathustra* as to who makes this statement, namely a little old woman, and even those who read it do not understand the mischievous humor of the whole chapter.[15]

We will return in a moment to the comment about not bothering to check up. The point here is that many accounts of Nietzsche's relations with women are consistent with Elisabeth Förster-Nietzsche's. Ida von Miaskowski, the wife of Nietzsche's colleague at the University of Basel, who, for a period was very close to Nietzsche, relates the following. (Such remembrances are valuable as well for the human light they throw on our journey's all-too-human guide.)

> In the [1880s], when Nietzsche's later writings containing some of the oft-quoted sharp words against women appeared, my husband sometimes told me jokingly not to tell people of my friendly relations with Nietzsche, since this was not very flattering for me. It was just a joke. My husband, like myself, always kept friendly memories of Nietzsche, whose intellectually lofty, yet humanly gracious and cheerful demeanor always remained unforgettable to everyone who knew him. And his behavior precisely toward women was so sensitive, so natural and comradely, that even today in old age I cannot regard Nietzsche as a despiser of women.[16]

Nietzsche, edited by John Richardson and Ken Gemes (Oxford: Oxford University Press, 2013), 46–63.
15 Gilman, *Conversations with Nietzsche*, 123.
16 Gilman, *Conversations with Nietzsche*, 52.

Of course, a cheerful, intellectually lofty man can still be a misogynist. And offering that you are "only joking" about these matters is no longer an accepted justification. Like many of today's canceled comedians, Nietzsche himself uses the "joke" defense to explain the remark in question. In a somewhat humorous anecdote, one young man, Sebastian Hausmann, relates the following. He was walking toward Silvaplana, the beautiful lake near Nietzsche's summer residence of Sils Maria, in Switzerland. Suddenly, Hausmann sees a man with "a commanding personality and a rather unusual appearance, whom one would therefore well remember: a large bushy mustache gave the face a martial air, a striking profile; involuntarily one would have thought a Prussian officer in civilian clothes, except that the head also showed signs of very extraordinary intellectual significance." When the mustached man unwittingly dropped something from his coat pocket—a letter, as it turned out—Hausmann retrieved it and ran up to him. Grateful, the man thanked Hausmann, and then reached "fleetingly for his hat and mumbled a name that sounded very similar to *Nietzsche*." This similarity jogged Hausmann's memory: the man looked like the pictures he had seen of the controversial philosopher. "Are you perhaps a relative of the famous philosopher Nietzsche?" Hausmann asks, to which the man replies, "No, I'm not related to him." "Well, thank God!" says Hausmann. The man, looking askance at Hausmann, inquires: "So you don't like the philosopher?" "No," Hausmann answers.

> After a few paces the man suddenly stopped and turned toward me with a good-humored, gentle smile: "Let us not play hide-and-seek. You were quite right to think of the philosopher Nietzsche at sight of me. I am really not related to your Nietzsche, for I am the man himself… But you must tell me frankly exactly what you disliked about my style of writing."

Now Hausmann is greatly embarrassed, for, like many critics, Hausmann had not even bothered to "get very far in reading, or rather, studying [Nietzsche's] writings." So:

> Frantically I searched my memory…Suddenly I thought of a statement that my circle of friends had discussed in detail: "Don't forget the whip, when you go to a woman!" or something similar. When I cited this example, he looked at me in astonishment: "But, I beg you, surely that cannot cause you any difficulty! I mean, it is clear and understandable

that this is only a joke, an exaggerated, symbolic mode of expression." [...] He also told me, moreover, that the much discussed and much misunderstood phrase had its origin in a personal memory.[17]

The personal memory was of a now famous photograph in which Nietzsche had posed years earlier with his friends Pau Reé and Lou (Louise) von Salomé. The image shows Salomé in a cart being "pulled" by Nietzsche and Reé. In her hand—in *her* hand—Salomé wields a small whip, gesturing toward the two men, as if whipping them to *giddyup!* In fact, when, as a young man, I first read the line about the whip in *Thus Spoke Zarathustra*, I had already seen the photograph. So I reflexively assumed that Nietzsche was reminding us to bring the whip for the use of the women we will encounter. What *that* meant, I had little idea—something about women ultimately dominating men, maybe? In any case, nothing that I had ever read in or about Nietzsche had primed me to consider that he was bringing the whip to whip the woman. Are Nietzsche's and my personal references still too meager to explain (away) "You go to women? Don't forget the whip!"? Let's dig deeper. Any of us who "bother to check up" will discover that the statement is drenched in Nietzschean references that span Greek tragedy, Menippean satire,[18] the myth of Dionysus, the eroticism (sado-masochism?) of reading and writing, textual *(Zarathustra)* and intertextual passages, and more.[19] In her book *Nietzsche and Gender: Beyond Man and Woman*, literary scholar Frances Nesbitt Oppel offers a thorough analysis of the very comment in question. The relevant chapter, titled "Zarathustra's Whip," has the very telling subtitle of "Disciplining Readers." Nesbitt Oppel points out that most readers have taken the whip out of the text and used it to flagellate *Nietzsche* over his perceived misogyny. Her conclusion is that:

---

17 Gilman, *Conversations with Nietzsche*, 135. This "surely" response seems all-too-frequent in Nietzsche's encounters with others. As the following anecdote suggests, however, Nietzsche might have expected too much of others' powers of observation. A colleague, Julius Piccard, reports that Nietzsche had played the piano at a dinner party one evening. As we might expect, his playing was "quite bewildering." Piccard relates: "On the way home he asked me what people had thought of it. I answered politely but asked about the meaning of a repeated staccato that had seemed somewhat peculiar to me and probably to others. 'But Piccard! You didn't understand that this was the stars in the sky during a walk in the night?' And the poor man became so sad that I felt very sorry for him." *Ibid.*, 34–35.
18 Menippus was a third century B.C.E Greek Cynic philosopher.
19 See, for instance, Kathleen Higgins, "The Whip Recalled," *Journal of Nietzsche Studies*, No. 12, *Nietzsche and Women* (Autumn 1996): 1–18; and Adrian Del Caro, "Nietzsche, Sacher-Masoch, and the Whip," *German Studies Review*, Vol. 21, No. 2 (May, 1998): 241–261.

The line about the whip, like the text in which it is embedded, is vastly overdetermined: it derives from a multitude of sources and explodes with many possible interpretations. As part of the parody of "old law-tables" [...] and Zarathustra's apparent subscription to them, it is a joke. As an embryonic hint of Zarathustra's future transformation, it is an exaggerated, *symbolic* mode of expression. And as a personal memory, it is raw emotion—anger, lust, resentment [...] The discourse itself is *symbolic* of man's domination of woman and has served, like a whip, to keep her in her place: loving, obeying, sacrificing, and pregnant.[20]

Disciplining implicated *readers*, indeed!

Does any of this mean that Nietzsche never exhibited misogynist views in his work or that you might not *still* find the whip statement misogynistic? No! Nietzsche's views on woman are complex, spanning a continuum from healthy reciprocal friendship to idolization to hostility. His view, moreover, changed throughout his life. To repeat, the important point in this exercise is that a general rule about the guide to our adventure is this: wherever he leads us into one of his many surprises, danger likely lurks; and where we catch the scent of danger, we must slow down. To be very clear, though, the point is *not* to bring our guide unscathed out of the danger—a *safe* Nietzsche, indeed, an uncomplicated Nietzsche, is no Nietzsche at all. But neither is the point to get *ourselves* out unscathed. Persisting in your reading, recall, you will become "a monster of courage and curiosity;…supple, cunning, cautious; a born adventurer and discoverer." But only if you *slow down* and *proceed*.

Blond beast. Many readers of Nietzsche to this day believe that only a Nazi can appreciate such a phrase. And this is by no means the only phrase like it in Nietzsche's corpus. Imagine the raw possibilities of such Nietzschean notions as *übermensch/superman, masters/slaves, beyond good and evil, supra-moral morality, immorality, strength/weakness, the antichrist, instinct, will to power, perfect nihilism, Dionysian passion, the death of God, anti-reason*, and more! Not to mention the fact that the man whom Hitler appointed to oversee the Holocaust was none other than the high-ranking SS official, instigator of the so-called *Kristallnacht*, and murder mastermind of the SA purge "Night of the Long Knives," Reinhard Heydrich, *aka*. The Blond Beast.

---

20 Frances Nesbitt Oppel, *Nietzsche and Gender: Beyond Man and Woman* (Charlottesville: University of Virginia Press, 2005), 152 and 153; emphases on "symbolic" added.

Cruelty, aggression, and misogyny are the danger lurking behind the *whip* remark. Nothing less than the unspeakable horrors of Nazi Germany lurk behind *blond beast*. Our bothering to check up on the *whip* remark will not absolve Nietzsche of nastiness toward women in every reader's eyes. Nonetheless, doing so reveals additional layers of interpretations worthy, I believe, of serious consideration. Is the same true for the *blond beast* trope? Or is Nietzsche irretrievably in cahoots with Nazis here?

Elisabeth Förster-Nietzsche's earlier remark contains instructive strategy for reading her brother. She insists, first, that we "bother to check up in" the text. More than any author with whom I am familiar, divining Nietzsche's meaning requires the reader to attend with acute sensitivity to *context*. She also insists, second, that we properly discern the *intended tone*. Is the statement intended as "mischievous humor"? Irony? Provocation? Inspiration? Satire? Counterpoint? Symbolism? Nietzsche employs all of these modes, and many more besides, in his highly stylized writing. Nietzsche is nothing if not entertaining to read. He is also *difficult*. Nietzsche is not an obscure writer. Yet, he is *elusive*. Nietzsche places strict demands on his reader, often creating exquisite labyrinths of intertextuality—beautiful to behold, but quickly turning dark and forbidding. "It is absolutely no objection to a book if anyone finds it unintelligible," he tells us in a section titled "On the Question of Intelligibility," "perhaps that was part of the author's intention—he did not want to be understood by 'anyone.'"[21] *Thus Spoke Zarathustra* is tellingly subtitled, *A Book for None and All*. It would be a fair question to ask: so, which is it? The answer, I believe, is both. Surely speaking of himself, Nietzsche further confesses:

> Every nobler spirit and taste, when it wants to communicate itself, always selects its hearers; by selecting them, it at the same time erects its barricade against "the others." All refined laws of a style have their origin here: they simultaneously hold off, they create distance, they forbid "access," intelligibility, as I said—while they open the ears of those who are, with their ears, related to us.[22]

Nietzsche's incredibly rich cache of (often explosive) ideas is open to all, as long as they do the required mining work. Conversely, his work is open to none as long as they refuse such work. I will have many opportunities to say more about this facet of Nietzsche throughout this book. Here, let us

21 *The Gay Science*, 381.
22 *The Gay Science*, 381.

consider this "disciplining" of the reader—to read carefully, slowly, expansively, with concentration and attention—as yet another important reason to read Nietzsche—particularly in a world where 3.3 billion people have installed TikTok on their phones and watch an average of 850 minutes (14 hours) a month.[23]

Nietzsche, in fact, often expressed sheer terror at the possibility of being misunderstood by the kinds of "reading idlers"[24] that, arguably, we have collectively become: "The worst readers are those who behave like plundering troops: they take away a few things they can use, dirty and confound the remainder, and revile the whole." This is precisely what the Nazis, aided by none other than Elisabeth Förster-Nietzsche, did with Nietzsche's work. Like the masterful totalitarian propagandists that they were, they plundered it for sound bites—*What does not kill me makes me stronger!*—that appeared to harmonize with their noxious ideology. In fact, I believe that it can be demonstrated that, in every instance, Nietzsche's intended meaning was virtually *the opposite* of what Goebbels and Co. claimed. In fact, one prominent Nazi scientist and pedagogue, Ernst Krieck, "sarcastically remarked that apart from the fact that Nietzsche was not a socialist, not a nationalist, and opposed to racial thinking, he could have been a leading National Socialist thinker."[25] Can we keep in our ears Nietzsche's exhortation, "*Above all, do not mistake me for someone else!*"[26]

So, when we bother to check up on the phrase in question, how do things look? The notorious *blond beast* turns up in three passages.[27] The short answer is this. By "blond beast" Nietzsche means *a lion*: "At the bottom of all these noble races we cannot fail to recognize the beast of prey, the splendid *blond beast* prowling avidly about in search of spoil and victory." In classic Nietzschean fashion, however, as the phrase "noble races" indicates, the matter is not so easily settled. While a full exegesis would be too much

---

23 "TikTok Statistics." https://influencermarketinghub.com/tiktok-stats. Accessed May 5, 2022. For the uninitiated, TikTok "hosts a variety of short-form user videos, from genres like pranks, stunts, tricks, jokes, dance, and entertainment with durations from 15 seconds to ten minutes." *Wikipedia*. https://en.wikipedia.org/wiki/TikTok. Accessed May 5, 2022.

24 *Thus Spoke Zarathustra*, "On Reading and Writing." The full quote is relevant: "It is not easy to understand the blood of another. I hate the reading idler."

25 Prideaux, *I Am Dynamite!*, 377.

26 *Ecce Homo*, Preface; emphasis in original. "I am frightened by the thought of what unqualified and unsuitable people may invoke my authority one day. Yes, that is the torment of every great teacher of mankind: he knows that, given the circumstances and the accidents, he can become a disaster as well as a blessing to mankind." Letter to Elisabeth Förster-Nietzsche, from Venice, mid-June 1884, quoted in Prideaux, *I Am Dynamite!*, 378.

27 The passages are at *On the Genealogy of Morals*, 1.11 (where it appears three times) and 2.17; and *Twilight of the Idols*, "The 'Improvers' of Humankind," 2.

at this point, let me emphasize, once again, that *complexity* (in our time of overhasty, overdetermining *opinions*, idle reading, cancelation, and so on) is part of the very reason I have selected this problematic phrase, indeed, written this book. We can, in fact, learn something about Nietzsche's notion of a "noble race" from the very danger ringing in our ears. The passage continues:

> This hidden core needs to erupt from time to time: the animal has to get out again, and go back to the wilderness: the Roman, Arabian, Germanic, Japanese nobility, the Homeric heroes, the Scandinavian Vikings—in this need they are all the same.

Obviously, something more than *a lion*, the beast of prey with its blond mane, is meant here. Is some sort of metaphor afoot? This is a good place to mention Nietzsche's talents as both a psychologist ("That a psychologist without equal speaks from my writings—this is perhaps the first insight gained by a good reader") and a political scientist ("Only beginning with me is there *great politics* on the earth").[28] Nietzsche is fascinated, indeed obsessed, with human types. We will see many examples as we proceed. Historically, for Nietzsche, "blond beasts" and "noble races" are synonymous types. Whether in Japan or Germany, this is a type who "leaves behind them the concept 'barbarian' wherever they have gone."[29] The blond beast is an essential force, or, in figurative speech, a *lion*, of higher culture. The noble race is comprised of such "beasts," and, as such, overcomes base human barbarism toward the creation of higher values. Such "bestiality" is precisely the "hidden core," the continual renewal required to calibrate a more just and humane culture. (Recall the enervation of zoo animals previously.)

Still, "wilderness" in the quote suggests an aspect that may ruin this somewhat pleasant-sounding idea for many readers. Nietzsche, recall, insists that *truth is hard.* Truth does not care about human utility. It cares even less about our feelings. What Nietzsche is describing here is an ongoing process of creation and overcoming. Yes, it involves what we *like* to consider "noble"— magnanimity, justice, insight, health, wholeness, a future worth having. *And* it involves a wilder, more bestial sense of nobility—"indifference to and contempt for security, body, life, comfort, terrible cheerfulness and profound joy in all destruction, in all the voluptuousness of victory and cruelty."[30] Is

---

28 *Ecce Homo*, "Why I Write Such Good Books," 5, and "Why I am a Destiny," 1.
29 *On the Genealogy of Morals*, 1.11.
30 *On the Genealogy of Morals*, 1.11.

this meant literally or figuratively? Does it name an actual historical process or an interior psychological one? Is it an apt metaphor or an overwrought symbol? Might each of these possibilities stand in a dialectical relationship to the other? Can we even conceive of *a future* without *destruction* of what currently is? What is going on here?!

The crucial question for us aspiring perfect readers is this: are we willing to summon the necessary courage and curiosity; are we willing to render our minds and emotions supple, cunning, and cautious; are we willing to embark with Nietzsche on an adventure as rich in discovery as it is *dangerous*?

HOW TO READ LIKE A COW

In a passage remarkable for its unambiguous prescriptiveness, Nietzsche lays out the conditions for our understanding him. Let's consider carefully what he says: "If this text is incomprehensible to anyone, and grates on the ears, the fault, I think, does not lie necessarily with me."[31] His writing, he insists, is "clear enough, assuming, as I assume"—and here begin the conditions—"that the reader has first read my earlier work, and spared no effort doing so." Perhaps some of *my* readers have already done so, to some extent. Great! You know firsthand that "these texts are not easily accessible." So it seems that even *that* condition is not enough. Take Nietzsche's most popular work, *Thus Spoke Zarathustra*. Our demanding author will "allow no one to be considered a Knower of Zarathustra who has not at times been deeply wounded by his every word, and, at times, deeply delighted." Is this an arbitrary condition, arising, as is not uncommon, out of the author's overweening ego? Nietzsche claims that, on the contrary, this condition is literally that—a *condition*, a necessary and unavoidable prerequisite for an intended result, like priming a wall before applying paint. The result, Nietzsche promises, is to have a "reverent share in the work's tranquil element...its sunny luminosity, distance, expanse, and certainty." Surely, such results are worth the effort?

But not so fast! Even further difficulties arise from Nietzsche's "aphoristic" style of writing. Most readers will hear that term and think of pithy quips like Tolstoy's famous opening to *Anna Karenina*: "All happy families are alike; each unhappy family is unhappy in its own way." Nietzsche, indeed, wrote some two thousand such (short) aphorisms. He expressly

---

31 This and the following quotes are from *On the Genealogy of Morals*, Foreword, 8.

admired, in particular, the seventeen-century French aphorists François La Rouchefoucauld and Jean de La Bruyère. His reasons for doing so are expressed in this, well, aphorism, by La Rouchefoucauld:

> As the stamp of great minds is to suggest much in few words, so, contrariwise, little minds have the gift of talking a great deal and saying nothing.[32]

As true as Nietzsche finds this statement to be, he also believes that *the form* in which it is expressed presents yet another obstacle to our understanding him: "Today, we do not take this form *serious enough*. An aphorism, properly stamped and poured out is, in being read, not yet 'deciphered.' More, its *interpretation* has only just begun—a practice requiring an art of interpretation." This book is really just the practice of this "art"; so, as we proceed, we will see just what such an art entails. But, if nothing else, the reader must perceive by now that it requires facility with seemingly atonal hues: seriousness without gravity; minute attention to details without conceptual myopia; antipathy without dismissal; criticism without ridicule; acceptance without acquiescence; poetry and passion without romanticism; humor without frivolity; joy without naiveté. Early in his life, Nietzsche believed that art could save us from cultural collapse and outright nihilism. So, given its obvious importance to him, we should linger a moment longer on that word, art. I think this image in *The Gay Science* is clearly that of the kind of artist that Nietzsche wants us, his readers, to become: "We, the thinking-feeling ones, are those who actually constantly fashion something that is not yet there: the whole eternally proliferating world of valuations, colors, accentuation, perspectives, scales, affirmations, and negations."[33] This is the language of painting and poetry and music. Unlike the merely practical person, the "contemplative" artist that Nietzsche has in mind is immersed in the *vis creativa*, the creative life.[34] In the last passage of *Beyond Good and Evil*, Nietzsche explicitly equates his own work with "written and painted thoughts." I will quote this statement at length because it captures crucial values that we, his aspiring perfect readers, must keep in mind.

---

32 *Maxims* 142. Quoted in Yunus Tuncel, "Nietzsche's Aphoristic Style: The Art of Concise and Polemical Writing," *The Agonist*, Vol. IX, Nos. I and II (Fall 2015–Spring 2016). http://www.nietzschecircle.com/Nietzsche_and_La_Rochefoucauld_Yunus.html. Accessed June 1, 2022.
33 *The Gay Science*, 4.301.
34 *The Gay Science*, 4.301.

Oh, what are you, after all, my written and painted thoughts! It was not long ago that you were so colorful, young, and evil, full of thorns and secret spices—you caused me to sneeze and laugh—and now? You have doffed off your newness, and some of you are, I am afraid, ready to become truths: so immortal they already look, so heartbreakingly righteous, so boring! And has it ever been any different? What things do we copy with our writing and painting, we mandarins with Chinese brushes, we externalizers of things that *can* be written, what then are we able just to paint? Oh, only that which wants to become wilted, and starts to stink! Oh, only ever passing and exhausted storms and yellowing belated feelings. Oh, only ever birds that flew tired and strayed and now can be snagged with the hand—with *our* hand! We eternalize what cannot live and fly much longer, only tired and worn out things! And it is only your *afternoon*, you my written and painted thoughts, for which I alone have colors, many colors perhaps, many colorful tendernesses and fifty yellows and browns and greens and reds:—but no one can guess from that how you looked in your morning, you sudden sparks and wonders of my loneliness, you, my old beloved—*wicked* thoughts![35]

Our Nietzschean text—so earnest, so serious, so *philosophical*—a text that *this book* consults to better understand our own time, is suffused in the ephemeral, in the vicissitudes of time, in a kind of lingering doubt, full, too, of playfulness, wonder, and joy, but also of withering, autumnal yellowing, and fading away. Can this describe how to read…*Nietzsche*?

It is probably obvious by now that the aphoristic genre, with its "poetic techniques such as pun, polemics, and sarcasm, and insightfulness, or psychological observation"[36] is well-suited to Nietzsche's complex personality. To the reader new to Nietzsche, however, I want to clarify that his "aphorisms" are typically *not* the pithy remarks of a dozen words or so that distinguish writers like La Rouchefoucauld.[37] Really, with the exception of three works—his first, *The Birth of Tragedy*, *Untimely Meditations,* and the "symphonic"

---

35 *Beyond Good and Evil*, 296.

36 Tuncel, "Nietzsche's Aphoristic Style."

37 To be clear, Nietzsche himself uses this term: "The aphorism, the pithy sentence, of which I am the first among Germans to master, is the form of 'eternity;' my ambition is to say in ten sentences what requires others an entire book to say—what others in a book *don't* say…(dots in original); *Twilight of the Idols,* in the aptly titled section "Raids of an Untimely Man," 51.

Thus Spoke Zarathustra[38]—Nietzsche's works consist in numbered sections or paragraphs ranging from several sentences to a few pages. The numbering allows for the breaks and jumps and asides and digressions and comparisons and seeming *non sequiturs*, etc., that a "proper," conventional argument does not. In addition, the typical Nietzsche paragraph, in German, is *full* of dots and dashes—ellipses and em dashes—commas and semicolons and scare quotes and italics and exclamation points and word lists...much like this one! More, a Nietzsche paragraph, may extend over two or three pages and yet lack indentations (hence, *paragraph* in the singular). And, finally, in a style not uncommon to German writing, a sentence may go on for several lines of text, albeit with all those markings just mentioned. This is not to say that a given sequence of paragraphs (typically divided into titled or numbered sections), much less his books, lack coherence. What it *does* mean is that the likelihood has increased that the writing "grates on the ears" of the uninitiated reader and so leads to an incomprehensibility that is not necessarily *Nietzsche's* fault...Not *necessarily*. To repeat the aphorism titled "The Question of Intelligibility," Nietzsche admits:

One not only wants to be understood when one writes, but also quite as certainly *not* to be understood. It is by no means an objection to a book when someone finds it unintelligible: perhaps this was precisely the intention of its author—perhaps he did not *want* to be understood by "just anyone."[39]

So, how might we aspiring perfect readers—no mere *anyones*!—negotiate this crucial issue of understanding, of *reading,* Nietzsche? We should consider a few possibilities. Some writers attribute Nietzsche's aphoristic writing style—and thus his *difficulty*—to his recurring bad health. Contrary to his robust appearance[40] (aided, certainly, by that majestic mustache), Nietzsche,

---

38 In a letter to his composer friend Peter Gast (Heinrich Köselitz) about *Zarathustra*, Nietzsche writes: "With this book I have stepped into a new *Ring*"—a reference to Richard Wagner's masterpiece. And later, writing again to Gast: "Under which rubric does this *Zarathustra* really belong? I almost believe that it comes under 'symphonies.'" The composer Gustav Mahler said of this work: "His *Zarathustra* was born completely from the spirit of music, and is even 'symphonically' constructed." See Friedrich Nietzsche, *Thus Spoke Zarathustra: A Book for All and None,* translated with an introduction and notes by Graham Parkes (Oxford: Oxford University Press, 2005), xxix.
39 *The Gay Science,* 381.
40 Peter Gast (Heinrich Köselitz) records that when he and a friend first encountered Nietzsche, "we were struck by his appearance. A military type! not a 'scholar'!" Gilman, *Conversations with Nietzsche,* 57.

as we saw, suffered throughout his life from debilitating illnesses accompanied by headaches, nausea, temporary blindness, and unrelenting insomnia, not to mention the mental effects of depression and outright desperation. We get a sense of his suffering from a letter to Peter Gast. Nietzsche writes: "My health is once again practicing its most miserable ways. The exhaustion on even supposed 'healthy' days is frightening. There are nights when I sink into such a despondency and desperation that I am suffused with shame."[41] The frequency of such nights helps us to understand Nietzsche's comment that "The thought of suicide is a great consolation: by means of it one gets through many a dark night."[42] (Against the mores of his age, Nietzsche supported a person's right to suicide.) In any case, the "illness" view holds that his difficult, seemingly disjointed aphoristic style is a reflection of his physical condition: Nietzsche could only write in spasmodic spurts of optimal health and clarity.

Even if that is true, I still take Nietzsche at his word that he does not want *just anyone* to understand him. Why not? I believe that if we could trace to a single root the multitudinous, thickly entangled, richly adorned network of conceptual branches that comprises Nietzsche's overall project, it would be: *subjectivity*—how to create the *type* (a recurring term in his work) of human beings who can then create beautiful and fulfilling worlds—or, in his own words, who can discover and enable "a happiness that humanity has not known so far."[43]

> I am not concerned with the problem of what should replace humanity in the order of being (—the human is an endpoint—): rather, which type of human we should *cultivate*, we *should want*, as a being of higher value, more worthy of life, more certain of a future.[44]

As the reference to "higher value" indicates, it is impossible to speak of subjectivity without also speaking of values. The question of *values* pervades Nietzsche's work. We will revisit this point throughout. I further believe that the *heartwood* of Nietzsche's project is identical to that of both Schopenhauer, his first philosophical love, and the Buddha, a peripheral but spectral "futural" figure in his work. The heartwood: *the revaluation of*

---

41 Reproduced in Volker Gerhardt's *Nachwort* (Afterword) to *Zur Genealogie der Moral* (Stuttgart: Philipp Reclam GmbH & Co., 2020), 172.
42 *Beyond Good and Evil*, 157.
43 *The Gay Science*, 337. I have to add, though, that this is subjectivity without a subject. I'll explain in the section on identity.
44 *The Antichrist*, 1.3. On "cultivate" for *züchten*, see "Overcoming" footnote 139.

suffering. The particular nature of Nietzsche's "difficulty," then, would be of a piece with his wish to *form a subject* (or, really, to incite us to *self-formation*) fit for his ultimate aim of a wholly new, more humane, world. Certain idiosyncrasies of style, of course, contribute to this subject-forming process that you, the aspiring perfect reader, must undergo. At times Nietzsche's stylistic idiosyncrasy may be rooted in necessity, such as illness, as we have seen. At others, in an acquired proclivity, such as his aversion to, indeed hostility toward, conventional scholarship, a style he happened to excel in as a young philologist. At still other times, his stylistic idiosyncrasy may result from a deep suspicion of *truths* and an honest refusal to play the part of the guru. This suspicion and refusal may lie behind his frequent unabashedly expansive experimentation—"Suppose," "Assuming, "Provided that" begin many passages; and "attempt" and "experiment" are frequently invoked. His easy openness to experimentation, furthermore, is perfectly consistent with his belief that our particular *perspective*—resulting from upbringing, experience, society, biology, physiology, and so on—plays a decisive role in our understanding of the world. In such a world of perpetual becoming and of infinite vantage points, we can really *only* ever experiment with modes of thought and being. If these qualities of fragmentation, epistemological promiscuity, fluid becoming against static being, complex intertextuality, and so on, resonate with poststructuralism and postmodernism, that is no fault (or merit) of Nietzsche's. But their perceived affinity to Nietzsche, like that of the earlier existentialists, must surely throw *some* light on the proper way to read him. Right? I'd like to think so. But here we are faced with yet another difficulty. Happily, Nietzsche himself will provide the solution. But first, let's consider an aphorism[45] that succinctly expresses the problem:

> *The worst readers*. The worst readers are those who proceed like plundering soldiers: they carry away a few things they can use, besmirch and befuddle the rest, and deride the whole.[46]

We will be besmirching, befuddling, and deriding nothing. In mining Nietzsche's work for insight into the issues of our day, might we nonetheless justifiably be accused of plundering, or indeed, of *forgery*? Let's consider.

Giorgio Colli, the preeminent coeditor of Nietzsche's complete works, issues this stern accusation: "A forger is one who interprets Nietzsche

---

45 Going forward, I will refer to a section of only a few sentences as an "aphorism" and as a "passage" if longer.

46 *Human, All Too Human*, "Assorted Opinions and Sayings," 137.

by using quotes taken from him. For, by slyly arranging authentic words and sentences, he can make those quotes say whatever he wants them to say."[47] Another distinguished Nietzsche scholar, Volker Gerhardt, somewhat concurs. "Considering the context" of Nietzsche's work, Gerhardt writes, "the denseness of the linguistic web, and the subtlety of the literary form," we can understand why Colli might hold the contrived cherrypicking of Nietzsche's passages to be inherently "dishonest."[48] Gerhardt is, mercifully, quick to add that Colli's "exaggerated" view cannot be sustained over time; for, using his standard, we would never be able to say *anything* about Nietzsche's work. Knowing what we now know about the disgusting perversions of Nietzsche's words by the Nazis, we should be able to appreciate Colli's protectiveness. But it is a fair question: can we not take isolated passages of text in good faith, and try mightily not to *forge* them for purposes foreign to the author? Colli's former student and editorial partner,[49] Mazzino Montinari, offers a way forward here. It involves a return to the procedure of reading as an "art." To read Nietzsche is an art, says Montinari, that requires that we not constrict our reading "through isolated phrases, through radicalizations, through taking statements literally, and yet nonetheless avoid sliding into non-committal vagueness."[50] That is, make justifiable determinations of meaning *without* being definitive. Read with precision and exactness *along with* openness and generosity of interpretation. Take Nietzsche at his word, *but not* too literally. Enable the dangerousness of an idea *without* radicalizing it. Okay, but this is difficult! I will briefly highlight an outcome of this difficulty as a warning—and example—to us aspiring perfect readers. And then, finally, I will let Nietzsche offer his own solution, which is to *read like a cow*.

The Nazis' embrace of Nietzsche is well documented. Less known is his embrace by the Nazis' archenemies: "left-leaning liberationist, progressive circles, including anarchists, socialists, feminists—both hard-boiled Marxist materialists and more aesthetically inclined romantic radicals."[51] (Feminists? Embracing a misogynist?) How can such ideologically disparate

---

47 Gerhardt, *Nachwort* (Afterword), *Zur Genealogie der Moral*, 181.

48 Gerhardt, *Nachwort* (Afterword), *Zur Genealogie der Moral*, 181.

49 Colli and Montinari are the editors of the German version of Nietzsche's works to which I am referring in this book, *Digitale Kritische Gesamtausgabe Werke und Briefe*. Also, *The Complete Works of Friedrich Nietzsche*, twenty volumes in English translation published by Stanford University Press, is based on the Colli and Montinari edition.

50 Gerhardt, *Nachwort* (Afterword), *Zur Genealogie der Moral*, 181.

51 Jennifer Ratner-Rosenhagen, *American Nietzsche: A History of an Icon and His Ideas* (Chicago: University of Chicago Press, 2012), 145.

groups employ the same writer for their purposes? Nietzsche was admired by both Benito Mussolini, the Italian Fascist leader, and Huey Newton, the American Black Panther leader. (Take a moment to let that sink in.) His views on education have been shown to be consistent with both Allan Bloom's reactionary *The Closing of the American Mind* and Paulo Freire's revolutionary *Pedagogy of the Oppressed.*[52] And then there is the sordid affair of Leopold and Loeb. Inspired in large part by Nietzsche's concept of the *Übermensch*, Nathan Leopold and Richard Loeb, two highly intelligent University of Chicago students, decided one spring evening in 1924 to test the theory. Tragically, they did so by kidnapping fourteen-year-old Bobby Franks on his way home from school and murdering him with chisel-blows to his head as he sat in the front seat of their car. Word started circulating about the young killers' fascination with a certain late German philosopher, one...*Friedrich Nietzsche*. And so the public judgment, fueled by the railings against "modernist ideas" and "salacious books" by conservative firebrands such as Billy Sunday and William Jennings Bryant, was that Leopold and Loeb killed because "they thought they were Nietzschean supermen."[53] Can a philosopher really have such an effect on people? Leopold expresses his (mis-)understanding of this concept in a letter to Loeb: "A superman [*Übermensch*]...is, on account of certain superior qualities inherent in him, exempted from the ordinary laws which govern men. He is not liable for anything he may do."[54] It was true! Leopold and Loeb killed to prove their "superman" status. Even their world-renowned lawyer, Clarence Darrow, argued as much during his twelve-hour summary for the defense.

> [Nathan Leopold] became enamored of the philosophy of Nietzsche...
> Here is a boy at sixteen or seventeen becoming obsessed with these
> doctrines. There isn't any question about the facts. It was not a casual
> bit of philosophy with him; it was his life. He believed in a superman.
> He and Dickie Loeb were the supermen. The ordinary commands of
> society were not for him.

Darrow, too, it turns out, was himself "enamored of the philosophy of Nietzsche."

---

52 Many additional incongruent connections can be made concerning music, spirituality, politics, even diet.
53 Ratner-Rosenhagen, *American Nietzsche*, 145.
54 Simon Baatz, *For the Thrill of It: Leopold, Loeb, and the Murder that Shocked Jazz Age Chicago* (New York: Harper Perennial, 2009), 53.

Your Honor, I have read almost everything that Nietzsche ever wrote. He was a man of a wonderful intellect—the most original philosopher of the last century. A man who probably has made a deeper imprint on philosophy than any other man within a hundred years, whether right or wrong.[55]

But unlike his clients, Darrow was a man of profound discernment. He possessed an unparalleled virtuosic reasoning ability. His life story is filled with examples of often debilitating self-sacrificing compassion toward outsiders, the poor, and the ailing. Were he and Leopold reading the same Nietzsche? I think my point is clear: we must treat Nietzsche's ideas as the "dynamite" they obviously are. I'll say it again: the volatility of Nietzsche's ideas, their raw playfulness and exuberant excess, their multifaceted nature enabling motley interpretations, and so on, are what make them of such great value to us at the beginning of the twenty-first century. In the remainder of this work, I hope to show that we have much indeed to learn from a self-described "immoralist."

But first, and finally, this crucial *solution* to the problem posed. Nietzsche, too, wants us—his perfect readers—to "practice reading as art." This practice requires one skill above all others. Nietzsche is not yet "readable," he says, because this skill has been forgotten. It is a skill that requires us to repudiate our desire to be a "modern person" (hasty, shallow, etc.) and to become "practically a cow." The skill: rumination—to chew, and then chew again; to go over, and then go over again; to harp on, dwell on, tarry in; to contemplate, deliberate, excogitate; to reflect on—again and again and again.[56] No small task in this age of infinite scroll, or, indeed, of infinite *feed*.

The reader can surely see that Nietzsche is a strong writer. By this, I mean that he is *demanding* of his aspiring virtuosos. As entertaining as he is, Nietzsche is not writing to entertain. His demands begin already at the level of comprehension. But I mean something else as well. Nietzsche is a strong writer because he is demanding no less than that each of his "perfect" readers labors to become an *Übermensch*. This, at least, is the thread that *I* follow throughout his work. Nietzsche says that "a good writer possesses

---

55 *Voices of Democracy: The U.S. Oratory Project.* https://voicesofdemocracy.umd.edu/clarence-darrow-plea-for-leopold-and-loeb-22-23-and-25-august-1924-speech-text. Accessed April 12, 2023.
56 *On the Genealogy of Morals*, Foreword, 8.

not only his own spirit, but also the spirit of his friends."[57] I read Nietzsche as a friend who is close to me in spirit. I imagine that I share this feeling with many readers. When we read, are we not constantly asking Nietzsche, *what do you want from me? What are you asking me to do?* I believe that Nietzsche's entire body of work contains the lineaments of a figure, a person—a *type*—to be realized. Recall that the quote opening this book already provides clues as to the qualities of this person. It is someone who is "a perfect reader" of the root texts—slow, deliberate, thorough, critical yet generous; it is someone who is "a monster of courage and curiosity"—always wanting to learn more, always wanting to consider a matter from multiple perspectives; never afraid of where thought might lead; a "supple, cunning, cautious" person" who, like the one of "great health" we just encountered, is "a born adventurer and discoverer."[58]

A strong writer, then, requires a strong reader. Indeed, Nietzsche's "perfect reader" is a strong reader in the sense that I intend. The text, as Umberto Eco evocatively expresses it, is merely a "lazy machine." It is mere text. The text gives us concepts, ideas, terms, figurative imagery; it offers us guidance and gives us signals; it creates an atmosphere of thought and a globe of perspectives; it stokes interest and incites desire or disgust. Embedded in this inert assemblage of concrete and abstract signs is what Eco calls the "model reader." The model reader is *in the text* in the form of a *prototype*. The model (strong, perfect) reader is but an *implicit* potential whose charge lies dormant in the text. What is required to release the potential is the collaboration of a living "empirical reader." This reader labors to generate the real-world effects that are encoded within the text's signals. Indeed, Eco insists that the process of fruitful reading—whether it be of a theatrical script, a road map, a brownie recipe, or a work of strange philosophy—begins only once the empirical reader consciously determines to *discern with care* the "intentions" of the text. This discernment is the beginning of the work that Nietzsche is asking us, his own readers, to do.[59]

---

57 *Human, All Too Human*, 180.
58 *Ecce Homo*, "Why I Write Such Good Books," 3.
59 See Umberto Eco, *Six Walks in the Fictional Woods* (Cambridge: Harvard University Press, 1994).

WHAT TO PACK
TRUTH, CONSCIOUSNESS, EMBODIMENT

GIVEN THE SOMETIMES ROUGH AND ROCKY JOURNEY AHEAD, I THINK IT WILL BE helpful to some readers to alert them to three concepts that are central to Nietzsche's philosophy: truth, consciousness, and embodiment. Although often implicit, these concepts are lifeblood coursing through Nietzsche's *corpus*. Each term, moreover, addresses a theme that continually fascinates and vexes thinkers in philosophy, psychology, neuroscience, anthropology, literature, the arts, and beyond. Truth, consciousness, and embodiment, however they are understood, are universally recognized as matters at the very core of our human self-understanding. A grasp of these terms, and specifically what Nietzsche means by them, is essential to understanding his thinking.

TRUTH

The ancient and famous question, whereby one thought to push the logicians into a tight corner and endeavored to bring them to the point to where they either fell into a dreadful circularity or were forced to admit their ignorance along with the vanity of their entire enterprise, is this: *what is truth?*[1]

Could any matter be more prodigious in human thought, indeed, in human *existence*, than that of "truth"? The German philosopher Immanuel Kant (1724–1804), whose shadow loomed even larger in Nietzsche's day than it does in ours, offered a definition that I think is close to our commonsense notion of truth—or, as this is sometimes referred to by philosophers, to our "folk" belief—namely, that it "consists in the agreement of cognition with

---

1 Immanuel Kant, in the section "On Transcendental Logic" in *Critique of Pure Reason*, 111–112, *Internet Archive*, German text of *Kritik der reinen Vernunft*, https://archive.org/details/kritikderreinenv19kant/mode/2up. Accessed April 13, 2023.

its object."[2] With that statement, Kant is giving us an answer to the question "what is the *nominal definition* of truth?" A nominal definition provides nothing more than a rough and ready description of how we might think about, indeed, of how we might communally speak about or *name* (hence, "nominal"), some X. For example, to the question "what is love," a nominal definition might be along the following lines: love is a condition of intimacy, when you feel deep affection for, attachment, and commitment to some person, idea, or object. The reader may well be thinking, *yeah, but what about...* The problem with nominal definitions is that they produce an infinite regress. For my proposition about love to be *true,* for it to constitute knowledge and not mere opinion, it must be grounded in a justification that makes it so. A justification is a category of knowledge rather than of mere opinion *if* it is supported by a reasonable "warrant," such as indubitable empirical evidence or unassailable logic. Is that ever the case? Can we not always point to some X that raises a question about a given aspect of the proposition-justification-warrant nexus? (Is it clear, for instance, that your warrant is not just a proposition in disguise?) Epistemologists—philosophers who give thought to the nature of knowledge—believe that, yes, we can indeed always raise an objection. Even Kant, who gives us his "mere nominal definition" of truth, sees the problem. "All I can ever pass judgment on," he recognizes, "is whether my cognition of the object agrees with my cognition of the object" (meaning that we can speak intelligibly only about our own cognitions, not about the "thing-in-itself," as Kant puts it). A nominal definition does not pretend to be anything more than that—a naming of X. A name can only hope to serve as a kind of caption to the thing it names, to declare it, to explain it, to bring it into a clearing, to clarify it. Indeed, the German term that Kant uses for "nominal" is *Namenerklärung,* which roughly means all these things.[3]

Another issue to consider as we go forward is that people generally confuse nominal definitions with *real* definitions. Kant is expressing the notion of a real definition when he says that people might want to probe beyond the "mere nominal" and ask: "what is the general and sure criterion

---

2 *Critique of Pure Reason*, 112. Interestingly, it appears that the very term "commonsense" was invented to validate the everyday person's ideas about truth over the muddled hairsplitting of the philosophers. This was argued in James Beattie's 1778 "An Essay on the Nature and Immutability of Truth in Opposition to Sophistry and Scepticism." In Joseph Ulatowski, "Folk-Theoretic Foundations of Truth Theory" in *Commonsense Pluralism about Truth.* (New York: Palgrave Macmillan, 2017), 1–28. https://doi.org/10.1007/978-3-319-69465-8_1. Accessed April 8, 2024.
3 *Critique of Pure Reason*, 112.

of the truth of each and every cognition?" It is understandable that we ask such a question, but can anyone reasonably answer it? What would such an account look like? Imagine we asked, "What is the general and sure criterion of love?" or of justice, beauty, goodness, and so on ad infinitum? It is legitimate, Kant says, to ask for a nominal definition because that is asking only for usages and approximations. To ask for a real definition, by contrast, is illegitimate because it is asking for an exactitude and certainty that cannot be granted. The question itself is "muddled." To ask it only creates "embarrassment" and "entices the incautious reader to the same muddled answers and to the ridiculous scene (of which the ancients told) of someone milking a he-goat while another holds a sieve beneath."[4]

In this, Nietzsche concurs with Kant. So where do we go from here? Nietzsche's solution is to persist in asking the question *what is truth*, but out from the tight corner of the logicians and cleansed of the philosophers' vanity. He does so by asking us to consider the question from three different vantage points: metaphysics, society, and life.[5] I will now briefly discuss each of these vantage points. Fuller accounts are provided throughout the book.

Metaphysics. According to the orthodox origin story, a certain ancient editor of the philosopher Aristotle (384–322 B.C.E.) assembled several of his treatises into a single work and then proceeded to include this collection after *(meta)* the book titled *Physics*, hence, *metaphysics*. Whether or not that is the case, the contents of *Metaphysics* have indeed become the concern of the philosophical subdiscipline called *metaphysics*. The meaning, import, interrelations, significance, and so on, of those contents are endlessly debated. Yet Stephen Makin, a translator of *Metaphysics*, writes: "In a way it is easy to state the aim of Aristotle's *Metaphysics*. The book explores the distinction between actuality and potentiality, between being actually and being

---

4 *Critique of Pure Reason*, 112. Kant is, of course, making these statements about the *truth* question. It is easy to extrapolate out from there to similar problems attending other (indeed all?) abstractions. The issue is different—though, according to Nietzsche, not entirely—with the sciences. To ask for an account of "the general and sure criterion of argon," for example, will produce much *real* knowledge.

5 Vanessa Lemm refers to the latter "genre" of Nietzsche's truth discourse as the "biopolitical." I say more about this term later. I want to acknowledge that this section, "What to Pack," was inspired by an online talk Lemm gave at the Institute of Philosophy and Technology, titled "Nietzsche: Truth, Embodiment and Consciousness." Watching her presentation, it occurred to me that treating these concepts at the outset would help the reader to frame what is to follow. I find Lemm to be the most original, insightful, and stimulating interpreter of Nietzsche's thought today. Her IPT talk can be viewed at https://www.youtube.com/watch?v=p7QQDJfDN64&t=2441s. Accessed April 13, 2023.

potentially, between the actual and the potential."[6] So, metaphysics wants to get at the "eternal things [that] are prior in substance to perishable things." Metaphysics aims to identify "being as such." It wants to get at the eternally unchanging *Being* that stands permanently prior to the infinitely protean swirl of impermanent *beings*. We get an even fuller sense of *metaphysics* from the contents of Aristotle's work: truth and falsity; change; potentiality; identity; causality; necessity; free will; mind; substance; beings; Being. As we will see, Nietzsche addresses—indeed, struggles mightily with—many of these notions throughout his own body of work. Just to give an indication of his stance, and of what is to come in this book, consider the following snippets:

—Every positive metaphysics is an error.
—What is "appearance" to me now? Certainly not the opposite of some being—what can I articulate about some being other than but the predicates of its appearance!
—You ask me, what is idiosyncrasy among philosophers?…for example, their lack of historical sense, their hatred of becoming… They believe they bestow honor on a matter when they dehistoricize it, *sub specie aeterni*,[7] when they have made a mummy out of it. For millennia, everything that philosophers have held in their hands were concept-mummies; nothing has come out of their hands alive.
—It is what we *make* out of the testimony of the senses that introduces falsehood into that testimony; for instance, the falsehood of unity, the falsehood of thingness, of substance, of permanence…"reason" is the cause for our taking the testimony of our senses as false. Insofar as the senses reveal becoming, passing away, change, they do not lie. Concerning this point, Heraclitus is eternally correct that being is an empty fiction. The "apparent" world is the only world: the "true world" is just *an appended lie*.[8]

---

6 Aristotle, *Metaphysics*, translated with an introduction and commentary by Stephan Makin (Oxford: Clarendon Press, 2006), xi.
7 Spinoza coined the phrase *sub quadam æternitatis specie,* "under a certain aspect of eternity," in his *Ethics* (Proposition XLIV, Corollary II). Philosophers have used it since in the form Nietzsche gives it. It means: from the perspective of eternity. The idea itself is found as early as Plato, who gives a good sense of its meaning in the *Republic* (486[a,b]): "Do you think that a mind habituated to thoughts of grandeur and the contemplation of all time and all existence can deem this life of man a thing of great concern?"
8 From, respectively: *Human, All Too Human,* 20; *The Gay Science,* 54; *Twilight of the Idols,* Reason, 1; *Twilight of the Idols,* Reason, 2. Heraclitus (flourished 500 B.C.E.) taught that, as Plato has Socrates recall, "all things go and nothing stays, and comparing existents to the

As it relates to our topic, metaphysics is concerned with TRUTH writ large—infinitely large (indeed, *sub specie aeterni*). What does Nietzsche think about this idea? Well, we might ask: what is a *name* for Truth such that "no imaginative force, no flight of the boldest fantasy, no abstract or deep thinking, no collected, devotional feeling, no delightful, enraptured spirit, has ever attained"?[9] That name, of course, is "God." That was how Nietzsche's contemporary, the doomed German philosopher and poet Philipp Mainländer (1841–1876), put it in his 1876 book *The Philosophy of Redemption.* Mainländer continues: "This spirit, its nature altered, has wholly and completely splintered into a world of multiplicity. The simple unity was; it is no more. God died, and his death was the life of the world."

The decay of metaphysics was in the air. If the reader knows one thing about Nietzsche, it is likely his infamous response to the stench of Truth Immemorial's disintegration in his nose: "God is dead!" In the longer version of this utterance, Nietzsche elaborates, if somewhat obliquely, on this pivotal idea. He communicates his view via a madman. Addressing the reader directly, Nietzsche asks us: "Have you not heard of the madman who, one bright morning, lit a lamp, ran into the market square, and repeatedly cried out: I seek God! I seek God!" And with oratory pitched perfectly to the terrible event that it portrays, he continues:

> Since many people were standing around who did not believe in God, the madman's words provoked uproarious laughter. "Has he gone missing, then?" someone said. "Is he lost, like a child?" said another. "Or is he perhaps hiding?" "Is he afraid of us?" "Did he board a ship?" "Emigrated?"—Thus did the people cry out and laugh together. The

---

flow of a river, he (Heraclitus) says you could not step twice into the same river" (*Cratylus* 402a.). The reason that all is in perpetual flux, according to Heraclitus, is that, contrary to traditional metaphysics, no unifying substance underlies the cosmos. The exact opposite was true for Heraclitus's near contemporary, Parmenides, who taught the primacy of permanence and substance. So the divided pathway between Being and Becoming is cut at the very outset of Western thought. Nietzsche, of course, follows Heraclitus in this regard.

9 Philipp Mainländer, *Die Philosophie der Erlösung. Erster Band.* Berlin, 1876: 108, *Internet Archive*, https://archive.org/details/mainlander-philipp-philosophie-der-erlosung-band-1/mode/2up. Accessed April 16, 2023. It seems certain that Nietzsche read Mainländer. He mentions him in several letters, notebook fragments (in which he cites passages and gives page numbers), and even published works (*e.g., The Gay Science,* 357). In 1876, the same year that Mainländer's book was published, Nietzsche writes his friend Overbeck, for instance, that "we have read a good deal of Voltaire; Mainländer is up next." *BVN*–1876, 573. Mainländer's work was also a probable stimulus for Nietzsche's eventual turn away from Schopenhauer. See Thomas H. Brobjer, *Nietzsche's Philosophical Context: An Intellectual Biography* (Champaign: University of Illinois Press, 2008), 69–70.

madman leapt among them and pierced them with his gaze. "Where has God gone?" he cried. "I will tell you! *We have killed him*—you and I! We are all his murderers! But how did we commit this deed? How did we drink up the sea? Who gave us the sponge to wipe away the whole horizon? What have we done by unchaining the earth from the sun? Whither is it moving now? Whither are we moving? Away from all suns? Are we not plunging incessantly ahead? And backwards and sideways and forwards and every which way? Is there even still an up and a down? Are we not wandering as through an infinite nothingness? Does empty space not breathe down our necks? Has it not become colder? Does night not continually fall, and always more night? Must lanterns not be lit in the morning? Have we not yet heard the racket from the gravediggers burying God? Do we not yet smell the stench of the divine decay—gods rot, too! God is dead! God remains dead! And we have killed him! How can we console ourselves, we murderers among all murderers? The holiest and most powerful being that the world has ever possessed has bled to death under our knives— who will wash this blood from our hands? With what water might we purify ourselves? What rituals of atonement, what holy games must we invent? Is not the magnitude of this deed too great for us? Must we not now become gods ourselves in order merely to appear worthy of such a deed? There has never been a more portentous deed—and, because of it, whoever is born after us belongs to a higher history than has ever existed in all of time!"[10]

The "madman" pretends to seek the very same God to whom the people continually pay lip service. Is "God" not the omnipotent guarantor of all that matters to them: value, meaning, morality, governance, power, truth, beauty, goodness, divine reward, eternal afterlife? Yet when faced with the madman's display of (feigned) God-intoxication, the people show themselves to be the disbelievers that they are. Few, in the West, still *believe* in the living presence, the colossal cosmic force, the eternal brilliant magnitude that "God" indexes. Sure, many *say* they believe, but who *lives* as if an omniscient, omnipotent, omnipresent God were a living actuality? For Nietzsche, the death of God, of course, means the death of any and all metaphysical certainties. As it turns out, the madman/Nietzsche is not really surprised by the people's disbelief—it is apparent in their speech and actions, in their

---

10 *The Gay Science*, 125.

consumerism and wheeling and dealing within the marketplace, and in their politics, perpetual warfare, and very way of life outside of it. No, what surprises him is the fact that the people do not recognize the *gravity* of the event. They do not recognize that the death of God/metaphysics will have profound long-lasting consequence both on society and on their personal psyches. In a recurrent theme in Nietzsche's work, the madman thus concludes that he has "come too early"—the implications of our unmoored situation have not truly dawned on us.

> With this, the madman went silent and looked at his listeners. They, too, were silent, and looked bewilderingly at him. Finally, he threw his lantern to the ground, smashing it to pieces and extinguishing its light. "I have come too early," he then said to himself. "The time is not right. This enormous event is still on the way, traveling—it has not yet reached the ears of the people. Lightning and thunder require time, the light of stars requires time, deeds require time, even after they have been done, to be seen and heard. This deed is more distant from them than is the most distant star—and yet, *they themselves have done it!*"—It is still told that on that same day, the madman forced his way into various churches and belted out the *requiem aeternam deo* prayer—"O, eternal peace to God!" Led out and confronted, he could only reply: "What are these churches now if not but the crypts and tombs of God?"

So, for Nietzsche, metaphysical truth lies lifeless in its cold crypt. Yet he recognizes that we cannot yet face that fact. And so we construct monumental truths—in society, morality, education, ideology, religion—that are emptied of value, mere wafts of empty space. And yet…

Society. And yet, construct we must. If we want to avoid the perpetual warfare of all against all, we must form ourselves into collective society. Nietzsche argues that an integral feature of such shared social life is, precisely, *untruth*. Or, a better way of putting it—and things get confusing here—is this: what we label as "truth" is often little more than what simply enables us to live together. "Truth" is thus not a logical or philosophical, or indeed scientific, category; it is a sociological, or indeed anthropological, one: "*Truth is a type of error* without which a certain type of sentient being could not live. The value to life is ultimately decisive."[11] "Truth" concerns

---

11 *NF*–1885, 34 [253].

social norms. It names what is practical, *practicable*, what serves communication and community with others.

Nietzsche's point is not that the very notion of *the truth of X* is nonsensical. Again, science can take us very far in determining hard-nosed truths about the material world. Nietzsche's point is, rather, that we "clever animals" are in the millennia-long habit of claiming X as the truth *not* because it meets some objectively prescribed, uncontested, ideologically-free standard of *actually being the case*, but because it serves our interests and has become a habit.[12] We get a facile version of this idea in the contemporary notion of "my truth." *You* cannot determine what is true *for me*; *the world* cannot determine what is true *for me*; *science* cannot determine what is true *for me*, and so on and so forth; only *I* can determine what is true *for me*. "True" here simply means something like "works for *me*" or "corresponds to my experience." I imagine my readers are with me in wanting to reject such a simplistic notion. Indeed, in our current Era of Conspiracy Theories and Alternative Facts, the notion is outright dangerous. And so this is a good place to mention a massive load-bearing feature of Nietzsche's overall approach. He himself sums up his approach as: "a yes, a no, a straight line, a *goal*." Taking this approach, Nietzsche says, we will discover "the formula for our happiness."[13] And by "our," Nietzsche—in an occasional move that I take to be a kind of esoteric initiation[14]—means any reader willing to experiment in his manner. Nietzsche, to elaborate, is first and foremost concerned with

---

12 As Thomas Kuhn's seminal work *The Structure of Scientific Revolutions* teaches us, advancement in science, too, is hindered by self-interest and disciplinary habit. Paul Feyerabend's *Against Method* makes a similar point about the overly rationalistic ethos of science. Nietzsche, I think, would concur with both authors on this critical point.

13 *The Antichrist*, Foreword, 1.

14 Nietzsche is occasionally quite explicit about his esoteric intentions. *Beyond Good and Evil*, 30, is worth quoting at length as an example. This passage also provides a crucial, if somewhat *esoteric*, clue to (i) the meaning of the dangerous idea of "beyond good and evil" itself, (ii) why Nietzsche believes in the importance of an "order of priority" or rank among people, and (iii) how all three of these matters relate. We are also given insight into why he is a critic of compassion and pity: "Our highest insights must—and should—sound like foolishness, and possibly like crimes, when they impermissibly fall on the ears of those who are not constitutionally capable and predetermined for them. The exoteric and the esoteric, as these were previously differentiated by philosophers, among Indians as among the Greeks, Persians, and Muslims, in short everywhere where people believed in an order of priority and *not* in equality and equal rights.—The difference does not consist so much in the fact that the exoteric stands on the outside and sees, estimates, measures, and judges from the outside, not the inside. The more essential difference is that the exoteric sees matters from below, while the esoteric *looks down from above*. There are heights of the soul from where even tragedy ceases to appear tragic; and combining all the pain of the world into One, who would dare to decide whether its view *necessarily* seduces and compels us to pity and thus to the doubling of the pain?"

considering *how it is* with us clever beasts. This consideration constitutes the "straight line." This line can extend very far indeed before we arrive at our yeses, noes, and goals. My impression is that many readers of Nietzsche commit errors in interpretation by virtue of not understanding the nature of this straight line, and by mistaking it for a yes, a no, or a goal in itself. So when Nietzsche discusses truth in relation to social norms, for instance, he is, in the first instance and for quite a while, plotting a straight line. When he says, for example, that "the intellect, as a means for preserving the individual, unfolds its primary strengths as dissimulation," he is not passing judgment on that posited state of affairs.[15] He is, at this stage, simply speculating on how we got here, and asserting that we will benefit from engaging a thought experiment in which this speculation is the case. It may help the reader to view Nietzsche not as a "philosopher" per se, but as a highly variegated thinker—part anthropologist, sociologist, psychologist, historian, philologist, poet, musician, literary stylist, *and* philosopher. Often, he is operating on several registers at once; and it is not always obvious on which one he is operating. When he is in his anthropologist-psychologist-historian mode, Nietzsche typically wants us to slow down and look with fresh eyes on the early historical moment of some phenomenon. He wants us to do so in order to examine the formative impulse of what has become a long, often tedious discourse on some matter (in the present case, *truth*). So, I hope the reader will catch wind that a speculative thought experiment is called for when Nietzsche says things like "Perhaps no one has yet been truthful enough about what 'truthfulness' is."[16]

And if we *were* to be truthful about truthfulness what might we come to consider? First, disabused of the pretense of metaphysical truth and the myopia of logical truth, we would recognize that we are dealing with a selective social phenomenon.

We want truth only in a limited sense. We desire the agreeable, life-preserving consequences of truth; are indifferent toward purely

---

15 *On Truth and Lies in an Extramoral Sense*, 1. Nietzsche never published this early (1873) essay. In using the term "extramoral" *(außermoralisch)*, Nietzsche is asking us to give thought to the nature of what we call "truth" and "lie" subtracted from, or prior to, the deeply ingrained system of (largely Christian) morality that has predetermined these matters for us. This task of thinking unconstrained by morality preoccupied Nietzsche throughout his life. Indeed, the term brings to mind two of his most important works, *Beyond Good and Evil* and *On the Genealogy of Morals*.

16 *Beyond Good and Evil*, Maxims and Interludes, 177.

inconsequential knowledge, and are even hostile towards possibly damaging and destructive truths.[17]

Second, we would recognize to what extent our professed truths involve dissimulation; indeed, that our societal status quo *depends on* the untruths of dissimulation. Think, for example, of the power dynamics that lie concealed in—and thus explain the actual impossibility of—our national Truths concerning "the American Dream," "all men are created equal," "liberty and justice for all," even the very notion that we are a "democracy." Nietzsche is arguing that such "truths" bind, or are intended to bind, society harmoniously together. When some fixed social truth is challenged—say, the idea that women are too politically unsophisticated to have suffrage or that enslaved Black people's cognitive capacity is too diminished for freedom—that harmonious binding comes undone.

> Since, out of both necessity and boredom, humanity wants to exist socially and in herds, it needs a peace treaty, and strives thereby to rid our world of at least the crudest form of *bellum omnium contra omnes* [war of all against all]. However, this peace treaty brings something along with it, something that we can view as the first step in the attainment of that enigmatic drive to truth. Now, namely, what henceforth is to be considered "truth" becomes fixed; that is, a consistently valid and binding designation of things is invented, and the legislation of language grants the first law of truth, for the contrast between truth and lie appears here for the first time: the liar employs the valid descriptors, the words, in order to make the unreal appear real.[18]

"Wealth and wellbeing await all who work hard enough." "There is no alternative to capitalism." "Volkswagen makes clean diesel cars." "E-cigarettes are safe." "The Goliath of totalitarianism will be brought down by the David of the microchip." "In the 21st century, you cannot live without a cell phone." "Free-range eggs are healthier than caged eggs." "Book banning is free speech." "Anti-aging cream is effective." "America is a democracy." "We will leave no child left behind." "Compassionate conservatism." "Inclusive liberalism." "Surveillance makes us safer." "Guns make us safer." "Presidential candidate X makes us safer." "The best way to secure peace is to prepare for war." "Work sets you free." "The truth will set you free."

---

17 *On Truth and Lies in an Extramoral Sense*, 1.
18 *On Truth and Lies in an Extramoral Sense*, 1.

—these are mere bumper sticker slogans. Yet long, complex, sophisticated ideologies are woven with the same threads of deception. The list of examples using valid descriptors to make the unreal appear real is literally endless. The reason for this all-too-easy dissimulation lies in the third point that Nietzsche would like us to consider on our way to becoming truthful about truthfulness: the nature of language itself.

> What is the status of those linguistic conventions? Are they perhaps products of knowledge, products of our sense for truth: do designations and things correspond? Is language the adequate expression of all reality? Only through forgetfulness can humanity ever come to imagine that it possesses a truth to that degree. If it is not content with truth in the form of a tautology, that is, with empty husks, humanity will forever swap illusions out for truths.[19]

And forget we do. With the utterance of every word, we intuitively feel as though our designations adequately correspond to the factual state of affairs that we call "reality." In each of those foregoing slogans it is demonstrable—some have even been disproven in courts of law—that no *correspondence* between the words and the world exists. And yet every one of those claims effectively functions as true in the world. This is the reason, in part, that Nietzsche wants us to take to heart the possibility that "the falseness of a judgment is, for us, no objection to that judgment…The question is to what extent the judgment is life-fostering, life-preserving, species-preserving, perhaps even species-cultivating."[20] Again, Nietzsche's task is not to convince us that humanity is one big gullible naif. Indeed, if anything, he wants us to see that the opposite is the case: "We may admire a people as a tremendous architectural genius, who, on [the] shifting ground and flowing water [of words], is able to amass an infinitely complicated concept cathedral."[21] Nietzsche's task, rather, is to incite "free spirits," those people who *do not forget*, and are thus better positioned to contribute to a wholly new conception of society and culture. (This idea is elaborated throughout the book.) One pivot point of continual remembrance occurs at the very instance of the *word*.

---

19 *On Truth and Lies in an Extramoral Sense*, 1.
20 *Beyond Good and Evil*, 4.
21 *On Truth and Lies in an Extramoral Sense*, 1.

What is a word? The representation of a nerve stimulus in sound. To further conclude an external cause from the nerve stimulus, however, is already the result of a false and unjustified application of the principle of sufficient reason.[22]

On what flimsy grounds we construct the truths of our shared world! Out of mere "arbitrary delineations," we fashion fortresses of unassailable certainty. Nietzsche offers as an example the trivial assertion that "the stone is hard." Well, who would want to argue with that assertion? Indeed, given the commonsensically uncontroversial correlation between "stoneness" and "hardness," the statement appears nearly tautological. *But*, Nietzsche asks us to consider, is it really so *obviously* the case that "hard" is a property of the *stone*, and not simply the result of "a wholly subjective stimulus"?[23] His answer is *no*, that is not at all obvious. In fact, what is obvious is precisely that hardness is an imputation from *our* side. It is a relative notion that is, moreover, "known" only through subjective, bodily experience. Hardness no more obviously inheres in the stone as masculinity does in a tree *(der Baum)* or femininity does in a plant *(die Pflanze)*.[24] Furthermore, how might a mosquito (Nietzsche's example) experience the stone? That question may strike the reader as ridiculous, but consider: does reflection on it not give the lie to the unambiguous, universal validity presumably required for a matter of "truth"? "Nature," Nietzsche reminds us, "knows neither forms nor concepts." We forget that fact, and so forget, too, that it is *we* who shroud the world with the particular concepts that we do and then attach to that enclosure the "utterly unintelligible" belief in the "thing-in-itself." We can sum up Nietzsche's view of the nature of "truth" in relation to our shared social life with one of his most famous passages.

So, what is truth? A mobile army of metaphors, metonyms, anthropomorphisms, in short, a sum of human relations that have been poetically and rhetorically intensified, transmitted, embellished, and which, after long use, appear to a people fixed, canonical, and binding: truths are illusions that we have forgotten are illusions, metaphors that have become worn out and sensuously sterile; coins whose image has faded

---

22 *On Truth and Lies in an Extramoral Sense*, 1. In its most basic form, the principle of sufficient reason says that "For every fact *F*, there must be a sufficient reason for why *F* is the case."

23 *On Truth and Lies in an Extramoral Sense*, 1.

24 *Der* and *die* are, respectively, the masculine and feminine definite articles in German.

and are seen now as mere metal, and no longer as coins. We still do not know from where the will to truth stems: for, until now, we have heard only of the obligation that society imposes in order for it to exist: to be truthful; that is, to use the customary metaphors, hence, morally expressed, the obligation to lie according to a fixed convention, to lie in droves in a style that is binding for everyone. Now, people forget, of course, that this is how it is with them; they therefore lie in the manner described unconsciously and after centuries-long habit —and so come, through precisely this unconsciousness, through precisely this forgetting, to the feeling for truth.[25]

CONSCIOUSNESS

Like "truth," for millennia hardly any matter has occupied the minds of thinkers as the nature of "consciousness." The very question of truth, in fact, is intimately bound up in the question of consciousness. Consciousness, as the seat of reason and the intellect,[26] is precisely our means of distinguishing truth from falsehood; indeed, it is the means by which we *know* at all. Consciousness, in this view, is the human organ of knowledge. It is, moreover, our highly developed intellect that distinguishes us humans from other animals. For these reasons, consciousness and its various properties— self-awareness, abstraction, judgment, discernment, reason, will, and so on—is universally hailed as cause for jubilation. And Nietzsche? As much as he loves to dance, he will not be joining this celebration.

In some remote corner of the universe brimming with countless shimmering solar systems, there was once a star on which clever animals invented knowledge. It was the most arrogant and dishonest minute of "world history"—yet, a mere minute it was. After nature had drawn a few breaths, the star froze, and the clever animals had to die.—One could invent such a fable and still would not have illustrated how miserable, how shadowy and fleeting, how pointless and arbitrary the human intellect appears within nature. For eternities it did not exist; and when its time has passed, nothing will have happened. For, no further mission exists for the intellect beyond human life. Rather, it is human, and only its possessor and producer accepts it so pathetically, as if the

---

25 *On Truth and Lies in an Extramoral Sense*, 1.
26 Following Nietzsche, I will use these three terms interchangeably.

world turned on its axis. If we could communicate with a mosquito, we would learn that it, too, floats through the air with this same pathos, and feels itself to be the flying center of the world. Nothing in all of nature is so reprehensible and meager that it would not immediately become swollen like a balloon with the slightest whiff of air from the power of that faculty of knowing.[27]

All of this is not to say that consciousness is an inconsequential faculty for us "clever animals." It is indeed important, but not in the ways that our celebratory humanists would have us believe. Consciousness, says Nietzsche, is "the last and most recent development of the organic, and, consequently, the most unfinished and least robust therein."[28] This immaturity gives rise to its propensity for "countless errors." The first error that it leads us into is precisely the notion that it, consciousness, constitutes the "unity of the organism," that it is "*the quintessence* of the person, that which is enduring, eternal, ultimate, original in him." Because we take it as a "fixed given immensity," we fail to register that consciousness is itself a product of organic history. This failure leads us into a "ridiculous overestimation and misjudgment of consciousness." On the evidence of *other* animals, for instance, we have no reason to doubt that we could not "think, feel, will, remember...and act...without it all 'coming into consciousness' (as we figuratively put it)." Nietzsche expands on his "extravagant conjecture" concerning this celebrated wonder of human evolution to consider that, in fact, "the entirety of life would be possible without it simultaneously seeing itself in the mirror [of consciousness], just as how, at present, the far better part of our lives plays out."[29] And so the

---

27 *On Truth and Lies in an Extramoral Sense*, 1. In an earlier version, Nietzsche has this fable spoken by an "insensitive demon" *(gefühlloser Dämon)*. His work is sprinkled with such ascriptions of comments to some character that his ordinary reader will, he assumes, consider a bad actor. It is a rhetorical warning that *you're not going to like this, reader!* By contrast, he just as often gives an esoteric wink and a nod to his "perfect reader," as I mentioned earlier. See *Über das Pathos der Wahrheit* [On the Pathos of Truth], http://www.nietzschesource.org/#eKGWB/CV.

28 This and the following quotes, *The Gay Science*, 11.

29 As this statement indicates, Nietzsche's questions concerning consciousness are *not* those of contemporary philosophy of mind. As if to anticipate the intractable tediousness of that discipline, for instance, he says that he leaves the question of whatever "the opposite of subject and object is to the epistemologists, who have become entangled in the grammar of folk metaphysics." (*The Gay Science*, 354). In particular, he has no interest whatsoever in the most animating question of all current discussions: how is conscious experience even possible? This is the so-called "hard problem" of consciousness. How is it that I *experience* the sour quality of the apple? The question is "hard" because it obtains even after all of the "easy" problems have been solved. It is "easy" to map the brain mechanisms that *give rise* to consciousness experience, such as perception, discrimination, categorization, conception,

question arises: "What use is consciousness, anyway, if it is so *superfluous*?" Three ways that Nietzsche answers this question are: consciousness is useful in terms of dissimulation, communication, and the future. We will briefly consider each.

Dissimulation. Recall Nietzsche's assertion that "the falseness of a judgment is, for us [*wink, wink*], no objection to that judgment."[30] He is asserting that in everyday life what we call a "judgment" is not obviously a matter of truth or untruth. The word "judgment" itself prejudices our view as to its function as a mode of *knowing*. Nietzsche wants us to consider, rather, that judgment operates in the mode of *maintenance*: it is a "life-fostering, life-preserving, species-preserving, perhaps even species-cultivating" function of consciousness. Thus, being the least robust of faculties, judgment lends consciousness an important utility: "The intellect, being a means for the preservation of the individual, manifests its principal strengths in dissimulation."[31] Dissimulation enables us to engage in numerous ways of being that are essential to social life. It is crucial to note that Nietzsche is, perhaps contrary to appearances, not being facetious or cynical here. He is seriously asserting that, far from being a *problem* in its role as dissimulator, consciousness is a valuable source of existential creativity.

> This art of dissimulation reaches its peak in human beings: the deception, flattery, lies and deceit, the talking-behind-the-back of others, the performance of social duties, the living in borrowed splendor, the masquerading, the camouflaged convention, the play-acting before others and before oneself.[32]

Nietzsche challenges us to consider that, in order to get along reasonably well with one another, a certain "benevolent dissembling" is required. For when someone inevitably engages in one of the above practices, we must act "as if the other's motives were not transparent." We could thus add to that list of dissimulations "holding our tongues" (or is holding your tongue

---

internal access, bodily response, verbalization. But neither in isolation nor in assemblage do these mechanisms account for "experience." Nietzsche takes brute awareness and subjective experience for granted. He is not interested in consciousness per se. In many passages, he seems to want us to understand "consciousness" as "self-consciousness," as he does parenthetically in *The Gay Science*, 354: "The problem of consciousness (more correctly: of becoming conscious of oneself)." His interest is ultimately in the role that consciousness plays in forming the subject in the world.

30 *Beyond Good and Evil*, 4.
31 *On Truth and Lies in an Extramoral Sense*, 1.
32 *On Truth and Lies in an Extramoral Sense*, 1.

a "social duty"?) The reader may be picking up on the fact that Nietzsche is not bemoaning the hopelessly opaque stupor of human consciousness. On the contrary, he is positing that consciousness provides us with an uncanny aptitude for discerning and navigating social "reality." For we only *pretend* not to notice what others are up to. What complex creatures we are! The instrument of this discernment, however, is precisely *not* some capacity of consciousness. "We possess no organ at all for *knowledge*," Nietzsche insists.[33] The instrument of "knowing" is, rather, a capacity of *instinct*. (More on this point in the section "Embodiment.") One answer that Nietzsche develops for his query into the use of our seemingly superfluous consciousness is this: since consciousness renders everything it touches "shallow, thin, relatively stupid, general, sign, mark of the herd,"[34] it makes, for this very reason, a superb instrument for our forming ourselves into community. In fact, it seems that consciousness arises precisely out of this interface between the individual and society. This point brings us to the next answer that Nietzsche develops for the use of consciousness.

Communication. Nietzsche, recall, believes that dissimulation is valuable because it enables us to engage in forms of life that are essential to society. And what could be more essential to shared existence than our ability to communicate with one another? In fact, the direct answer that Nietzsche gives for his "extravagant conjecture" concerning the use of consciousness is that "the subtlety and strength of consciousness always stands in relation to a human's (or an animal's) *capacity for communication,* and this capacity, in turn, stands in relation to the *necessity for communication.*" The pressure from living in a hostile and chaotic environment necessitated our ability "to communicate quickly and delicately." So Nietzsche emphatically concludes:

> *Consciousness generally developed only under pressure from our need for communication.* From the outset, consciousness was necessary and useful only between person and person (between those who command and those who obey, in particular), and also developed only in proportion to this utility. Consciousness is actually only a connectivity network between person and person—only as such was it compelled to develop: reclusive and wild people had no need for it. The fact that our actions, thoughts, feelings, and movements even come into consciousness—or at least that some portion of them do—is the consequence of a terrible, prolonged "must" reigning over us: humans, as the most endangered

---

33 And following quotes until otherwise noted, *The Gay Science*, 354.
34 Earlier in this passage, Nietzsche calls humans "sign-inventors."

animal, *required* help and protection, they needed equals, they had to be able to express their distress, to make themselves understood—and for all of this they needed, in the first instance, "consciousness"; thus, they needed to "know" what was missing, needed to "know" how they feel, needed to "know" what they think.

As a "connectivity network," consciousness gave rise to language itself: "The development of consciousness (*not* of reason, but only of the becoming-conscious of reason) and the development of language go hand in hand." And it is not only spoken language that functions as a communicative "bridge" between people, but also our very gaze and gestures. Out of necessity, we became experts in giving "signs" to other people. It is thus "as a social animal that humans learned to become conscious of themselves." Nietzsche's extravagant yet compelling speculation on the use of the seemingly superfluous phenomenon called consciousness, finally, asks us to consider that "consciousness does not actually belong to the individual existence of a person, but rather much more to that which is of the nature of the community and the herd in the individual." We have, he says, developed the "demanding" capacity to "back-translate" the individual into the "not-individual," into the "average," into the "herd perspective." This exacting proclivity toward "the herd" is nothing less than the "genius of the species."[35]

The future. As ingenious as consciousness may well be, we will nonetheless have to find a way to *overcome* its current functions and limitations. As I read Nietzsche, his abiding concern is how our species might come to use its capacities—its "genius"—for the creation of a civilization worthy of the name. These themes are addressed throughout *Nietzsche NOW!* Here, I would like briefly to register Nietzsche's contention that our tangled and troublesome capacity for consciousness might have a role to play toward this end.

Our ability to form into community is the necessary condition for civilization. Yet, in Nietzsche's estimation, the civilization that we have created for ourselves is in bad shape—it is decadent, life-denying, narcotized,[36] sick; in a word, nihilistic. Our civilization produces much unnecessary suffering,

---

35 Nietzsche puts this phrase in quotes because he is borrowing it from Schopenhauer's essay "The Metaphysics of Love." For Schopenhauer, the genius of the species manifests as the spirit of *eros*, in the love between a man and a woman that has as its end the reproduction, hence perpetuation, of the species. That "unegoistic" compulsion toward collective maintenance is, for Schopenhauer, what constitutes the "genius of the species."

36 See *The Gay Science*, 86.

but most of all "we *suffer* from human beings."[37] Our civilization produces "tame people" who complacently enable this suffering because they are precisely "hopelessly mediocre and insipid people" who, in a feat of tragic self-delusion, "have learned to feel themselves as the goal and pinnacle, as the meaning of history, as 'higher people.'" And, Nietzsche grants, they have a point, "insofar as they feel themselves at a distance from the abundance of wayward, sickly, exhausted, spent people of whom Europe today is beginning to stink." We are at a dangerously low point when such people count as "at least relatively composed, at least still capable of life, at least yea-saying to life" in comparison with the vast majority of humanity. Nietzsche is convinced that he is writing in the late stage of Western culture's decisive inundation by the torrent of nihilism. Nietzsche's use of this term is idiosyncratic. For him, nihilism is not primarily the *rejection* of meaning, morality, values, and grounds for knowledge, as the conventional view holds. Nihilism is the *acceptance* of those matters as they currently circulate in our society. Surely, this sounds counterintuitive. So let us ask the decisive question for determining whether a value, and so on, is nihilistic: is it life-affirming or life-denying? What Nietzsche means by life-affirming and life-denying is a central theme of this book. In brief, a moral system, and so on, is life-affirming if it is rooted in an immanent view of the human being, that is, the view from *this* world, *this* body, *this* experience. It is life-denying if it is rooted in a transcendent view, that is, a view from *another* world (Christian heaven, Buddhist *nirvana,* Plato's forms, Kant's thing-in-itself), a *purified* nonanimalistic body, and an *idealized* experience. In Nietzsche's view, the entire Western philosophical tradition from Plato forward is nihilistic in this life-denying sense. So are science and religion, and particularly Christianity The proof lies in the fact that we are destroying ourselves. He says that if we are "to keep from destroying ourselves,"[38] we must "set ourselves ecumenical goals, embracing the whole earth," and that this project requires that we "first discover *knowledge of the conditions of culture.*" Such knowledge will "surpass all previous knowledge" and be adequate to the ecumenical challenges facing us. Significantly, Nietzsche adds that "herein lies the enormous task of the great spirits[39] of the next century." Once Nietzsche has completed his genealogical analysis of our past and performed his critical operations on our present, his thought becomes urgently oriented toward our future. Our

---

37 This and following quotes, *On the Genealogy of Morals,* 1.11.
38 This and following quotes, *Human, All Too Human,* 25.
39 This word, *Geiste,* could also mean "minds." Nietzsche, however, often singles out "free spirits," *Freigeiste,* as those who will undertake this task.

current situation has been a long time coming, he observes, and so, assuming that we largely agree with his diagnosis of our culture, we must labor under no facile delusion that solutions will be smooth and swift. However, with his help, Nietzsche believes, we are at last discovering the *"knowledge of the conditions of culture"* that will prove decisive in our civilizational and cultural renewal. Can it possibly be the case that our Immoralist believes in *progress*?

In an unusually programmatic passage, Nietzsche almost apologetically argues for the *"possibility of progress."*[40] He realizes that in declaring that "progress is *possible*," he risks being accused of "an intolerable obtuseness and an equally disagreeable over-enthusiasm." His future-orientedness, however, saves him from this judgment. Nietzsche's insistence that any greatness that might have existed in the past "can never again be fresh" is a crucial point to keep in mind throughout this book. Indeed, his unwavering belief in the unrecoverability of past glory is what animates his future-looking philosophy. In this passage, Nietzsche argues that human beings "can with *consciousness* determine to develop themselves forward into a new culture." With an eye to the features of consciousness that we have already discussed, and will discuss further in the following section, Nietzsche adds, "whereas humans earlier developed themselves unconsciously and by chance." It is *possible* that we develop consciousness in this direction. In the sunnier appraisals of humanity that are more typical of his middle period works (1878–1885), Nietzsche argues that, in relation to the history of human consciousness:

Humanity can now create better conditions for the formation of people, their nourishment, upbringing, instruction. We can now steward the entire earth economically, can weigh and employ the energies of people against one another. This new, conscious culture kills the old culture, which, taken as a whole, led an unconscious animal and plant life; it also kills the mistrust of progress—progress is *possible*. What I mean to say is that it is premature and almost nonsensical to believe that progress must *necessarily* result; but who can deny that it is possible? On the other hand, progress in the sense and in the footsteps of the old culture is not even conceivable.

---

40 This and following quotes, *Human, All Too Human*, 24.

So what is entailed by Nietzsche's postulation that we can "with *consciousness*" create better conditions for ourselves now? In a passage that reverberates throughout his entire body of work, indeed, may even be said to permeate virtually every other passage, Nietzsche articulates an essential feature of progress. He calls this feature "intellectual conscience." And while "conscience" *(Gewissen)* is not "consciousness" *(Bewusstsein)* per se, it is, like reason, will, intellect, judgment, and so on, certainly an essential *component* of it.[41] So I want to give the full passage here without commentary (I will provide some later in the book) with the hope that you will allow it to suffuse your continued reading.

> *Intellectual conscience.* I have the same experience over and over, and resist it anew each time. I do not want to believe it even though I grasp it with my hands: *the vast majority of people lack an intellectual conscience.* Yes, it has often seemed to me as if someone demanding such a conscience would be as lonely in the most populated cities as in the desert. Everyone looks at you with strange eyes and works their weighing scales as before, calling this good and that evil; nobody blushes with shame when you let it be known that their weights are underweight—nor do they respond with outrage toward you; perhaps they laugh at your doubts. What I want to say is: *the vast majority of people* do not consider it contemptible to believe this or that and to live accordingly *without* first becoming aware of the final and most certain reasons *for and against,* and without even troubling themselves about such reasons afterward: even the most gifted men and the noblest women belong to this "vast majority." But what are good-heartedness, refinement, and genius to me when the person possessing these virtues tolerates lax feelings in belief and judgment and when the *demand for certainty* is not his innermost longing and deepest necessity—as that which separates the higher human beings from the lower! I discovered in certain pious people a hatred against reason, and that was fine with me: at least this hatred revealed their bad intellectual conscience! But to stand in the midst of this *rerum concordia discors* [discordant harmony of things] and the whole wonderful uncertainty and ambiguity

---

41 The English and German terms equally indicate the quality of *knowing.* "Conscience" and "consciousness" derive from Latin *scire (to know > scientia, a knowing),* while "Gewissen" and "Bewusstsein" derive from *wissen (to know > Wusst, a knowing).* For *Wusst,* see *Deutsches Wörterbuch von Jacob Grimm und Wilhelm Grimm, s.v.* Wust, https://www.woerterbuchnetz.de/DWB. Accessed May 3, 2023.

of existence *without questioning*, without trembling with the longing and rapture of questioning, without at least hating the person who questions, perhaps even taking a dim delight in him—that is what I feel to be *contemptible*, and it is this feeling that I first look for in everyone—some sort of foolishness keeps convincing me that every person must have this feeling, simply as a human being. That is my type of injustice.[42]

EMBODIMENT

We can rephrase that penultimate sentence in the foregoing section to stimulate the following positive hypothesis: *a person who poses questions while standing within the discordant harmony of things, within the whole wonderful uncertainty and ambiguity of existence, will tremble with the longing and rapture of that questioning [...] that is my type of justice.* To phrase it like this brings out Nietzsche's valorization of what he calls "embodiment." For the situation assumes that the prime nexus of concern for those of us who want to practice intellectual conscience is that between the world and our body. The questions are discharged at precisely this volatile point of contact. Nietzsche's description is suffused with the energetic frisson of the body suddenly immersed in the questions catalyzed by the world—trembling, longing, rapture, full sensorial presence, rapt engagement. For Nietzsche, ever the psychologist, this immersion is redoubled by the fact that much of the questioning concerns precisely the subjective experience of *a body in the world* and, by the same token, of *the world in a body*. All of a sudden, the atavistic propensity of consciousness to live in borrowed splendor, masqueraded and camouflaged, leaks its hidden charge. Do you want to detonate that charge, Nietzsche asks. If so, you must become a "thinker."

The thinker: that is now the being in whom the drive to truth and those life-preserving errors fight their first battle, now that the drive to truth has *proven* itself to be a life-preserving power. In relation to the importance of this fight, all others are unimportant: the final question concerning the conditions of life is here posed, and the first attempt is here made to answer this question with an experiment. To what

---

42 *The Gay Science*, 1.2. This important extract is also quoted in full in the chapter "Wokeness and Ideology."

extent does the truth bear embodiment?—that is the question, that is the experiment.[43]

For virtually all of prior philosophy, the nexus of truth was most certainly *not* between the world and the body but rather between the world and some higher *contemplative faculty*, such as exalted reason, rarefied mind, luminous intuition, pure spirit, sanctified soul. Plato, for instance, considered the body to be an outright *hindrance* to truth. Its messy, eternally unsatisfied physical and emotional needs distract the soul from its contemplation: such "companionship disturbs the soul and hinders it from attaining truth and wisdom." Plato continues:

> The body is constantly breaking in upon our philosophical studies and disturbing us with noise and confusion, so that it prevents our beholding the truth, and in fact we perceive that, if we are ever to know anything absolutely, we must be free from the body and must behold the actual realities with the eye of the soul alone.[44]

Nietzsche was contending, too, with no less a power than all of Christendom, whose magistrates admonished its citizens to "put to death the components of your earthly nature,"[45] for although "it is sown a natural body, it is raised a spiritual body."[46] Dead though God may be, his "massive, gruesome shadow" may darken our "caves" for millennia to come in this regard.[47] Someone who poses as "the thinker" should offer us light. Yet the most influential ideas of his day—such as Kant's "thing-in-itself," Hegel's "world spirit," Descartes's *cogito, ergo sum*, and Schopenhauer's "disinterested will"— were, in Nietzsche's diagnosis, contaminated with "theologian's blood." It is for this reason, too, that morality itself has become "counter-nature."[48] Thus, "we free, *very* free spirits"[49] must vanquish not merely God, but God's shadow as well. We can only begin to do so, Nietzsche informs us, insofar as we "translate the human back into nature" and come to know once again "the terrible basic text of *homo natura*."

---

43 *The Gay Science*, 110.
44 *Phaedo*, 66a, 66c,d,e, in *Plato in Twelve Volumes*, vol. 1, translated by Harold North Fowler (Cambridge: Harvard University Press, 1966).
45 Colossians 3:5.
46 1 Corinthians 15:44.
47 *The Gay Science*, 108.
48 "Morality as Counter-Nature" is a chapter in *Twilight of the Idols*.
49 This and following quotes, *Beyond Good and Evil*, 230.

As *Nietzsche NOW!* unfolds, the reader will come to understand what Nietzsche means when he says that the record of the human as part and parcel of nature is "terrible." Before we move on from this section, I want to mention another profoundly significant assumption informing Nietzsche's conception of the human being.

As we have seen, Nietzsche constantly hedges on the significance, much less the primacy, of consciousness as the decisive human faculty. He does so literally and directly; but he also does so parenthetically, as when he says, for instance, that our thoughts, and so on, come into consciousness, *or at least some of them do*, or when he speaks of the development of consciousness and adds "*not* of reason, but only of the becoming-conscious of reason." The root of this hedging is found in a thesis of Nietzsche's that anticipates Freud and all of twentieth-century psychology and psychoanalysis.

> The entirety of life would be possible without its seeing itself in a mirror, so to speak: as in fact even at present the far greater part of our life plays out without this mirroring —and indeed even our thinking, feeling, volitional life as well, however offensive this idea may sound to an older philosopher.[50]

If "a mirror" stands for conscious life, then "without a mirror" stands for unconscious life. An "older philosopher," and those among us who continue to think in this fashion, would axiomatically assume a self-theory with a fully *conscious* agent at the center. Nietzsche thinks of existence as a "monster of energy."[51] But if there is any such thing resembling a *center* to this maelstrom, it is the body—indeed, as we will see, it is the *human-animal* body.

> Behind your thoughts and feelings, my friends, stands a mighty commander, an unknown sage—called the self. This self lives in your body, is your body. There is more intelligence in your body than in your best wisdom. And who knows why your body requires your best wisdom?[52]

Nietzsche is asking us to consider that truth is not a function of divine revelation or of contemplation of eternal forms or of linguistic representation or

---

50 *The Gay Science*, 354.
51 *NF*–1885, 38[12].
52 *Thus Spoke Zarathustra*, "On the Despisers of the Body."

of philosophical investigation or of logic or even of reason. *Truth*, Nietzsche is asking us to consider, *is* a function of a properly attuned *body*. What can this possibly mean? *Nietzsche NOW!* is an attempt to wind our way toward something like an answer.

DEMOCRACY

Is Democracy withering in the world? According to the near unanimous opinion among independent pro-democracy watchdog organizations "the long democratic recession is deepening." In its recent report, "Democracy Under Siege," Freedom House, for example, shows that forces such as economic insecurity, internal dissension, violent conflict, immigration, and pandemic measures have "shifted the international balance in favor of tyranny."[1] And yet, as these watchdogs tell it, the new tyranny is *not* appearing in the form of totalitarian one-party dictatorships, as in China or the old Soviet Union. Rather, it is appearing in the guise of self-professed *democracy*. The new tyranny is being erected on the venerable mantel of democracy itself. The reader may ask, *how can this be?* But this state of affairs would not surprise Nietzsche at all. In his later view, the two, *tyranny* and *democracy,* are never far apart. A crucial reason why this is so, says Nietzsche, is that democracy breeds mediocrity at best, stultification at worst. Most alarmingly, it breeds *herd mentality*. In this chapter, we will consider where our wild guide might take us in reconsidering a value that we rarely, if ever, challenge: democracy itself.

I assume that my reader will agree that if it is true that democracy is giving way to tyranny around the world, then it is patently dangerous to bring the former into question. For that assumption is grounded in another one, namely, that the two systems are mutually exclusive. But what if democracy were itself amenable to tyranny? What if the very seeds of tyranny lay dormant *in* democracy? This fear has been present since the first inkling, in fifth century B.C.E. Athens and other Greek city-states, that "rule by the people" (*dēmos*: people; *krátos*: force, strength) might be a good idea. So, along with this inkling glinted another: *power to the people* can easily slip into *rule of the mob (ochlocracy)*. Indeed, the *dēmos* is not the *óchlos*. The former is a special class of people—typically landowning men of the dominant social caste—while the latter are the *hoi polloi*, the many, the mob, the

---

1 "Democracy Under Siege," *Freedom House,* https://freedomhouse.org/report/freedom-world/2021/democracy-under-siege. Accessed September 13, 2022.

masses or, in one of Nietzsche's favorite words, "the rabble" *(Pöbel)*. And wherever humans have fashioned governments, the political potential of "the masses" has terrified the "special class." In the fledgling United States of America, for instance, James Madison, having studied dozens of historical examples of democracy, convinced his fellow constitutional Framers that "in all very numerous assemblies, of whatever characters composed, passion never fails to wrest the scepter from reason. Had every Athenian citizen been a Socrates; every Athenian assembly would still have been a mob." Thus, the most important feature of "a well-constructed Union" is the constitutional ability "to break and control the violence of faction."[2] The result, of course, is not a direct democracy, but a representative republic. In the Framers' thinking, the latter centered on an enlightened "special class"—privileged people like themselves, for example—while the former was centered on the quite unenlightened, endlessly fractious, passionately unpredictable masses.

We can get a quick read on Nietzsche's view of democracy by asking what he would have made of Madison's contention. As with all things Nietzsche, to do justice to his view we must wind our way slowly. But let's not be precious here. Nietzsche could hardly agree with anything more than that we must find a way to sift out from the populace the people most equipped to make compassionate, wise decisions that impact our shared civic life. In fact, given his distrust of the mask of reason, Nietzsche would have gone a step farther than Madison and argued that *even* an assembly full of Socrateses would have devolved into a mob. Let us provisionally consider the hard proposition that Nietzsche the Founding Father would have argued for more safeguards against the tyranny of the mob, against the *We*, in *We, the people*, than is present in the American *Constitution*. But wind our way we must.

This distinction between representative democracy and direct democracy raises another question lurking in the background: what do *we*, much less Nietzsche, even mean by the term? In a recent survey, Jean-Paul Gagnon calculates that "democracy" appears in the political science literature with at least 2, 234 significant descriptors.[3] By "significant" I mean that the modifiers are demonstrably substantive in terms of actual practice. For example, clearly, *authoritarian* democracy, with its motto of "confidence from below, authority from above," would function in real terms quite differently from a leaderless, stateless *inclusive* democracy. (The former prevailed in Bonapartist France and Bolsonaro's Brazil, and the latter, in contemporary

---

2 *Federalist Papers,* Nos. 55 and 10.
3 See Jean-Paul Gagnon, "2, 234 Descriptors of Democracy: An Update to Democracy's Ontological Pluralism," *Democratic Theory,* No.5, Vol. 1 (2018), 92–113.

Rojava and Chiapas.) In Nietzsche's case, we have at least this bare definition: "*Goal and method of democracy*. Democracy wants to create and
guarantee *independence* for as many people as possible, independence of
opinion, of lifestyle, and of occupation."[4] He is quick, however, to mention
that he is "speaking of democracy as of something to come" in the future.
So what of Nietzsche's present? We could narrow "democracy" down to
the form that was practiced in Bismarckian Germany. We might call this
Junker—quasi-feudal landholding elite—democracy. However, Nietzsche
typically throws contemporary German democracy onto the same pile as
contemporary English (parliamentary democracy) and American (representative democracy) as well as ancient Greek forms (limited direct democracy).
How can such divergent varieties of citizen participation and governmental
assembly be characterized by the single term "democracy"? Perhaps Alexis
de Tocqueville, the famous author of *Democracy in America* (1835), had
stumbled on a *feature* of democracy when he lamented its broad definitional
lack of clarity. Unless we can say precisely what constitutes democracy, he
said, people will continue to "live in an inextricable confusion of ideas, much
to the advantage of demagogues and despots."[5] Given that in the supposed
bastion of democracy, the United States, votes cast in midterm elections in
recent decades have typically struggled to reach forty percent of eligible
voters[6]—so that Candidate X might be elected with a mere *twenty percent* of
the total vote—and that voter suppression is practically as old as American
democracy itself,[7] it is safe to assume that the powers-that-be—who, incidentally, spent $14 billion on election races in 2020 alone[8]—have no such
clarification forthcoming. Indeed, one wonders why it has taken so long for
the Stockholm-based International Institute for Democracy and Electoral
Assistance to declare the United States a "backsliding democracy."[9]

But as valuable as it is to debunk the deeply ingrained cultural myth that
"democracy is the worst form of government except all those other forms that
have been tried from time to time," as Winston Churchill famously quipped,
it is neither the lack of clarity concerning the definition of democracy nor

---

4 *Human, All Too Human*, "The Wanderer and His Shadow," 293.
5 Quoted in Gagnon, "2, 234 Descriptors of Democracy," 93.
6 See *FairVote*, https://fairvote.org/resources/voter-turnout. Accessed November 1, 2022.
7 Terrance Smith, "Timeline: Voter Suppression in the US from the Civil War to Today,"
ABC News. https://abcnews.go.com/Politics/timeline-voter-suppression-us-civil-war-today/
story?id=72248473. Accessed November 1, 2022.
8 *Reuters*, https://www.reuters.com/graphics/USA-ELECTION/SENATE-FUNDRAISING/
yxmvjeyjkpr/.. April 3, 2024.
9 See its "Global State of Democracy Report 2021," https://www.idea.int/gsod. Accessed
November 1, 2022.

democracy's failures that animate Nietzsche's criticism. He is even less interested in the hand-wringing about whether democracy is truly "of the people, by the people, for the people," as Abraham Lincoln summed it up. His concern lies much deeper. His attention would be piqued, for example, by the fact that someone like Adolf Hitler could be appointed chancellor of a parliamentary democracy such as the Weimar Republic; or, indeed that a wealthy racist, misogynist, illiberal, unabashed *enemy* of democratic institutions such as Donald Trump could be elected president of a representative democracy outright. Such results are possible, Nietzsche believes, *not*, in the first instance, because of the political formation known as democracy. They are possible because of the democratic "mentality"—the democratic "taste," "disposition," "bad habit," "diverse wanting," "prejudice"[10]—that pervades our shared social consciousness. For Nietzsche, what he commonly refers to as the "democratic movement" and our "democratic epoch" is but a *symptom* of this mentality.

A general feature of Nietzsche's thought is once again coming into focus: his interest ultimately lies less in (mass) *politics* and more in (individual) *psychology*. Taste, disposition, habit, wanting, and prejudice are elements of "mentality." Certain mentalities have a way of spreading throughout the social field. In his 1976 book, *The Selfish Gene*, evolutionary biologist Richard Dawkins coined the term "meme" to describe the way this transmission occurs. Similar to genes, which "propagate themselves in the gene pool by leaping from body to body via sperms or eggs," memes "propagate themselves in the meme pool by leaping from brain to brain via a process which, in the broad sense, can be called imitation."[11] (The term "meme" thus plays on both "gene" and "mimetic," imitative.) A meme is a unit of cultural information—a catchy tune, like "Shallow"; a cliché, like "it is what it is"; clothing fashions, like skinny ripped jeans; greeting decorum, such as shaking hands, cheek-kissing, or bowing; or ideas, like God, MAGA, and, indeed, democracy—that gets passed from mind to mind via non-genetic means, such as language and speech, ritualized practices, symbols, imagery, advertisement representations, conspiracy theories, and so on. For Nietzsche, acquiescence to the memes of the moment is the way of the lowly "last

---

10 Respectively: notebook fragment: *NF*–1875, 6[28]; *Beyond Good and Evil*, 204, 44; *Gay Science*, 103; *Beyond Good and Evil*, 208; *On the Genealogy of Morals*, 1.4.

11 Richard Dawkins, *The Selfish Gene* (Oxford: Oxford University Press, 1976), 249.

mortal,"[12] the *letzter Mensch*. The "higher type," the capacious *Übermensch*, for whom Nietzsche is writing, is constituted to no small degree in *resistance* to the seemingly natural and inevitable stream of memes that buffet them: "One must be a sea to absorb a dirty stream without becoming unclean."[13]

In what follows, we will consider Nietzsche's statements about the "democratic movement," the political formation as well as the psychological "democratic disposition" that pervades our social mentality to this very day. As we do so, remember that a central thesis of this book is that if we look to Nietzsche for *answers* to questions, such as, in this case, *what is the best form of government?*, we are courting frustration. Nietzsche is neither a pundit nor a self-help guru. He does not offer answers to such questions. Nietzsche is a guide to thinking. If we look to him for a *procedure,* for an approach to arriving at *our own* answers, we will discover an abundance of riches. So let's proceed.

DEMOCRACY AS AN ANTIDOTE TO TYRANNY

In his earliest texts, Nietzsche makes statements that can be garnered in favor of democracy, as both mentality and movement. His 1872 fragment "Homer's Contest," for instance, is concerned with the role that interpersonal *agon*—struggle, rivalry, contestation—played in the life of ancient Greek society. If we want to understand the Greeks' conviction that *agon* is vital to the well-being of the state, he says, "then we should consider the original meaning of *ostrakismos* [ostracism]." He then cites Heraclitus (fragment 121) quoting the Ephesians on the occasion of their banning of one Hermodor: "Among us, nobody should be the best; but if somebody is the best, let him be so elsewhere, with other people." Although he does not include this additional statement in his quote, Nietzsche seems to disagree with Heraclitus's further assertion that: "The Ephesians deserve, from the young men to the old, to be hanged, and to leave the city to the beardless youths, since they cast out Hermodor, their best man."[14] On the contrary, in defense of the Ephesians, Nietzsche reasons: "For why should nobody

---

12 This is my gender-neutral translation of *letzter Mensch,* typically rendered "last man." Concerning its relationship to the *Übermensch*, Nietzsche writes in a note that "the opposite of the *Übermensch* is the "last mortal." Everything that has the quality of the *Übermensch* appears to people as sickness and insanity. I created them at the same time." *NF*–1882, 4[171].
13 *Thus Spoke Zarathustra,* "Zarathustra's Preface," 3.
14 *Wikisource*, "Fragments of Heraclitus," https://en.wikisource.org/wiki/Fragments_of_Heraclitus#Fragment_121. Accessed November 5, 2022.

be the best? Because if someone were the best the contest would dry up and the everlasting basis of life in the Hellenic state would be endangered." Hermodor was apparently so talented at whatever it was he did—perhaps music, oratory, or athletics—that he discouraged his competitors to the point of enervation. Such a result, says Nietzsche, dampens desire in the other participants for achievement and for continuous self-overcoming, thereby endangering the growth not only of individuals but also of society as a whole. Therefore, Nietzsche further reasons, "The outstanding individual was removed in order that the competition of forces might be awakened." The purpose of ostracism is thus to inject a "stimulant" into the social body. In a very interesting move, Nietzsche says that the underlying assumption here is that the necessity of such exclusivity lies in the fact that

> in the natural order of things there are always *several* geniuses, who incite one another to action as much as they hold one another within the bounds of moderation. That is the kernel of the Hellenic conception of competition: it abhors autocracy/monopoly, and fears its dangers; it demands, as a *protection* against the genius—a second genius..[15]

I find this remark interesting for three reasons. First, it bears on a core concern of Nietzsche's entire body of work: the relationship between "genius" and "culture." Although his understanding of the term "genius" changes somewhat over time, Nietzsche consistently wants culture to serve the production of geniuses—ultimately, that means creators of new life-enhancing values, institutions, ideologies, and forms of life. Second, on the face of it, the remark contradicts Nietzsche's later adamant and somewhat hostile position (as we will see) against what he calls democracy's "leveling" tendency. I can imagine the later Nietzsche arguing that it is the exclusion of figures like Hermodor that precisely *threatens* the well-being of society. Why? Because it results in a "mediocritization" of competition. The third reason, however, is the most significant and Nietzschean of all. Nietzsche is suggesting that in the interest of social well-being—a necessary prerequisite for the creation of outstanding people, "geniuses"—a highly sensitive balance between the "competition of forces" is essential. If the force of competition is too weak, we will never test ourselves, and culture will suffer. Lacking challenge, we will never develop our abilities—"Every natural talent must develop itself in struggle," he says. Without the struggle, properly modulated, no "second

15 *The Nietzsche Channel*, "Homers Wettkampf," http://www.thenietzschechannel.com/works-unpub/five/hcg.htm. Accessed November 5, 2022.

genius" can even *recognize* himself or herself, much less *arise*. If the force of competition is too strong, however, "*Alleinherrschaft*" ensues. I double-translate this term of Nietzsche's as "autocracy/monopoly" because it simultaneously suggests a dictatorial leader on the political stage and a domineering fellow participant on the stage of everyday activity. Both figures achieve their superiority not through society-enhancing democratic *agon* but through the "harmful and destructive means" of *disabling agon* through monopolizing a situation.

Have we not all experienced the imbalance of which Nietzsche, via the Greeks, is wary? Think of the conversation-suffocating "expert" in a group discussion. The loudest, most aggressive colleague in a staff meeting. The know-it-all professor in whose stultifying presence the students must sit effectively dumb and mute. Who knows what genius lies buried in the presence of such Hermodors? I know Hermodors from my days as a musician— the virtuoso players whose impossibly good chops in a jam session paralyze everyone else. By contrast, a common cliché in sports is that one great player can raise the game of his or her teammates. If that is true then it would be an example of the *proper* balance being achieved; it would assume a kind of democracy of play. Just as often, though, we hear of the ball hog, whose combined athletic talent and overconfident personality serve to cancel out the abilities of his or her teammates.

Such examples may seem trivial. But Nietzsche is asking us to recognize an issue that, he believes, lies at the very heart of "politics," namely, the intertwined relationship between the ostensibly "honorable 'Above'" of our government and the "habitually humble 'Below'" of us *hoi polloi*, for whom such Hermodors in my examples are all too real.

> The relationship between the people and the government is the strongest model of a relationship, according to whose image other dealings are automatically patterned: teacher and student; householder and servants; father and family; military officer and soldier; master and apprentice.[16]

Nietzsche is going as far as to argue for the *fractal* nature of the state-people relationship. A fractal is a pattern that replicates itself across different scales—Above as Below, Below as Above. You can observe fractals in the repeated patterns found in snowflakes, lightning bolts, trees, ocean waves,

---

16 *Human, All Too Human*, "A Look at the State," 450.

shorelines, mountains, clouds, geographic terrains, seashells, craters, DNA, and…societies. You can see the fractal form equally in the cosmos, in a molecule, and in Romanesco broccoli, somewhere in between. Take a tree as an example. The patterning within the tree's cellular DNA is replicated in the tiniest twigs of the tree, which, again, resemble the patterning found within the large branches of the tree, which in turn resemble the patterning of the tree's trunk. I read Nietzsche here as such a fractal thinker. It is only because of his ultimate concern with the Below—with human subject formation and with the foundational culture within which that takes shape—that Nietzsche must give thought to the Above, to that element of culture we call "the state." He is not interested in politics per se. (This qualification may be why traditional political thinkers find Nietzsche so evasive on the subject.) In "Homer's Contest," he is sensitive to democracy's function as a "safety valve" against some "great competing politician and party leader [who] feels himself incited in the heat of the conflict towards harmful and destructive measures and alarming *coups d'état.*"[17] Such a figure from Above, replicated in our interrelations Below, spells disaster for culture. Whether in the sphere of everyday interactions, heightened ritualized competition, or politics and statecraft, democratic *agon* serves as a kind of kill switch for tyrannical domination, thereby enabling additional "geniuses" to emerge.

> *Hundred-year quarantine.* Democratic institutions are quarantine establishments against the ancient pestilence of tyrannical lust: as such, they are very useful and very boring.[18]

> *The danger of kings.* Completely without violence, and through constant constitutional pressure alone, democracy is able to render the offices of king and emperor *hollow*, until but a Nothing remains.[19]

For the earlier Nietzsche, democracy's usefulness thus lies in the "*prophylactic measures*" it enacts against tyrannical tendencies—in everyday life as in national politics. In a passage prefaced *The age of cyclopean building*, Nietzsche argues that the nascent democratic edifices being raised in his midst are, like cyclopean walls, near-mythically colossal fortifications against past forms of tyrannical domination, both mental and physical.

---

17 *The Nietzsche Channel*, "Homers Wettkampf," http://www.thenietzschechannel.com/works-unpub/five/hcg.htm. Accessed November 11, 2022.
18 *Human, All Too Human*, "The Wanderer and His Shadow," 289.
19 *Human, All Too Human*, "The Wanderer and His Shadow," 281.

The democratization of Europe, it seems, is a link in the chain of those tremendous *prophylactic measures* that constitute the thinking of this new era and through which we distinguish ourselves from the Middle Ages. Only now has the age of cyclopean building arrived! At last, securing the foundations so that the whole future can build on it without danger! Hereafter, it is impossible that the fruit fields of culture will again be destroyed overnight by wild and senseless mountain torrents! Stone dams and protective walls against barbarians, against epidemics, against *bodily and mental servitude*.[20]

DEMOCRACY AS TYRANNY

The careful reader will have noticed Nietzsche's "very boring" comment earlier. So let's slow down. It is clear that Nietzsche views democratic institutions as "very useful" because of the measures against tyranny that they introduce. But why does he add that they are at the same time "very boring"? "Homer's Contest" argues, if indirectly, that we must include among our "prophylactic measures" the society-enriching fostering of *pluralism*. Nietzsche is nothing if not a fierce champion of pluralism—pluralism of human "types" as well as of conceptual perspectives. So, in light of the pluralistic Nietzsche, it is noteworthy that, in "Homer's Contest," inclusion comes at the price of *exclusion*. In this case, the exclusion is, moreover, of the too-excellent Hermodor. Hence, Nietzsche's snipe about democracy's boringness. When the democratic prophylactic, when the taste for and mentality of democracy, slips from being a cautiously regulated "stimulant" *for* dynamism, to being a crude "safety valve" *against* dangerous tendencies, then it becomes a "bad habit." Nietzsche's earlier statement about government's being the "strongest model of relationship" shows that at stake is the fractal pattern being replicated. That statement continues:

All of these relations [teacher-student, father-family, etc.] now somewhat rearrange themselves under the influence of the reigning constitutional form of government: they *are becoming* compromises. But how they will have to turn and twist, change their names and nature, when that very latest concept [*i.e.,* constitutional democracy] has gained mastery in everyone's mind![21]

---

20 *Human, All Too Human*, "The Wanderer and His Shadow," 275.
21 *Human, All Too Human*, "A Look at the State," 450.

As is so often the case with our wild guide, Nietzsche catches sight of objections to a view that he is offering *in the very process of offering it*! Indeed, as Ulrich Baer writes, "Nietzsche does not only argue his points; he performs them."[22] Observing the almost mythic nature of democracy's cyclopean construction, Nietzsche cannot but notice the *toll* it is taking on its builders.

> One can feel anxious about those who are toiling consciously and honestly for this future [*i.e.*, for the "democratic path"]. Something desolate and monotonous lies in their faces, and the gray dust [of construction] seems also to blow into their brains. Still: it is possible that posterity will laugh at our anxiety and consider the democratic labor of a succession of generations as we do the construction of stone dams and protective walls—as an activity that necessarily gets a lot of dust on clothing and faces, and perhaps makes the workers a bit stupid, too. But who would therefore wish such work undone?[23]

So, yes, a robustly balanced agonal, democratic *Above* equates to a robustly balanced agonal democratic *Below*. But what about a *compromised* Above? What about a *stupid* Below? In the fractal model, the presence of desolation, monotony, stupidity, dust, and harm *Below* are evidence *from Above*, and *vice versa*. I imagine that Nietzsche must have seen the nature of this compromise in his very example of Hermodor. The compromise, namely, is that of the "leveling" that occurs in "Homer's Contest." From this point on, "tyranny" and "democracy" will remain bound in Nietzsche's writing, but no longer as antagonistic tendencies. Rather, in this view, democracy breeds—indeed, is itself—a quite particular variety of tyranny. Let's consider this shift in Nietzsche's perspective.

Nietzsche's sympathetic view supports, to a great extent, our contemporary social myth of liberal democracy as a way of shoring up against the tyrannical genius, whether in the form of an enervating Hermodor of culture or a domineering Napoleon of politics. It shares, too, one of the central assumptions of liberal democracy, namely, the nonnegotiable necessity of *pluralism*. Nietzsche, I think, offers us insights for seeing through our social myth. Indeed, he does so on the very grounds of a value that is supposedly inextricable from that myth: the pluralist assumption. His logic goes something like this: The task of a philosopher is to think through the optimal conditions

---

22 Ulrich Baer, in his revised translation of *Beyond Good and Evil* (New York: Warbler Press, 2021), 187.
23 *Human, All Too Human*, "The Wanderer and His Shadow," 275.

for the cultivation of optimal humans. A finely calibrated democracy is such a condition—it enhances human growth and well-being—*because* it enables pluralism. This condition obtained for a brief moment, perhaps, in ancient Greece. But, viewing our contemporary society, we see that it no longer holds: our form of democracy breeds ill-health—it encourages human diminution and decadence—*because* it disables pluralism. Therefore, as a system of governance as well as a cultural "taste," "habit," "prejudice," and so on, democracy is now undesirable. In a passage that is vague yet deeply suggestive, Nietzsche bluntly states, "This is how it is":

> The diminution and leveling of Europeans harbors *our* greatest danger, for the sight of this person is exhausting…We see nothing today that wants to become greater, we suspect that everything will go further down, down into what is thinner, more good-natured, more clever, more comfortable, more mediocre, more indifferent, more Chinese, more Christian—humanity is, without doubt, always becoming "better."[24]

Nietzsche's use of a characteristically charged term, "more Chinese," will help us understand what he sees as the dangerous diminution of people under democracy. His elucidation, nested within a criticism of Immanuel Kant (1724–1804), is, in short, of a universal human type. As such, we should view it as something more nuanced than the brute racialized stereotype that it might appear on first sight.[25] In *The Antichrist*, Nietzsche argues that Kant is "damaging" because of his *moralizing*:

> "Virtue," "duty," the "good-in-itself," the good with an impersonal and universal character—a fantasy in which the decline, the final enervation of life, the Königsbergian Chinesism expresses itself.[26]

---

24 *On the Genealogy of Morals*, 1.12.
25 Nietzsche's interest in Asian culture and thought goes back to his youth. As a teenager, he requested A. E. Wollheim's *Mythologie des alten Indien* [Mythology of Ancient India] (Berlin, 1856) as a Christmas gift. His sympathetic interest intensified at Pforta and peaked with his absorption in Schopenhauer. Thereafter, he continued to read widely in Asian thought, though now mainly as a foil to his own philosophy. He writes to his old friend, Paul Deussen, the Sanskrit philologist, thanking him for sending his recently published work on the Indian philosophy *Vedanta*: "I read page for page with complete 'malice'—you cannot desire a more grateful reader, my friend! As it happens, a manifesto of mine is at this moment being printed [*Thus Spoke Zarathustra*], which, with approximately the same eloquence, says Yes! where your book says No!" On the substantial evidence for Nietzsche's reading in Asian thought, see Thomas H. Brobjer, "Nietzsche's Reading About Eastern Philosophy," *Journal of Nietzsche Studies*, Autumn 2004, No. 28: 3–35. See also "Reader, Nietzsche," footnote 28.
26 *The Antichrist*, 11.

"Chinesism" [*Chinesentum*], first of all, indicates our tendency toward obedient passivity and complacency in relation to received ethical norms. Two of the most important, indeed related, themes in Nietzsche's work are the contingent nature of "good and evil" and the repressive nature of morality as such. In this sense, "Chinesism" denotes our uncritical acceptance of norms. In Nietzsche's reading, Confucianism provides the norms in China, whereas Christianity does so in Europe (and as Buddhism and Brahmanism do in India). Second, the term indicates the ages-old philosophical tendency toward a flattening of human experience. Somehow, the infinite variety, the ungraspable complexity, the unfathomable richness of human desire and motivation can be reduced to a generic rule of morality. Kant, in a move of "Königsbergian Chinesism," names this reduction the "categorical imperative."[27] Nietzsche, recognizing the high and repressive cost of this increasingly popular view in Europe, calls it a "Moloch of Abstraction," and is astounded that people have not experienced it as "dangerous to life."

A virtue must be *our* invention, *our* personal self-defense and necessity: in every other sense it is merely a danger. What does not determine our life *harms* it: a virtue merely out of a feeling of respect for the concept "virtue," as Kant wanted it, is damaging [...] The reverse is offered by the deepest laws of preservation and growth: that we each discover *our* virtue, *our* categorical imperative. A people perishes when it confuses *its* duty with the duty concept in itself. Nothing ruins more deeply, more interiorly, as that "impersonal" duty, that Moloch of Abstraction.[28]

"Chinesism" is, in fact, virtually synonymous with other Nietzschean usages highlighting our duty-motivated tendencies, such as "the herd," "the

---

27 In *The Groundwork of the Metaphysic of Morals*, Kant defines the categorical imperative as: "Act only according to that maxim whereby you can, at the same time, will that it should become a universal law." This imperative "act" is "categorical" because it is a nonnegotiable, unconditional, ethical *requirement*, one that must be practiced as an inherently justified end in itself. This imperative is to be fulfilled, moreover, regardless of any seemingly mitigating circumstances, such as lying to the police about the presence of your crime-committing friend in your room. Emphasizing the action itself, the categorical imperative is an example of "deontological," duty- or rule-bound ethics, in distinction to "consequentialism," which considers the outcome or consequences of an action. "Königsbergian" is a reference to Kant, who lived his entire life within the medieval walls of the Prussian city Königsberg (present day Kaliningrad, in Russia). Moloch was a Canaanite god who required child sacrifice. In modern times, "Moloch" refers to a power that demands a dire sacrifice.

28 *The Antichrist*, 11.

last mortal," "the passive nihilist," "the decadent," "European Buddhism," and, most scathingly, "Christian." And it is precisely *in democracy*, in the democratic taste, the democratic habit, the democratic mentality, and the democratic government, that Nietzsche places the blame for enabling these dehumanizing tendencies to infiltrate society. The ultimate, damning consequence of democracy, one of such severity that it could well take generations to reverse, is "the human's mediocritization and degradation."[29]

> Precisely here lies the undoing of Europe—along with our fear of humanity we have lost our love of it, our reverence for it, our hope in it, indeed, even the will to it. The view of humanity now makes us weary—what is nihilism today if not *that*?—We are weary of *humanity*.[30]

MASTER MORALITY AND SLAVE MORALITY

Our "undoing" is encapsulated in the case of Hermodor. Ultimately, the democratic habit reveals itself to be hostile to life because it represses, indeed even punishes, displays of strength, intelligence, and ability that challenge the status quo. In our democratic banishing of Hermodors, we may be removing tyrannical threats, but we are introducing a new, indeed all-encompassing, singular threat. In the former case, tyranny takes the form of *domination*, of monopolization and enervation, by a single dominant individual. In the latter case, it takes the form of *consensus*, of "mediocritization" and "leveling," by "the people" as a whole. The people do this, Nietzsche holds, through the imposition of uniformity, or, what amounts to the same thing, through the exclusion of difference. In a deceptively dense fragment from 1880, Nietzsche writes:

> The more that the feeling of unity with others gains the upper hand, the more people become uniform, the more severely they experience difference as immoral. Thus arises, necessarily, the sand of humanity: everyone very similar, very small, very round, very harmless, very boring. Christianity and democracy have hitherto led humanity the farthest along the path to sand. A small, weak, faintly good little feeling spread equally over everyone, an improved and exaggerated

---

29 *Beyond Good and Evil*, 203.
30 *On the Genealogy of Morals*, 1.12.

Chinesism—is that the final image that humanity can offer? On our current track of moral sensibility, it is unavoidable. Profound consideration is required. Humanity must perhaps draw a line under its past, or perhaps it must direct a new rule *(Kanon)* to all individuals: be different from all others, and be pleased when someone is different from the others. The most uncouth monsters have, of course, been eradicated under the present regime of morality—this was its very purpose; we do not want to continue to live thoughtlessly under a regime of fear of wild beasts. For so long, for all-too long, the motto has been: One like All, One for All.[31]

On whatever modern formation Nietzsche sets his gaze—politics, education, customs of speech and dress, newspaper and magazine journalism, morality, religion, literature, theater and music, scholarship, philosophy—he sees the dual phenomena of individual "sandification" and mass cultural mediocritization at work. For an agonistic pluralist like Nietzsche, this leveling homogenization is, of course, detrimental enough for society. But what it brings in its wake is even worse. Nietzsche is claiming that we have come to experience difference not on rational grounds, but on *moral* ones. A person's difference from some social norm, concerning, say, political opinion or sexual orientation, is not considered good, bad, better, worse, or neutral as a matter of reasoned evaluation; it is rather considered so as a matter of moral judgment. In the logic of democratic mass culture, to be outside of the boundaries of accepted norms, Nietzsche holds, is to be bad, even evil. Now, I can imagine that this claim goes too far for many readers. Surely, it is overly simplistic if not outright wrong? After all, diversity is considered to be as intrinsic to liberal democracy as are liberty, equality, and justice.[32] Let's slow down here. Nietzsche's reference to "the feeling of unity with others" involves a claim about the general parameters of our "moral sensibility." So first we must ask: where does this sensibility play out, where does the actual imposition of uniformity occur? Well, Nietzsche argues, where else could it play out but in our families, in our schools and universities, in friend groups and relationships, in local communities, in the workplace, in our online feeds? Given Nietzsche's fractal logic (as Above, Below; as Below, Above), we must, of course, include politics here. The reader may wonder: unity of moral sensibility—in politics? Consider that, in the United

---

31 *NF*–1880, 3[98]. See also *Dawn*, 174.
32 See, for instance, Ryan Muldoon, *Social Contract Theory for a Diverse World: Beyond Tolerance* (New York: Routledge, 2016).

States, liberal democrats and conservative republicans differ about virtually every specific policy under the sun—student debt relief, marriage equality, reproductive rights, the death penalty, and so on. However, they absolutely, without question, are one-hundred percent in agreement about, indeed, they *dogmatically assume*, the value, necessity, inevitability, goodness, rightness, and so on and so forth, of *the state* and of all that that entity encompasses: the nation, the government, the security apparatus, the free market, the justice system; in short, all existing institutions that constitute our democratic republic. Nietzsche would agree with Slavoj Žižek's contention that this liberal-conservative dogma gives the lie to our social myth of "actual freedom," producing instead mere "formal freedom," namely, "freedom of choice *within* the coordinates of the existing power relations."[33] Noam Chomsky's similar comment about the very real but largely invisible nature of our limiting parameters is helpful, and also quite Nietzschean in spirit:

> The smart way to keep people passive and obedient is to strictly limit the spectrum of acceptable opinion, but allow very lively debate within that spectrum—even encourage the more critical and dissident views. That gives people the sense that there is free thinking going on, while all the time the presuppositions of the system are being reinforced by the limits put on the range of the debate.[34]

Chomsky is making a quintessential anarchist claim here. Anarchists invoke this argument when confronted with the inevitable claim by liberals that they (liberals) represent a genuine political alternative to conservatives. Anarchists consider the liberal-conservative distinction superficial and the liberal alternative to conservatism inconsequential. Nietzsche is ultimately against the anarchists, who are literally dynamiting their way into public consciousness as he is writing. Yet he is in perfect unison with them concerning their critique of the "presuppositions of the system" that liberals and conservatives equally hold legitimate. In particular, he agrees with them about what lies at the very *root* of the cultural enervation in his midst: "State? What is that? It is the coldest of all cold monsters."[35] For both the anarchists and Nietzsche, "the state" is the bedrock presupposition on which rests the "hellish hoax"

33 Slavoj Žižek, "A Plea For Leninist Intolerance," *Critical Inquiry*, Vol. 28, No. 2 (2002), 542–544.
34 Noam Chomsky, *The Common Good* (Berkeley: Odonian Press, 1998), 43.
35 Unless noted, this and the following quotes in the paragraph, *Thus Spoke Zarathustra*, "On the New Idols."

that is our society as spectacle, where "all are drinkers of poison…where all lose themselves…where the slow suicide of all is called 'life.'" The "feeling of unity" that Nietzsche mentions is locked in place by our shared "moral sensibility" about what is good and proper, what is right and wrong, within our everyday formations. Crucially, for both Nietzsche and the anarchists, a profound distinction is at hand here: that between *state* and *culture*. Think of a workplace scenario. "Below" are the workers who, hands on, actually produce the product. "Below" is where intimate knowledge of the details of the workplace exists. "Above" are the rules, regulations, and traditions that determine the limits of the workers' application of their knowledge. "Above" is where the managers and executives maintain the limiting structures that Chomsky mentions. In this example, "Above" is the state and "Below" is culture. Nietzsche and the anarchists are equally adamant that "the state" means domination, fixity, uniformity, stultification, and death, while "culture" means innovation, fluidity, diversity, intelligence, and life. The state at the heart of any given formation—from a relationship to a workplace to a nation—"suffocates" us in the "fumes" of *its* world, *its* presuppositions. And so, says Nietzsche, we should at all costs "smash its windows and leap to freedom." The culture at the heart of any given formation, by contrast, is the sum total of all those matters "for whose sake it is worth living on earth: for example, virtue, art, music, dance, reason, spirituality—[matters] transfiguring, refined, mad, and divine."[36] Indeed, together with the utopian anarchists, Nietzsche, finally, implores us: "Where the state ends—look there, my friends! Do you not see it, the rainbow and the bridges of the *Übermensch*?"

We, however, are currently nowhere near *where the state ends*. We are deep in the midst of "the steam of human sacrifices"[37] that constitutes our ongoing state of affairs. Nietzsche's question whether this state of affairs is "the final image that humanity can offer?" is profoundly significant. For his entire project is precisely to present his reader with the lineaments of *a wholly other* image of humanity. We will remain impervious to such an image as long as we are vulnerable to the "preachers of death" in our midst—those people who insist on the inevitability and naturalness of the current, democratic, status quo. We will remain blind to all new images of humanity until we find a way to exit from "our current track of moral sensibility."

What makes such a renewed vision of our collective lives so difficult to achieve? The answer to this question takes us to the very heart of Nietzsche's

---

36 *Beyond Good and Evil*, 188.
37 *Thus Spoke Zarathustra*, "On the New Idols."

project. The answer is: Christianity. More specifically, it is the fact that Christian "moral sensibility" continues to exert a decisive influence on our way of life in the West, far removed though we are from the days of deep religious conviction and ecclesiastic control of daily life: "God is dead; but given the way of people, there will still be caves for perhaps thousands of years in which his shadow will be cast. And we—we still have to vanquish his shadow, too."[38] You and I must not explicitly subscribe to Christian values in order to absorb Christian morality. Christian beliefs and imperatives—concerning pity and sympathy, kindness and neighborliness, right and wrong, industry and work, family and friendship, sexuality and gender, weakness and humility, human rights and equality, and much more—Nietzsche suggests, make up the very atmosphere—the "steam"—in which we live. We cannot help but inhale it. More to the point for our purposes, Nietzsche holds that the same is true for democracy. With its emphasis on equality and all the rest, democracy, it turns out, is a direct offspring of Christianity: "The *democratic* movement claims the inheritance of the Christian movement."[39] "One like All, One for All" is, for Nietzsche, the original sin of Christianity and its progeny. "One like All, One for All" is the moral sentiment that breeds the homogenizing "feeling of unity with others." Incidentally, I said earlier that Nietzsche and anarchism were in agreement concerning their views on the detrimental effects of the state for the advancement of culture. It may be instructive briefly to note that Nietzsche ultimately rejects the emerging socialism of his day for the same reason he rejects democracy. For communism, one brand of socialism, holds fast to nothing if not "One like All, One for All," and anarchism, another brand of socialism, is nothing if not "democracy taken seriously."[40]

This, then, is the problem at the heart of Nietzsche's project: first, "Christianity and democracy have thus far led humanity the farthest along the path to sand"—to, that is, an homogenized uniformity and massified conformity regarding our culture-shaping moral values—*and,* second, Christianity and democracy are inextricably and invisibly bound up in that very path, in our very way of being. Christian and democratic morality are simply *given*, they are granted axiomatically as what is good and right. So how might we act free from their influence? Who, among my readers, is ready to reject those imperatives listed previously? Who is prepared to

---

38 *The Joyful Wisdom*, 108.
39 *Beyond Good and Evil*, 202.
40 Edward Abbey, *One Life at a Time, Please* (New York: Henry Holt and Company, 1978), 26.

declare our notion of kindness or neighborliness not only problematic but…
evil? Well, Nietzsche is. To understand why, we have to give thought to a
dangerous thesis of his: *slave morality*. For, ultimately, we are stuck on our
path to sand because we collectively embrace the central conceit of slave
morality, which is none other than "One like All, One for All." It is precisely
such morality, Nietzsche holds, that blocks our path to a "higher" culture,
indeed, to a future in which an *Übermensch,* and not, as at present, a *letzter
Mensch*, will feel at home.

So what is slave morality? Nietzsche asks us to engage in a thought
experiment: "Suppose that moralizing is done by people who are violated,
oppressed, suffering, unfree, lacking confidence, and weary." Imagine that
what we collectively hold as "moral" were determined by such weary people.
What would be the defining spirit of their moralizing? What, in other words,
would count as "good" and what as "bad" and "evil"? Nietzsche answers:

> Probably, a pessimistic suspicion against the entire condition of
> humanity would come to expression, perhaps a condemnation of
> humanity along with its condition. The gaze of the slave looks unfavor-
> ably toward the virtue of the powerful: he is skeptical and distrustful,
> he possesses an *acuteness* of distrust concerning all the "good" that
> is honored there—he would like to convince himself that even their
> happiness is not genuine.[41]

So, first of all, if our shared moral code were devised by the weary, etc.,
it would *not* be that of "the powerful." It would not, indeed could not, be,
in Nietzsche's terminology, a *master morality*. A master morality can be
summed up negatively as that which has "contempt for the cowardly, the
anxious, the petty, for those who consider narrow utility; also for the dis-
trustful ones with their unfree gazes, the self-demeaning, the doglike people
who allow themselves to be mistreated, the begging flatterers, especially the
liars."[42] I think it is important to note, as we rock a bit in these choppy waters,
that "slave" and "master" indicate, in the first instance, that the dignity of a
person is *not* a matter of birth, class, gender, ethnicity, or nationality. Rather,
it is a matter of disposition and behavior. We will return to this point in
a moment. To continue with the slave morality that Nietzsche believes is
permeating democratic modernity, consuming the populace, and disabling
higher culture:

---

41 *Beyond Good and Evil*, 260.
42 *Beyond Good and Evil*, 260.

Conversely, certain qualities that serve to ease the suffering of existence would be brought out and bathed in light: here are honored pity, the obliging helpful hand, the warm heart, patience, industry, humility, and friendliness—for these are the most useful qualities for, and practically the only means of, enduring the pressures of existence. Slave morality is essentially a morality of utility.[43]

We consider qualities such as humility and friendliness morally "good" because they make life easier for us. Going around thinking you are better than everyone else and being unfriendly to, say, work colleagues, simply has no practical utility: people will dissemble around you, avoid and shun you if possible. Imagine a time you were in a meeting with colleagues or at a gathering of friends. One of them says something cringey or phony or dishonest. How do others react? Chances are, they chuckle nervously (at most), and let it go. They *exhibit*, regardless of whether they actually *feel*, a warm heart and patience. It is rare that someone responds in a way that upsets the "feeling of unity with others." It is unlikely that anyone will explicitly challenge the "presuppositions of the system," and likely that they will reinforce those presuppositions by acquiescing to the tacitly agreed on necessity of accepting the reigning power dynamic and, in short, of *being nice*. The democratically ingrained Christian and generally conformist value of "One like All, One for All" becomes an unconscious force of self-inhibiting censorship. The alternative would be a seemingly hostile act of what Sara Ahmed calls "killing joy." The "joy" comes from upholding the system of social hierarchies and ideological presuppositions that have somehow been deemed right, proper, and good. The killer of joy is, by contrast, deemed an undesirable troublemaker who risks tearing apart our carefully constructed social net for the sake of—what, honesty, integrity, difference?[44] Ahmed's killer of joy and Chomsky's denier of the limiting spectrum might have in common with Nietzsche's smasher of windows that they are all practicing master morality. As such, their examples offer our best hope for altering our "current track of moral sensibility" and for courageously applying the decidedly nonutilitarian new rule proposed by Nietzsche: "be different from all others, and be pleased when someone is different from the others." But beware: as in the case of Hermodor, difference in a democratic setting can too quickly provoke ostracism.

---

43 *Beyond Good and Evil*, 260.
44 See Sara Ahmed, *The Promise of Happiness* (Durham: Duke University Press, 2010).

So what is this master morality that offers some hope? First of all, it does not involve the puerile impulse of being different merely for the sake of being different. Being different involves the necessity of resistance specifically within the modern world with its many defects, which Nietzsche tirelessly enumerates. Being different means becoming a new subject, a new *type* of person, within this world. It means becoming a nomad, a heretic, a stranger, an *Übermensch*. Indeed, Nietzsche's favorite adjective for this different person is *noble*. Throughout his work, he names many characteristics of nobility. It involves "insight, justice, magnanimity, capability of bestowing, dancing, singular, having a sense of order or rank, active, 'natural,' health, wholeness, concern for the future, and [is] dialectically related to barbarism."[45] Difference—of types, of opinions, of actions, of abilities, and so on—is also, for Nietzsche, an essential feature of a vibrant, robust, creative culture. But perhaps the most salient feature of master morality, and indeed a major means for difference to appear in social life, is that "it is *value-creating*": "The noble type of people feel themselves to be *value-determining*. They do not feel it necessary to be granted approval."[46] In our example of the uncomfortable conversation with colleagues or friends, it is the "contemptible" person, the practitioner of slave morality, who, with warm heart and friendliness, participates in the perpetuation of the dishonest, lazy, or cringey status quo. By contrast, the practitioner of master morality, the "noble" person, acts in a way that "is to open a life, to make room for life, to make room for possibility, for chance," as Ahmed says of the killjoy.[47] Of course, in *making room* you may be showing yourself the exit. This is often the cost of nobility among the cowardly and self-demeaning.

We can be more specific about the values driving master morality. But it will not be pretty. Indeed, Nietzsche accurately points out that this type of morality "is for the most part alien and embarrassing to contemporary tastes." It is particularly so given "the severity of its basic principle, namely, that we have duties only toward our peers; that toward people of lower ranks and toward everything that is alien to us we may act according to our own discretion or 'as the heart desires,' and in any case 'beyond good and evil.'"[48] (Yes, the sky is darkening and the waves are swelling.) Let us put aside the fact that Nietzsche is almost certain to temper such provocative statements

---

45 See Douglass Burnham, *The Nietzsche Dictionary* (London: Bloomsbury Academic, 2015), 239.
46 *Beyond Good and Evil*, 260.
47 Ahmed, *Promise*, "Introduction."
48 *Beyond Good and Evil*, 260.

elsewhere in his work. For instance, concerning the "duty" of the noble, he seems to contradict himself by insisting that "if the exceptional person handles the mediocre person more tenderly than he does himself or his peers, this is not mere politeness—it is simply his *duty*."[49] Discounting such perspectival equivocations, we must ask: are we not in Leopold and Loeb territory here? Recall that Nathan Leopold brutally murdered poor Bobby Franks because, as his own lawyer, the legendary Clarence Darrow, admitted, "He believed in [Nietzsche's] superman…The ordinary commands of society were not for him."[50] Leopold and Loeb were, if nothing else, "beyond good and evil" in the flesh. The question, though, is whether they were *noble*, whether they had *earned the privilege* to act contrary to accepted norms. We might ask the same questions about figures like Napoleon and Caesar, indeed, like Trump and Hitler. Certainly, these men feel themselves to be profoundly "value-determining"; they are in need of enemies and revenge, they are strong and aggressive, and they stand far beyond any requirement to ask for permission or forgiveness in light of their transgressive actions— all noble qualities, for Nietzsche. Are they therefore noble practitioners of master morality? Nietzsche is aware that such figures exhibit certain "noble" qualities, as those mentioned. But that is not enough. In fact, it is *far* from enough. Napoleon, for instance, represents, for Nietzsche, "the embodiment of the problem of *nobility in itself*. One might well consider *what* kind of problem it is: Napoleon, this synthesis of inhuman [*Unmensch*] and overhuman [*Übermensch*]."[51] (Elsewhere, he calls such seemingly masterful people as our spiritual gurus "ghastly mixtures of sickness and will to power."[52]) In fact, as we saw in the passage that opens this section, one of the achievements that slave morality has to recommend it is that "the most uncouth monsters have, of course, been eradicated under" its regime of democracy. In any case, the likes of Leopold and Loeb come nowhere near the strict demands of the "superman" they so yearned to emulate. I think that Nietzsche would see their efforts to act "beyond good and evil" as a wholly predictable perversion of the *Übermensch*. The perverting elements, furthermore, he would say, are furnished by modern democracy, specifically, by the elements of human diminution and decadence that we have been discussing. Leopold and Loeb's "*Übermensch*" is what Nietzsche's *Übermensch* looks

---

49 *The Antichrist*, 57.
50 *Voices of Democracy: The U.S. Oratory Project*. https://voicesofdemocracy.umd.edu/ clarence-darrow-plea-for-leopold-and-loeb-22-23-and-25-august-1924-speech-text.
51 *On the Genealogy of Morals*, 1.16.
52 *Ecce Homo*, Preface, 4.

like in a Democratic Hall of Mirrors. Indeed, Nietzsche argued that, in his time at least, it was still too soon for the goal of democracy—namely, a fully independent individual, one capable of responsibly going beyond arbitrarily accepted norms of good and evil—to be realized. Why? Because of the influence that Christian-democratic-conformist-slave morality still exerts on us. Recall that Nietzsche expressed his hopes for democracy as a matter for the future.

> I am speaking of democracy as of something to come. That which currently goes by that name differs from the older forms of government only in that it drives with new horses: the streets are the old ones, and the wheels of the carriage are the old ones as well.—Has the danger presented by these wagons of public weal really been diminished?[53]

We, of course, may—indeed, must—ask whether the time has come to change out those wheels and lay new roads. *How* to do so, and *who* to do it, follow quickly behind that *whether.* Nietzsche has much to offer us here, although, again, we need to slow down.

"TO WHERE MUST WE REACH WITH OUR HOPES?"

Nietzsche's complex view of modern democracy as championing mediocrity at the cost of excellence is summed up in this passage from *Beyond Good and Evil*:

> We who are of a different faith—we who view the democratic movement not merely as a decayed form of political organization but rather as a decayed, that is to say, diminutive, form of the human, as the human's mediocritization and degradation of worth: to where must we reach with our hopes?[54]

Let us conclude this chapter by giving careful thought to that final question. Significantly, and wholly consistent with his overarching concern with *types,* Nietzsche's most substantial answer to this question comes not in terms of anything resembling political theory but rather in terms of a human subject, a model of his desired person. That topic, however, requires a thorough

---

53 *Human, All Too Human,* "The Wanderer and His Shadow," 293.
54 *Beyond Good and Evil,* 203.

treatment of its own, and this must await the final chapter. Here, I would like to present some ideas that appear, to a degree at least, as more in line with "political organization," as Nietzsche himself calls it. So the question I am addressing here is, "to what kind of political organization must we reach with our hopes?"

The short answer is: toward "aristocratic radicalism." But before we consider what this term means, we should be clear that Nietzsche did not expect democracy in its various guises to disappear anytime soon. He speaks of "the slow arising of the democratic order of things" and of democracy's inevitability.[55] So the answer to our question is, once again, future oriented. "Aristocratic radicalism" was the term that the renowned Danish literary critic Georg Brandes (1842–1927) used to describe what he understood to be Nietzsche's implicit political theory.[56] Fortunately, Brandes mentioned this term in a letter to Nietzsche, and we have his reply from a letter six days later:

> The expression "aristocratic radicalism" that you employ is very good. It is, if I may say so, the most astute term that I have read about myself so far. How far this mindset has already informed my thinking, and how far it will continue to do so—I am almost afraid to imagine this.[57]

So how might we understand this term, "aristocratic radicalism"? Brandes explains what *he*, at least, means by the term. Nietzsche reveals himself an aristocratic thinker, says Brandes, in that he promotes the thoroughly aristocratic notion that "humanity must work unceasingly for the production of solitary great men—this and nothing else is its task." Nietzsche constantly and emphatically endorses this notion, thus "aristocratic radicalism"—leadership by the most capable people for a specific job.

Nietzsche, as we should expect by now, offers nothing even remotely resembling a blueprint for a system of aristocratic radicalism. Indeed, he never uses that term himself. He does, however, have a lot to say about

---

55 *Beyond Good and Evil*, 261.
56 Georg Brandes, "An Essay on the Aristocratic Radicalism of Friedrich Nietzsche," 9, Internet Archive, https://archive.org/details/essayonaristocra00bran. Accessed April 3, 2024. The original essay was published in Danish in 1889. In 1899, Brandes added his correspondence with Nietzsche on this and other matters. This part consists of ten letters from Brandes and twelve from Nietzsche. A memorial essay written on Nietzsche's death in August 1900 was then added. Finally, on the publication of *Ecce Homo,* in 1909, Brandes included a review essay on that book.
57 *BVN*–1887, 960.

"nobility" and the "aristocratic." So in yet another candidate for an imaginary book titled *Nietzsche's Most Cancelable Quotes*, the following passage is worth a slow, careful look:

Every enhancement of the type "human" has thus far been the work of an aristocratic society—and so will it always be: a society that believes in a long ladder of ranking and in variations in value from person to person and one that requires slavery in some form or another. Without the *pathos of distance*, which grows out of embodied differences of status, out of the ruling caste's constant looking out from afar on and looking down on the subjects and instruments, and out of its equally constant practice of obeying and commanding, keeping down and keeping distant, that other more mysterious pathos could not have grown, that longing for always new increasing of distances within the soul itself, the development of ever higher, rarer, more distant, more wide-ranging, more comprehensive conditions, in brief, even the enhancement of the type "human," the continued "human self-over-coming," to use a moral phrase in a super-moral sense. Of course, one should not give in to humanitarian delusions about the historical origins of an aristocratic society (and thus of the preconditions of that enhancement of the type "human"): the truth is hard. Let us admit to ourselves, without being precious, how every higher culture on the earth has *begun!* People whose nature was still natural, barbarians in every terrible sense of the word, predators still in possession of an unbroken strength of will and lust for power, thrust themselves onto weaker, more civilized, more peaceful, perhaps trading or cattle breed-ing races, or onto old crumbling cultures in which the final life force flickered in brilliant fireworks of spirit and corruption. The noble caste was in the beginning always the barbarian caste: its predominance lay not primarily in its physical strength, but in its strength of soul—they were the *more whole* people (which, at every level, also means as much as "the more whole beasts.").[58]

Whole beasts, predators, obeying and commanding...slavery?! As Nate Anderson, quoting another eminently cancelable Nietzsche passage, says:

---

58 *Beyond Good and Evil*, 257.

"If you think this sounds like a quote from the *Jerkwad Manifesto*, you're not alone."[59] So, yet again, we are called to slow down.

First of all, we should be clear that Nietzsche is being descriptive here, not prescriptive. That is, he is not saying that this is how it *should* be. Rather, he purports to be telling us something that is historically verifiable. This is important since, as both a "genealogist" and a "psychologist," Nietzsche wants his claims, however speculative, to be grounded in plausible history and observable human proclivities. Specifically, he is asserting that human beings have advanced in particular ways *as human beings*, have grown and improved in quite particular ways, in short, have been "enhanced," only under the "rule *(krátos)* of the best *(áristos)*." The pivotal terms here, "enhanced" and "best," are, of course, highly evaluative and subjective—who decides what "the best" is; one person's "enhanced" is another's "diminished," and so on. In Nietzsche's case, however, these terms constitute the core of his overall concern; and so I trust that the reader is slowly gaining a cumulative effect of what *he* means by them. Now, having said all of that, we should recognize two additional matters. First, rhetorical descriptiveness aside, throughout his work Nietzsche clearly does advocate for some sort of aristocratic formation. Second, in terms of "history," Nietzsche's view is, on the whole, limited to ancient Greece and, in the present case, to the Renaissance as well. Those two reference points are left implicit in the passage. I will elaborate these points in a moment.

Next, we get an elucidation of "aristocratic society." It is, namely, a highly hierarchical society based on personal qualities and one that requires an underclass to support the cultivation of a higher culture. Nietzsche's use of the word "slavery" is obviously packed with explosives. He cannot possibly mean actual enslavement, can he? But what else might he mean? Is his thinking here as profoundly noxious as it appears? Let us take Nietzsche's own advice and "admit to ourselves, without being precious" the fact that—the line between description and prescription here being razor thin—Nietzsche might actually be *advocating* for slavery in the service of humanity's overall "enhancement." Sure, if we take the passage as genuinely descriptive, we can let Nietzsche off the hook. For, *observing* that, historically, slavery has underwritten the enhancement of society is a long way off from holding slavery as a social good, much less from advocating outright for it. (Indeed, that a society's wealth is grounded in slave labor is the central argument for the reparations movement in the United States.) But what if we do not take it this

---

59 Nate Anderson, *In Emergency, Break Glass: What Nietzsche Can Teach Us About Joyful Living in a Tech-Saturated World* (New York: W. W. Norton and Company, 2021), 68.

way, as truly descriptive? I count, after all, three hundred and seven references in Nietzsche's *Collected Works*[60] to some variety of the term—slaves, slavery, enslavement, slavish, slavelike, and so on. The concept clearly plays *some* role in his thought. One scholar of German intellectual history, Martin A. Ruehl, of Cambridge University, argues that Nietzsche scholars have been far too ready either to treat his slavery comments as metaphorical or to ignore them outright. Those who read Nietzsche as a political thinker in the support of "radical democracy," Ruehl further argues, walk on eggshells around his slavery remarks. I think we can all agree that Ruehl is correct to consider the issue a serious desideratum of Nietzsche scholarship. Whether the failure to do so "has left us with an impoverished understanding of his moral and political philosophy"[61] remains, of course, to be determined.

From my own rough examination of all three hundred and seven instances where a variation of "slavery" appears in the *Collected Works*, I tentatively conclude the following. Of 307 entries, 272 occur in the *Notebooks*. Usage of the *Notebooks*, indeed, of the *Nachlass* in general, is a contentious matter in Nietzsche scholarship.[62] (I personally refer to material from the *Notebooks* only if I can locate a similar idea in one of the authorized texts.) The 272 occurrences of "slavery," and so on, that I count are strictly from one of the 106 notebooks, dating from 1869 to 1888.[63] As the term suggests, these

---

60 See "Democracy" footnote 57.

61 Martin A. Ruehl, "In Defence of Slavery: Nietzsche's Dangerous Thinking," *Independent*, https://www.independent.co.uk/news/long_reads/nietzsche-ideas-superman-slavery-nihilism-adolf-hitler-nazi-racism-white-supremacy-fascism-a8138396.html. Accessed December 30, 2022. The précis for the article reads: "Artists, adolescents, and assorted free spirits venerate him as the prophet of total liberation. But Nietzsche did not think all should be free. Martin A Ruehl reveals a disturbing and politically incorrect aspect of the great philosopher." Two observations. First, a close reading of the whole of Nietzsche's work complicates that "should" enormously. Better word choices, I think, are "can realistically be"; "are capable of being"; "want to be"; "are feasibly." Second, a central contention of *Nietzsche NOW!* is that, like it or not, eliminate Nietzsche's "disturbing and politically incorrect" aspects, and you eliminate Nietzsche. And while on the topic—why "adolescents"?

62 See, for instance, William A. B. Parkhurst, "Does Nietzsche Have a 'Nachlass'?" *Nietzsche-Studien* 49 (2020), 216–257. The word *Nachlass* indicates material that was unpublished in the author's lifetime. Parkhurst compiled the following list from various Nietzsche scholars: "personal and professional correspondences; unpublished writings; unpublished papers; unpublished notations; unpublished notes; texts and notes left unpublished; lectures; posthumously published writings or writings published posthumously; posthumous writings; posthumously published materials; posthumously published notebooks; notebooks; manuscripts; manuscript remains; suppressed manuscripts; fragments and jottings; and even, handwritten manuscripts, published and unpublished."

63 The terms are as follows: slavery *(Sklaverei)*; slaves *(Sklaven)*; male slave *(Sklave)*; female slave *(Sklavin)*; enslavement *(Sklaventhum)*; slave-like *(Sklavenhaft/Sklavenhafte)*; slavish *(sklavisch/sklavischen)*; and slave rebellion *(Sklavenaufstand)*.

notebooks contain material that is sketchy (literally and figuratively), fragmentary, experimental, and occasionally often quite outlandish. We may find many versions of a notebook turn of phrase or indeed an entire passage in the published work. The invariable difference is that the published version is more circumspect—the Immoralist is fully aware when he is playing with fire. I treat Nietzsche's notebooks as I would someone's diary; namely, as consisting of highly intimate, private, potentially reckless, conceptually unformed, and fluid thoughts. Close to 90% of his written mentions of slavery are contained in these raw thought-diaries. Are some noxious? I'm sure the reader knows the answer: "Slavery should not be eradicated. It is necessary."[64] Vastly more, however, are of the Dada-like nature of a note to be followed up later, such as, "Newspaper-Slavery";[65] and "Utopia. Slavery. The wife. Herodotus on foreign lands. Wandering. Hellenistic delusions. Revenge and justice."[66] Many are historical: "Slavery as something instinctual among the Hellenes."[67] Some are of a piece with his scathing critique of Christianity: "Christianity has no more dislike for slavery than it has for marriage and the state. It is an altogether different matter when it comes to emancipation."[68] Really, the bulk of the additional references can be found in letters and early unpublished works. For instance, he writes to his mother and sister: "One knows that life is full of suffering, one knows that we are slaves to life the more we want to enjoy it."[69] And, more unfortunately, to the Overbecks: "I would at least like to have a slave, like even the poorest Greek philosopher had. I am too blind for so many things."[70] Finally, I would argue that Nietzsche's most emphatic point about slavery is that which is summed up in a fragment from 1870: "Enslavement belongs to the essence of a culture."[71]

Ruehl, who strikes me as overall critical of Nietzsche's remarks on slavery, generously allows that "if we approach Nietzsche's philosophy in [a contextualized nineteenth-century] way, we allow it truly to challenge our liberal, humanist assumptions. That would make his 'dangerous thinking' even more dangerous."[72] I think Ruehl is right, and, more importantly, that

---

64 *NF*–1881, 11[221].
65 *NF*–1874, 32[4]. "Newspaper-Slavery" was intended as one of the *Untimely Meditations*.
66 *NF*–1869, 3[73].
67 *NF*–1869, 2[4].
68 *NF*–1870, 8[115].
69 *BVN*–1865, 486.
70 *BVN*–1884, 488.
71 *NF*–1870, 7[16].
72 Ruehl, "In Defence of Slavery."

this is right where *we*—the readers and the writer of this book—want to keep Nietzsche. Yes, he believes that creating a culture, a world, that is capable of cultivating human beings of the highest possible caliber, of, in a word, human "enhancement," requires, indeed, is *predicated on* "slavery in some form or another." It is difficult to imagine a notion that is more anathema in liberal and humanist circles. But does that fact invalidate the claim? I recall an incident following the tsunami that devastated the northeastern Japanese coast in 2011. The disaster killed 20,000 people and caused billions of dollars in property damage. A nuclear plant was in imminent danger of a potentially catastrophic meltdown. So when a marine biologist went on television to extol the many tremendous and absolutely essential "positive effects" of the tsunami, people around the world were outraged. The colossal biological fecundity caused by the tsunami, the replenishment of minerals and redistribution of nutrients along the coast, the creation of new sea and land habitats, the improved changes in landscape, the creation of new economic and scientific study opportunities—does any of this matter when human lives are lost? The uncomfortable point of this quite Nietzschean biologist was that natural disasters create *the very conditions for life*. From such a perspective, what does it mean to call them "disasters" at all? I can image the reader replying, "from the only perspective that matters—ours!" We are right back at the "challenge [to] our liberal, humanist assumptions" that such a view entails. Nietzsche is in similar, and similarly dangerous, territory as the biologist here. So before we move on, I would like to consider Nietzsche's claim about slavery a bit further.

The claim is well represented in the 307 notebook entries and can be summed up in an entry from 1870: "slavery is generally visible, although it does not admit it."[73] This statement is a corollary to the overall main point that "enslavement belongs to the essence of a culture." So, all together, the claim is that (i) the enslavement of people is everywhere and at all times staring us in the face; (ii) enslavement is woven into our culture; and (iii) slavery denies that it is in fact what it is. Let's consider. Fasten your seat belts.

"It is hard to find any ancient civilizations in which some slavery did not exist," writes Peter Hunt in *The Cambridge World History*.[74] "Slavery was common to all ancient societies. It was nowhere condemned, not even

---

73 *NF*–1870, 8[115].
74 Peter Hunt, "Slavery," in *The Cambridge World History, Volume 4: A World with States, Empires and Networks 1200 BCE–900 CE* (Cambridge: Cambridge University Press, 2015), 76–100.

in the Old and New Testaments" we read in *The Ancient City*.[75] Indeed, as evidenced in texts such as the *Code of Hammurabi*, the very first civilizations, Sumer and Mesopotamia, had robust institutions of slavery. Slavery existed as far back as the Shang dynasty (18th–12th century B.C.E.) in China.[76] Some evidence even exists of slavery in prehistoric hunter-gatherer societies. In short, indisputable evidence of the systematic enslavement of people exists around the globe: Greece, Rome, the Akkadian Empire, Egypt, Assyria, Babylonia, Persia, pre-Columbian civilizations of the Americas, Israel, India, China, Korea, Japan, Indonesia, Nepal, throughout the Middle East, throughout Western and Central Europe, Russia, Scandinavia, Britain, Sub-Saharan Africa, North Africa, American indigenous societies from Alaska to California, among the Creek and Comanche Amerindians, throughout Central and South America, Canada, the United States, French and British Caribbean, Hawaii, New Zealand, Easter Island. It is no exaggeration to say that we could extend this list by dozens of places. In considering Nietzsche's claim, it is also important to note that the number of enslaved people in these regions typically ranged from 5% to as much as 50% of the entire population.

Hunt sums up the prevalence of slavery throughout history like this: "Slavery is rare among hunter-gatherers, is sometimes present in incipient agricultural societies, and then becomes common among societies with more advanced agriculture. Up to this point slavery seems to increase with increasing social and economic complexity."[77] That last comment should send chills up our spines. For when has a more socially and economically complex global society ever existed than our own? Incredibly, then, by Hunt's reckoning, slavery should be even more prevalent today than in the past. Is that possible? An article tellingly titled "One in 200 People is a Slave. Why?" has the lede: "Slavery affects more than 40 million people worldwide—more than at any other time in history."[78] Here are some statistics. Of these 40 million people currently subjected to conditions of enslavement, nearly three-quarters are female, with one-quarter of those being a mere child.

---

75 Peter Connolly and Hazel Dodge, *The Ancient City* (Oxford: Oxford University Press, 2001), 9.

76 All remaining information in this paragraph is derived from Richard Hellie, "Slavery," *Encyclopedia Britannica*, https://www.britannica.com/topic/slavery-sociology. Accessed December 31, 2022.

77 Hunt, "Slavery."

78 Kate Hodal, "One in 200 People Is a Slave. Why?" *The Guardian*, https://www.theguardian.com/news/2019/feb/25/modern-slavery-trafficking-persons-one-in-200. Accessed December 31, 2022.

Most modern-day slavery is in Africa, Asia, and the Pacific. North Korea has the highest per capita slavery rate (one in 10 people). India has the most slaves altogether, with 8 million. Russia has nearly 800,000. Slavery also exists, at present, in significant numbers in China (3.86 million), Pakistan (3.19 million), North Korea (2.64 million), Nigeria (1.39 million), Iran (1.29 million), Indonesia (1.22 million), the Democratic Republic of the Congo (1 million), and the Philippines (784,000), Eritrea (with 9.3% of the population), Burundi (4%), Central African Republic (2.2%), Afghanistan (2.2%), Mauritania (2.1%), South Sudan (2%), Pakistan (1.7%), Cambodia (1.7%), and Iran (1.6%). At no other time in the history of the world has slavery been so prevalent and so profitable (an estimated $180 billion in profits annually to enslavers) than at present.

Let's consider Nietzsche's claim that "slavery is generally visible, although it does not admit it." On the one hand, "currently, slavery is recognized in essentially the same way it has been throughout history…[namely, being] forced to work without pay under threat of violence and unable to walk away."[79] On the other hand, one way that slavery refuses to admit itself is in the very nomenclature we use for it today: human trafficking. The United Nations' definition for human trafficking, though, reveals that the means of enslavement have, in fact, been made easier, are more visible, and yet less recognizable. That definition is: "the recruitment, transportation, transfer, harboring or receipt of people through force, fraud or deception, with the aim of exploiting them for profit." How many times have you stared "slavery in some form or another" in the face and not seen it? It's right there: "in domestic work; in agriculture and farm work; in traveling sales crews; in restaurant and food services; in health and beauty services; in hotels; in bars; on the street."[80] The *Global Slavery Index* offers this illuminating view:

It is a confronting reality that even in the present day, men, women and children all over the world remain victims of modern slavery. They are bought and sold in public markets, forced to marry against their will and provide labour under the guise of "marriage," forced to work inside clandestine factories on the promise of a salary that is often withheld, or on fishing boats where men and boys toil under threats of violence. They are forced to work on construction sites, in stores, on farms, or in homes as maids. Labour extracted through force, coercion, or threats

---

79 Micah Hartmann, "Does Slavery Exists in America Today?" *The Exodus Road*, https://theexodusroad.com/does-slavery-exist-in-america-today. Accessed December 31, 2022.
80 Micah Hartmann, "Does Slavery Exists in America Today?"

produces some of the food we eat, the clothes we wear, and the foot-balls we kick. The minerals that men, women, and children have been made to extract from mines find their way into cosmetics, electronics, and cars, among many other products…This is modern slavery. It is widespread and pervasive, [and] often unacknowledged.[81]

By this definition, at present over 400,000 people live in slave conditions *in the United States.* This number does not include the 1, 304, 200[82] people locked up in American prisons who, under the Thirteenth Amendment of the US Constitution may be legally submitted to conditions of enslavement: "Neither slavery nor involuntary servitude, *except* as a punishment for crime whereof the party shall have been duly convicted, shall exist within the United States, or any place subject to their jurisdiction" (emphasis added). According to the *Prison Policy Initiative*, prisons pay inmates on average between $0.14 cents and $1.41 per hour for their labor (in manufacturing, agriculture, prison facility maintenance).[83] In a story straight out of the dark-est dystopian farce, the state of California recently "employed" over 2,000 prisoners as firefighters against raging forest fires. And by "employed" I mean paid them $1 a day.[84]

But perhaps the single greatest reason that the fact of slavery is denied or suppressed is that it rakes in billions and billions of dollars annually in profits that are *not* illicit. Two recent examples are particularly instructive because they involve matters in which you and I are likely complicit. *The truth is hard.* The first example is the 2022 soccer World Cup in Qatar. FIFA, the sponsoring organization, earned an estimated $4.7 billion from the event.[85] Hundreds of millions of viewers from around the world watched the matches. It was an all-around highly celebrated international event. And

81 *Global Slavery Index*, https://www.globalslaveryindex.org/2018/findings/global-findings. Accessed December 31, 2022.

82 *Bureau of Justice Statistics*, "Prisoners in 2021," https://bjs.ojp.gov/library/publications/prisoners-2021-statistical-tables. Accessed December 31, 2022.

83 *Prison Policy Initiative*, https://www.prisonpolicy.org/blog/2017/04/10/wages. Accessed December, 31, 2022.

84 "Prison Inmates Are Fighting California's Fires, But Are Often Denied Firefighting Jobs After Their Release," *CNN*, https://www.cnn.com/2019/10/31/us/prison-inmates-fight-california-fires-trnd/index.html. Accessed December 31, 2022.

85 Matt Craig, "The Money Behind the Most Expensive World Cup in History: Qatar 2022 By the Numbers," *Forbes*, https://www.forbes.com/sites/mattcraig/2022/11/19/the-money-behind-the-most-expensive-world-cup-in-history-qatar-2022-by-the-numbers/?sh=24052edcbff5. Accessed January 1, 2023.

it was made possible because of slavery. In short, the substantial report[86] of the human rights organization *Equidem* evaluating worker-abuse allegations confirms the ubiquitous headlines that tracked the lead-up to the event. The most common refrain of these headlines was, bluntly, "A World Cup Built on Slavery." Amnesty International avoids the term "slavery," but that is precisely what it documents in its report "Qatar World Cup of Shame."[87]

The second way that most of us are ensnared in this noxious phenomenon that is "generally visible, although it does not admit it" is through our dependence on cobalt. Cobalt is the mineral that allows us to recharge the lithium-ion batteries in our seemingly indispensable electronic devices, such as mobile phones, smartphones, laptops, tablets, cameras, and electric vehicles. The story of how it is mined, particularly in the Democratic Republic of Congo, is gruesome beyond belief, involving, in short, some 100,000 "artisanal miners" (yes, that's how the literature refers to them), some 40,000 of whom are children as young as seven years old:

> work in wretched conditions that are extremely dangerous to their health—often with no safety equipment or protective clothing [no industrial tools, no protective clothing, no hard hats, not even facemasks to shield toxic dust or shoes]. They are exposed to a near invisible poison, cobalt dust, which can cause fatal hard metal lung disease. Work hours are long, and miners labour in tunnels that are not properly supported. Rainfall can cause large areas of cobalt mines to suddenly collapse. At least 80 artisanal miners died underground in the DRC between September 2014 and December 2015 alone, and the bodies of children and adults alike are often left buried in the rubble.[88]

All of this for $2 a day, if they are paid at all. If you earn your living on Wall Street, this is good news—and it's only getting better. When Tesla, for example, increased its production of electric vehicles to 500,000 a few years ago, it bought some 8,000 tons of cobalt. What will be the state of cobalt slavery

---

86 *Equidem.* "The Legacy of Qatar FIFA World Cup." https://www.equidem.org/blogs/the-legacy-of-qatar-fifa-world-cup-2022. Accessed April 7, 2024.
87 For instance, at *Yahoo! News*, https://news.yahoo.com/world-cup-built-modern-slavery-173027855.html. See also "Qatar World Cup of Shame," *Amnesty International.* https://www.amnesty.org/en/latest/campaigns/2016/03/qatar-world-cup-of-shame. Accessed January 2, 2023.
88 "Modern Slavery: The True Cost of Cobalt Mining," *Human Trafficking Search*, https://humantraffickingsearch.org/resource/modern-slavery-the-true-cost-of-cobalt-mining. Accessed January 2, 2023.

when Tesla reaches its goal of 40 million cars by 2030, requiring 640,000 tons of the mineral?[89] And that smartphone in our pocket? In a world of 8 billion people, 8.02 billion devices have been sold.[90] (Yes, you read that right—more phones than people.) Exacerbating this voraciously increasing consumer demand is the cruel fact that at present there exists *"no regulation directly covering the cobalt market."*[91]

This lack of regulation leads us to the final point I would like to make in considering Nietzsche's comment about slavery. It is, in fact, one that Nietzsche himself makes. While Nietzsche can only make this point somewhat obliquely, since he is living at its beginning, we can make it with deadly precision: modern slavery is joined at the hip to modern capitalism, which, in turn, is joined at the hip to modern democracy. The logic goes roughly along the following lines. On the supply side of the supply-demand nexus, capitalism requires an impoverished underclass in order for shareholders, manufacturers, investors, and so on, to reap their profits. Capitalism has spread throughout the world, always under the banner of democracy. Thus, capitalism is now a global phenomenon, creating "poverty-as-vulnerability" worldwide. The creation of vulnerability is strengthened by the ever-present cuts in, if not outright denial of, access to the commonwealth—health care, education, clean water, housing, labor protections, human rights, and so on. The result is that "there exists, across the world a layer of impoverished labour that can be plunged into modern slavery because it is vulnerable."[92] At the heart of the demand side is nothing short of the everyday corporate practices that fuel our neoliberal economy. To take but one example, just consider that of the "over 3.8 million people living in conditions of modern slavery in China,"[93] nearly 2 million of them alone work assembling our cell phones. The demand, in short, for workers to continuously produce the goods that we desire is bottomless. The solution?—a global network of "labour market intermediaries," essentially "brokers who profit from

---

89 Charles P. Pierce, "The Real Cost of the I-phone in Your Pocket," *Esquire*, https://www.esquire.com/news-politics/politics/news/a49363/cobalt-miners-congo-smartphones. Accessed January 2, 2023.

90 See, for instance, C. Well, "How Many Smartphones in the World," *Uniwa*. https://www.cwelltech.com/how-many-smartphones-in-the-world. Accessed January 2, 2023. These numbers are as of January 2021.

91 "Modern Slavery: The True Cost of Cobalt Mining." Emphasis added.

92 John Westmoreland, "Modern Slavery Finds Its Roots in Capitalism," *Counterfire*, https://www.counterfire.org/article/modern-slavery-finds-its-roots-in-capitalism. Accessed January 2, 2023.

93 *Global Slavery Index*, https://www.globalslaveryindex.org/2018/findings/country-studies/china. Accessed January 2, 2023. This number is for 2016.

workers' vulnerability at the bottom end of the labour market, sometimes through business models deliberately configured around practices of human trafficking and forced labour."[94] Finally, speaking of "supply and demand," we should consider the grisly fact that in 1850, a slave cost roughly today's equivalent of $40,000, while today a "human trafficker"—I think Nietzsche would prefer the term "enslaver"—will sell you a human being for $90 on average.[95] Do not Nietzsche's comments about humans' "degradation of worth" under democracy take on a grim, disturbing aspect in light of all of this?

Let us end our consideration of Nietzsche's comment on slavery with a passage directed to the workers he sees toiling all around him, workers caught up in "factory slavery," those among the haggard, dust-covered stultified builders of democracy mentioned in an earlier quote. Nietzsche has something serious to convey to these people, unless, that is, "they do not consider it at all a disgrace to be *used*, as they are, as screws and stopgaps in the machine of human invention!" What does he want to tell this mass of people who produce the very goods that we so voraciously demand? And, of course, by "mass of people," he ultimately means *us*—we who spend our lives in a modern democracy.

To hell with believing that by increasing their wage the *essential* nature of their suffering, that is, their impersonal enslavement, can be rendered! To hell with talking oneself into the belief that through an enhancement of this impersonality, from within the machinic gearworks of a new society, the disgrace of slavery could be turned into a virtue! To hell with having a price through which a person becomes a screw! Are you the coconspirators in the current folly of nations that desire, above all, to produce as much, and become as wealthy, as possible? It should be up to you to reproach them with a counterclaim: what great sums of *inner* worth are thrown away for such external goals! But *where* is your inner worth when you no longer know the meaning of breathing freely? When you barely have any command over yourselves? When you, like a stale drink, become tired of yourselves? When you eavesdrop on the newspapers and squint at your wealthy neighbors, rendered lustful by the rapid rise and fall of power, money, and opinion? When

---

94 Westmoreland, "Modern Slavery Finds its Roots in Capitalism."
95 See *CNN Freedom Project*, "How Much Does A Slave Cost?" https://edition.cnn.com/videos/world/2017/01/05/freedom-project-slave-cost.cnn, which quotes *Free the Slaves*, https://freetheslaves.net. Accessed April 7, 2024.

you no longer have faith in a philosophy that is wrapped in rags or in the sincerity of a person who has few needs? When you have rendered laughable the voluntary, idyllic poverty and rejection of work and marriage—which the more brilliant among you should well adopt?

Nietzsche continues in a vein that explicitly condemns socialism and capitalism, both of which, in cahoots with democracy, instigate "slavery in some form or another" precisely through the "degeneration and diminution of the human into a perfect herd animal."

On the other hand: the piping of the socialist ratcatchers reverberating perpetually in your ears, wanting to make you rut with insane hope? who tell you to be *ready* and nothing more, ready from today to tomorrow, so that you wait and wait for something to come from outside and continue to live as you have always lived—until this waiting becomes hunger and thirst and fever and madness, and finally dawns in all glory as the day of the *bestia triumphans*[96]? Against this, each of you should think: "It is better to migrate to wild and fresh regions of the world, seeking to become *master*, and especially master of myself; changing my dwelling place whenever a sign of slavery beckons me; not to evade adventure and war, and, for the worst of circumstances, to be prepared for death: only no longer this indecent enslavement, only no longer this becoming-sour, becoming-poisonous, becoming-conspiratorial!" This would be the right attitude: the workers in Europe should from

---

96 *Triumphant beast*. This may be a reference to Giordano Bruno's (1548–1600) work, *The Expulsion of the Triumphant Beast*. Nietzsche was well aware of Bruno. He writes to his friend Heinrich von Stein: "These poems [you have sent me] by Giordano Bruno are a gift for which I am grateful from the bottom of my heart. I have permitted myself to appropriate them as if I had written them myself for myself—and 'taken' them as *strengthening* drops. Yes, if you knew *how* rare it is that something so strengthening comes to me from the outside!" (*BVN*–1884, 514). Nietzsche must have felt a deep kinship with Bruno. A Dominican friar, poet, and philosopher, Bruno was burned at the stake as a heretic. Among other horrendous blasphemies, he dared to assert that many of the stars shining in the night sky are actually distant planets, and even, here and there, the occasional sun. We should not be surprised that *The Expulsion of the Triumphant Beast* was written and published in absolute secrecy since it is "a bold indictment of the corruption of the social and religious institutions of its time." 'Triumphant beast' signifies the reign of multiple vices. Written in the form of allegorical dialogues, Bruno's work presents the deliberations of the Greek gods who have gathered to banish from the heavens the constellations that remind them of their evil deeds. The crisis facing Jupiter, the elderly father of the gods, is symbolic of the crisis of a Renaissance world deeply troubled by new religious, philosophical, and scientific ideas." https://www.abrahamicstudyhall.org/2021/11/05/the-expulsion-of-the-triumphant-beast-giordano-bruno. Accessed January 2, 2023.

now on declare themselves, *as a class*, to be a human impossibility, and not only, as mostly happens, as something set up [in society] to be hard and unsuitable; they should lead the way to an epoch of massive swarming in the European beehive, the likes of which have not yet been experienced, and through this act of generosity, protest, in grand style, against the machines, against capital, and against the looming decision confronting them of having to become either a slave of the state or a slave of some subversive party.[97]

Nietzsche would agree with the Soviet folk saying that "under capitalism man exploits man; under socialism the reverse is true." The problem was that, in his day, these were the only two viable possibilities for an economic system to accompany the democratic "political organization" that was spreading. That both systems, combined with democracy, amount to a death cult, wherein human life is not only cheap and easily replaceable but outright expendable, was as clear to Nietzsche as it was to Marx. So in the face of such "human impossibility," which arguably confronts us even more directly today, Nietzsche's recommendation of "aristocratic radicalism" burrows deep. As he tells us, he is a "subterranean" thinker who "bores, mines, and undermines." The question for *us* is whether we, too, toiling in the dark, "have eyes for such labor in the deep."[98] Let's continue mining our passage.

In terms of equality, a central premise of liberal democracy—"One like All, One for All"—Nietzsche's speculative aristocratic radicalism is, for many readers, I imagine, a disturbing challenge. Worse, in the place of equality, he recommends what he calls "the pathos of distance," an affect and an action that he defines as "growing out of embodied differences of status." Nietzsche aims at nothing less than the undermining of our two millennia-long belief in "the equality of souls before God." His basic conviction is that this Christian ideal is a "fraud, a pretext for the *rancor* of all low-minded people."[99] Although equality is one of the "most often recited tunes and teachings" of modern democracy, it is nonetheless "laughably superficial." He says this, in any case, of the "levelers," who advocate for such modern ideals as equality. These "falsely so-called 'free spirits'" are "eloquent and prolific slaves of the democratic taste and its 'modern ideas:' all of them are…awkward well-behaved people whom we should not deny either courage or respectable morals—only, they are precisely unfree and

---

97 *Dawn*, 206.
98 *Dawn*, Preface, 1.
99 *The Antichrist*, 62.

laughably superficial."[100] The pathos of distance is an emotion that catalyzes us to *recognize* that what we call "equality" is similarly "unequal and laughably superficial." Nietzsche challenges us: show me an instance of equality, not in theory or in grand pronouncements such as "all men are created equal" or "equal rights for all!" but in real life. Differences are real for Nietzsche. For a thinker who so highly values *agon*, multiplicity of all kinds, including those of "rank," is profoundly fecund. If we ignore them, or pretend otherwise, we only perpetuate the "fraud" in which we are all so deeply ensconced. It is crucial that we get right the "long ladder of ranking and in variations in value from person to person." Let us consider an example from everyday life. Although it risks oversimplification, I find it helpful to test the theories we encounter with instances from our own lives. Any workplace scenario will do. I will take as my example a university department. Consider the "ladder of ranking" in play. At the top is the department chair. Then come the full, associate, and assistant professors, respectively. Then comes the senior office administrator, followed by two junior staff. Then come advanced doctoral students all the way down to first-year undergrads. At the very bottom of the ladder are the night janitorial staff. Is every one of these individuals equal to the others in terms of absolute human dignity? Of course! Human dignity is not in question. Human equity before the law is not the question. Nietzsche is thinking through the way in which a society must be organized if it is to realize its optimal version of itself. How must the academic department be organized hierarchically to ensure the excellence worthy of the name "academic department"? Nietzsche concludes that whether we are organizing a workplace or a society, it must operate under the "rule of the best" *(áristokratíā)*. What constitutes "the best" will always be contested—and that's the point! But in my example, the criteria for the respective positions on the ladder should be obvious. When Nietzsche mentions "variations in value from person to person," he means something obvious: "value" is context dependent. Now, given that most, if not all, workplaces *are* organized along such lines, we might say that the workplace *already is* an aristocracy in Nietzsche's sense. No one becomes a professor or an office administrator by birthright. So aristocratic radicalism is not aristocracy in the strict historical sense of the term. Neither are we involved in meritocracy. The janitor cannot become a professor even if he becomes an expert in the field. Some workplaces, of course, are ruled as monarchies. We have seen that Nietzsche wants nothing to do with such tyrannical forms of

---

100 *Beyond Good and Evil*, 44.

organization because, among other means of diminishment, they prevent the appearance of additional "geniuses." If some workplaces are ruled by the *demos*, Nietzsche will suspect that, in that case, a great deal of talent and ability is being stunted by the presence and undue influence of those of lesser ability. Only when the spirit of aristocracy prevails can workers practice the pathos of distance and thereby "seize the right to create values and to coin names for values."[101]

How such a model gets scaled up to society as a whole is not Nietzsche's concern. In terms of historical antecedents, it might be interesting to note the following. For Nietzsche, *aristocracy* lay in the distant past. His model was not medieval or modern European but Homeric Greek and Renaissance. *Monarchy* was crumbling before Nietzsche's eyes in the present. *Democracy* was rising and spreading inevitably into the future. He sums up these three modalities as follows:

> According to whether the people feel that "the few have the right, the insight, and the ability to lead, etc.," or whether "the many" do—there will be an *oligarchical* or a *democratic* regime.
>
> Monarchy represents the belief in a wholly superior person, a leader, a savior, a demigod.
>
> Aristocracy represents the belief in an elite-humanity and a higher caste.
>
> Democracy represents the *disbelief* in great humans and elite society: "each is equal to everyone else." "At bottom, we are, every one of us, self-serving cattle and rabble."[102]

That last jab at democracy points to an additional objection Nietzsche has with it: "What they are trying with all their strength to achieve is a common green pasture of happiness for the herd, with safety, security, comfort, ease of life for everyone."[103] Who can argue with that goal? The problem, for Nietzsche is that without the perpetual infusion of "greatness," that end can never come to pass. Again, think about "greatness" not as some kind of disembodied platonic form but rather in terms of an actual community with which you are familiar, like a workplace or a neighborhood. What qualities would a "great" neighbor, administrator, boss, student, and so on, exhibit? What would constitute, for you, a great workplace? Might some people be

---

101 *On the Genealogy of Morals*, 1.2.
102 *NF–1884*, 26[282].
103 *Beyond Good and Evil*, 44.

intimidated by such displays of greatness? Yes, they might; hence, *agon*. Indeed, Nietzsche predicts that people will display all sorts of traits that the moralists and liberal democrats among us consider awful. Chief among these traits is, in fact, the one I just mentioned, *agon*: "the necessity of having enemies (as drainage ditches, so to speak, for the affects of envy, quarrelsomeness, boisterousness—at bottom, in order to be capable of being good *friends*)."[104] But we need agonistic others not only as drainage ditches, as the lesson of Hermodor taught us, but as worthy challenges to our own development.

Nietzsche, however, has in mind a much more severe proposition. It is this: At the heart of our inability to arrive at a "common green pasture of happiness" nests democracy's original sin: its intractable refusal to come clean about the world. I will leave the reader with a passage to contemplate, and a few final remarks. Speaking to readers who feel themselves opposed to those people who "are trying with all their strength to achieve a common green pasture of happiness for the herd," Nietzsche offers this:

> We who are contrary, who have opened our eyes and conscience to the question of where and how the plant "human" has grown mightiest into the heights, suspect that in every case this has occurred under the contrary conditions, that for such growth the dangerousness of the plant's situation must first grow to enormity, its power of invention and imagination (its "spirit") must develop under long periods of pressure and compulsion into subtlety and boldness, its life-will must be intensified into unconditional power-will. We suspect that hardness, forcefulness, slavery, danger in the alley and in the heart, seclusion, stoicism, the art of the tempter and devilry of every type, that everything evil, terrible, tyrannical, predator-like and snake-like in the human being serves the enhancement of the species "human" as much as its opposite.[105]

The truth is hard if Nietzsche is on to something with all of this. He knows just how "alien and embarrassing to contemporary tastes"[106] his assertions are. But does our unwillingness, our embarrassment, even to *think the thought* make any of it untrue? How distant we are from the "Just Be Nice!" ethos that permeates our social sphere! Contrary, in fact, to *ethos*, Nietzsche is

---

104 *Beyond Good and Evil*, 260.
105 *Beyond Good and Evil*, 44.
106 *Beyond Good and Evil*, 260.

immersing the reader in *pathos*. In Greek rhetoric, *ethos* is the appeal to character. Good people are nice; nice people are good. Just look at the beloved,[107] ever-smiling Dalai Lama. He never tires of telling us Westerners, "My religion is very simple; my religion is kindness," and exhorting us to "Be kind whenever possible; and it is *always* possible." Nietzsche knows that the "distance" that ensues from his *pathos of distance* is painful to us. It is, moreover, a particular kind of pain, that of *pathos*. One afternoon, he tells us in a passage titled *Looking back*, "a few notes of music recalled to my memory a winter and a house and a life of utter seclusion and, at the same time, the feeling in which I was living at that time…I understand now that it was wholly pathos and passion, something comparable to this painfully spirited, comforting music."[108] This is the pain, the poignancy, of loss. We certainly lose something when we take on Nietzsche's view of democracy, much less his suspicion toward the ethos of politeness. But what is lost, exactly? Certainly, we "find ourselves at the *other* end of all modern ideology and wishful thinking of the herd: as their antipodes, perhaps?"[109] That is a painful place to be. Yet, again, pain is not a repudiation of the truth. The passage directly following the one I just quoted is titled *Wisdom in pain*. In it, our immoral guide wants us to consider that "there is in pain as much wisdom as in pleasure. Like pleasure, pain is a species-preserving energy of the first order. If it were not, it would have disappeared long ago. That it hurts is no argument against it—hurting is its very essence."[110]

---

107 Jessica Ravitz, "Why Do Americans Love the Dalai Lama?" *CNN*, https://www.cnn.com/2010/LIVING/02/22/americans.love.dalai.lama/index.html. Accessed January 9, 2023.
108 *The Gay Science* 317.
109 *Beyond Good and Evil*, 44.
110 *The Gay Science,* 318.

IDENTITY

Basic issues are driving us into mutually hostile camps. Think of politicians posturing around, for instance, personal pronouns, gender, race, and ethnicity, and women's and LGBTQI+ rights. What makes these contentious matters so fundamental is that they revolve around *identity*. Some people claim for themselves identities and identity markers that are, they contend, a matter of life and death. Others consider those same identity markers wrongheaded, outrageous, or even dangerous to society. Why identity? Philosophically, nothing is more basic to the establishment of knowledge than what is called the *principle of identity*; it is the very foundation of logic. Psychologically, nothing is more central to our personal subjective experience than *identity formation*; it is the very foundation of the self. Politically, nothing is more basic than the communities, castes, classes, and other person groupings than *identity conferral* and *adoption*; it is the very basis of society. Although the strict meaning of "identity" varies between these three usages, Nietzsche connects them in ways that are nothing short of startling. In fact, it may be his treatment of identity that makes Nietzsche such a revolutionary thinker for our times. Let's see what we might learn from our Immoralist here. As always—buckle up!

Identity issues of the psychological and political variety are ubiquitous in the public sphere. As evidence, consider a 2023 headline regarding a certain "unsettling interview": "Gwen Stefani Says, 'I'm Japanese' to an Asian Reporter."[1] (We will have a closer look below.) Just a few years ago, the daily news was not complete without a slew of headlines such as "Battle of the Bathroom."[2] Talk about basic! Complex issues around the dignity of people who identity as transgender and nonbinary were being reduced to where they may pee. You may now infer the politics of your local café proprietors based on whether or not they have an "All Gender Restroom"

1 Elyse Wanshel, "Gwen Stefani Says, 'I'm Japanese' to an Asian Reporter," https://www.huffpost.com/entry/gwen-stefani-japanese-allure-interview_n_63bddbe8e4b0d6724fc82241. Accessed January 11, 2023.
2 Michael Sherer, "Battle of the Bathroom," *Time*, https://time.com/4341419/battle-of-the-bathroom. Accessed January 11, 2023.

sign hanging on the bathroom door. For getting a sense of the high stakes involved, how about this recent headline: "Pronoun Controversy: Teachers Will Not Get Prosecuted In Sweetwater County For 'Misgendering' Students."[3] It turns out that even though federal civil rights law might be construed as treating "misgendering" as a form of sexual harassment or even abuse, it is not a crime in this teacher's case, at least not according to the prosecutor's "reading" of his state's statutes. Not *yet*, anyway, one gets the sense. Indeed, the stakes of the "21st century bathroom wars" are so high, said Lieutenant Governor of Texas Dan Patrick six months prior to the 2016 election of Donald Trump, that the issue "is going to probably define who the next President is."[4] Patrick hit on an issue that many people have indeed used to explain the seemingly inexplicable defeat of Hillary Clinton: identity politics.[5]

As uniquely contemporaneous as they feel to us, none of these issues, like so many hot button topics of our day, are really anything new. Reviewing this point briefly will allow me to frame the issue as one of contemporary relevance. It will also enable us to get some distance from the emotional heat that surrounds identity issues today. Perhaps we might even broaden our horizon to fuse with that of Nietzsche's, within which *identity* and *power* are coextensive. In fact, let's begin there. Take the "battle of the bathroom," for instance. Surely it could only be an early twenty-first century culture war issue, right? In fact, Terry S. Kogan, a law professor who studies, of all things, the legal history of gender-specific bathrooms, tells us that until 1887, neither law nor custom dictated gender-segregated public bathrooms.[6] It would not be until the 1920s that most US states adopted similar laws. From

---

3 *Cowboy State Daily*, https://cowboystatedaily.com/2022/09/15/pronouns-controversy-teachers-will-not-get-prosecuted-in-sweetwater-county-for-misgendering-students/. Accessed April 3, 2024.

4 Sherer, "Battle of the Bathroom."

5 For readers unfamiliar with the term, this neutral definition should be helpful: "Identity politics is a people-based political approach and analysis [by people] who prioritize concerns most relevant to their particular racial, religious, ethnic, sexual, social, cultural, or other identity, and form exclusive political alliances with others in this group, rather than to get involved in the more traditional party politics and broad base. Those who prioritize their particular type of identity politics may promote the interests of their group without regard to the interests of larger and more diverse political groups that are based on shared theory." Everett Vazquez, "What Is Identity Politics? Definition and Effects," *Polling Place Photo Project*. https://pollingplacephotoproject.org/what-is-identity-politics-definition-and-effects. Accessed January 17, 2023.

6 Terry S. Kogan, "Sex Separation: The Cure-All for Victorian Social Anxiety," in Harvey Molotch and Laura Norén, *Toilet: Public Restrooms and the Politics of Sharing* (New York: New York University Press, 2010), 145–154.

ancient Greece and Rome down to the early twentieth century, men, women, boys, and girls, simultaneously occupied the same public bathroom space.[7] So why, after millennia, did it change? Kogan's short answer is given in his article's subtitle: social anxiety. More specifically, it was social anxiety about women entering workspaces and thereby upsetting the millennia-long status quo of "separate spheres"—women at the hearth, men at the plow, so to speak. Nothing less than the "cult of true womanhood"—the sentimental myth of women as necessarily weak, dainty, virtuous, nurturing, and domestic—was being threatened by images of women in dirty bathrooms alongside workingmen. The deeper underlying anxiety for this change, however, was a desire to maintain ages-old power relations between the genders. A change in the general identity of "woman" means a change in the general identity of "man," and *that* entails far-reaching, and undesirable (for many men), changes in the social status quo.

We can discern a similar threat in Jim Crow America. "Will the white girls be forced to take their showers with Negro girls?"[8] This question, posed in a segregationist newspaper in 1957 and in various similar formulations throughout the South, was, of course, no question at all. It was, in microcosm, both an expression of the fear of change being aroused by racial integration and an incitement to its refusal. The fear was that a change in the perceived identity of Blacks, much less in their own self-identity, from *lesser than* to *equal to* whites, would erupt in a cataclysmic change in existing power relations. And, of course, the fears of the race-segregationists, like those of the gender-segregationists, are well-founded: identity realignment entails power realignment.

This brings us back to the headline: "Gwen Stefani Says, 'I'm Japanese' to an Asian Reporter." Or, as another headline more dramatically put it, "Gwen Stefani Sparks Outrage with Shocking Announcement: 'I am Japanese.'"[9] This is the issue in a nutshell. In an interview with the beauty magazine *Allure*, Stefani[10] talked about the influence that Japanese culture had on her growing up in southern California. Her father frequently traveled to Japan

---

7 You can see a drawing of such a scene in Peter Connolly and Hazel Dodge, *The Ancient City* (Oxford: Oxford University Press, 2001).

8 Sherer, "Battle of the Bathroom."

9 *MSN*, https://www.msn.com/en-us/news/world/gwen-stefani-sparks-outrage-with-shocking-announcement-i-am-japanese/ar-AA16roSx. Accessed January 11, 2023.

10 Gwen Stefani (b. 1969) is primarily known as the multi award-winning singer-songwriter for the pop band No Doubt. She has also had success as a fashion designer, actress, perfumer, and philanthropist. The music network, and home to MTV, voted her #13 in its 2012 list of the 100 "greatest women in music." Gwen Stefani," *Wikipedia,* footnote 15, https://en.wikipedia.org/wiki/Gwen_Stefani. Accessed April 3, 2024.

on business. What stood out most for Stefani were his stories about the Harajuku district of Tokyo, with its "performers cosplaying as Elvis and stylish women with colorful hair." Stefani enthusiastically offered: "That was my Japanese influence, and that was a culture that was so rich with tradition, yet so futuristic, [with] so much attention to art and detail and discipline and it was fascinating to me." When, as an adult, she visited Japan, she said to herself, "My God, I'm Japanese and I didn't know it."[11] Part of the reason that her remark is felt to be so "weird" is that Stefani is, as virtually every article mentions, "Irish-Italian American." Bad enough. Making matters worse, she made her remark to an "Asian reporter." The reporter, Jesa Marie Calaor, is a "Filipina American." The even bigger problem, however, is that Stefani, being white, is a member of the dominant social group in the United States, while Calaor, being Brown, belongs to a historically marginalized, indeed, oppressed group. So even though Stefani's attraction to Japanese culture was driven by admiration and inspiration, her membership in the "dominant group" renders the relationship illicit. This, at least, is the logic of identity in the United States today. Calaor says as much. She sought an expert on the issue to "make clear the road between inspiration or appreciation and appropriation." (In identity discourse, "appropriation" means *to take possession of something belonging to others for oneself, typically without permission.*) The expert explained that "cultural appropriation is the usage of one group's customs, materials tradition, or oral traditions by one other group" and involves two additional "vital elements…commodification and an unequal energy relationship."[12] Did Stefani commodify the elements of Japanese culture that she appropriated? Yes, with great success. According to the financial magazine *Forbes*, Stefani's 2007 Harajuku-themed tour and fashion line earned $27 million.[13] Does her case involve an "unequal energy relationship"? It does. In such a relationship "the dominant group has the ability to take the marginalized group's customs and practices, and provides these traditions without the unique context or significance."[14] In other words, it is Stefani's identity as a member of the dominant social group that enables her to appropriate Japanese cultural elements to *her* desired ends, in complete disregard of the historically conditioned and culturally embedded *Japanese* ends. In her defense, Stefani offered the following:

11 Elyse Wanshel, *Huffington Post*, https://www.huffpost.com/entry/gwen-stefani-japanese-allure-interview_n_63bddbe8e4b0d6724fc82241. Accessed January 11, 2023.
12 Jesa Marie Calaor, https://www.allure.com/story/gwen-stefani-japanese-harajuku-lovers-interview. Accessed April 3, 2024.
13 Lacey Rose, "World's Best-Paid Music Stars," *Forbes*, September 2008 issue.
14 Calaor, 2023.

If we didn't buy and sell and trade our cultures, we wouldn't have so much beauty, you know? We learn from each other, we share from each other, we grow from each other. And all these rules are just dividing us more and more[15]... If [people are] going to criticize me for being a fan of something beautiful, and sharing that, then I just think that doesn't feel right. I think it was a beautiful time of creativity...a time of the ping-pong match between Harajuku culture and American culture. [It] should be okay to be inspired by other cultures because if we're not allowed then that's dividing people, right?

Be *inspired by*? Yes, of course. Appropriate? Well, no. Profit by? ABSOLUTELY NOT! The logic of identity does not include in its calculation the appropriator's positive motivation for the appropriation. The logic of identity is cold and uncompromising. Explanations like Stefani's simply do not matter. Motivations like Stefani's do not matter. Love and admiration like Stefani's do not matter. Only one thing matters in Stefani's case: her identity.

So what is this thing, "identity," and why does it pack such volatile cultural powder? First, Nietzsche wants us to disabuse ourselves of "identity." Before we become what we are—as opposed to what we ourselves or others identify us as being, we must empty ourselves of identity altogether. "To become what one is requires that one has not the vaguest notion *what* one is."[16] Does such self-abnegation strike you as a little too mystical, a little too Zen-like? Or maybe it sounds like a self-serving idea that benefits the dominant class at the expense of marginalized people? Let us slow down and, like Nietzsche's perfect reader, "think through the reasons for this and resist all sentimental frailty."[17]

THE PRINCIPLE OF IDENTITY

Identity is the very basis of Western thought. It is the bedrock of any and all matters we label *knowledge*. Adding to its already granite ballast, it is supported by two additional rock-hard principles: the principle of

---

15 Kalhan Rosenblatt, *NBC News,* https://www.nbcnews.com/news/asian-america/gwen-stefani-says-japanese-response-cultural-appropriation-charges-rcna65203. Accessed January 18, 2023.

16 *Ecce Homo*, "Why I am So Clever," 9.

17 *Beyond Good and Evil*, 259.

noncontradiction and the principle of the excluded middle. Altogether, these three principles make up the "laws of thought." Indeed, as *laws*, they must never be transgressed. When you do transgress them, you will have left the bright clearing of knowledge and descended into the murky pit of nonsense. Aristotle is unequivocal: "The most indisputable of all beliefs is that contradictory statements are not at the same time true."[18] Knowledge traditions around the world have no patience for anyone who tries to dispute these laws. In imagery that evokes the fate of heretics at the stake, the great Persian polymath Avicenna (980–1037) made his impatience abundantly clear:

> Anyone who denies the law of noncontradiction should be beaten and burned until he admits that to be beaten is not the same as not to be beaten, and to be burned is not the same as not to be burned.[19]

Despite their erudite-sounding nomenclature, these three laws are extraordinarily simple.

The principle of identity: a = a; whatever is, is.

The principle of noncontradiction: not (a and not-a); nothing can both be and not be.

The principle of the excluded middle: (a or not-a); everything must either be or not be.

It is even clearer in everyday terms. So, to take our examples from the Stefani identity drama.

The principle of identity: it *is* the case that an Irish-Italian American (a) is an Irish-Italian American (a).

The principle of noncontradiction: it is *not* the case that an Irish-Italian American (a) is Japanese (not-a).

---

18 Aristotle, *Metaphysics*, https://www.csus.edu/indiv/m/merlinos/arimetaiv.html. Accessed January 19, 2023.
19 Avicenna, *The Metaphysics of the Healing*, translated by Michael E. Marmura (Provo: Brigham Young University Press, 2005), I.11.105a4–5.

The principle of the excluded middle: Gwen Stefani is *either* Irish-Italian American (a) *or* Japanese (not-a).

Who would want to refute such basic axioms? You guessed it—Nietzsche would! That's right: with a full frontal assault on the very laws of thought, Nietzsche aims to obliterate the time-honored foundations of knowledge and along with it the basis for identity. To his thinking, these laws add up to nothing more than a "prejudice," to "dogmas" and "imperatives" disguised as incontrovertible truths. Let's work our way through the material now. As we do so, it might be useful to keep in mind that, as abstract as it may seem, this *philosophical* issue of identity ultimately comes to bear on the *psychological* and *political* issues as well. We will consider all three in turn.

Nietzsche sums up the basic claim thus: "The foundational principles of logic, the principle of identity and the principle of contradiction, are forms of pure knowledge because they precede all experience." That's the ancient claim. Closer to Nietzsche's time, it was employed by Immanuel Kant (1724–1804). Kant held that the laws of thought are a priori; that is, they are, like $2 + 2 = 4$, deducible through reasoning prior to any empirical investigation or experiential encounter with the world which might inform that reasoning. Nietzsche's response to this bedrock premise of the most influential philosophical system of his day, indeed, of the modern era, is succinct and unequivocal: "But these are not forms of knowledge at all! they are *regulative articles of faith.*"[20] That is, like religious articles of faith, the laws of thought are summary statements of foundational beliefs that, furthermore, guide, indeed, *determine*, further beliefs and practices. Like the law of salvation—*Christ died for our sins*—the law of identity—*a = a*—is held to be an essential truth, out of which all subsequent forms of thought, belief, and action must necessarily emerge.

Nietzsche's objection to this ostensible "ultimate ground of all demonstration"[21] could hardly be clearer. According to Nietzsche, in formulating the principle of contradiction (as he calls it), Aristotle was doing one of two things: Either (i) claiming something about "reality, being," namely, that "contradictory predicates *could* not be ascribed to it." If this is the case, then Aristotle had to have already ascertained this knowledge from somewhere else. And from where might that be? Where else but precisely *from* "reality, being" itself? In that case, the laws of thought are not purely rational a priori at all. Or (ii) claiming that "contradictory predicates *should* not be ascribed

---

20 *NF*–1886, 7[4].
21 *NF*–1886, 7[4].

to it." In that case, "logic would be an imperative, *not* to knowledge of the truth, but rather to the establishment and arrangement of a world *that we are obligated to call true.*"[22] This obligation, of course, would be derived *not* from "reality, being," but from the logical imperative itself.

Nietzsche is anticipating the ground-shaking insights of Ludwig Wittgenstein (1889–1951), insights that would contribute to the cataclysmic poststructuralist shift in thought that continues to define our postmodern present.[23] To the unending annoyance of the two greatest logicians of the early twentieth century (who also happened to be his dissertation advisers), Alfred North Whitehead (1861–1947) and Bertrand Russell (1872–1970), Wittgenstein declared, indeed, for many, *proved*, that:

> The propositions of logic are tautologies.
>
> The propositions of logic therefore say nothing.
>
> One cannot say that two objects have all their properties in common.
>
> Roughly speaking: to say of *two* things that they are identical is nonsense, and to say of *one* thing that it is identical with itself is to say nothing.
>
> The identity sign [=] is therefore not an essential constituent of logical notation.[24]

As counterintuitive as it may seem, this *a* is not identical to this *a*. Not in actual reality, not outside of the logical conceit *a = a*, anyway. In unison with Nietzsche, Wittgenstein is claiming that logical formulations such as the

---

22 *NF*–1886, 7[4].

23 I can sum up these two terms for readers unfamiliar with them as follows. Poststructuralism and postmodernism are two closely related theories, movements, or, indeed, worldviews. They indicate a decisive turn away from the preceding related theories, movements, or worldviews known as *structuralism* and *modernism*. The *post* criticism revolves around the refutation of the structuralist conviction that through an analysis of the "structure" (the network, pattern, organization, system) that underlies any given phenomenon (such as language, culture, consciousness, a text), it can arrive at inherent, stable, and universal knowledge of the world. Permeated by structuralist assumptions, modernism was characterized by belief in fixed meanings, universal truths, and all-encompassing explanatory models or "grand narratives." Poststructuralism holds that attention to the actual world in history reveals that such putative "structures" are neither obviously inherent in the phenomenon they analyze nor unchanging over time and place. As such, postmodernism challenges the stability of meaning and the coherence of meta-explanations. As such, poststructuralism/postmodernism sees linguistically- and socially-embedded interpretations where structuralism/modernism sees universal fact.

24 *Tractatus Logico-Philosophicus* (1921): 6.1, 6.11, 5.5302, 5.5303, and 5.533, respectively. https://www.wittgensteinproject.org/w/index.php/Tractatus_Logico-Philosophicus_ (English). Accessed April 3, 2024.

principle of identity are purely *formal*. That is, they are notational ways of establishing and arranging the world, and as such are in themselves devoid of all knowledge content. In a fulfillment of his prophecy of himself as a precursor to mighty events yet to come, Nietzsche wrote, before Wittgenstein was even born:

> In short, the question remains open: are logical axioms adequate to reality; or are they standards and means for *creating* the concept "reality" for us in the first place?...To be able to affirm the first possibility, one must, as previously said, already have knowledge of being, which absolutely is not the case. The principle [of contradiction], therefore, is *no criterion of truth*, but rather an *imperative* concerning *what should be counted as true.*[25]

How does all of this somewhat abstruse philosophy relate to the contemporary discourse on identity? Let's consider further.

PERSONALITY CRISIS

Resisting all sentimental frailty, the reader may already suspect that the short answer to the preceding question was just given. Assume that Nietzsche's statement applies to the Gwen Stefani case: the logic of identity is *"no criterion of truth*, but rather an *imperative* concerning *what should be counted as true.*" In this reading, the principle guiding our contemporary popular notions of identity "has behind it the 'apparent fact'"[26] that reality is so construed as not merely to validate, but to validate *lawfully*, our identity claims. We are now, of course, shifting from a philosophical concept and critique of identity to a psychological concept and critique. As we move through our material, the reader may want to keep the following question both *in mind* and *open,* for now: Might it be true that identity operates philosophically and psychologically as a fiction, but nonetheless has real force politically (socially, culturally)?

Nietzsche states his general position on psychological identity in a rich notebook fragment. The key concept here is the noun "complex":

---

25 *NF*–1886, 7[4].
26 *NF*–1885, 36[23].

If we abandon the effective *subject* then we also abandon the *object* on which the subject operates. Duration, identity with itself, and being inhere neither in what is called subject nor what is called object: they are complexes of events, seemingly durable in relation to other complexes…If we abandon the concepts "subject" and "object," then also the concept *"substance"*—and consequently its various modifications, for instance, "matter," "mind," and other hypothetical beings [such as] "eternity and immutability of matter," etc. We are rid of *materiality*. Duration, identity with itself, being are inherent neither in that which is called subject nor in that which is called object: they are complexes of events apparently durable in comparison with other complexes.[27]

In short, then, Nietzsche wants us to follow him in abandoning the idea of anything like a "soul," and thus to "deny the 'personality' and its ostensible unity, and [instead] find in every person the stuff of too many 'personae' (and masks)." He asks us to consider along with him that any notion of a stable, inherent, unitary entity such as a self, a personality, or, indeed, an identity, is a "mythical creature." He then offers a clue as to why this is so. Behind terms such as "unitary self," "stable identity," and so on, "is poorly hidden a *contradictio in adjecto*." That is, the noun contradicts the adjective: "stable identity" is no more coherent than "square triangle."[28] What this leaves us with is identity as a "complex of events." Nietzsche, in short, wants us to be "rid of *materiality*" altogether. He wants us to see that what appears to be a self-contained discrete material entity (a self, an identity, indeed even a chair, a table, or a flesh and blood Irish-Italian American) existing fully *from its own side*, is a "complex" entity existing to a decisive degree *from our side*, from our linguistic categories and social practices. The materiality of even something as concrete as a table does not account for the *being* of the table. That may sound preposterously esoteric to many readers. But consider: is it not the case that the "being" of your table extends far beyond its concrete materiality and includes its ideas, parts, and uses? If we want "being" to mean anything beyond a brute description, it must encompass reality in all of its fullness. It follows that we, too, must be "rid of *materiality*."

Let's relate all of this to our test case: "Gwen Stefani Says, 'I'm Japanese' to an Asian Reporter." Nietzsche will argue that in granting such significance to the identities in play, we are erroneously subscribing to "one of the best

---

27 *NF*–1887, 9[91].
28 *NF*–1885, 36[17].

refuted theories that there is."[29] That theory is called "materialistic atom-ism." Nietzsche gives the gist of this theory in citing the Copernican discovery that "contrary to the senses, the earth does *not* stand fast." He expands on this: "[The astronomer] Boscovich taught us to swear off the belief in the final part of the earth that 'stood fast,' namely, the belief in 'substance,' 'matter,' in the earth-remnant, and the clumpy atom."[30] We may nonetheless speak, indeed may be *compelled* to speak, of static atomistic identity in our everyday shared speech but only "as an abbreviated means of expression." The danger in doing so, however, is that the habit of speech becomes a habit of perception. Language has a conjuring effect. Claim with enough force and persistence that the Loch Ness Monster is in the lake, and *behold, there's Nessie!* Similarly, get enough people to claim with insistence that "some detail in us" profoundly matters, and add to that insistence a tacit or explicit moral imperative that *at least it matters to good people* and so *should* matter to you, and *voila!*—our "Shocking Announcement" that Gwen Stefani said, "I am Japanese" becomes viral on the internet.

Nietzsche argues against atomism by noting that "contrary to the senses, the earth does *not* stand fast." His point is even more pertinent to our issue, for regarding identity beliefs we are led astray by something even more subtle than our sensorium. Nietzsche, namely, gives us good reasons for understanding psychological identity as *largely* a matter of linguistic grammar and of social practice. I will say something here about the first matter—the role that language plays in identity formation—and discuss the social aspect in the next subsection, on the political ramifications of it all.

---

29 All the quotes in this paragraph, *Beyond Good and Evil*, 12.

30 Ruđer Josip Bošković (1711–1787), known in the Anglophone world as Roger Joseph Boscovich, was a Jesuit priest and astronomer. The term that I am translating as "clumpy atom" is *Klümpchen-Atom*. Nietzsche is subscribing to Boscovich's account that "what appears as matter is made up of indivisible, immutable, non-extended mathematical points exerting attractive force at relatively large distances and repulsive force at very small distances." See Rachel Cristy, "Commanders and Scientific Labourers: Nietzsche on the Relationship between Philosophy and Science," *Proceedings of the Aristotelian Society*, Vol. 122, (2022): 97–118. Nietzsche's choice of the term "earth-remnant" *(Erdenrest)* evokes Goethe's verse in Faust, spoken, we should note, by the "more perfect angels" to the "younger angels": "A remnant of earth *(Erdenrest)* remains/painfully embarrassing to bear/and even if it were made of asbestos/it is not clean." The rest of the verse, I think, can also be considered a poetic expression of the general point that I am trying to make here about Nietzsche's understanding of psychological identity: "When strong mental power/has gathered/the elements near to itself/no angel can separate/the unified dual nature/of the two intimate ones/Eternal love only/is able to separate them." As unpopular as the question is today, we can still ask, might such "love" have a role to play in overcoming our cultural divisions?

I say "largely" because all this talk of nonidentity, empty tautologies, and confused perceptions does *not* mean that we have abolished *the person*. In fact, Nietzsche, having refuted "soul-atomism," whispers an esoteric secret in our ears: "Just between us," he says, "it is completely unnecessary to get rid of 'the soul' itself, and thereby to renounce one of the oldest and most venerable hypotheses." Rather, he wants to disable the "atomistic need" driving our conception of "soul." Like its counterpart, "metaphysical need," this "atomistic need"—our emotional longing for a unified self-identity—"still leads a dangerous afterlife in places where no one suspects it." Both of these human needs generate hallucinations—they enable misapprehensions of, respectively, worlds beyond and selves within. Yet not abandoning the hypothesis "soul" (inherent, stable self-identity) and instead subjecting it to a critique of the laws of thought, we glimpse a surprising result:

> The way to new versions and refinements of the soul hypothesis stands open: and concepts like "mortal soul" and "soul as subjective multiplicity" and "soul as a social structure of drives and affects" want henceforth to have citizenship in the sciences and humanities.

I hope the reader will at least consider that "identity" can fruitfully stand in for "soul" in Nietzsche's treatment throughout this section. If so, what we have is a tool for complicating the everyday understanding of our very own self-identity, and for critiquing the way "identity" is wielded in today's cultural discourse. Nietzsche's psychology is very complex. As the preceding passage clearly indicates, he wants us to retain a notion of soul/self/identity but to inject it with a massive dose of *actual reality*. In actual reality, soul/self/identity is interminably complex and mutable. In fact, he goes even further with his notion of "subjective multiplicity" in offering that "our body is but a social structure composed of many souls."[31] This is a way of speaking about a *real* feature of ourselves—multiplicity, division, rupture. We remain, however, unaware of the very multiplicity whirling within us because of another old habit of speech: the "synthetic concept 'I.'"[32] Our capacity for gathering together multiple strands of self into a single, seemingly coherent "I" runs deep within us. Why? In several instances, Nietzsche speaks of the "unconscious domination and command" that we undergo by means of "grammatical functions."[33] What can this possibly mean?

31 *Beyond Good and Evil*, 19.
32 *Beyond Good and Evil*, 19.
33 *Beyond Good and Evil*, 20.

Grammar is implicated in the "error and deceptiveness" of matters for two main reasons. First, in beholding ourselves and others (Nietzsche's example is the sun), it is "our *language* itself that pleads" for such qualities as "unity, identity, permanence, substance, cause, matter, being."[34] Our language does so because of the second reason for the role that grammar plays in bewitching us. Nietzsche asks us to consider that "from its origin, language belongs to the time of the most rudimentary form of psychology."[35] We see this rudimentary form at work in Descartes's epoch-making employment of the assertion *I think, therefore I am* as an—indeed as *the*—unassailable bulwark against doubt. Nietzsche, however, wants us to see that Descartes is expressing nothing at all here beyond his "belief in grammar."[36] That is, the very syntax of the sentence *I think, therefore I am* tricks Descartes into taking the subject of the sentence *(I)* as the condition of that which is conditioned, the predicate *(think)*. Nietzsche notes that I may indeed *feel* as though I have willed a thought (and thereby established the certainty of I/soul/identity), but this feeling only occurs in retrospect. It follows from the old habit of language-thought mentioned earlier: the application of the "synthetic concept 'I.'" This subjective feeling and the perceptual habit it engenders unleashes "a whole chain of erroneous conclusions, and, consequently, false evaluations."[37] "I think" is but one of the most basic of those evaluations. It is akin to concluding that the sun orbits the earth. Resisting the pleas of language, is it not clear that "thinking occurs" and that the "synthetic I" claims the thinking only in retrospect?

Nietzsche's critique of identity remains at this level of "the metaphysics of language."[38] His resolution of the Gwen Stefani affair would not require a sorting out of who is allowed to claim what identity when and why and for what purpose and to which ends. Analogously to the much later "linguistic turn" in philosophy, Nietzsche asks us to look at how the language around the affair functions. His critique of psychological identity operates at that point where explanatory concepts, such as identity, burrow deeply into the roots of grammatical reasoning. Nietzsche thus gives us material for considering identity as a "moralistic-optical delusion."[39] The delusion is optical because we see something that is not there, like a mirage. It is moralistic because of the implicit *ought* embedded in that very seeing. Our current ideology

---

34 *Human, All Too Human*, "'Reason' in Philosophy," 5.
35 *Human, All Too Human*, "'Reason' in Philosophy," 5.
36 *Beyond Good and Evil*, 54.
37 *Beyond Good and Evil*, 19.
38 *Human, All Too Human*, "'Reason' in Philosophy," 5.
39 *Human, All Too Human*, "'Reason' in Philosophy," 6.

of identity thus leaves little to no room for negotiating the complexities of "Gwen Stefani Says, 'I'm Japanese' to an Asian Reporter."

Noting the power that subject-object predication has over our cognition and perception, Nietzsche famously concludes, "We will never be free of God as long as we believe in grammar."[40] How truer is that statement for a phenomenon as near to us as our personal identity! And yet, whatever its ultimate nature, there is hardly anything more real than personal identity.

POLITICAL RAMIFICATIONS

In this section, we return to the question: might it be true that self-identity operates philosophically and psychologically as a fiction or even an error, yet still has significance politically? Throughout, I am using "political" synonymously with "social" and "cultural." So in short, we are asking whether our treatment thus far makes any real difference for the lived everyday ramifications of identity.

Do the insights of philosophy and psychology matter in the end? Just ask the 80% of Americans who believe in at least one irrefutably disproven conspiracy.[41] No amount of science or empirical evidence, much less the considerations of philosophy and psychology, can dissuade them from believing that lizard people run the world or that the 1969 moon landing was a Hollywood hoax. The role that "the intellect—that master of dissimulation"[42] plays in the creation of our self-identity and, indeed, of our very world, is a momentous theme running throughout Nietzsche's work. His thinking on the relation between truth and untruth is, moreover, highly counterintuitive. In short, Nietzsche believes that our "invincible tendency to let ourselves be deceived"[43] is not necessarily a bad thing. Why not? Because such deception often serves life. Now, given our "post-truth" moment in history, such a notion is easily misunderstood. So let's look at Nietzsche's fuller statement to this effect. It is an important passage for approaching an answer to our question about the real-world ramifications of self-identity.

---

40 *Human, All Too Human*, "'Reason' in Philosophy," 5.
41 See *PsychCentral*, "Why Do Some People Believe in Conspiracy Theories?" https://psychcentral.com/blog/conspiracy-theories-why-people-believe. Accessed February 12, 2023.
42 *On Truth and Lies in an Extra-Moral Sense*, 2.
43 *On Truth and Lies in an Extra-Moral Sense*, 2.

The falseness of a judgment is, for us, no objection to that judgment; it is here perhaps that our new language sounds the strangest. The question is to what extent the judgment is life-fostering, life-preserving, species-preserving, perhaps even species-cultivating. And we are fundamentally inclined to maintain that the most false judgments (to which belong synthetic judgments a priori[44]) are the most indispensable to us; that without an acceptance of logical fictions, without a measuring of reality against the purely invented world of the unconditional and self-identical, without a constant falsification of the world by means of numbers, humans could not live—the renunciation of false judgments would be a renunciation of life, a denial of life. To admit untruth as a condition for life: that means, of course, to resist in a dangerous way the accustomed sensation of values; and for this reason alone, a philosophy that dares to do this places itself beyond good and evil.[45]

Nietzsche's new language strikes us as so strange because it flows against the two millennia-old raging torrent of that which we call "philosophy." The question that initiated this primordial surge was "What is truth?" In a brief note, Nietzsche captures his relationship to both this question and the tradition that poses it: "Parmenides said 'we cannot think what is not.' [I am] at the other end and say, 'what can be thought must certainly be a fiction.' Thinking has no grip on reality, rather only on——"[46] Only on what? We can safely fill in the blank in Nietzsche's notebook with "utility." Our heaviest load-bearing concepts—good, right, proper, correct, moral, true—are, in

---

44 Nietzsche is taking a dig at Immanuel Kant's epistemology. In short, Kant attempted to combine elements from the seemingly irreconcilable rationalist and empiricist theories of his day. Rationalism holds that reason is the primary source and justification for knowledge. Empiricism holds that sensory experience is the only source and justification for knowledge. Knowledge derived from reason is a priori because it comes from *(a)* that which is former *(priori)* to experience. That "all bachelors are unmarried" is known a priori because it is self-evident. Empiricism is knowledge that comes from that which follows *(posteriori)* sensory experience. That "Mr. Rogers is unmarried" is known only through real-world investigation. Kant sought a mix of the two positions, stating, "But, though all our knowledge begins with experience, it by no means follows that all arises out of experience. For, on the contrary, it is quite possible that our empirical knowledge is a compound of that which we receive through impressions, and that which the faculty of cognition supplies from itself (sensuous impressions giving merely the *occasion*)." See *The Critique of Pure Reason*, Introduction, 1 (1781). Nietzsche is not granting Kant the validity of a priori judgment.
45 *Beyond Good and Evil*, 4. On the term "species-cultivating" *(Art-züchtend)* see "Overcoming" footnote 139.
46 *NF*–1888, 14[148].

Nietzsche's eyes, rarely but convenient expressions of *what is useful*, perhaps even necessary. Is political identity—that is, one's relation to other identities and to the power nexus as a whole—one such "life-fostering, life-preserving, species-preserving, perhaps even species-cultivating" fictional utility? Following our Guide, our task is precisely to give thought to the matter. So, first, we will consider an affirmative answer to that question. Then, we will turn to a negative answer.

To delineate here yet another instance of Nietzsche's starkly divided pathway between a life-affirming creativity and a life-negating nihilism, I think it will be helpful to take as our working material the contemporary matter of "identity politics." I believe it will become clear that Nietzsche himself had something similar in mind when he diagnosed the ailments of "the political," broadly conceived, in his own day. After all, he located the origin of the psychological, social, and cultural illness that he observed to be at the very heart of liberal democracy itself. In particular, he pinpointed the debilitating moment of tension between the age-old dueling values of individual freedom and social equality. These two quintessential liberal values are at odds with one another. Individual freedom engenders profound *difference* (in access to and share of the commonwealth, in power dynamics, in identity categories), while social equality necessitates *sameness* (of share and access, political power, and identity categories) at the cost of personal limitation (think: Hermodor). So it is precisely *personal identity* that drives the demands of individual freedom, and, conversely, *human universalism* that animates the dream of social equality.

Are we presently on the same trajectory, dealing with the same ailments, that Nietzsche diagnosed? That is a matter for the reader to decide. Remember: we are following Guide Nietzsche *not* to a cache of neatly wrapped prefabricated answers. We are following him in order to walk the path of thinking itself.

So, on to the affirmative utility of our topic. The term "identity politics" was coined by the Combahee River Collective, a group of Black feminists founded in 1974. The following passage from their "Statement" makes the case for identity per se and explicitly in politics.

Our politics evolve from a healthy love for ourselves, our sisters, and our community which allows us to continue our struggle and work. This focusing upon our own oppression is embodied in the concept of identity politics. We believe that the most profound and potentially most radical politics come directly out of our own identity, as opposed to working to end somebody else's oppression. In the case of Black women this is a particularly repugnant, dangerous, threatening, and therefore revolutionary concept because it is obvious from looking at all the political movements that have preceded us that anyone is more worthy of liberation than ourselves.[47]

Clearly, there is nothing feigned in the sense of urgency here. "Identity" is presented in the Statement not as some frivolously chosen lifestyle moniker. It is presented as a matter of life and death. Indeed, identity is presented as not a *choice* at all. Elsewhere, the Statement refers to the default identity against which all others are ranked: "Black women's extremely negative relationship to the American political system (a system of white male rule) has always been determined by our membership in two oppressed racial and sexual castes." If we add a few modifiers, we have a largely uncontroversial (because demonstrable[48]) name for what amounts to the ostensible nonidentity that determines the identity values of all other groups: white heterosexual cisgendered middle-class Christian male. As the Statement makes clear, an all-too common theme in a group's articulation of its identity is the very real threat that it faces in relation to the dominant status quo. The list is long: women, gays, lesbians, transgender people, nonbinary and queer people, Blacks and other people of color, the physically disabled, the mentally ill, indigenous Americans, Little People, homeless people, economically impoverished people, certain ethnic groups, Muslims, Jews, the elderly, and more. Throughout American history, the struggle of these groups is in large part the result of being identified as something other than the largely invisible identity of white heterosexual cisgendered middle-class Christian male. Recognizing the role that identity "caste"—indeed, even the combination of identities (Black *and* female) that law professor Kimberlé Crenshaw

---

47 Combahee River Collective Statement, https://combaheerivercollective.weebly.com/the-combahee-river-collective-statement.html. Accessed April 7, 2024.

48 See, for instance, Anagha Srikanth, "Changing America," *The Hill*: "A new study found that white men hold 62 percent of all elected offices despite being just 30 percent of the population," https://thehill.com/changing-america/respect/diversity-inclusion/555503-new-study-finds-white-male-minority-rule; and Michael Allen, "Diversity and Inclusion," *Physics World*: "White heterosexual men have systematic advantages in science, finds study," https://physicsworld.com/a/white-heterosexual-men-have-systematic-advantages-in-science-finds-study/. Accessed March 11, 2023. There is also a large body of academic work on the topic. For instance, Ashley Jardina, *White Identity Politics* (Cambridge: Cambridge University Press, 2019), Eric Kaufmann, *Whiteshift: Populism, Immigration, and the Future of White Majorities* (New York: Abrams Press, 2019), and many others.

calls "intersectionality"—plays in their oppression, the Combahee River Collective concludes that it is incumbent on the members of the particular identity group to unite and fight.

Perhaps the reader can make additional identity-affirmative arguments. I can think of none, however, that is stronger than the *argument from survival.* Certainly, this argument places identity within Nietzsche's high stakes criterion of being a life-preserving "truth." Again, we are speaking here of the ways that identity plays out in our political—social, cultural, statist—sphere. The Combahee River Collective articulates the dire necessity of formulating, making explicit, and rallying around an identity marker. It also argues for the fact that the struggle of each of the "castes" that I listed is unique in itself and so is best served by as robust a formulation, explication, and rallying around as possible.

What argument can Nietzsche possibly make that challenges the necessity of identity when survival is at stake? Moreover, since, for Nietzsche, life-denial is a definitive feature of nihilism, would not any such argument be, by definition, nihilistic? In fact, Nietzsche's argument against identity in the political sphere is as surprising as it is devastating. The following is going to be rough going for some readers. So hold on!

We begin by returning to the theater of modern political life: liberal democracy. Recall that for Nietzsche the state is "the coldest of all cold monsters."[49] (Think of "state" as the collusion of the governmental apparatus with the status quo: the affairs of state = the state of affairs.) The state's coldness lies in its *enervation* of life. It does so the better to gain social control toward its goal of equality and power. Moreover, as a *liberal* state, it must simultaneously permit a splintering of the social body along the lines of freely competing individual and group agendas. Hence, the proliferation of identity categories that we see among the populace in modern mass culture (see my previous list of examples). The conundrum here is that the identity marker being rallied around for the purpose of heightened political visibility doubles as a ranking and disciplinary tool for the status quo. The identity, furthermore, is integral to the social powerlessness that those bearing the marker experience. One final wrinkle. The ultimate goal of identity politics is for the marginalized group to attain the access, privileges, and goods that are perceived to be enjoyed by those with the ostensible nonidentity. Indeed, the marginalized group's very claim to exclusion and injury rests on its very *difference* from the privileged group. So, in the end, if the affirmative

---

49 *Thus Spoke Zarathustra*, "On the New Idols."

argument places identity within Nietzsche's high stakes criterion of being *life-preserving*, it simultaneously places those who do the affirming in a condition of *perpetual injury*. This is a terrible contradiction. Fortunately, it is one for which Nietzsche offers a solution.

Nietzsche, I think, would see identity in our current sense as a differential *position* in relation to power. For, as we saw earlier, he argues that psychological identity is not an ontological category but a relational one. In fact, consistent with a formally ubiquitous, now largely bygone, trope, he would agree with the social constructedness thesis of identity categories. In the Gwen Stefani story, I think he would lament the hardened overdetermination of the identity markers in play. Recall that he does not want to get *rid* of the "soul [self, integral identity] hypothesis"; rather, he wants it to refer to "a social structure of drives and affects," to an intra- and inter-relational "subjective multiplicity." We are certainly no *single* identity. If anything, Nietzsche would enthusiastically endorse Crenshaw's concept of "intersectionality," namely, that we are multiple intersecting identities all at once. But he would do so with the proviso that we must not take this idea too literally. And he certainly would not want us to invest energy into the maintenance of a given identity marker, much less a complex of identities.

Why not? Nietzsche offers an argument with several threads running through it. As a general background to what follows, I will ask the reader to bear in mind two ideas from the preceding section, on psychological identity. Recall that Nietzsche asks us to resist subscribing to "one of the best refuted theories that there is," namely, that of "materialistic atomism."[50] When he adds that "we must go even further...and declare war, relentless war unto death" on any and all notions of this reifying phenomenon, he is not engaging in mere rhetorical hyperbole. Nietzsche's alpha and omega is that if we are ever going to achieve a breakthrough into genuinely new and "healthy" cultural possibilities, we must not shy away from danger, either in thought or in action. And, as the Combahee River Collective Statement's concept of identity politics makes clear, it is certainly a dangerous move to be "rid of *materiality*" concerning how we treat identity. Juxtaposed with the Combahee argument from survival, the arguments Nietzsche makes may even strike readers as dangerously irresponsible. Yet the danger-immune "intellectual conscience" boldly responds: but does that necessarily render them *untrue*?

---

50 *Beyond Good and Evil*, 12.

The main thread in Nietzsche's argument against thinking of ourselves in terms of identity groups is that doing so fosters "herd mentality." As the metaphor suggests, the benefit of herding together is that protection and power are to be found in numbers. Indeed, this is the primary rationale for identity politics in the Combahee River Collective Statement. Nietzsche sees two problems, however, that outweigh this benefit. The first problem is that group consciousness entails repudiation of one's individuality, or, in his neologism, it entails "unselfing."[51] In our final chapter, we will explore Nietzsche's preferred self-model. That model involves what he terms "types"; and types prevail precisely at the expense of identities. The difference between a type and an identity involves that between *transformation* and *assertion*. A type is created through conscious self-becoming, whereas an identity involves adapting to an already (socially) given self-being. A type, furthermore, is present-future oriented, whereas an identity is present-past oriented. The crucial point here is that "the morality of unselfing is the morality of decadence par excellence."[52] In short, the desired cultural breakthrough will never occur as long as the reigning morality ranks group identification over individual self-becoming. Indeed, the problem with such a morality is that, like Nietzsche's categories of passive nihilists, last mortals, and Christians, "fundamentally, it negates life." The paradox is that danger lurks in the very heart of the safety that is "the herd."

> *Herd instinct.* Wherever we encounter a morality, we find an assessment and ranking system of human drives and actions. These evaluations and ranking systems are always the expression of the need of a community or herd: that, to which the community or herd avails itself in the first place—and in the second and third as well—is at the same time the highest standard of the worth of every individual. Through morality, the individual is taught to be a function of the herd, and only as such a function to ascribe worth to him- or herself.[53]

The problem that Nietzsche sees here is that the potentially transformed individual *type* gets hopelessly subsumed within the group *identity*. Being subjected to the identity community's "assessment and ranking system," being bound to a necessarily narrow ideological conception of which "human

---

51 *Ecce Homo,* "Why I Am A Destiny," 7. Nietzsche's neologism is *Entselbstung,* "unselfing" or "de-selfing."
52 *Ecce Homo,* "Why I Am A Destiny," 7.
53 *The Gay Science,* 116.

drives and actions" are desirable and permissible, the individual undergoes the very "leveling" that we saw in the chapter on democracy. An additional problem in Nietzsche's view is that group "moralities" are endlessly prolif-erating—they are forever altered, contested, modified, splintered, scraped, rejected, disbanded.

> Since the conditions for preserving one community have been very different from those of another community, there exist quite distinct moralities. And with regard to still to come essential transformations of herds, communities, countries and societies, we can prophesize that there will be seriously deviating moralities yet. Morality is the herd instinct in the individual.[54]

The Combahee River Collective itself is an example of this process. It was originally a splinter group from two national movements, women's libera-tion and civil rights. Discerning racism in the former's policies (it consisted mainly of white feminists) and misogyny and homophobia in the latter's (its leadership consisted largely of Black men), certain members left to form the Collective. And a mere six years after forming, owing to irreconcilable inter-nal dissension, the Collective itself was disbanded. In part, it was a contested "assessment and ranking system of human drives and actions" concerning education and class distinctions that led to the Collective's dissolution.[55] The point here is that a "morality" that is grounded in a particular identity is not sustainable because "fundamentally, it negates life." It does so, for instance, by discounting the multiplicity of subjective views, and, in particular, in disabling the human diversity that gives rise to the group's existence in the first place. Nietzsche's hope for a healthy, new culture rests firmly on the creation of healthy, new human types. As we will see in the final chapter, one of the defining characteristics of his new type is the ability to resist the very *modus operandi* of "the herd": identity or "virtue" labeling.

> If you have a virtue and it is your virtue, then you have it in common with nobody else. Of course you want to call it by name and caress it…And behold! Now you have the virtue's name in common with the people and have become one of the herd and people with your virtue! You would do better to say: "Inexpressible and nameless is that which

54 *The Gay Science*, 116.
55 See Kimberly Springer, *Living for the Revolution: Black Feminist Organizations*, 1968–1980 (Durham: Duke University Press, 2005), 128ff.

gives my soul suffering and sweetness and also is the hunger in my gut." Your virtue is too exalted for the familiarity of names. And if you must speak of it, do not be ashamed to stammer.[56]

Identity-driven groups are not sustainable because no real single "identity" ever exists within the group in the first place. Again, the reason for this impossibility rests on Nietzsche's refutation of the principle of identity. "Identity," namely, is never an ontological category; it is always a relational one: "That there exists same things," he insists, results from mistaken apprehension.[57] So why do identity groups have such a hold on us? Nietzsche offers two reasons. The first is superficial, but the second is profound.

To what extent active people are lazy. I believe that everyone must have their own opinion about anything for which an opinion is possible. The reason is that each person is their own unique thing, which takes a new, never-before existing position to all things. But laziness, which lies at the bottom of active people's souls, prevents them from drawing water from their own wells.—As with the freedom of opinion, so with health: both are individual; from neither can a generally applicable concept be erected. That which is necessary for one individual's health is grounds for another's sickness, and some means and ways to freedom of the spirit may, for more highly developed natures, be means and ways to bondage.[58]

Is it *laziness* that leads us to join some "herd"? I say that this reason is superficial because it is eminently reversible. Indeed, Nietzsche's theory of types is predicated on such reversibility. I do not think it is too much of a stretch to say that, in the much deeper, and so less readily reversible, reason that he offers, Nietzsche anticipates the findings of, for instance, cognitive science and evolutionary biology. In short, the issue is this: "More ancient is delight in the herd than delight in the I; and as long as the good conscience is identified with the herd, only the bad conscience says: I."[59] In a striking early passage that bridges Nietzsche's "laziness" and "bad conscience" theories, he makes explicit his underlying universal principle: "every person is a unique miracle."

---

56 *Thus Spoke Zarathustra*, "On Pleasures and Passions."
57 *NF*–1885, 36 [23].
58 *Human, All Too Human*, 286.
59 *Thus Spoke Zarathustra*, "On the Thousand and One Goals."

A traveler who, having seen many different lands and people and continents, is asked which human characteristic he encountered everywhere, replies: they have an inclination toward laziness. Some would think that that person would have more correctly and validly said: they are all fearful; they hide themselves behind customs and opinions. At heart, everyone knows full well that he appears but once, uniquely, in the world, and that no strange coincidence will mix together for a second time such a curiously colorful variety as the single entity that he is. He knows it, but buries it like a bad conscience. Why? Out of fear of his neighbor, who demands the conventionality in which he wraps himself. Yet, what is it that compels the individual to fear the neighbor, to think and act herd-like, and not to be happy with himself? Modesty, perhaps, for some and few. For most, the reason is comfort, inertia, in brief, that inclination toward laziness about which our traveler spoke. He is right: people are lazier than they are fearful, and they fear most the discomfort with which unconditional honesty and nakedness would burden them.[60]

Rehearsing his eventual theory of types, Nietzsche completes the above passage with the solution to the problem of group conformity. He does so by invoking his earliest figure of the antiidentified social outsider: the artist.

Artists alone hate this casual adoption of borrowed manners and protruding opinions, and reveal the secret, the bad conscience of everyone, the principle that every person is a unique miracle. Artists dare to show us how the human being, down to every twitch of his muscles, is himself alone. And more still, that in this strict consequence of his uniqueness he is beautiful and worthy of regard, is new and incredible like every work of nature, and by no means boring.

What about this idea that we take "delight in the herd" over our very sense of self and that our "good conscience is identified with the herd," while a sense of self elicits "bad conscience"? The famous Asch Conformity Experiments provides insight into the nature of "herd mentality." When Nietzsche uses this term, it has a ring of derision to it. Yet it is an actual category of investigation in social psychology. Also referred to as mob mentality and pack mentality, herd mentality denotes a proclivity in humans toward

---

60 *Untimely Meditations*, "Schopenhauer as Educator," 1.

"groupthink" and "deindividuation." (In Nietzsche's language, these two terms translate as "the neighbor" and "unselfing.") In the Asch experiments, people consistently chose conformity to the group over the unambiguous contrary evidence before their very eyes. Imagine you were asked to determine which of the following lines are equivalent to line (a):

(a) _____

The choices are:

(i)_____
(ii) _____
(iii)_____
(iv)_____

In the experiment, each one of the coached participants intentionally chooses the same obviously incorrect answer, while a lone random participant goes last, having observed the selection made by the previous participants. In over 75% of the trials, the random participant simply goes along with the group and selects the same incorrect answer.[61] Incredible, isn't it? Researchers hypothesize various reasons for such herding behavior, but Nietzsche's "comfort, inertia" strikes me as plausible as any.

The longer version of Nietzsche's theory is as follows. As I said, it is roughly in the same vein as the current cooperation between disciplines such as cognitive science, evolutionary biology, historical anthropology, behavioral ecology, and social psychology—a cooperation that endeavors to arrive at acquired naturalistic explanations for social phenomena.

The herd's sting of conscience.—In the longest and most distant time of humanity, there existed a wholly different sting of conscience than that of today. Today, people feel responsible only for what they themselves want and do and have pride in themselves: all our legal scholars proceed from this sense of self and desire of the individual, as if the source of law had always sprung from here. But for the longest time throughout humanity's history, nothing was more terrifying than feeling singular. To be alone, sensing by oneself, neither to obey nor to

---

61 See, for instance, "Conformity, Compliance, and Obedience," *Pressbooks*, https://opentext.wsu.edu/psych105nusbaum/chapter/conformity-compliance-and-obedience. Accessed March 17, 2023.

command, to count as an individual—this was, back then, no pleasure but rather a punishment: a person was condemned "to individuality." Freedom of thought was considered disquiet in itself. Whereas we experience law and order as coercion and loss, back then one experienced egoism as a painful matter, as an actual affliction. To be oneself, to value oneself according to one's own measure and weight—back then that was considered tasteless. The tendency to do so would have been experienced as a case of insanity: for, being alone was associated with every form of suffering and fear. Back then, the "free will" had as its nearest neighbor bad conscience: and the more unfree a person acted—the more an action spoke from the herd instinct and not from personal meaning—the more the person valued himself morally. Everything that caused harm to the herd, whether it was something the individual wanted or not, instigated in the individual—and in his neighbor and, yes, in the entire herd!—a sting of conscience. In this matter, we have relearned the most.[62]

We might have "relearned" our relationship between the individual I and the herd conscience, but we have not *unlearned* it. Laziness, the desire for comfort, and inertia were still the order of the day in Nietzsche's time. Are they still so in ours? It is true that Nietzsche offers up some harsh reasons for our "herd instinct," or, expressed with more compassion, for our deep-seated need to associate with like-minded people. In the final thread of his argument, Nietzsche's language will sound even harsher to some readers. His reason, again, is that he feels we are engaged in a momentous struggle against the raging torrent of cultural nihilism. Some readers may feel that we are on dangerously thin ice in considering that the existence of identity in the sense we have been discussing in this section is a symptom of nihilism, of life-negation. Perhaps. In the case of such danger, let us recall that Nietzsche is addressing a reader who is a "monster of courage." "Monster" conjures images of inhuman transgression, repulsive otherness, and ominous presence. Nietzsche's reader must be willing to engage in all of these unpleasant things, and more besides. Following Nietzsche as our guide to thought, however hesitantly and temporarily, we simply cannot avoid the stubble fields of divisive politics, group moralizing, and the suspicious gaze of "the neighbor."

---

62 *The Gay Science*, 117.

I offer these comments as a kind of prophylactic or hedge against the reader's immediate rejection of what follows. Some readers will hear the distinct voice of conservatism (or worse) as we proceed. Indeed, some readers have likely heard that voice throughout this book. I can only intone again the premise driving this book: it is precisely Nietzsche's utter disregard for our political-social-cultural tribalism that makes him such a necessary guide today. In fact, he himself is laboring like a monster to unsettle what he views as the very "moralities," the interminable, overbearing, overdetermining systems of "assessment and ranking...of human drives and actions" that circulate within any given "herd." Recall that he is asking us to consider that these systems "are always the expression of the need of a community or herd" and *not* of a unique, free-thinking individual. There is always something nomadic, even heretical, about the individual for Nietzsche. Invoking once again one of his favorite figures, the artist, Nietzsche asks the following pertinent, if severe, questions. (Imagine his remark as a response to the accusation that some comment of his is "conservative" or "liberal" or "masculinist" or "hetero-normative" or, indeed, simply "dangerous" and therefore *necessarily* disqualified.)

> Yes, well, what compels us to assume that there is an intrinsic opposition between "true" and "false"? Does it not suffice to assume degrees of apparentness and, so to speak, lighter and darker shadows and whole tones of appearance—different "values" *(valeurs)* to use the language of painters?[63]

This is not an anything-goes, post-truth evasion of taking a stand. It is an assertion about the uncomfortable work required to take a stand at all. For *taking a stand* is diametrically opposed to *subscribing to a program*. I think Nietzsche would agree that the intractability of today's political discourse is in no small part a result of our knee-jerk resistance to any idea, sentiment, claim, argument, indeed, *word*, that does not bear the imprimatur of our particular group's "morality." This lack of sanction does not condemn an idea or a word to eternal Wrongness. Listening in on the rancorous "debates" that resound through our public spaces, you would think that it does. Perhaps we would want to reject the way in which an idea, argument, and so on, is put to *use* within some ideological whole. That is understandable. But that move does not preclude our consideration of the idea as a potentially

---

63 *Beyond Good and Evil*, 34.

viable element and even to employ it within a different whole.[64] The pressing question, then, is: can we boldly cross boundaries between our endlessly and increasingly fractured "herd" communities? If we answer "no," then, well… around and around we go, getting nowhere. And if we answer "yes"?

Let's experiment. Imaginè someone were to respond to the Gwen Stefani incident by arguing that, on the whole, no harm was done. She expressed her deep appreciation for Japanese culture. As an "influencer," her appreciation further spread through her fanbase, further raising appreciation for Japanese pop culture. Yes, by that same token, she profited off her appropriation. Yes, we can imagine different contexts in which a privileged white woman claiming that she is Japanese is highly problematic; for instance, if she means it *literally*, as in the Rachel Dolezal case.[65] But when we consider the details of the Stefani case—the context, the backstory, the spirit in which she said it—is it *necessarily* problematic? Could it conceivably be considered wholly inconsequential? In today's environment, such queries almost predictably meet with a resounding *NO! It caused injury. That* [*word, idea, comment, claim, clothing, image, post, joke, show, article, question, belief, gesture, action, inaction, ad infinitum*] *is hurtful personally and injurious historically, and so must be reckoned with accordingly.*

In our own day, we are mired in "the politics of resentment" and "grievance politics." Our public discourse—a "*moralized* manner of speaking," says Nietzsche[66]—is driven by "snowflakes"[67] on the liberal left, "angry radicals" on the libertarian left, "aggrieved anti-elitists" on the working-class right, and "outrage" among well-heeled conservatives. "This is our politics now,"

---

64 The debate on increased primary and secondary education spending is one example. Democrats and Republicans of all stripes agree on the principle and even on the amount but disagree on the methods, aims, and ends. The difference, of course, results from the "assessment and ranking system of human drives and actions" that define the respective political ideologies of the two parties. For many other examples, see "100 policies supported by majorities of Democrats and Republicans," *YouGov America*, https://today.yougov.com/ politics/articles/44463-policies-supported-by-democrats-and-republicans?redirect_from=% 2Ftopics%2Fpolitics%2Farticles-reports%2F2022%2F11%2F17%2Fpolicies-supported-by-democrats-and-republicans. Accessed April 3, 2024.

65 Rachel Dolezal (currently: Nkechi Amare Diallo) is a woman of German, Czech, and Swedish descent who claims to be a "transracial" Black woman. Her situation was uncovered during her tenure as a chapter president for the National Association for the Advancement of Colored People.

66 *On the Genealogy of Morals*, 3.19.

67 "Snowflake" is a derogatory slang term referring to someone whom some people consider to be too delicate, too easily offended, and who feel themself to be special and unique. *The Guardian* declared it "the defining insult of 2016." See Rebecca Nicholson, "Poor Little Snowflake," https://www.theguardian.com/science/2016/nov/28/snowflake-insult-disdain-young-people. Accessed October 23, 2023.

decries one astute observer: "No uplifting rhetoric about 'hope' or 'a shining city on the hill.' No poetry. No norms. No decency. It is grievance, revenge, and identity, all the way down."[68] In short, we are engulfed in a cauldron of "victimization." (If this characterization strikes the reader as overwrought, I recommend a twenty-minute perusal of social media, network and cable news, and virtually any daily newspaper.)

Nietzsche's ears buzzed with a similar cacophony in his own day. His response, in a (French) word: *ressentiment*. In the nineteenth century, this term was reserved for a particular variety of *resentment*. It names an affect, an emotional charge, that arises when we believe we have been slighted or harmed yet find ourselves incapable of redressing the offense. *Ressentiment* is an affect of the powerless. It differs from *resentment* precisely in this regard. A person with the means for redress or revenge can feel *resentment* and respond accordingly. The attitude of *ressentiment*, by contrast, is: "I suffer: someone must be to blame for it."[69] Passive "blame" fills the space where effective redress otherwise manifests. Connecting this notion to the earlier discussion, we can say that it is precisely the frustrated freedom of access to the commonwealth that fuels *ressentiment* in a suffering identity group: "This *instinct for freedom*, forcefully rendered latent," says Nietzsche, "repelled and repressed, is incarcerated within us and ultimately able to discharge and vent itself only on itself."[70]

> Suffering people are altogether awfully eager and inventive in finding pretexts for their painful affects: indeed, they enjoy their suspiciousness, their brooding over misdeeds and imaginary impairments, they rummage through the entrails of their past and present looking for dark, questionable narratives.[71]

Nietzsche the psychologist even surmises on the "actual physiological cause of *ressentiment*."

---

68 William Falk, "The Politics of Grievance," *The Week*, https://theweek.com/articles/799887/politics-grievance. Accessed March 17, 2023.

69 *On the Genealogy of Morals*, 3.15.

70 *On the Genealogy of Morals*, 2.17.

71 *On the Genealogy of Morals*, 3.15. Quoting the entirety of this passage, political theorist Wendy Brown adds: "Nietzsche's elaboration of this moment in an economy of suffering could easily characterize the rancorous tenor of many contemporary institutions and events in which politicized identity is strongly and permissibly at play." See Wendy Brown, "Wounded Attachments," *Political Theory*, Vol. 21, No. 3 (August, 1993): 410.

Every sufferer instinctively seeks a cause for his suffering. More precisely, he seeks a perpetrator. More precisely still, he seeks a *guilty* perpetrator who is himself susceptible to suffering—in short, something living, onto which he can, under some pretense or other, discharge his affects in actuality or in effigy: for, the discharge of affect is the greatest attempt of relief for the sufferer, namely, *anaesthetization*, his involuntarily desired narcotic against pain of any kind. Here alone, I conjecture, is to be found the actual physiological cause of *ressentiment*, vengeance, and the like: in a longing for *anaesthetization of pain by means of affect.*[72]

With this, we can sum up Nietzsche's argument against identity as a valid political (cultural, social, statist) category as follows. Identity communities emerge in response to a sense of disenfranchisement or injury. Identity-allegiance thus ensconces the person in a protective community. But it does so by enabling "herd mentality" at the expense of individual development. Perpetrators of injustice, the perceived agents of disenfranchisement or injury, are singled out. The protective identity marker simultaneously marks the identity holder as susceptible to the disciplinary and hierarchical categories of the dominant group and thus in need of perpetual protection. This state of affairs incites the affect of *ressentiment*—righteous anger, frustrated hostility, and so on. At the same time, it creates a target for affect discharge, enabling release. Release, finally, results in the "anaesthetization of pain." And so the process continues. Hence, perpetuating things as they are, it is at heart nihilistic.

"That sounds harsh," Nietzsche admits. However, in the last word that we will permit him on this topic, he offers a justification for this harshness. For some readers, it will just increase the harshness. If nothing else, it is a remarkably *current-sounding* statement that he makes.

That sounds harsh…But why stroke the pampered ears of our modern softies? Why should *we* yield a single step to their foolishness of words? For us psychologists, it would be a *foolishness of deed* to do so: quite apart from the fact that doing so would make us nauseous. For, if a psychologist today has any *good taste* (some would say "honesty"), it lies in his resistance to the shamefully *moralized* manner of speaking

---

72 *On the Genealogy of Morals*, 3.15.

with which virtually all modern judgments about people and things are besmeared.[73]

Harsh, severe, cutting. For some readers, Nietzsche may have reached the end of his usefulness as a cultural diagnostician here. I, personally, have sometimes had difficulty squaring my lifelong commitment to collective transformative solutions with Nietzsche's emphasis on individual innovation. More decisive than my certainty of conviction, however, is my desire to become "aware of the final and most certain reasons *for and against*," as Nietzsche says of intellectual conscience. To read and think as Nietzsche demands is to "stand in the midst of this *discordant harmony of things* and the whole wonderful uncertainty and ambiguity of existence"; it is to "tremble...with the longing and rapture of questioning," perhaps even "hating the person who questions" or, who knows, "even taking a dim delight in him."

---

73 *On the Genealogy of Morals*, 3.19.

WOKENESS AND IDEOLOGY

WHAT DOES NIETZSCHE OFFER THAT MIGHT HELP US NAVIGATE THE CONTEN-tious issue of "wokeness"? As I am using this term, the reader should always read it with implied scare quotes. I say this for several reasons. One, the term is increasingly being disavowed by the very people who recently wore the badge with pride.[1] Two, the term has an unclear and controversial referent. Three, what it is held to refer to and what value it is granted or denied has become deeply politicized. The right often uses "wokeness" as a catchall for everything it imagines "the left" to advocate for, particularly concerning issues around justice, gender, and equality. Yet, somewhat con-fusingly, a powerful critique of "wokeness" has also emerged *from the left.* For different reasons, centrist liberals, socialists, communists, and anarchists are articulating their particular versions of "anti-wokeness."

As murky as it might be, "wokeness" is a phenomenon to be reckoned with in early twenty-first-century America and possibly beyond.[2] I will make

---

1 In "The War On Wokeness," for instance, opinion columnist Charles Blow concludes: "The opponents of wokeness are fighting over an abandoned word, like an army bombarding a fort that has been vacated: They don't appear fierce, but foolish." *New York Times*, November 10, 2021.

2 Consider, for example, that "ending wokeness" is a central talking point, perhaps even *the* central talking point, of Republican candidates in the United States 2024 presidential election. Governor Ron DeSantis constantly barks that "Florida is where wokeness goes to die." Former United Nations ambassador Nikki Haley proclaims that "wokeness is a virus more dangerous than any pandemic." Former US secretary of state Mike Pompeo tweets that "our internal threats—especially those trying to corrupt our kids with toxic wokeness—are more serious than our external threats." In addition, Leonard Lee, the cochairperson of the conservative libertarian legal organization The Federalist Society, recently announced his intention to create similar organizations at American vortices of power, such as Wall Street, Silicon Valley, journalism, and academia. His goal is to transform "American culture and American life where things are really messed up right now." And where is that? Among other places, "wokeism in the corporate environment, in the educational environment, in entertainment that is really corrupting our youth." Is this obsession with "wokeness" just another conservative foil, like "communism" in the 1950–1980s and "crime" from the 1980s till today? Maybe. But that fact, to my mind, strengthens, not lessens, the importance of engaging the discourse. Lee, furthermore, is the force behind the elevation of Donald Trump's three Supreme Court appointments. That means that he was a decisive force behind no less than the reversal of Roe Vs. Wade. He knows what he is doing. The $1.6 billion in dark money

that point clear as we proceed. To begin with, it will be useful to highlight the phenomenon. In doing so, it should also become clear that the issue is much bigger than contemporary "wokeness" talk. Indeed, we are really dealing here with the age-old phenomenon of *ideology* as a whole. What I say here about the ideas, attitudes, and actions that have coalesced around an ostensible wokeness apply to the elements of any given worldview, or indeed to an ideology outright. Ideologies circulate and are contested in *public*. So, turning to Nietzsche, I then say something about his views on *public opinion*, whatever form it takes, and his appreciation for *agon*—struggle, strife, contest, whatever form *it* takes. Finally, we will consider his ideas about *perspective*. Here we go. Buckle up!

WOKENESS?

Let's start at the most perilous place possible: with a definition. Pollsters who try to gather opinions about ostensible "woke" issues are unanimous on one matter: "wokeness" is a "conceptually squishy" concept.[3] Indeed, it is. I would argue, however, that the same is true for every other ideological conception. If you drill down far enough into, say, what it means to be a "democrat," a "sports fan," or an "American," you eventually reach a big blob of limp conceptual squishiness. Each of those terms means quite varied and sometimes internally contradictory things. That's how language works. It proliferates meanings. It is flexible, fluid, and resistant to being nailed down. In addition to this lexical variation of a word, there is its history. Like human beings, words have genealogies. In fact, Nietzsche himself was the progenitor of the genealogical method of analysis. To him, concepts are products of a history that we, the user of the concepts, have likely forgotten. Like a human being, the term "woke" has a complex lineage, tangled branches, ancestors (both honored and dubious), progeny (both refined and unruly). So while we reflexively ask what a word *means*, a genealogical awareness prompts us to ask the better question of how a word *functions*. This is a good place to present the first thing about concepts that Nietzsche would ask us to bear in mind, namely, its shifting foundation.

---

he has received for his anti-wokeness transformation of America means the "wokeness" issue will have staying power. See Michelle Goldberg, "The Right's Obsession with Wokeness is a Sign of Weakness," *The New York Times*, Opinion, March 10, 2023. https://www.nytimes.com/2023/03/10/opinion/republican-woke-focus.html. Accessed April 3, 2024.

3 Matthew Crowley, "What Does It Mean to Be Woke," *Politifact*, https://www.politifact.com/article/2023/mar/07/what-does-it-mean-to-be-woke. Accessed March 8, 2023.

Like the Romans and Etruscans, who cut up the heavens into rigid mathematical lines and, as in a *templum*, banished a god into each delineated space, so, too, above every people hovers such a mathematically divided concept heaven, and, under the demands of truth, people understand that every concept-god may be sought in *its* sphere *only*. Here, we may admire a people as a tremendous architectural genius, who, on shifting ground and flowing water, is able to amass an infinitely complicated concept cathedral. Of course, to find support on such a foundation, the construction must be made of spiderweb—so gentle as to be carried away on the waves yet so firm as not to be blown asunder by the wind. As an architectural genius, such a people rises far above the bee. The bee builds with wax that it gathers from nature. A people builds with the much more delicate material of concepts, which it must first fabricate from out of itself.[4]

Since it is the manifold *we* who is fabricating the concept "woke," how could it not function in multiple, complex, and often mutually exclusive ways? So how might we outline a definition of the term that is delicate enough to allow for the inevitable lexical shifts and firm enough to say *something*? One way is to return to the pollsters that I mentioned previously. In the end, they have to get a read on the real world. Simply put, they do so by formulating questions that they feel best home in on the respondents' positions concerning an issue. I suggest that questions *answered in the affirmative* concerning the following matters would, to a pollster, constitute "being woke," to some degree or another, in the sense that is in play in politics and popular culture today. So, dear reader, you can play along and answer the following questions:

- Is racism in America exclusively and/or primarily systematic?
- Are concepts like "white fragility" and "toxic masculinity" legitimate descriptors of most white/male people?
- Is it possible that a person be "assigned" the "incorrect" gender at birth?
- Is it acceptable that children under the age of twelve receive "gender-affirming" treatment?
- Should the police be defunded?
- Should people who engage in acts deemed "offensive" by some be "canceled."

4 *On Truth and Lies in an Extra-Moral Sense*, 1.

- Should far-right figures be prevented from speaking on college campuses?
- Does gender exist on a nonbinary continuum?
- Should we accommodate pronoun requests of nonbinary people?
- Do you favor "safe spaces" and the use of "trigger warnings"?
- Should group identity play a decisive role in policy decisions?
- Do you hold that anyone who disagrees with any or most of the foregoing is necessarily conservative or "reactionary"?

Questions like these are "simultaneously irresistible and silly," as Janine A. Parry, a political science professor and pollster, says of "provocative culture war-type constructs such as 'woke.'" They are irresistible because it is precisely such matters that are in play at our cultural moment, and we have to get somewhere with our questions. They are silly because they can lead to caricatures and misrepresentations. Yet, as Parry points out, "despite being conceptually squishy—loud swaths of the electorate have staked out hyperbolic positions on"[5] our term, and so here we are…and here we go.

"THE WOKE MOB IS EVERYWHERE!"

In a world where cancel culture and political correctness are reshaping how citizens across the United States interpret the political and social climate around them, another term has become as prominent in the mainstream: "wokeness."

Thus begins a recent article in *The Elm*, the student newspaper of Washington College, titled "The Meaning of 'Wokeness,' Explained."[6] The piece elicited the following exchange. The article, I should mention, was admirably nonpartisan, and the (hyper-partisan) comments were perfectly par for discourse around the issue—online, in print, or in person.

PETE: Pretty interesting discourse […] No group in our history has been without struggle, without injustice and without privilege and benefit… We have an opportunity despite the hindrances. If we focus on access to the opportunities, it becomes more of an assessment of individual

---

5 Crowley, "What Does It Mean to Be Woke."
6 "The Meaning of 'Wokeness,' Explained." https://blog.washcoll.edu/wordpress/theelm/2020/10/the-meaning-of-wokeness-explained. Accessed May 24, 2002.

talent and willpower than it does about class suppression. One view-point unites. One viewpoint divides. I ask which one will make a better tomorrow for all people in this country?

NOBODY: So you agree that right wingers are whiny children that need to grow the fuck up then. Good.

WAKEUP: You are a real idiot! That is not even close to what Pete said, he had no hint of right or left, just what is best for all Americans [...]

RTFORD: It's really very simple. Wokeness equals self-righteousness.

NOBODY: Good to know that wanting black people to have the same rights as white people is equal to self-righteousness for you. To me, wokeness is just showing basic respect and dignity to your fellow human beings, no matter their appearance. If that's self-righteousness, then I'm glad to be self-righteous. Fucking manchild.

Whew! What is it about "wokeness" that elicits such heated reactions? Clearly, something of great importance is felt to be at stake here.[7] But what is it, exactly? I will give a brief overview of the increasingly treacherous "wokeness" terrain, and then consider how our Immoralist might help us navigate through it.

Warnings about wokeness are issuing from all points on the American political spectrum. The right bellows that "THE WOKE MOB IS EVERYWHERE!"[8] And by "everywhere" they mean that it has "infiltrated every industry, from the military to media to philanthropy" to publishing to higher education, and, of course, to government. The essential *danger* of wokeness for those on the right is that it is destroying America. How? By conditioning us Americans to hate ourselves and our nation. Conservatism

---

7 *The Global Language Monitor* ranks "woke" as #3 in its list of top words for 2021. The ranking is based on global English usage. It would have been ranked first if not for "Covid" (#2) and "numerals" (#1, because of "19" after "Covid" and other numerals after some "variant"—#4). Wokeness-inspired "pronouns" are ranked #5. The site provides the following (somewhat snarky?) definition of the term: "Wokeness—The state of being awakened to the social distresses found amongst us. Though this appears to occur for every generation it is used by politicians as a never-before-witnessed phenomenon. Favored by Progressives." https://languagemonitor.com. Accessed June 26, 2022.

8 *Fox News,* "The Woke Mob is Everywhere," https://www.foxnews.com/media/the-woke-mob-is-everywhere-heres-where-it-came-from-and-victor-davis-hansons-solution-for-stopping-it. Accessed April 3, 2024.

sees wokeness as a "radical progressive ideology" that is leading to a "soft totalitarianism"—a societally induced subservience to the state. The danger is that the "softness"—a result of its ostensibly "therapeutic" and "liberal democratic" nature—will eventually give rise to a brutal *hardness*. Imagine *The Handmaid's Tale*, but with hippie-inspired Whole Foods instead of the biblically inspired Milk and Honey.[9] Liberalism, by contrast, sees wokeness as a "messaging problem," one of unnecessarily alienating language (Latinx instead of Latino/Latina/Hispanic, community of color in place of neighborhood or simply community) and unpopular solutions to social ills (defunding the police, educational innovations such as ethnomathematics and Black English Vernacular).[10] The perceived danger is thus that wokeness *threatens the election* of centrist liberals to political office. The New York legislature, for example, must redraw the state's congressional district map because of the results of the 2020 census. And "Although there are plenty of places to cut, New York Dems"—that's *Dems*—"are reportedly eyeing Alexandria Ocasio-Cortez's Bronx district for elimination." Alexandria Ocasio-Cortez is, of course, a member of the so-called "woke squad"—denigrated on the right as a "cabal of Marxists who hate this country"[11]—consisting of three other female POC members of Congress. The reason given for eliminating her district?—"Because she's been out of sync with state-level Democrats who control the process."[12] For "out of sync" read: *woke*. Finally, those who are left of liberal proclaim that wokeness has "congealed into a stifling morass of political correctness and competitive victimhood." The socialist-oriented left, as expected, decries the fact that, with wokeness, "class politics has given way to identity politics." The perceived danger is that we are yet again distracted by manufactured superficialities, enabling the oppressive status quo to continue unhindered.[13]

---

9 See Rod Dreher, "Why are Conservatives in Despair?" *The American Conservative.* https://www.theamericanconservative.com/dreher/why-are-conservatives-in-despair. Accessed June 9, 2022; and David Brooks, "This is How Wokeness Ends," *The New York Times.* https://www.nytimes.com/2021/05/13/opinion/this-is-how-wokeness-ends.html.

10 See Sean Illing, "Wokeness Is a Problem and We All Know It," an interview with centrist Democratic extraordinaire James Carville. *Vox.* https://www.vox.com/22338417/james-carville-democratic-party-biden-100-days. Accessed June 8, 2022.

11 See "AOC's 'Squad' Blasted as 'Marxist Cabal Who Hate the US,' Book Claims." *The Sun.* https://www.thesun.co.uk/news/15349099/alexandria-ocasio-cortez-squadmarxist-cabal-new-book. Accessed June 9, 2022.

12 *The Daily Wire*, "NY Dems Are Redrawing Congressional Districts." https://www.dailywire.com/news/new-york-dems-are-redrawing-congressional-districts-and-it-could-put-alexandria-ocasio-cortez-out-of-a-job. Accessed June 8, 2022.

13 For this point and the last two quotes, see Fraser Myers, "Meet the Anti-Woke Left," *Spiked.* https://www.spiked-online.com/2019/07/04/meet-the-anti-woke-left. Accessed June

As evidence of how deeply and insidiously wokeness has infiltrated our nation's most influential—or, in the language of the conservative/right, our *elite*—institutions, news agencies spanning the political continuum mockingly point to a recent CIA recruitment video. I think it will be useful to say more about this video because it, and the pushback against it, illuminates central issues hovering around the phenomenon of "wokeness."

In the viral video, one in a series titled "Humans of CIA" (which also features a gay librarian and a blind receptionist), an intelligence officer named Mija casually strolls through the agency's Langley headquarters describing herself. She begins by telling us that on her college application she quoted Zora Neale Hurston: "I am not tragically colored. There is no sorrow damned up in my soul nor lurking behind my eyes." Mija tells us that she is a daughter of immigrants, is bilingual, and is a skilled multitasking mother. Then comes the part that met with mockery, right, left, and center.

> I am a woman of color [...] I am a cisgender millennial who's been diagnosed with generalized anxiety disorder. I am intersectional but my existence is not a box-checking exercise. I am a walking declaration. A woman whose inflection does not rise at the end of her sentences, suggesting that a question has been asked. I did not sneak into the CIA [...] I earned my way in…I used to struggle with imposter syndrome, but at thirty-six I refuse to internalize misguided patriarchal ideas of what a woman can or should be. I am tired of feeling like I am supposed to apologize for the space I occupy [...] I am unapologetically me. I want you to be unapologetically you, whoever you are.

As I said, the responses to this video momentarily united the fractured American political spectrum. In short, the responses were consistent with what I described earlier, as the perceived *dangers* of wokeness by the respective political positions. Conservatives and the right decried its dangers to national security; liberals were embarrassed at how Chinese and Russian officials must be laughing uproariously at us. And a discussion on the hard left facetiously asks, "Intersectional regime change? Queer drone strikes?" The two interlocutors in that discussion go on to analyze the way that the promotional video "weaponizes identity politics and left buzzwords to woke-wash imperialism and advance the agendas of war and empire."[14]

9, 2022.

14 *BreakThrough News*, "New Woke CIA Ad." https://www.breakthroughnews.org/post/new-woke-cia-ad. Accessed June 9, 2022. Watch journalists Katie Halper and Rania Khalek

Wokeness is routinely referred to as "liberal" or "progressive" or "leftist." It is sometimes even viewed as being of a piece with extremist thought, as with the characterization of it as a "soft totalitarianism." The right calls it left; the left calls it liberal; liberals call it progressive; progressives call it conservative. An obvious question is now staring us in the face: if even liberals and leftists find basic woke ideas such as intersectionality "cringe-worthy,"[15] where is wokeness positioned on the political spectrum? Rania Kalek of the "anti-capitalist and leftist"[16] news outlet *BreakThrough News* refers to "Woke millennial language for people in their 30s," as if wokeness were a generational linguistic phenomenon more than a universal political one.[17] As someone who has tried to live by anarchist values since a teenager, I personally find it irritating when wokeness is referred to as a variety of left-ist thought. So I just stack that assertion up to a deep ignorance of its cardinal values, such as knowing who the *real* enemies are (the ruling class, etc.), hence, unity over division, and universal solidarity as opposed to identity particularism, as we explored in the previous chapter. I also feel it ignores the fact that a "leftist" orientation worthy of the name requires robust dialogue and debate, reasoning and counter-reasoning, argument and response. So when some manifestation of "the left" (roughly from democratic liberalism through socialism and communism to anarchism) points to *its* left, and calls wokeness *that*, things get very weird. In any case, with this question about the political orientation of woke thought, I'm afraid that the matter becomes even more complex. Following Nietzsche's "genealogical" approach, we have to dig deeper into the family tree of the very term "woke."

In "Weaponizing 'Woke:' A Brief History of White Definitions," Michael Harriot, a self-described "world-renowned wypipologist,"[18] tells the origin story of the term:

> Fourscore and three years ago [in 1938], Huddie "Lead Belly" Ledbetter...explained how he came to create one of the first racism carols. Named after nine young Black men who had been falsely

discuss the video at the same URL.

15 Katie Halper in the "New Woke CIA Ad" video.

16 Mary Retta, "How to Radicalize Your Parents," *Vice*. https://www.vice.com/en/article/n7v53z/how-to-radicalize-your-parents-prison-abolition-anti-capitalism. Accessed June 10, 2022.

17 *BreakThrough News*, "New Woke CIA Ad."

18 That's *white-people-ologist*. He defines that term on his personal website: "A professional who has specialized knowledge in the field of Caucasian culture, including the political, economic, and social habits of white people and their history." https://www.michaelharriot.com. Accessed June 9, 2022.

accused of raping two white women, "Scottsboro Boys" was a protest and a warning to Black people about the evil that awaited anyone who dared traverse the borders of Alabama. At the end of the song, he told the story of meeting two of the wrongly convicted men and—just before the recording faded into silence—the legendary singer coined a phrase that would become a clarion call to Black America until white people discovered it eight decades later: "I advise everybody to be a little careful when they go down through there," Lead Belly said of Alabama. "Just stay woke. Keep your eyes open."[19]

Harriot shows that wokeness, as originally conceived "had nothing to do with progressive ideas or politics." Nothing to do with pronouns and gender identity and safe spaces? What, then? "It was about white people." It was, quite pointedly, "a warning to Black people *about white people.*" The term has not only been contorted beyond recognition with its emphasis on "identity," but has been outright "repurposed for the advancement of whiteness." This is why *New York Times* columnist Amanda Hess's widely adopted characterization of "'woke' as the inverse of 'politically correct'" misses the mark. She writes that calling someone "politically correct" was intended as a "taunt from the right, a way of *calling out* hypersensitivity in political discourse." Similarly, calling someone "woke" is now "a back-pat from the left, a way of *affirming* the sensitive." And calling yourself woke "means wanting to be considered correct, and wanting everyone to know just how correct you are."[20] How does this miss the mark? According to Harriot:

> By co-opting and transforming "woke" into a beacon for self-congratulatory allyship, white *wokeness* has been reversed-engineered into the actual thing that Black people need to stay woke about.

19 Michael Harriot, "Weaponizing 'Woke:' A Brief History of White Definitions," *The Root.* https://www.theroot.com/weaponizing-woke-an-brief-history-of-white-definitions-1848031729. Accessed June 9, 2022.

20 Amanda Hess, "Earning the 'Woke' Badge," *New York Times.* Emphases added. https://www.nytimes.com/2016/04/24/magazine/earning-the-woke-badge.html. Accessed June 9, 2022. I think that even this characterization is changing. The term "woke" is undergoing what historical linguistics refers to as "perjoration." This term denotes a form of semantic drift from being an acceptable, inoffensive term to being a negative, pejorative term. One reason for the current disavowal of the term by people who until recently accepted it as a "back-pat," is this shift, occasioned in part by conservatives' successful demonization. Adding to the general confusion around the term, a recent *USA Today* survey found that "By 56%–39%, Americans…see the word 'woke' as a positive attribute, not a negative one." https://www.usatoday.com/story/news/politics/2023/03/08/gop-war-woke-most-americans-see-term-positive-ipsos-poll/11417394002.

That "actual thing," is, again, "a warning to Black people *about white people.*" And what is it about white people that Black people need to be warned about? It is, of course, the fact of white supremacy. Harriot gives two "translations" of this term.

> *Black translation:* A system or ideology that preserves the social, political or economic power of white people over non-white people.

> *White translation:* Like racism, but intentional and supersized.

So at the root of "woke" is a life-or-death admonishment to remain vigilant in the face of deeply entrenched dangers. It is not something you *are* but something you *do,* and something you do not ever stop doing: *I stay woke!* sings Erykah Badu in "Master Teacher."

But family trees grow and change and sometimes bear unrecognizably strange fruit. Coursing through the woke family tree is the sap that nourishes Black Lives Matter, for whom *stay woke!* is an imperative for remaining vigilant in the face of brutal police tactics when demonstrating and when *living*—in a world constructed by and for white people. The same sap nourishes the sentiments behind the identity-oriented "People of CIA" videos, where "woke" is either a demonstrative, *I am woke,* or an interrogative, *are you woke?* Both usages are held by their proponents to be in the service of radical, even revolutionary, change. So we can question each of these positions. To the first, we might ask: does the insistence that the hindrance to change is an impersonal, omnipresent, and supposedly intransigent *system* offer a way forward, or does it only sow further entrenchment, hostility, and division? To the second, can language that is so easily coopted by the CIA—*the CIA!* not to mention by corporations such as Pepsi, American Express, Pfizer, and the Bank of America—*really* be all that radical, all that emancipatory, all that interested in *change*?

We can see the confusion wrought by this genealogical equivocation of terms in the public comments that opened this section. Wokeness is self-righteousness; it is a divisive viewpoint; a mature counter to the whiny immaturity of right wingers; it is what is best for all Americans; it is simply wanting Black people to have the same rights as white people; it is showing basic respect and dignity to your fellow human beings. Well, can we at least agree that it certainly is *a pretty interesting discourse*? Nietzsche would think so, at least. Let's see what else he might say about the matter. Once again—buckle up!

PUBLIC OPINION

To say it again—public opinions, private laziness.[21]

Recall the "discussion" that opens this chapter. I think we can all be excused for seeing it as little more than a nasty, thoughtless exchange. Even if it does reflect some basic issues concerning the general discourse on the topic discussed, it cannot be said to be all that *edifying*. Cannot the same be said of social media and online discussions, in general? Indeed, can it not be said of platforms for the expression of *public opinions* generally? I think it is worth considering that the situation is like that of the "great city" in front of whose gates Zarathustra finds himself one day. He is accosted there by a "foaming fool" who warns Zarathustra not to enter the city. "Oh, Zarathustra, here you have nothing to find and everything to lose. Why do you want to wade through this sludge? [...] Here great thoughts are boiled alive and cooked until they are small." It is a place that "steams with the stench of slaughtered spirit." In this city of public opinion, souls are hung out to dry "like limp, dirty rags." And it is out of these rags that *newspapers* are made. And yet, somehow, although it is a place where "all desires and vices are at home," we may nonetheless still find "virtuous people" to interact with there.[22]

I am suggesting that Nietzsche, first of all, would have us see the phenomenon of wokeness, as it currently circulates in mainstream society, whether fairly or not—namely, in the version expressed in the CIA video rather than the Black Lives Matter version—as one of *public opinion*. In Nietzsche's day, such opinion was formed, articulated, consumed, and disseminated mainly through newspapers, as well as through popular magazines, political gazettes, and the endless glut of information coming over the telegraph. All of our versions of the same can be found, of course, on the internet today. Nietzsche's point would be that, whether in his time or in ours, such public organs serve simultaneously as mirrors reflecting culture as well as instruments for influencing, indeed, for *creating* culture. Herein lies their extreme importance. Together with educational institutions, organs of public opinion play a decisive, outsized role in the creation of the very *ground* on which we live. If that ground is cultivated to a great extent by "devout sycophants" who "stir each other up and know not to what end" and who "overheat each other and know not why," well, so, too, goes the culture.[23]

---

21 *Human, All Too Human*, 482.
22 *Thus Spoke Zarathustra*, "On Passing By."
23 *Thus Spoke Zarathustra*, "On Passing By."

"Culture" is a massive load-bearing term in Nietzsche's thought. It was the central concern of his earliest works, *The Birth of Tragedy* and the four essays comprising *Untimely Meditations*. (Highlighting the role that public discourse plays in the creation of culture, an early plan of the latter work was to include an essay titled "Newspaper Slavery.") Nietzsche holds that a key requirement for "*not destroying ourselves*" is to acquire an unsurpassed "knowledge of the conditions of culture."[24] Without knowing the conditions that have formed, and that continue to form, our culture, we cannot properly diagnose it, and without a proper diagnosis we cannot change it. You may ask: And is our culture necessarily in need of change? Let us note briefly and emphatically that Nietzsche believed his nineteenth-century German culture was in dire need *of changing course*:

What I relate is the history of the next two centuries. I describe what is coming, what cannot but come: *the rise of nihilism*. This story can already be told, for necessity itself is at work here. This future already expresses itself in a hundred signs, this destiny announces itself every-where; all ears are already pricked up for this music of the future. For long now, our entire European culture has been twisting in a tortured tension that increases decade by decade, as if towards a catastrophe: restless, violent, rash—it is like a torrent rushing to *reach its end*, no longer reflecting, afraid to reflect.[25]

The point here is that Nietzsche wants us to consider whether an ideological discourse is being driven largely by "devout sycophants" or by "virtuous people." The former contribute to the rushing torrent that is cultural nihilism seeking its end. The latter contribute to nihilism's *overcoming*. Our cultural situation is, for Nietzsche, a divided pathway, where the way of devout sycophancy is broad and the way of virtue is narrow. As its agricultural metaphor suggests, culture is the soil from which actual people spring. It is the ground out of which we fashion our collective form of life. Echoing one of our earlier commenters, we have to ask: is "woke" discourse, from whatever direction, contributing to a *genuine* culture—namely, one that is *unified*, in Nietzsche's definition—or an inauthentic culture, a "pseudo-cul-ture"—one characterized by *dispersion and division*?[26] Before you answer, please consider this: some eighty-six percent of Americans get their news

24 *Human, All Too Human*, 25.
25 *NF*–1887, 11[411].
26 *Untimely Meditations*, "David Strauss: The Confessor and the Writer," 1.

and opinions from digital devices,[27] a quarter from podcasts,[28] millions from sites that "mix news with social connection, problem solving, social action, and entertainment,"[29] and all of that in a Wild West of anything-goes information-gathering options, of rabid, irreconcilable partisanship, surrealistic misinformation, totalitarian-inspired fake news, AI-enhanced deep fakes, algorithmic myopia, Orwellian perversions of language, and dystopian manipulation of our personal news feeds by Google and other tech leviathans. Is "wokeness" just more flotsam and jetsam in this steaming sea of public opinion? Or is it a cultural *countercurrent* to the violent torrent rushing unreflectively to its end? Something else altogether? How can we make such determinations? How can we get some clarity in this haze? Nietzsche recommends an approach that will sound counterintuitive to many readers. You want clarity? he asks. Then *fight, argue, struggle against one another.* In short, engage in *agon,* a form of contest radically at odds with our current rancorous arguing.

AGON

Courageous, unconcerned, mocking, violent—thus wisdom wants us: she is a woman and always loves only a warrior.[30]

Wisdom loves only a warrior because without a *struggle* against an opponent there is no wisdom to be had. Struggle, contest, *agon*, is a necessary condition for a relationship with wisdom. The stakes involved in winning the love of wisdom could not be higher; so let's slow down here. For Nietzsche, "wisdom" is nothing less than "life" itself. Not to win wisdom's heart is thus to live alienated from life. "In my heart do I love only Life," says Zarathustra. "But I am affectionate towards Wisdom, and often too affectionate, because she reminds me so very much of Life!"[31] He remonstrates

---

27 Mason Walker, "Nearly a quarter of Americans get news from podcasts," *Pew Research Center.* https://www.pewresearch.org/fact-tank/2022/02/15/nearly-a-quarter-of-americans-get-news-from-podcast. Accessed April 7, 2024.

28 Elisa Shearer, "More than eight-in-ten Americans get news from digital devices," *Pew Research Center.* https://www.pewresearch.org/short-reads/2021/01/12/more-than-eight-in-ten-americans-get-news-from-digital-devices. Accessed April 7, 2024.

29 *American Press Institute*, "How Millennials Get News: Inside the habits of America's first digital generation." https://www.americanpressinstitute.org/publications/reports/survey-research/millennials-news. Accessed June 9, 2022.

30 *Thus Spoke Zarathustra*, "On Reading and Writing."

31 *Thus Spoke Zarathustra*, "The Dance Song."

against his seeming infidelity: "How can I help it if both are so alike?" When Zarathustra spoke to Life of Wisdom's qualities, Life "laughed maliciously, and shut her eyes." "Of whom do you speak? Perhaps of me?" What, then, are the qualities that describe equally Life and Wisdom?

> And when Life once asked me, "Who is she then, this Wisdom?" I eagerly replied, "Ah, yes! Wisdom!"
>
> One thirsts for her and is not satisfied, one looks through veils, one grasps through nets. Is she beautiful? What do I know! But the oldest carps are still lured with her. She is capricious and defiant. I have often seen her bite her lip and drag the comb against the flow of her hair. Perhaps she is evil and false, and in all things a woman; but it is when she speaks ill of herself that she seduces most.

Might the seductive quality of speaking "ill" of herself come from Life-Wisdom's *honesty*? Surely, the most basic requirement of a figure that we anoint with the exalted name of "wisdom" is that it reveals what is *true of life*. Is life always, or even necessarily, *beautiful*? Can anyone other than the proudest Pollyanna deny life's occasional malice and falsity, much less its vicissitudes *and* intransigence? What might further honest reflection on life reveal? Remember: *truth is hard*!

> If we wanted to take this principle [of politeness] further, and possibly even to make it the *basic principle of society*, it would immediately be revealed for what it is: as a will to *deny* life, as a principle for dissolution and decline. We must thoroughly think through the reasons for this and resist all sentimental frailty: Life itself is *essentially* appropriation, injury, overpowering strangers and weaker people, oppression, severity, forcing one's own ways on others, annexation, and at the very least, at the very mildest, exploitation.[32]

For Nietzsche, life is *agon,* a struggle that unfolds at every level of existence. It is, moreover, not a question of the scholar's abstract theory but of everyone's practical, *verifiable,* experience. The struggle occurs in the microbiological sphere of human physiology, where organs and cells fight for nutritional resources. "Our body is but a social structure composed of many souls," insists Nietzsche.[33] So it occurs in the affective sphere of

---

32 *Beyond Good and Evil*, 259.
33 *Beyond Good and Evil*, 19.

human psychology, where our various "wills," conscious and unconscious, vie against one another for dominance (should I go to the gym or take a nap?). It occurs at the social and political levels, where worldviews, parties, and even armies clash for supremacy. And it occurs in the cultural sphere, where beliefs about who we are, or should be, as a people compete for maximal influence. What would prevent the reader from viewing the contemporary discourse on wokeness—whether you are for or against—in the terms Nietzsche gives here? One objection might be that it is talk like that in the previous passage that makes Nietzsche guilty in many contemporaries' eyes of macho, perhaps even "toxic," masculinity. But does that make his claim *untrue*? Does the aggression of the formulation disqualify it as a perspicuous insight *into life*? In fact, Nietzsche recognizes the risk he is taking, and so offers: "why should we keep using this kind of language, language that has from time immemorial been infused with a slanderous intent?" Fair enough, he concedes. But we *do* have a monumental reason, he tells us in the next breath, for *not* speaking in less "slanderous" terms. The reason is that *Life will have none of it*.

> I recently gazed into your eyes, oh Life! And there, into the unfathomable, did I appear to sink. But you pulled me out with a golden angle; you laughed mockingly when I called you unfathomable.
>
> "This is the language of all fish," you said; "what *they* do not fathom is unfathomable. But capricious am I only, and wild, and in all things a woman, and not a virtuous one at that—though I be called by you men the 'profound one,' or the 'faithful one,' 'the eternal one,' 'the mysterious one.' But you men endow us always with your own virtues—ah, you virtuous ones!"

Okay. Who can argue with Life? But perhaps we can find a good reason for refraining from such severe language in an appeal to simple *politeness*. Nietzsche will allow the possibility:

> Abstaining from injury, violence, or exploitation toward one another; to equate our own will with another person's will: this can, in a certain crude sense, develop into good manners between individuals.[34]

So can we all not just get along? Can we not intone with the Dalai Lama that "My religion is very simple. My religion is kindness." Sure. We can. But not

---

34 *Beyond Good and Evil*, 259.

yet! That would be a colossal mistake. The greatest argument against a facile, comes-too-early *kindness*, against cozy membership in a *mutual agreement society*, in which everyone feels safe from any semblance of *agon,* is that it is antithetical to the very conditions of cultural *health*. Cultural health, like personal health, consists in growth, increasing wholeness, becoming what we are individually and collectively. The forging of these qualities requires struggle. Rhetorically, at least, Nietzsche will refrain from language that some feel is "infused with a slanderous intent," but he does so only to implode that language into an even more volatile, and more essential, point: *the will to power*—a scary term that Nietzsche wants us to see not as a mere "innovative theory" but as a *"primordial fact"* of existence.[35] The will to power is a complex idea that we will encounter again; but for our present purpose, it entails making an evaluation (about some aspect of the culture war, for instance) and striving to give your view as capacious an expression as possible, perhaps even exerting influence over others regarding your evaluation.

So much for us all-too-virtuous ones, so quick to cover Life's blemishes and scars with the lovely platitudes of yet another toxin of public opinion— *toxic positivity*. Nietzsche, like Barbara Ehrenreich, believes that "there is a vast difference between positive thinking and existential courage."[36] In a seemingly direct reproach to the "sentimental frailty" of "snowflakes," liberal or conservative or whatever, Zarathustra bellows: "Life is hard to bear: but do not affect to be so delicate! We are all fine beasts of burden, us male and female asses."[37] Regarding both the pervasiveness and continual necessity of *agon*, I hope at least some of my readers—my fellow asses— will agree with Nietzsche that "people should be honest with themselves at least that far."

To sum up *agon*: A crucial assumption, woven like a thread throughout all of Nietzsche's work, is that "every natural gift must unfold in contest."[38] We come to know ourselves—our beliefs, our character, our abilities and capacity, our relation to others and to the whole—only in robust engagement with people. Indeed, *agon* is a pervasive condition throughout existence, pertaining as much to the microscopic and the psychological as to the social

35 *Beyond Good and Evil*, 259.
36 Barbara Ehrenreich, *Bright-Sided: How the Relentless Promotion of Positive Thinking Has Undermined America* (New York: Metropolitan Books, 2009), 6.
37 *Thus Spoke Zarathustra*, 1.7, "On Reading and Writing."
38 "Homer's Contest," *The Nietzsche Channel*, "Homers Wettkampf," n.p. http://www.thenietzschechannel.com/works-unpub/five/hcg.htm. Accessed June 16, 2022.

and cultural. If we are to create values that give meaning, *agon* cannot be circumvented. Life is struggle. Can any of us honestly deny *that*?

It would seem, then, that those less-than-edifying comments on the college woke article might be on the correct path after all. Surely, *agon* is on display there. But does it rise above the lowly level of mere *public opinion*? Does it unshackle itself from the bonds of *herd mentality*? It certainly doesn't do so to my liking. It might nonetheless spark insight in another reader. What is at issue is the much larger contestation of *ideology*. Wokeness is just another instance of ideology.[39] Although Nietzsche rarely uses that term,[40] I think he would agree that, ultimately, at stake in the *agon* is what constitutes the proper—the *most healthy*, in Nietzsche's language—image of society. For he is asking questions that are ideological in nature, such as: For *what* does our educational system educate us—for commerce and obedience or for the arts and idiosyncrasy? Do our politics genuinely have a healthy society as their objective, or are they focused on the special interests of commerce and the state? What kind of people are we creating, anyway? The sort who, like Nietzsche himself, are virulently anti-antisemitic, antistatist, anticonformist, or ones who show animus toward others based on some perceived "racial" difference, who happily submit to the norms of "the neighbor"? In short, what are the defining *values* of our society? Proponents of wokeness believe that their ideas self-evidently lead to a more just society, a more livable world, for all. Critics of wokeness believe that it is a divisive belief system sowing seeds of totalitarianism. To some, "labeling something as 'woke' as a means of arrogantly dismissing it, often feels like a convenient cop out for those who seem allergic to self-reflection, thoughtful analysis...or maybe accountability." To others, "*woke* is an example of good intentions leading us to hell."[41] Can we ever get a clear perspective on this, or on *any* ideology's, viability? A pervasive theme in Nietzsche's work is, in fact, *getting*

---

39 In Louis Althusser's classic definition, an ideology is a strategy that "represents the *imaginary* relationship of individuals to their real conditions of existence." See Louis Althusser, *Lenin and Philosophy and Other Essays*, translated by Ben Brewster (New York: Monthly Review Press, 2001 [1971]), 109, emphasis added. "Imaginary" should be understood in relation to the sense provided by psychoanalyst Jacques Lacan, namely, as referring to internalized images of self and reality.

40 See *Beyond Good and Evil*, 44, for instance. He is more apt to use the broader *Weltanschauung* (worldview), particularly in his letters and notebooks.

41 Both quotes from Dana Brownlee, "Exhibit A Bill Maher: Why White People Should Stop Using The Term 'Woke'...Immediately," *Forbes*, https://www.forbes.com/sites/danabrownlee/2021/04/19/why-white-people-should-stop-using-the-term-wokeimmediately/?sh=1176f0367779. Accessed April 3, 2024. Ellipsis in the original.

perspective. He wants us to see, however, that a perspective is never more than just that—*a* perspective. His thinking may prove useful to us here.

PERSPECTIVE

> To speak of spirit and the good as Plato did meant standing truth on its head and denying the perspectival itself, the basic condition of all life.[42]

How did Plato so grievously violate the truth, and what, exactly, does his violation have to do with our discussion on woke discourse? Nietzsche goes even further in castigating "Plato's invention of pure spirit and of the good in-itself" as "the worst, most prolonged, and most dangerous of all errors to this point in time." ("Pure spirit is pure lie."[43]) Plato's costly mistake is, in short, "the dogmatist's error." Nietzsche believes that Plato enshrined a way of thinking that has proven catastrophic to the West down to the present day. Not only philosophy and, for our purposes, ideology, but even physics and other sciences are trapped in "the dogmatist's error" initiated by Plato, Nietzsche holds. So what is this error? It involves the assumption of an eternal, unchanging, transcendental order, an Other World. Plato posited such a world, moreover, precisely to *enable* Truth. For only perpetual *contingency*—the opposite of Truth—is ever possible in a world of temporality, change, and immanence. To "speak of spirit and the good"—and indeed of justice, beauty, right and wrong, good and evil, even of everyday material objects like chairs—"as Plato did" means to locate their ultimate being, their essence, in a transcendental "idea" *(eidos)*. The object of contemplation or investigation, then, becomes these *ideal* forms, rather than actual, particular, perpetually becoming real instances of the form. What was Nietzsche's evaluation of such idealism? We can sum it up in one brutal judgment:

> Plato is a coward in the face of reality—*consequently*, he takes refuge in the ideal.[44]

Nietzsche denigrated any and all refuge-takings in an ideal *Hinterwelt*, a world somewhere, somehow, beyond, behind, *this* world. Throughout his

---

42 *Beyond Good and Evil*, Preface.
43 *The Antichrist*, 1.8.
44 *Twilight of the Idols*, "What I Owe the Ancients," 2.

work, Nietzsche specifically derides the Christian heaven, Buddhist nirvana, Platonic forms, and the Kantian thing-in-itself as such refuges. His main objection is that all such ideas are ultimately world-denying. Crucially, by "world," Nietzsche emphatically means *this* world, the ever-present, discernible world of our sensorium; and by "denying" he means a nihilistic negation of the very reality in which we are submerged. Plato desires a perfectly stable world *outside* of this one, a world in which we can make incontestable, definitive claims about the *Truth* of some matter, or indeed about the Whole. The consequence of Plato's desire is the obscuration of the hard *truths* that whirl around us: finitude, change, contingency, immanence. Where Plato desires the stasis of eternal Being, Nietzsche can discern only the flux of temporal becoming and so postulates that "there is no substratum, no 'being' behind [*hinter*, as in *Hinterwelt*] doing, effecting, becoming."[45]

The consequences of Nietzsche's view are enormous. Zarathustra offers the short version of those consequences: "'That is *my* way—where is *yours*?' Thus did I answer those who asked me 'the way.' For, *the* way does not exist."[46] Zarathustra does not mean this as a license to a relativistic anything-goes for the people coming to him seeking *a* way. We hear such relativism in notions such as "alternative facts" and the insistence that "X is *my* truth—you have no say in the matter." Although the former is more likely to issue from the mouth of a MAGA supporter, and the latter, perhaps, from a mainstream proponent of wokeness, each amounts to nothing more than a "pretentious substitute for 'non-negotiable personal opinion.'"[47] Zarathustra is prescribing nothing if not a *hard* way, a way of extraordinary commitment and perpetual "overcoming"; but exactly what that way is for any given individual, no one *but the individual* can ultimately say. Nietzsche is, in other words, much too focused on his positive goal of the *Übermensch* to be concerned about such a facile repercussion. Always risking being misunderstood, he nonetheless insists that we can *never* escape evaluating a matter from a relative standpoint, from *a* particular perspective.

There is *only* a perspective seeing, *only* a perspective "knowing"; and *the more* affects we allow to speak about one matter, *the more* eyes,

---

45 *On the Genealogy of Morals*, 1.13.
46 *Thus Spoke Zarathustra*, "On the Spirit of Gravity," 2.
47 *Urban Dictionary*, s.v. "My Truth," https://www.urbandictionary.com/define. php?term=My%20Truth. Accessed June 26, 2022.

different eyes, we can use to observe one matter, the more complete will our "concept" of this matter, our "objectivity," be.[48]

Is it not self-evident that the more eyes that view some X and the more angles from which they view it and the more emotional energies brought to it, the less subjective will be any one final estimation? Still, it assumes that we allow in other voices and other perspectives to intermingle with our own. Given his poor estimation of us (barely) humans, Nietzsche has little faith that we will ever actually do the work required to come to a more complete view of any given matter. "The vast majority of people," he says, "lack an intellectual conscience."

> What I want to say is: *the vast majority of people* do not consider it contemptible to believe this or that and to live accordingly *without* first becoming aware of the final and most certain reasons *for and against*, and without even troubling themselves about such reasons afterwards: even the most gifted men and the noblest women belong to this "vast majority."[49]

Agon can take us some of the way toward developing such an intellectual conscience, but only if we are open, precisely, to *other perspectives.* Let's look at a current example. Alexandria Ocasio-Cortez recently took to task her fellow Democrats who, in one reporter's words, "refuse to adopt the woke vernacular"[50] of terms such as "Latinx" (pronounced: Latin-ex) for "Latino/Latina/Hispanic." Let's review a couple of points before we look at what the progressive congresswoman said. First, language changes all the time. According to the Global Language Monitor, "a new word is created every 98 minutes, about 14.7 words a day or 5400 words a year."[51] English-language dictionaries add around one thousand of these new words every year.[52] Surely, seeking a gender-neutral term like Latinx, particularly in an arguably (obviously?) patriarchal world, is an honorable project. Think

---

48 *On the Genealogy of Morals*, 3.12.
49 *The Gay Science*, 2.
50 Chris Enloe, "AOC attacks members of her own party," *Blaze Media*, https://www.theblaze.com/news/alexandria-ocasio-cortez-rant-democrats-latinx. Accessed June 26, 2022.
51 *The Global Language Monitor*, https://languagemonitor.com/category/number-ofwords. Accessed June 26, 2022.
52 See Andy Bodle, "How New Words Are Born," *The Guardian*, https://www.theguardian.com/media/mind-your-language/2016/feb/04/english-neologisms-new-words. Accessed June 26, 2022.

of the widespread adoption of "Ms." in the 1970s as a parallel to "Mr.," obscuring marital status. Second, in terms of mainstream American politics, I admire Alexandria Ocasio-Cortez more than any other active US politician, both for the majority of her policy positions and for her personal courage and integrity. I mention this to disabuse anyone of the notion that I am biased against her here. In fact, my close political alignment with her allows me all the better to make my point about the importance of broadening our—my— perspective. So what did Ocasio-Cortez say in her Instagram story?

> In the spirit of pride [day], I wanted to have a note on gender inclu- sivity in the Spanish language. People sometimes like to make a lot of drama over the term "Latinx." [...] Gender is fluid, language is fluid. [You] don't have to make drama over it. There are some politicians— including Democratic politicians—that rail against the term "Latinx." And they're like, "This is so bad. This is so bad for the party like, blah, blah blah." And like, it's almost as though it has not struck some of these folks that another person's identity is not about your re-election prospects. Like, this is not about you.

If a community of people wants to be referred to by a certain term, then so be it—*this is about them, not you or me.* The issue hardly seems controversial. But what if the community in question does *not* want to be referred to by the term? Gallup recently asked people who identified as "Hispanic" whether they preferred the term "Hispanic," "Latino," or "Latinx." Only 4% said they prefer "Latinx."[53] A similar survey by the left-leaning news source *Politico* arrived at a mere 2% result.[54] One Democratic congressman, Ruben Gallego, of Arizona, who does not permit his office workers to use "Latinx" in their official correspondence, offers an explanation. He says, "When Latino polit- icos use the term, it is largely to appease white rich progressives who think that is the term we use. It is a vicious circle of confirmation bias."[55] An uncomfortable question for liberal readers, at least concerning the issue at hand: might *Fox News* have a point when it proclaims that "wokeness...has

53 *Gallup,* "No Preferred Racial Term Among Most Black, Hispanic Adults," https:// news.gallup.com/poll/353000/no-preferred-racial-term-among-black-hispanic-adults.aspx. Accessed June 26, 2022.

54 *Politico,* "The Use of 'LatinX' by Hispanic Voters," chrome-extension:// efaidnbmnnnibpcajpcglclefindmkaj/https://www.politico.com/f/?id=0000017d-81be-dee4- a5ff-efbe74ec0000. Accessed June 26, 2022.

55 Chris Enloe, "AOC attacks members of her own party," *Blaze Media,* https://www. theblaze.com/news/alexandria-ocasio-cortez-rant-democrats-latinx. Accessed June 26, 2022.

succeeded in spite of a lack of public support."[56] Another obvious question arises: if not "the public," whom *does* the term "Latinx" serve?

Critics of wokeness have an answer to that question. Their answer also serves as their explanation for the discrepancy between Ocasio-Cortez's belief that "Latinx" is a term of "inclusivity" and its preference for a mere 4% of *actual* "Latinx" people surveyed. The answer: elitism. Let's be clear. When American conservatives say "elite" they *do not* mean the "75,000 Americans whose wealth is actually higher than $50 million"[57] or even the 664 American billionaires, whose collective wealth increased by $1.3 trillion after less than a year into the coronavirus pandemic.[58] No. They mean anyone they perceive as possessing the following attributes: highly educated, cultured, living in a coastal urban area, in a position of influence, and *not conservative*. Republican presidential nominee John McCain summed up the conservative definition of the term for a reporter who asked him to define "elite." McCain, in a presidential campaign against Barack Obama at the time, said, "I know where a lot of them live—in our nation's capital and New York City—the ones [that running mate Sarah Palin] never went to a cocktail party with in Georgetown—who think that they can dictate what they believe to America rather than let Americans decide for themselves."[59] Thus did longtime Washington insider, John McCain,

> the son and grandson of admirals, a millionaire who couldn't remember how many houses he owned, accuse his mixed-race opponent, raised by a single-mother and only a few years past paying off his student loans, of being the real elite candidate in the campaign.[60]

What makes Obama "elite" in conservative circles is that the attributes I mentioned apply to him. Thus, he is supposedly presumptuous, arrogant, out of touch with "real people," and so on.

56 Kelsey Koberg, "The Woke Mob is Everywhere." *Fox News.* https://www.foxnews.com/media/the-woke-mob-is-everywhere-heres-where-it-came-from-and-victor-davis-hansons-solution-for-stopping-it. Accessed June 8, 2022.
57 Nancy LeTourneau, *Washington Monthly*, "Republicans are the Party of the Wealthy Elite," https://washingtonmonthly.com/2019/10/22/republicans-are-the-party-of-the-wealthy-elite-2. Accessed June 26, 2022.
58 "Billionaires Are $2.2 Trillion Richer Since 2017 Trump-GOP Tax Law." https://americansfortaxfairness.org/billionaires. Accessed June 26, 2022.
59 Jacob Weisberg, "Elite Nonsense," *Slate*, https://slate.com/news-and-politics/2010/10/the-right-s-favorite-scare-word-is-elitism-what-does-it-mean.html. Accessed June 27, 2022.
60 Weisberg, "Elite Nonsense." Accessed June 27, 2022.

As we saw previously, when conservatives and right wing pundits scream that "THE WOKE MOB IS EVERYWHERE!"[61] they mean that institutions as diverse as the military, news media, philanthropy, publishing, higher education, and government are unduly influenced by "the elite" in their very midst. By far the worst culprit of woke influence, however, is the press, particularly *The New York Times*. So let's consider whether there might be merit to the conservative/right wing contention that media is, via its influence on institutional leaders, driving woke discourse ever more deeply into our collective social consciousness. If it is true, might that shift in perspective lead to a sharpened "intellectual conscience" for us?

Conservatives recognize that "if your aim is to change the world, journalism is a more immediate short-term weapon," as playwright Tom Stoppard says. That is the actual epigraph for a study titled, "Expertise in Journalism: Factors Shaping a Cognitive and Culturally Elite Profession."[62] That study shows that, yes, "almost half of the people who reach the pinnacle of the journalism profession"—namely, *The New York Times* and *The Wall Street Journal*, the subjects of the study—"attended an elite school and were likely in the top 1% of cognitive ability." However, I want to call your attention to another data-driven study. In "How the Media Led the Great Racial Awakening," Zach Goldberg, a self-described "Wokeness Studies scholar researching all things woke," aims to show that "the explosion in the usage of racialized terminology and ideological constructs isn't simply a neutral reflection of an increase in racial incidents." Key "woke" concepts, of course, center on race and racial justice, including notions such as *white privilege, intersectionality, microaggression, Black erasure,* and *white fragility.* So Goldberg wants to show that by drastically increasing their usage of such language in their reporting by some 700–1000% in recent years, publications such as *The New York Times* "have helped normalize among their readership the belief that 'color' is the defining attribute of other human beings." If true, one of the ramifications of this "normalization" would be that "it has made stereotypes socially acceptable, if not laudable." In place of his many graphs and statistics, I give you Goldberg's conclusion.

What the data presented here suggests is that editorial decisions made over the past decade at some of the most powerful media outlets in

---

61 *Fox News,* "The Woke Mob is Everywhere."
62 By Jonathan Wai and Kaja Perina, in the peer-reviewed *Journal of Expertise,* https://www.journalofexpertise.org/articles/volume1_issue1/JoE_2018_1_1_Wai_Perina.html. Accessed June 27, 2022.

the world about what kind of language to use and what kind of stories merited coverage when it came to race—whatever the intention and level of forethought behind such decisions—has stoked a revival of racial consciousness among their readers. Intentionally or not, by introducing and then constantly repeating a set of key words and concepts, publications like *The New York Times* have helped normalize among their readership the belief that "color" is the defining attribute of other human beings. For those who adopt this singular focus on race, a racialized view of the world becomes the baseline test of political loyalty. It requires adherents to overlook the immense diversity among so-called "People of Color" and "People Not-of-Color" (*i.e.*, whoever is being lumped together as "white" according to the prevailing ideological fashion). In doing so, it has made stereotypes socially acceptable, if not laudable.

Now, many left-leaning readers will likely reject this conclusion, indeed, the very data, because it turns out that Goldberg is a fellow of the Manhattan Institute of Policy Research. According to *Media Bias/Fact Check*, Manhattan Institute is "moderately to strongly biased toward conservative causes through story selection and/or political affiliation." Does that fact, however, invalidate his data and make his argument *wrong*? Here's another wrinkle: much of Goldberg's data is drawn from "least biased" PEW Foundation and "left-center biased" institutions such as the Kaiser Family Foundation, *The New York Times*, *The Washington Post*, and *The Los Angeles Times*.[63] Do those sources make it more credible (or perhaps less credible) for you? We can quibble endlessly about the methodology, analysis, and conclusions of Goldberg's study. So, to make my point clear, let's try a Nietzschean experiment. Suppose you *reject* the conservative contention that woke concepts such as white privilege and intersectionality are fueled by "elitist" institutions. Suppose, now, that Goldberg's data and conclusion prove to be indisputably correct. Think about it. Has your perspective shifted? How? Now, consider the fact that Goldberg himself is right-leaning. Does your perspective shift again? How, exactly, and *why*—remember, in our thought experiment his data and conclusion are indisputably correct. Finally, consider that much of his data is taken from *liberal-leaning* sources. Take it all in. What is your final perspective?

---

63 *Media Bias/Fact Check*, https://mediabiasfactcheck.com. Accessed July 27, 2022.

Nietzsche is well aware of what is at stake in exercising your intellectual conscience. Your in-group will give you strange looks. You will feel isolated. You might even be ostracized. But what is the alternative to living with your intellectual conscience robustly activated? The strange thing is that *doing* so—that is, longing to consider reasons *for and against*—is considered contemptible, while remaining snug in our in-group's perspective is considered honorable. Perhaps that is why the "vast majority" of us prefer groupthink to intellectual conscientiousness. Here's Nietzsche in full.

Intellectual conscience. I have the same experience over and over, and resist it anew each time. I do not want to believe it even though I grasp it with my hands: *the vast majority of people lack an intellectual conscience.* Yes, it has often seemed to me as if someone demanding such a conscience would be as lonely in the most populated cities as in the desert. Everyone looks at you with strange eyes and works their weighing scales as before, calling this good and that evil; nobody blushes with shame when you let it be known that their weights are underweight—nor do they respond with outrage toward you; perhaps they laugh at your doubts. What I want to say is: *the vast majority of people* do not consider it contemptible to believe this or that and to live accordingly *without* first becoming aware of the final and most certain reasons *for and against*, and without even troubling themselves about such reasons afterwards: even the most gifted men and the noblest women belong to this "vast majority." But what are goodheartedness, refinement, and genius to me when the person possessing these virtues tolerates lax feelings in belief and judgment, and when the *demand for certainty* is not his innermost longing and deepest necessity—as that which separates the higher human beings from the lower! I discovered in certain pious people a hatred against reason, and that was fine with me: at least this hatred revealed their bad intellectual conscience! But to stand in the midst of this *rerum concordia discors* [discordant harmony of things] and the whole wonderful uncertainty and ambiguity of existence *without questioning*, without trembling with the longing and rapture of questioning, without at least hating the person who questions, perhaps even taking a dim delight in him—that is what I feel to be *contemptible*, and it is this feeling that I first look for in everyone—some sort of foolishness keeps convincing me that every person must have this feeling, simply as a human being. That is my type of injustice.[64]

You may doubt whether there is indeed pleasure to be had in such questioning, much less pleasure enough to make the social and emotional risks worthwhile. Nietzsche himself seemed to find at least a dim delight in his compulsion to consider an idea from discordant perspectives. An *incomplete* reading of his work could justify the perspective that Nietzsche praised and recommended Kant, Schopenhauer, Spinoza, and other thinkers. Another *incomplete* reading could justify the perspective that he disparaged those same thinkers. Incomplete readings of his work could justify the perspective that he by turns admired or despised figures such as Napoleon and Machiavelli, by turns advocated or barred reasoning, the will, the passions, even pity and compassion. A *complete* reading, however, entails another perspective entirely, one that requires us to stand courageously in the midst of the *discordant harmony of things*. Let's briefly take as an example one of Nietzsche's most fervent love/hate relationships: Socrates. In a section titled "The Problem with Socrates," Nietzsche writes:

> From his very origins, Socrates belongs to the lowliest of people: Socrates was rabble...Not only the acknowledged desolation and anarchy of the instincts point to Socrates's *décadence*: there also points to the double pregnancy of the logical and misshapen malice that characterize him. And let's not forget those aural hallucinations, which were interpreted in a religious sense as the "dæmon of Socrates." Everything about him is exaggerated, buffoonish, caricature. At the same time, everything is hidden, ulterior, subterranean.[65]

Socrates is a problem, too, because of his unleashing of "tyrannical rationality" into Greek culture, spelling the doom of one of the noblest cultures ever for Nietzsche, the Greek Archaic. Worse, Socrates's life-exhaustion, his low estimation of *this* life, his hatred of becoming and longing for being, make him the instigator of accursed "modern" ways of (nihilistic) thinking and action. So for Nietzsche, Socrates is, indeed, a noxious influence on Western culture. And yet, looked at from another perspective:

---

64 *The Gay Science*, 1.2
65 *Twilight of the Idols*, "The Problem with Socrates," 3, 4.

I have given reasons why Socrates can be repellant: it remains all the more necessary to explain why he fascinates. The first is that he discovered a new type of *agon*, that he was its first fencing master in Athens' most noble circles…But Socrates discovered something more. He saw *behind* the noble Athenians; he grasped that his case, his idiosyncratic case was already *not* the exception. The same type of degeneracy was spreading in silence all over: the old Athens was coming to its end. And Socrates understood that the entire world needed him—his medicine, his cure, his personal artfulness for self-preservation.[66]

Socrates *must* be considered from various perspectives because, for better or for worse, he became for us a healer, "a physician, a savior." In fact, Socrates is the very model of "how a philosopher ought to behave toward men," namely, "as their physician, as a gadfly on the neck of man."[67] You might ask: a savior *and* a buffoon…*and* a model philosopher? From another perspective entirely, Nietzsche, the self-proclaimed first psychologist among the philosophers, the man who Sigmund Freud reportedly said "had a more penetrating knowledge of himself than any other man who ever lived or was ever likely to live,"[68] offers us a perspective from within his psyche, so to speak: "Socrates, just to confess it, is so close to me that I almost constantly fight with him."[69] Also from *deep down*: "I have a terrible fear that I will one day be pronounced holy…I do not want to be a holy man, rather a buffoon— perhaps I am a buffoon."[70] Like…*Socrates*?

Nietzsche recognizes the complex contradictoriness of the matters he takes up because he intimately *lives* them. Might that, too, be a recommendation to us? Nietzsche admits that he is "at the same time a *decadent* and a *beginning.*" Can we admit the same for ourselves? We, too, are functioning as *decadents* when we respond to woke/ideological discourse and its many issues concerning social justice without *longing to consider reasons for and against* its positions. In eschewing such "rapture of questioning," decadents, by definition, betray a deep *exhaustion*, one that amounts to denial of life itself. I will leave it to the reader to decide if such woke-inspired phenomena

---

66 *Twilight of the Idols*, "The Problem with Socrates," 8, 9.
67 Cited and translated in Walter Kaufmann, *Nietzsche: Psychologist, Philosopher, Antichrist* (Princeton: Princeton University Press, 2013 [1950]), 398.
68 Ernest Jones, a member of Freud's close inner circle, reports this secondhand. He heard Freud say it during the 1908 meeting of the Vienna Psychoanalytic Society. Ernest Jones, *The Life and Work of Sigmund Freud*, Vol. 2 (New York: Basic Books, 1955), 344.
69 *NF*–1875, 6[3].
70 *Ecce Homo*, "Why I Am A Destiny," 1.

as safe spaces, trigger warnings, tiptoeing around pronouns, fear of misgendering and of simply using the wrong word for some X in conversation—all very real in many circles today—constitute evidence of "pathological" oversensitivity.[71] But for Nietzsche, such ideological reactivity, such sensitivity, is always a sure sign of cultural decadence and, even worse, an ominous symptom of creeping nihilism. But there is an alternative. And that is for us to function as *beginnings*. We do so when we act on our intellectual conscience, risking censure and ostracization. The risk is necessary if culture is to be *healthy*, which means ascending, growing, increasing our collective intelligence, tending toward *unification* rather than division. Nietzsche says that it is his honest recognition of being potentially either a *decadent* or a *beginning* that "explains that neutrality, that freedom from all partiality in relation to the total problem of life, that perhaps distinguishes me…I know both. I am both."[72]

Tarrying in perspectival contradiction is crucial for two specific benefits it enables. First, it jolts us out of our narrow, preservation-driven, groupthink: "Insight: every value judgment concerns a specific perspective: *preservation* of an individual, a community, a race, a state, a church, a belief, a culture. By virtue of *forgetting* that there is only perspective evaluation, everything teems with contradictory evaluations and, *consequently*, with *contradictory drives in a single person*."[73] Such a condition of momentary forgetting of our narrow perspective leads to the second benefit: "this creature, so full of contradictions, has in his very being an excellent method of acquiring *knowledge*: he feels many pros and cons, he attains to *justice*—to a comprehension of *evaluating beyond good or evil*. The wisest person is *richest in contradictions*."[74] Mention of "knowledge" should disabuse any readers that Nietzsche is an anything-goes relativist: "In so far as the word 'knowledge' has any meaning at all, the world is knowable: it can, however, be interpreted variously, it has no meaning hidden behind it, but rather innumerable meanings which can be assigned to it—'perspectivism.'"[75] Hence, too, the *necessity* of actively seeking different perspectives, of interminably cultivating our intellectual conscience.

---

71 *Twilight of the Idols*, "What the Germans Lack," 6.
72 *Ecce Homo*, "Why I Am So Wise," 1.
73 *NF*–1884, 26[119].
74 *NF*–1884, 26[119].
75 *NF*–1886, 7[60].

FOUR READINGS

In the spirit of inciting the cultivation of *intellectual conscience,* I'd like to present several passages that speak to the matter. The first two are remarkably (for Nietzsche) *prescriptive* in nature. These passages will be most interesting if you bear in mind, as you read, an actual ideological commitment of yours. (Think: a conviction from religion or spirituality; politics; the culture wars; technology; LGBTQI+ issues; race and ethnic issues, and so on.)

1. In the first selection, Nietzsche explains his method of "waging war." By "war" we should understand the struggle of *agon.* Nietzsche's preliminary rule for *waging war* is to engage people at your own level of capability. Only then is the engagement just: "Where one feels contempt, one *cannot* wage war; where one commands, where one sees something beneath oneself, one has no grounds for waging war." He then sums up his practice:

First. I only attack matters that are already victorious—I even wait if necessary until they are victorious.

Second. I only attack matters where I would find no allies, where I stand alone—where I compromise myself alone [...] I have never taken a public step where I did not compromise myself. That is *my* criterion of right action.

Third. I never attack people. I use people as a strong magnifying glass with which one can make visible a general, lingering, and barely tangible difficulty…

Fourth. I only attack things where every personal disagreement is excluded, where any background of bad experience is lacking. On the contrary, attacking is for me evidence of goodwill, under certain conditions, even of gratitude. I honor, I distinguish a matter or a person by relating my name to them: for or against—that does not matter to me.[76]

2. Nietzsche began his writing career at a time of great social promise. Under the iron-fisted conservative chancellor Otto von Bismarck, German unification had just occurred. For a brief moment, social, political, and cultural

---

76 *Ecce Homo,* "Why I Am So Wise," 7.

institutions were open to transformation. The tension of such a moment, however, meant that simultaneously, a great *Kulturkampf*, much like our own "culture war," was being waged. Nietzsche's greatest concern at this initial opening was for educational innovation. He lectured publicly and wrote privately advocating his ideas, and his hope, for an educational system that would serve his high conceptions of culture. But it quickly became clear that any such hope would be cruelly dashed by Bismarck's *"defeat, indeed extirpation, of the German spirit in favor of the 'German Reich.'"*[77] The "German spirit" was capable of a cultural renewal, if only the educational system would stimulate creativity and genius. Instead, the system that the bureaucrats were crafting ensured that the spirit of creativity would be "swept away by the despicable money economy…a *rapid* education, so that one quickly becomes a money-earner." In this passage, under the guise of a general program of education, Nietzsche offers three suggestions on how to foster a "noble culture."

Learn to *see*—accustom the eye to composure, patience, to allowing it to come-into-its-own; to postponing judgment, to learn to survey and grasp a single matter from all sides. This is the *first* preliminary lesson in intellectuality: *not* to react immediately, but rather to take control of the inhibiting, the finalizing, instincts. Learning to *see*, as I understand it, is nearly that which unphilosophical language calls strong will: the essential point here is precisely *not* "willing," being *able* to forego a decision. All unintellectuality, all coarseness, touches on the inability to resist a stimulation—one *must* react, one follows every impulse. In many cases, such a *must* is already pathology, decline, a symptom of exhaustion—nearly everything that unphilosophical rawness characterizes as a "vice" is merely this physiological inability *not* to react. A practical application of having-learned-to-see: as a *learner*, one becomes generally slow, suspicious, reluctant. With an initial hostile silence, one allows everything that is strange, *newness* of every kind, to draw near—one pulls his hand away from it.[78]

3. A recent article in *Psychology Today* says that "thinking unconditionally, or un-contextually, characterizes wokeism."[79] We can, of course, say the same

---

77 *Untimely Meditations*, "David Strauss, the Confessor and the Writer," 1. Italics in original.
78 *Twilight of the Idols*, "What the Germans Lack," 6.
79 Michael Karson, "The Psychology of 'Wokeism,'" *Psychology Today*, https://www.psychologytoday.com/us/blog/feeling-our-way/202108/the-psychology-wokeism. Accessed

for *any and all* forms of rigid ideological commitment. *Context* complicates matters—indeed, often to the point of eradicating our very position, of evaporating our cherished belief. Recall that Nietzsche labels Plato a "coward" precisely because of his insistence on the *unconditionality* of truth.

> Objection, infidelity, cheerful mistrust, delight in mockery are signs of health: everything unconditional belongs in pathology.[80]

4. The "philosopher" is often a symbol of Nietzsche's ideal subject as thinker and investigator. As our final passage tells us, the "philosopher" must *of necessity* be filled with the very "if and buts" of "surveying and grasping a single matter from all sides."

> With the same necessity that a tree bears its fruit, out of us grow our thoughts, our values, our yeas and nays, our *ifs* and *buts*—related and connected to one another and witnesses of *one* will, *one* health, *one* earth, *one* sun. Do these fruits of ours taste good to you? But what does that matter to the trees! What does that matter to us philosophers![81]

In honor of the discordant harmony of things, may we know *one will, one health, one earth, one sun.*

June 27, 2022.
80 *Beyond Good and Evil*, 154.
81 *On the Genealogy of Morals*, Prologue, 2.

OVERCOMING

WE NOW COME TO THE QUESTION OF WHAT TO DO. IN THE BROADEST TERMS, Nietzsche's answer is: *overcome!* Our way to this conclusion, to this destination, will be winding and steep, and not without danger. Before considering what Nietzsche means by "overcoming," I will warn the reader of the greatest danger that lurks in this chapter. The danger is *the animal*. This danger, though, is *not* the animal as predatory beast among whom we must warily live and struggle. This danger is also not the excessively aggressive *human* understood metaphorically as animal. Neither is it the *animal within*, awaiting its every opportunity to slip the precarious binds of human reason and unleash bestial violence on ourselves and on others. None of this is the danger that we face in this chapter. The danger lies in the fact that Nietzsche wants to convince you that you *are* an animal, and that that's a good, or in Nietzschean terms, a *necessary* thing. For Nietzsche, the real danger—to ourselves, to society, to the future—is that we humans *forget* our animal inheritance. This inheritance is, for Nietzsche, a living treasure, one that we must not only continually remember, but actively draw on in the present. The danger here deepens: Nietzsche wants you to realize that the animal means *culture* while the human means *civilization*. It gets steeper still: animal-culture means openness, creativity, possibility, and human-civilization means constriction, conformity, monotony. In short, Nietzsche wants to convince us that "the terrible basic text of *homo natura* must again be recognized."[1] Nietzsche describes this text as one that aims "to translate the human back into nature." And the human in nature is, as we admit, animal. Civilization is our supposed saving grace *from* nature, *from* the animal; so what can Nietzsche possibly be asking of us here? Ultimately, the danger is that the reader will reject this "terrible" possibility out of hand, and we will have gotten nowhere. So, yet again, let's slow down.

What follows is organized according to the following logic. First, we will review the *reason* that Nietzsche engages in his philosophy at all. In Nietzsche's thinking, the very soil of our civilization is steeped in a

---

1 *Beyond Good and Evil*, 230.

contaminant so noxious, so insidious, that it affects everything that touches it. That contaminant is *nihilism*. Second, once we recognize this fundamental condition of our modern civilization, we can begin our resistance to its virulent effects. We do so by *becoming who we are*. What we *are* is something other than the "tame, hopelessly mediocre, and insipid people"[2] that nihilistic civilization has twisted us into. Just to disabuse any readers who sense that Nietzsche might be playing the spiritualist guru here, or indeed the neoliberal life coach, I will repeat that this *becoming* involves a close, all-too-close, identification of the human with *the animal*. Nietzsche, note, is not being metaphorical here. Third, we will consider more closely Nietzsche's interconnected conceptions of *nature, body,* and *animal* and how these interact with "civilization." Fourth, to get a better sense of how Nietzsche connects "nature," and so on, with *becoming who you are*, we will consider a few exemplary types. Mostly, these types are abstract, such as *the free spirit, the Hyperborean, the artist, the new philosopher, the immoralist*, and the omnipresent *We*. In a few instances, however, Nietzsche names historical figures, such as Goethe, Cesare Borgia, and Napoleon (it's not what you think!). Fifth, we will turn to Nietzsche's most famous figure and exemplar extraordinaire, *the Übermensch*. Finally, we will consider formative Nietzschean values: curiosity, courage, pathos of distance, solitude, and humor. Here we go. Buckle up!

NIHILISM

Recall that Nietzsche insists that if we, as a civilization, are "to keep from destroying ourselves,"[3] we must "set ourselves ecumenical goals, embracing the whole earth" and that this project requires that we "first discover *knowledge of the conditions of culture*." What are these conditions of culture of which we must become aware? The first and foremost condition is the fact of *nihilism*. The catalyst of Nietzsche's entire *oeuvre* is founded on what he presumes to be a discernment of a cultural-civilizational condition of such enormity that the only way forward is to experiment with new personal subjectivities, fresh forms of thought, and free-spirited ways of life. In killing God, the source of our meaning and the guarantor of our values for millennia, we all-too clever moderns have severed the seam of the Great Chain of Being. In so doing, we murderers among all murderers have opened up

---

2 *On the Genealogy of Morals*, 1.11.

3 This and following quotes, *Human, All Too Human*, 25.

an unfathomable abyss of loss. Although still as oblivious to the fact as the madman's mocking interlocutors in the marketplace, we are mired in an existential crisis so thick, so opaque, that we cannot even discern it. Indeed, Nietzsche speaks of nihilism as if it were a kind of dark matter that is simultaneously hidden and hyperreal. At his most general, Nietzsche's treatment of nihilism brings to mind Mark Fisher's haunting description of capitalism as "a pervasive atmosphere, conditioning not only the production of culture but also the regulation of work and education, and acting as a kind of invisible barrier constraining thought and action."[4] Nihilism is simply in the air, indeed, *is* the air; it is the very chemical essence of the stuff we breathe. As such, it courses continuously through our consciousness and bodies, singly and collectively, resulting in "the radical repudiation of value, meaning, and desirability" that swirls in our midst. When Nietzsche evokes "the uncanniest of guests" lurking perpetually at our doorways, he is presenting an image of inescapability. To get anywhere, to do anything, must you not first pass through your doorway? In this image, nihilism cannot be avoided. Nihilism saturates our civilizational soil the way pesticides, lead, radon, asbestos, petroleum products, assorted chemicals, solvents, and heavy metals permeate our earthly soil. It follows, then, that no production of the culture arises unscathed by the contaminant nihilism. We can, of course, tighten up the metaphor and name the corrupting contaminants. As we have seen, they are basically the moral fallout from the epochal death of God, in short: "poison, slander, negation of life, hatred of the body, the degradation and self-violation of humans through the concept of sin."[5] We can add other ideas associated with Christianity: resentment; meekness; obedience; equality; love of the neighbor; belief in another, truer world; postmortem existence; ascetic innervation of passion. These qualities are nihilistic because they serve the repudiation of *this* world, the diminishment of *this* life, and the denigration of *this* body.

It is important to note two matters concerning Nietzsche's thinking on the topic of nihilism. The first matter is that he was still in the process of working out his conception when his mental collapse brought an end to his work. What we have are numerous fragments. He is, however, explicit about his general intention. In a passage discussing the problem of meaning, Nietzsche announces that he intends to probe the matter "more thoroughly

---

4 Mark Fisher, *Capitalist Realism: Is There No Alternative?* (Winchester: Zero Books, 2009), 2.
5 *The Antichrist*, 56.

and rigorously"[6] in a section titled "On the History of European Nihilism." Although he conceived of the book in which this history would be contained as *The Will to Power: Attempt at a Revaluation of All Values*, the book that we currently have under that title is the concoction of his sister, Elizabeth Förster-Nietzsche and Nietzsche's old friend Peter Gast (Heinrich Köselitz). The notes that we have are extensive, rich, and highly suggestive, yet incomplete notes just the same. The second matter is that, in those initial notes, Nietzsche takes pains to bring nuance to his examination of European nihilism. For example, he speaks of "the most extreme form of nihilism: nothingness ('meaninglessness') eternal!"[7] This idea—that nihilism holds that nothing ultimately exists and so there can be no basis for meaning—seems to be the form that the concept takes in the popular imagination today. He also names a *radical nihilism* and defines it as "the conviction of an absolute untenability of existence when it comes to the highest values that we recognize, including the insight that we possess not the slightest right to postulate a beyond or an in-itself, which is held to be 'divine,' morality incarnate."[8] Indeed, this statement echoes one of Nietzsche's most well-known definitions of the term: "Nihilism: the goal is lacking; the answer to the question 'why?' is lacking. What does nihilism mean?—*that the highest values devalue themselves*."[9] Why do our highest values devalue themselves? I imagine that Nietzsche's logic here will strike many readers as counterintuitive. Basically, it goes like this. Our values are like promissory notes that we slap on our moral convictions; and our moral convictions are like contracts with the force of a medieval indulgence. The empty core of this value-morality nexus is derived from the severe fact that *existence contradicts it*: "*This is the antimony*: in so far as we believe in morality, we *condemn* existence."[10] Having struggled for survival over millennia, however, we have, in addition to moral values, cultivated a "will to existence."[11] And it is due to the impetus of this will that we have, finally, "nurtured 'truthfulness.'"[12] Ultimately, this is the reason that our precious values inevitably devalue themselves. Our drive for the truthfulness of some matter eventually uncovers the hollow core of our moral concepts. Even the highest of high values, "God," became, over centuries of honest inquiry, "God is dead."

---

6 *On the Genealogy of Morals*, 3.27.

7 *NF*–1886, 5[71].

8 *NF*–1887, 10[192].

9 *NF*–1887, 9[35].

10 *NF*–1887, 10[192].

11 *NF*–1887, 10[192].

12 *NF*–1887, 10[192].

Nietzsche emphasizes that we have now reached the point in history where nihilism *"is a normal condition."*[13] Indeed, Nietzsche adds two nuances that give the reader a feeling of *no escape* from perverse normalcy. I am referring to his distinction between *passive nihilism* and *active nihilism.* In short:

Nihilism as a sign for the *increased power of spirit*: as active nihilism.

Nihilism as *decline and regression of the power of spirit*: passive nihilism.[14]

Passive nihilism is what most of us think of as nihilism per se. It is a condition characterized by exhaustion. Have you ever found yourself complaining that everything is meaningless, that your actions are pointless, that the world is Hell and nothing can be done about it, that nothing will ever fundamentally change, that nothing really matters, and so on and so forth? If so, you might be a passive nihilist! This is not to say that you may not also be *correct* in your dire assessments. The passive nihilist sees into the hollow core of our "highest values" and is overcome by a deep sense of futility. Their depression makes them incapable of creating new values and meanings. New values? Won't they, too, merely reveal themselves to be hollow? A crucial nuance of Nietzsche's view is that a nihilistic outlook must never be but a passing stage.

Nihilism represents a pathological *intermediary stage* (pathological is the massive generalization it entails, the conclusion that there is *no meaning whatsoever*): either the productive forces are not yet strong enough, or decadence still hesitates and has not yet invented its remedies.[15]

When the passive nihilist does start inventing remedies, these always come in the guise of some external form. As long as the passive nihilist at least keeps going, something that "refreshes, heals, calms, and numbs will come into the foreground under various *disguises*, be they religious, or moral, or political, or aesthetic, etc." As this point shows, invention is not sufficient for evading nihilism if it involves a nihilistic disguise masked as a "solution."

---

13 *NF*–1887, 9[35].
14 *NF*–1887, 9[35].
15 *NF*–1887, 9[35].

In contrast to passive nihilism, *active nihilism* is energetic. In fact, Nietzsche contends that in the active nihilist "the spirit may have grown so strong that its 'convictions,' articles of faith, become inappropriate." They become inappropriate, of course, because they have been revealed to be hollow and proven to be impotent. So let's take the active nihilist test. Do you experience a persistent, gnawing apprehension about the actual *value* of your values and of those in your social circle? Do you find that this apprehension arouses in you a desire to struggle with the doubt, perhaps even spurs intimations of a *new passion*, a seeking mind, a will to meaning, a newfound *fertility* of inner resources? Have you ever experienced active nihilism's "maximum of relative strength as a power of destruction?"[16] If you answered *yes*... Nietzsche, in fact, offers himself as an example of the active nihilist.

> On the genesis of the nihilist. The courage to face what one knows to be the case comes only too late. I have only recently admitted to myself that I have always been a nihilist to the core: the energy, the radicalism with which I proceeded as a nihilist deceived me about this fundamental fact. When we move toward a goal, it seems impossible that "goallessness in itself" can be our underlying belief.[17]

And yet, move forward we active nihilists must: We can't go on. We'll go on.

Perhaps the reader is wondering why Nietzsche considers this active condition *nihilistic*. Is it not affirmative to a significant degree? The answer was suggested earlier; namely, two thousand years of Christian values and morality permeate our culture as life-denying minerals. Anything we might fashion *out of those materials* will of necessity be contaminated by this nihilistic material. The goal, however, cannot be to reject that legacy outright but must lie elsewhere. The reader may ask: why not reject the legacy outright? To do so would be to lapse yet again into passive nihilism. More importantly, Nietzsche is adamant about the fact that values are, in the end, needed. We cannot do without them. The following somewhat rough note is highly suggestive of a crucial feature of Nietzsche's thought: *the revaluation of all values*.

---

16 *NF*–1887, 9[35].
17 *NF*–1887, 9[123].

To what extent perfect nihilism is the result of our received ideals—we are surrounded by imperfect nihilism, its forms. Attempts to escape nihilism without revaluing those received values produces their opposite, intensifies the problem.[18]

As this fragment suggests, nihilism as our normal condition can be overcome. But *how*? Nietzsche insists that the solution to any nihilistic value *cannot* be through the mere negation of that value. We must not "rush headlong into the *opposite* values with the same measure of energy with which we have been Christians—with which we [had accepted] the nonsensical exaggerations of Christianity."[19] Slowing down, we have a chance to recover "the decisive thing on which our lives depend."[20] Our task is indicated in Nietzsche's subtitle: *the revaluation of all values.* But any glimmer of a golden solution should be viewed through Nietzsche's prism of perfect nihilism. How far-reaching is it? It seeps into our psychology as pathology, pessimism, anxiety, and depression; it rattles our cognitive apparatus as delusion, deceit, hallucination; it infects our ontology as emptiness in place of essence; it undermines our epistemology as a lack of foundations; it circulates in our very environment as an atmospheric background; it shatters the grandeur of our most cherished ideals concerning morality, religion, and the universe itself. Nihilism is not only an uncanny guest but also an utterly exacting one. As this brief survey of its nuances shows, it is not only the assertion "God is dead" that is nihilistic, but also the assertion "God." It is not only the naive superstitions of folk belief that are nihilistic, but also the rigorous certainties of science. It is not only decadence that is nihilistic but also morality.

Why is Nietzsche so convinced that he is writing during the advent of Western civilization's inundation by the torrent of nihilism? Is it not obvious, he asks us, that two millennia of Christianity have created in us a "wayward, sickly, exhausted, spent people" who can barely muster the energy to believe in a future worth living or, indeed, in the value of "the human" itself?[21] Are we still even human beings, Nietzsche asks, "or perhaps only thinking,

---

18 *NF*–1887, 10[42].
19 *NF*–1887, 11[148]. The specific "exaggerations" that Nietzsche mentions here are the following: "1. The 'immortality of the soul;' the eternal value of the 'person;' 2. The solution, the direction, the evaluation [judgment] in the 'beyond;' 3. Moral worth as the highest value; the 'healing of the soul' as cardinal interest; 'sin,' 'earthly,' 'flesh,' 'lusts,' stigmatized as 'the world.'"
20 *NF*–1887, 11[148].
21 *On the Genealogy of Morals*, 1.11.

writing, and speaking machines?"[22] At the dawn of the OpenAI revolution, is the answer not less obvious than it seems?

We open the door to nihilism, and the question *now, what will you do?* stares us in the face.

BECOMING WHO YOU ARE

Nietzsche's last sustained writing project was his intimate-intellectual auto-biography *Ecce Homo*. The subtitle to this strange, spirited, provocative, hilarious, nutty book is *How One Becomes Who One Is*. When I first read this book many years ago as a young man struggling to find his way in the world, I was excited by that title. Eyeing sections declaring "Why I Am So Wise," "Why I Am So Clever," "Why I Write Such Good Books," and "Why I Am A Destiny," I could only respond with an enthusiastic *yes, please tell me, Nietzsche, I want to know!* For my driving interest in reading the book was indeed to behold *(ecce)* this remarkable man *(homo)*, Friedrich Nietzsche, so that, in understanding how *he* became who *he* was, *I* might better understand how I might become who *I* was.

Is this not a perennial preoccupation of youth—becoming who you are? Nietzsche presses the point throughout his work. Already in "Schopenhauer as Educator" (1874), he writes that "the person who does not want to belong to the masses needs only to stop being comfortable with himself and to follow his conscience, which calls to him 'Be yourself! You are more than what you now do, think, and desire."[23] Similarly, in *The Gay Science* it becomes an explicit prerogative of conscience: *"What does your conscience say?*—'You should become the one who you are.'"[24] In a letter to his friend Erwin Rohde, Nietzsche indicates that he was inspired in this notion by the Second Pythian Ode in which Pindar also admonishes his reader to "become who you are."[25] Apparently, Nietzsche and Rohde had once created a "monument" on the bank of the river in Leipzig, baptized it "Nirvana," which bore "the solemn words, which have proven victorious, γένοι'οῖος ἐσσί [become who you

---

22 *Untimely Meditations,* "The Use and Abuse of History for Life," section 5.
23 *Untimely Meditations,* "Schopenhauer as Educator," section 1.
24 *The Gay Science,* 270.
25 It is line 73 of that work. Interestingly, Nietzsche omits the word "learn" from Pindar's imperative: *Learn, and become who you are.* But does not the epigram that begins this book— *Learning changes us*—show that Nietzsche agrees with Pindar even more than he lets on?

are]." Nietzsche assures his friend that these are "the best words that I can carry in my heart for you."[26]

As lovingly as Nietzsche might have intended it, is it not a questionable notion, *becoming* who you are? Are we not *already* who we are? The imperative is particularly questionable for a thinker like Nietzsche who, as we have seen, emphatically eschews any and all notions of an essentialized self and of being or even of becoming *toward* some final state of being. We saw that Nietzsche is forcefully countering the entire history of philosophy, which, he is convinced, follows Plato on his misguided search for the stasis of eternal Being. Nietzsche, recall, insists that "there is no substratum, no 'being' behind doing, effecting, becoming."[27] So is *becoming who you are* an interminable process? Is it coextensive with *living* itself?

Nietzsche occasionally offers us a clue as to his meaning. For example, he draws an instructive contrast in *The Gay Science*. On the one hand, "the many, the vast majority" engage in "the whole moralistic twaddle" and have "nothing better to do than lug the past a bit further through time." *We,* Nietzsche's "friends" and perfect readers, act wholly contrary to such lugging. His elaboration is instructive.

> *We want to become who we are*—the new, the unique, the incomparable, the self-legislating, the self-creating! And to this end, we must become the best learners and discoverers of everything lawful and necessary in the world: we must become *physicists* in order to be, in that sense, *creators*—whereas till now all valuations and ideals have been constructed in *ignorance* of, and in *contradiction* to, physics. And thus: Cheers to physics! And an even louder cheers to that which *compels* us to physics—our honesty![28]

By "physics" Nietzsche is indicating the naturalism that we have encountered throughout our journey in this book. We will return later to the centrality of "honesty" in Nietzsche's value system.

He also, as we will see in a moment, uses the trope of "youth" as an image of hope, possibility, and urgency in this matter of *becoming who you are*. Here, he glosses again his meaning in the form of a programmatic statement.

---

26 *BVN*–1867, 552.
27 *On the Genealogy of Morals*, 1.13.
28 *The Gay Science*, 335.

The most guaranteed sign of their own stronger health should be precisely that they—I mean the youth—can use no concepts, no group-speak from the currently circulating currency of words and concepts to characterize their nature, and that they are, rather, convinced only by a power acting within them, a fighting, eliminating, dividing power, and by an always heightened feeling for life in every good hour.[29]

Whatever else it might involve, *becoming who you are* entails a degree of estrangement from social norms. Even the speech, the word choice, of a person in such a condition of becoming will have a unique, strange quality. This quality, however, must not be contrived. Nietzsche makes it clear in this passage that the quality flows out of the person's very way of living. When *estrangement* and alienation are the topics at hand, Nietzsche's figure of Zarathustra is never far off. Indeed, in another passage, Zarathustra himself offers us an account. In the passage, he waits high in the mountains, casting his happiness far and wide as bait to lure the "strangest human-fish." Cunning and mocking, this "most malicious of human-fish catchers" casts and waits and casts and waits, until one of these human-fish bites the sharp tip of his hidden hook and rises up, is pulled up, to Zarathustra's lofty level.

> For *that* is what I have been doing at bottom and since the beginning: reeling, raising up, pulling up, bringing up, a reeler, a cultivator and disciplinarian, who once said to himself, not without reason: "Become who you are!"[30]

The resonance of the German words here—*heranziehend, aufziehend*, etc—with *erziehend* (upbringing, training, teaching) and *Erziehung* (education) bring us back again to our epigram, *Learning changes us,* as well as to Pindar's *Learn, and become who you are.* But learn what? Can it really be as simple as that—*just take the bait*, the Nietzschean bait? What about that uncanny guest darkening our doorway? Nietzsche wants us to *feel* the strict demands of nihilism, he wants us to *sense* it lying everywhere in wait, particularly around those corners where solution-bearing improvers of humankind have hung their shingle. Having just now turned such a corner, perhaps, we must, once again, slow down.

---

29 *Untimely Meditations*, "The Use and Abuse of History for Life," section 10.
30 *Thus Spoke Zarathustra*, "The Honey Sacrifice."

In his essay "The Use and Abuse of History for Life," Nietzsche discusses how an entire culture might *become what it is*. Such cultural becoming is in opposition to what a culture *has been*. History, of course, is the discipline of what has been, what once was. As the title indicates, Nietzsche is concerned with discerning the ways in which our internalization of history might by turns enervate or innervate us *for life*, that is, for living in our present and toward our future. He gives the essence of his argument in the opening sentence of the essay. It is a quote from Goethe: "Incidentally, I hate everything that merely instructs me without increasing my activity or directly innervating it."[31] Nietzsche does not offer Goethe's attitude as a counter to nihilism, but I think it can be read as an important clue.

In the essay, Nietzsche argues that a civilization's youth possess an instinctive urge to overcome nihilism, and this urge is tightly intertwined with the question of *becoming who you are*. Youth's counter-nihilist urge reveals itself most directly in their "desire to experience something for themselves and to feel growing in them a coordinated and living system of their own experiences."[32] Nietzsche is expressing here a major premise of his overall work. This is the premise of the priority of "life." Wary of making an overtly metaphysical claim, Nietzsche defines "life" impressionistically, as, for instance, "life alone, that dark, driving, insatiable self-desiring power."[33] Nietzsche wants to distinguish the promise-rich chaos of "life alone" from the "animal-taming" order of life's mere "decoration." The former is culture, the latter, civilization. I will return to this distinction in a moment. The point here is that, through education, youth's impulse for *life* is "narcotized and, as it were, made drunk through the opulent deceptions about" culture. How could this not be the result? For culture cannot be prescribed by an education or in any other manner. Textbook knowledge of culture is never but a stiff, lifeless *caricature* of culture. And yet the "monotonous orthodoxy" of our educational systems fatally holds that "the young person has to begin with a knowledge of culture, not at first with a knowledge of life, and even less with life and experience themselves." Such a culture is "poured out like a sugar drink," and so can be nothing but "untruthful and infertile." Nietzsche asks us to consider that precisely the opposite is the case: "culture can only grow up and blossom forth out of living."

---

31 *Untimely Meditations*, "The Use and Abuse of History for Life," Preface.
32 Unless otherwise stated, *Untimely Meditations*, "The Use and Abuse of History for Life," section 10.
33 *Untimely Meditations*, "The Use and Abuse of History for Life," section 3.

In Nietzsche's diagnosis, because we desire "flowers without roots and stalks," we are not only bereft of anything resembling an education but also "ruined for life, for real and simple seeing and hearing, for the fortunate grasping of what is near and natural, and lack even the foundation of culture, because we are not even convinced that we have within us a genuine life." And so youth declares: "First, give me life, and I will create a culture out of it for you!" This imperative is rooted in an "instinct of nature" that some fortunate youth are able to maintain even through education's nihilistic life-denying attempt to break them. Here, Nietzsche introduces a significant clue for our query of *what to do*. It comes in the form of a kind of conspiracy of resistance:

> Whoever wants to break this education in its turn must assist youth in finding their expression. He must illuminate their unconscious resistance with the luminosity of concepts, and turn it into a deliberate and loudly spoken consciousness.

And how might we attain such a "strange goal"? We may do so negatively by helping to ruin one another for the "superstitions" that education discharges into the world, and so by extension, for the spectacle of civilization. We may do so positively by helping to create the conditions for realizing the age-old command to "know thyself." Know where *you* stand on, say, the volatile social issues swirling in your midst. Know what *you* value. Know what *your* needs are. Know how *you* should live, think, speak, respond, act, be. How can you know? Only through living, only through life, indeed only through *your* singular, concrete life. Concepts, ideas, philosophies can never serve but as preestablished *scripts* to an abstract life.

Three crucial assumptions lie behind these imperatives. Nietzsche's first assumption is that a powerful counterforce is at work to convince you that your security, indeed your very life, can be found only in conformity to the social status quo. "Know thyself" can thus function as a gauge to our proximity to "the herd." His second assumption is that *we can know* precisely all of this and more. What is required is, among other values and dispositions that we will consider later, the "honesty" I referred to in earlier quotes. The third assumption is that "this is a parable for every individual among us." Although Nietzsche poses the issue in terms of youth in his essays on education, *becoming who you are* is a matter that attends us during every phase of our life. Nietzsche, moreover, predicates each of these assumptions on one essential, explosively controversial, claim: *homo natura*.

BEING–NATURE

We have already encountered Nietzsche's idea that if any worthy future is to be had, it will require that "the terrible basic text of *homo natura* must again be recognized."[34] He then explains his meaning:

> To translate the human back into nature; to become master of the many vain and overly enthusiastic interpretations and subtexts which up to now have been scribbled and painted over the eternal basic text of *homo natura*; to ensure that, henceforth, human stands before human, as they already stand today before the *other* nature, having become hardened through the discipline of science, with fearless Oedipus eyes and covered Odysseus ears, deaf to the temptations of the old metaphysical bird catchers, who have warbled at them for all too long: "you are more! you are higher! you are of a different origin!"—that may be a strange and insane task, but a *task* it is—who would deny that! Why did we choose it, this insane task? Or, put differently, "why have knowledge at all?"—Everyone will ask us this question. And we, pressed in this manner, we, who have asked ourselves this very question a hundred times, we have found and find no better answer...[35]

Let's slowly unpack this cardinal Nietzschean passage. Let's note the central function that *homo natura* serves in Nietzsche's conception of *embodiment*. Whatever else *homo natura* might entail, it entails the primacy of the human body. Although Nietzsche uses the term "nature," all of us good readers know to eat a lump of antimetaphysical salt here. So "to translate the human back into nature" means, in the first instance, to rethink what the human being is from the lived reality of the human body. We live in our bodies. Everything, literally everything, every sensory stimulus, every thought and conception, every emotion and feeling, every fear, every desire, every single instance of our lived subjective experience is through and through a bodily phenomenon. Even every conceivable external phenomenon with which we interact—sound waves, light waves, tactile masses, olfactory effluvium—is *incorporated*.[36] Even if there is some *supernatural* Real operating in our midst, it is only through our *natural* embodied sensorium that we could engage with it. This is why Nietzsche says that "really, 'the spirit' is most

---

34 *Beyond Good and Evil*, 230.
35 *Beyond Good and Evil*, 230.
36 The German term is *einverleiben*.

similar to the stomach."[37] Nietzsche is not being funny here. If we are "to become master of the many vain and overly enthusiastic interpretations and subtexts which up to now have been scribbled and painted over the eternal basic text of *homo natura,*" we must first become clear about what this "up to now" entailed, namely, *"The Christian interpretation of the body."*

> *The Christian interpreters of the body.* Whatsoever originates in the stomach, the entrails, the heartbeat, the nerves, the gall bladder, semen—all of those upsets, debilitations, overexcitements, the entire randomness of the machine so unknown to us!—A Christian such as Pascal must take all of that as a moral and religious phenomenon, with the question of whether God or Satan, whether good or evil, whether salvation or damnation are lying therein! Oh, such an unfortunate interpreter! How he must twist and torment his system! How he must twist and torment himself in order to be right![38]

We are the unfortunate interpreters. And the twisting and tormenting comes from our refusal to realize "the *other* nature," the one whose image is evaded by "the old metaphysical bird catchers"—the acolytes of science, anthropology, religion, humanism. Our other nature is, of course, *animal.* As in so many passages, Nietzsche is fully aware of the precariousness of the "insane" task he is promoting. Beholding the fact of *homo natura,* we risk the gruesome fate of an Oedipus gauging out his eyes. Hearing of it, we risk the fate of an Odysseus binding himself to resist the bewitching, deadly, song of the Sirens. Both figures did what they did as a response to a *recognition of reality.* Although these two examples might seem overwrought in the current context, Nietzsche's question, "why have knowledge at all?", grants the reader that to "translate the human back into nature" comes at a terrible cost, one that, may not be deemed worth it.

I'd like to mention two more points. Reading about those warbling old metaphysical bird catchers, the reader can be excused for protesting: *wait, that sounds like Nietzsche!* For, does Nietzsche not incessantly warble at full throttle that "you are more! you are higher!" I advise the reader not to let go of their skepticism too soon (recall that we perfect readers must remain "supple, cunning, cautious"). I will only mention here that, contrary to the bird catchers, Nietzsche most adamantly does *not* warble that "you are of a different origin!" His conceit of *homo natura* is intended precisely

---

37 *Beyond Good and Evil,* 230.
38 *Dawn,* 86.

to emphasize this point. Well, given Nietzsche's irony, it's a bit complicated here. So his version might go something like this: you are "less," you are "lower," you are of a different origin *than you think! Less* and *lower* are in scare quotes because it is only due to the millennial-long warbling of the metaphysical bird catchers—you are the children of God, you possess divine Souls, you are endowed with luminous Reason, you are spiritually evolved Humans—that species exceptionalism is so deeply seared into our consciousness. Actually, Nietzsche thinks that, when all is said and done, we are indeed, in some important sense, *higher* than we currently believe—but only once we go "lower."

Finally, in giving thought to what Nietzsche might want us to understand by "translating the human back into nature," we should bear in mind the following passage. In it, he denigrates a common trope in "back to nature" discourse.

> "According to nature" you want to *live*? Oh, you noble Stoics, what a swindle of words! Consider a being such as nature, wasteful beyond measure, indifferent beyond measure, lacking intentions and consider-ations, lacking mercy and justice, terrible and desolate and uncertain all at once, consider this indifference itself as power—how *could* you live according to this indifference? Life—is that not precisely a want-ing-to-be-other than this nature? Is living not estimating, preferring, being unjust, being limited, wanting-to-be-different? And suppose that your imperative "live according to nature" means at bottom no more than "live according to life"—then how could you *not*? Why make a principle out of that which you are and must be?[39]

This passage makes clear crucial features of Nietzsche's conception of nature. First, it is neither that of Hobbes nor of Rousseau nor of the Romantics. Unlike them, when Nietzsche says *nature,* he does not ask you to picture trees and water and birds and grazing animals and roaming bands of wild humans. He is not positing a *place*—brutal, benign, sublime, or otherwise. Indeed, to Rousseau's famous call to return to nature, Nietzsche somewhat snarkily asks, "To where did he actually want to return?"[40] For Nietzsche, because nature is not a place, it can have no *outside.* Hence, the notion of a

---

39 *Beyond Good and Evil*, 9.
40 *Twilight of the Idols*, "Raids of an Untimely Man," 48. In the same passage, Nietzsche calls Rousseau "this grotesque freak who sets up camp on the threshold of the new age."

return to nature in the classical, Romantic, or modern sense is nonsensical. We have, however, seen that Nietzsche himself uses such language.

> I, too, speak of a "return to nature," although it is not actually a going back but a *going up*—up into the high, free, even terrible nature and naturalness, such a nature as can play with great tasks, that *may* thus play.[41]

This passage is titled *Progress in my sense*. We are making progress toward *becoming who we are* when we finally turn away from the spatial conceptions of Rousseau, Hobbes, *et al.* and toward the *terrible*, wasteful, indifferent, inconsiderate, merciless, unjust, uncertain "monster of energy"[42] in whose midst we find ourselves. And while we do, of course, find ourselves in the midst of trees and sky, and so on, Nietzsche wants to home in as close as possible into the midst of where we ultimately and unequivocally find ourselves.

> *The forgotten nature.* We speak of nature and forget ourselves in the process: we ourselves are nature, *quand même* [all the same]. It follows that nature is something completely different from that which we feel when we utter its name.[43]

BEING–BODY

The "going up" that constitutes our "progress" begins with a going *into* the body. As coterminous with nature-as-outside as the body may be, Nietzsche's focus is on the body in and of itself. The great master of up-goings, Zarathustra, is explicit on this point in his speech "On the Despisers of the Body." Because this passage contains central features of Nietzsche's human-as-animal-as-nature psychology in a nutshell, it will be worth quoting at length:

> "I am a body and a soul"—thus speaks a child. And why should we not speak as children?
> But the awakened one, the knowing one, says: I am body through

---

41 *Twilight of the Idols*, "Raids of an Untimely Man," 48.
42 *NF*–1885, 38[12].
43 *Human, All Too Human*, "The Wanderer and His Shadow," 327.

and through, and nothing besides, and soul is only a word for something bodily.

The body is a great intelligence,[44] a multiplicity with a single sense, a war and a peace, a herd and a shepherd.

An instrument of your body is also your little intelligence, my friends, which you call "spirit," a small tool and toy of your great intelligence.

You say "I" and are proud of this word. But even greater is that which you do not want to believe—your body and its great intelligence: it does not say I, it does I.

What the senses feel and what the spirit recognizes never has its end in itself. But the senses and the spirit would like to convince you that they are the end of all things: so vain are they.

Tools and toys are the senses and the spirit: behind them lies yet the self. The self also sees with the eyes of the senses and also hears with the ears of the spirit.

The self constantly hears and seeks: it compares, forces, conquers, destroys. It rules and is also the ruler of the I.[45]

Behind your thoughts and feelings, my friend, stands a mighty commander, an unknown sage—it is called the self. It lives in your body, it is your body.

There is more intelligence in your body than in your best wisdom. And who knows, then, to what ends exactly your body needs your greatest wisdom?

Your self laughs at your I and its proud leaps. "What are these leaps and flights of thoughts to me?" it asks itself. "A detour to my purpose. I am the restraining leash of the I and the instigator of its concepts."

The self says to the I: "feel pain here!" And the I suffers and wonders

---

44 The term that I am translating as *intelligence* here, *Vernunft*, is typically rendered as *reason*, as in the *rational* cognitive apparatus that *reasons*. But I don't think that translation makes sense here. My thinking is as follows. First, throughout his work, Nietzsche is hostile to the Enlightenment's near-deification of Reason. Second, Nietzsche values precisely the body's potential for *irrationality*. Third, Nietzsche would have been aware of the older sense of *Vernunft* as Latin *intellectio*, intellection or grasping with the mind. Fourth, Nietzsche values precisely the body's capacity for a *sui generis* intelligence.

45 As with Freud a few decades later, the German term universally translated into English as "ego" is "das Ich," literally, "the I." "Ego" is, of course, the Latin first person singular pronoun, "I." Freud's first English-language translators, the married couple James Strachey (1887–1967) and Alix Strachey (1882–1973), were, and still are, criticized for introducing unnecessary "scienticisms" into Freud's otherwise clear language. Even though "ego" has such wide currency today, I choose not to muddy Nietzsche's meaning in the same way.

how it might no longer suffer—and exactly thus should it think.

The self says to the I: "feel pleasure here!" And the I rejoices and wonders how it might often feel such pleasure—and exactly thus should it think.[46]

Ultimately, Zarathustra rejects the despisers of the body because they are most definitely "not bridges to the overhuman." Why not? First of all, they— we?—still believe in mind-body dualism. Does not virtually every single one of us readers likewise believe that the body is one thing and the mind or "spirit" is another? Our lingering dualistic Enlightenment legacy goes even further. It insists that the mind takes precedence over the body. Specifically, the exalted mental faculty we call "reason" has the final say on all matters— mental, emotional, sensorial, bodily, or otherwise. Zarathustra insists that this view is childish and deluded. Yes, "reason" is an ability that we possess. That's obvious, isn't it? What Zarathustra asks us to recognize is that "reason" is only one of numerous "tools and toys"—faculties, drives, urges, instincts, tendencies, dispositions, and so on—competing for dominance at any given moment. Is that not equally obvious? (Once again, should I go to the gym or take a nap?)

In the discussion on identity earlier, I tried to show that Nietzsche rejects any and all notions of a unitary self. Instead of an essentialized individual, Nietzsche sees a cacophonous internal society of diverse, competing interests. (This is yet another instance of the wholistic mirroring of inner and outer in Nietzsche.) So why does he warble about "the self" here? Indeed, why does he go as far as to say that the self "rules and is also the ruler of the I"? Nietzsche could not be any more explicit: *the self is the body*. It is the *body* that is "a mighty commander, an unknown sage" possessing great intelligence. The perfect reader will have some questions here: Are we to take this claim literally? If so, is "the body" not just "the soul" in disguise? And even if Nietzsche's assertion could be proven, what are the real-life ramifications?

BEING–ANIMAL

We are indeed to take this claim literally. What might doing so entail? To begin with, "we must relearn here, in the same way that we had to relearn

---

46 *Thus Spoke Zarathustra*, "On the Despisers of the Body."

about heredity and the 'innate.'"[47] That is, once we gained knowledge about the role that genetics plays in forming individuals, virtually everything regarding our understanding of human agency changed. We will see later that Nietzsche does not subscribe to anything like biological determinism. He does, however, believe—observe?—that "the greater part of conscious thinking must still be included among the instinctual activities... 'Consciousness' is in no decisive sense the *opposite* of that which is instinctive."[48] Anticipating Freud's third Copernican revolution, Nietzsche held that most of what comes into our conscious awareness "is secretly led through [our] instincts and forced into certain channels." It *feels* to us as if that manifest element of consciousness were *us*, were the mighty commander and sage that is our *I*. Again, this is just the "absurd *overestimation of consciousness*" that has been drilled into us.[49] Consciousness, says Nietzsche, is "only a means" toward survival. As such, it is constantly competing with other means. Every instinct, drive, proclivity, urge, and so on is but a "quantum of energy" within the whole.[50] As Zarathustra taught us, each drive, and so on, possesses its own "little intelligence," its own reasoning power. Hence, our internal struggle:

> In all instances of becoming-conscious a discontentment of the organism expresses itself: something new should be tried, nothing is sufficiently right for it, there is hardship, tension, overstraining—that is precisely what becoming-conscious is...The genius is in the instinct; likewise the good.[51]

The "genius" of which Nietzsche speaks here is, more specifically, the "animal functions." And with this, we finally recognize "the terrible basic text of *homo natura*."

> The animal functions are fundamentally millions of times more important than all of the refined states and heights of consciousness: the latter are a surplus insofar as they must not necessarily be tools for those animal functions. All of our *conscious* life, the mind together with the soul, together with the heart, together with goodness, together with

---

47 *Beyond Good and Evil*, 3.
48 *Beyond Good and Evil*, 3.
49 *NF*–1888, 14[146].
50 *NF*–1887, 10[138].
51 *NF*–1888, 15[25].

virtue: in whose service does it then labor? It labors toward the greatest possible perfection of the means (of nourishment, of increase) of the basic animal functions: above all, *the increase of life*. That which used to be called "body" and "flesh" is of such unspeakably more importance: the rest is an insignificant accessory.[52]

In formulating his notion of *overcoming*, Nietzsche does not end with "the animal." That would be too simplistic. Rather, he asks us to *begin* here: "Starting point, from the body and physiology: why?" An excellent question! The short answer: "Because we gain the proper picture of the nature of our subject unity."[53] To return to the "basic text of *homo natura*" means to give thought to what we *are* from the perspective of precisely that which is most *basic* to our very being: the embodied human animal. Abandoning once and for all the fantastic delusions of the metaphysical birdcatchers—you are Soul, Reason, Self!—we can finally give honest thought to what we might *become*. Or can we? In an effort once again to evoke the danger involved, Nietzsche conjures the seductions of Circe, the goddess who transformed humans into animals: "*Truth as Circe*. Error has turned animals into humans; might the truth be able to turn humans back into an animal?"[54]

We will continue to work our way toward a fuller answer to that and other questions that were raised in this section. Now, a certain matter looms: *civilization*.

CIVILIZATION

Earlier, we heard youth trumpet, "First, give me life, and I will create a culture out of it for you!" Note that youth does not ask for *a* life. "Life," we learned, is the name for the turbulent monster of energy in whose midst we find ourselves. And as we also saw, "life" is an insatiable, dark, driving, self-desiring force; it is Dionysian chaos; it knows nothing of measure or morality. "Living," then, is that way of being that hews closely to "life." Living is what happens when we place ourselves under the spell of "Dionysian magic."

---

52 *NF*–1887, 11[83].
53 *NF*–1885, 40[21].
54 *Human, All Too Human*, 519.

Under the charm of the Dionysian, not only is the bond between human and human renewed: but also alienated, hostile, or subjugated nature celebrates once again its feast of reconciliation with its prodigal child, humankind.[55]

I noted that youth asks not for *a* life, but for *life*. In his first book, *The Birth of Tragedy,* Nietzsche makes clear the reason for youth's specific request. The "bond" between us humans is that we participate together in the "mysterious primordial unity" that is, precisely, life. Yet is it not obvious to every reader that such a spirit of unity is nowhere to be found? Could we humans be any more atomized and divided than we presently are? The very thought of the primordial unity that binds us together, Nietzsche says, clearly incites in us a frightening, disorienting "*intoxication*." And so, as a comforting balm, we resort to the "joyful necessity of the dream experience." And what is the "beautiful illusion" that we collectively dream up to stave off the terrible truth of our nature? Here, Nietzsche quotes the greatest early influence on his thought—Arthur Schopenhauer's *The World as Will and Representation*:

As if in the raging sea, unbounded in all directions, roaring mountains of waves rising and falling, a sailor sits in a small boat, trusting in his frail vessel; thus, in the midst of a world of suffering sits calmly the individual person, protected by and trusting in the *principium individuationis*.

The "principle of individuation," originally articulated by Aristotle, has played a decisive role in philosophical and psychological thought through the ages down to the present day. The principle simply holds that *this is not that; this is its own unique thing*. In the section on the principle of identity we saw what Nietzsche thinks of this idea. Yet here, he recognizes that, however we may ultimately evaluate it, the principle of individuation constitutes a powerful "drive" in human experience. Indeed, it constitutes a counter-drive to that of the Dionysian dissolution of the individual life—of *a* life—into the "primordial unity" of *life*. Nietzsche characterizes this individuating drive as "Apollonian," giving to it the name of the Greek god Apollo.

Yes, it can be said of Apollo that in him the unshakable confidence in that *principium* and the calm sitting of the person set on it have come to

---

55 Until otherwise noted, *The Birth of Tragedy*, 1.

their most sublime expression, and we would like to designate Apollo himself as the glorious divine image of the *principii individuationis*, out of whose gestures and glances the entire joy and wisdom of "illusion," together with its beauty, might speak to us.

Nietzsche asks us to consider, along with the ancient Greeks, that a basic understanding of reality can be gained by recognizing an *"Apollonian* and *Dionysian* duality." The Apollonian represents the "drive" or inclination toward *"dreams"*; and the Dionysian, that toward *"intoxication."* Apollo represents light, symmetry, order, healing, the plastic arts, rationality, and prophecy. The Dionysian, as we have seen, represents darkness, imbalance, chaos, destruction, music, irrationality, and forgetting. (Note that a far-reaching ramification of Nietzsche's division here is that dreaming and reasoning are on the same continuum.)

Given all of the characteristics that I have mentioned, it should not be difficult to view *civilization-society* as Apollonian and *culture-nature* as Dionysian. Not insignificantly, Apollo is also the god of herds. This is instructive; but although Nietzsche persistently denigrates "herd" mentality throughout his work, in *The Birth of Tragedy* his central point is that the genius of Greek civilization and culture lay in the symbiosis of the two drives. For Nietzsche, in other words, there is certainly value in civilization—it provides security, necessary structure and order, organized forms of life, and so on. The crucial point for our purposes here is that *civilization* must be grounded in *culture*, which must be grounded in *life*, which must be grounded in remembrance of our *animal* nature, which must be recognized as grounded in our very *body*. So while Nietzsche's dualisms *might* be reconciled into wholes, it is not inevitable. What he says here about the civilization-culture dualism may equally be said of the dualisms of Apollonian-Dionysian and human-animal.

> The high points of culture and civilization are separate from one another: we should not allow ourselves to be misled by the abyssal antagonism between culture and civilization. The great moments of culture were, morally speaking, periods of corruption. On the other hand, the epochs of the artificial and forced *animal taming* of the human being ("civilisation") were times of intolerance of the most spirited

and boldest natures. Civilization wants something different from what culture wants: perhaps something that is the contrary.[56]

I read Nietzsche's use of "corruption" as ironic. As he notes, a culture is "corrupt" only within the framework of "morality." It is precisely *civilization*, and not nature, that marks this distinction. The primary definition of "corrupt" is: *marked by immorality and perversion; depraved*. Indeed, one of the very defining characteristics of "civilization" is that it marks the distinction between itself as essentially "civilized" and "something that is its opposite." What might that "something" be? The following definition of "civilization" from an etymological dictionary matches Nietzsche's usage: "civilized condition, state of being reclaimed from the rudeness of savage life...serving as an opposite to barbarity."[57] Recall that, eschewing our "humanitarian illusions" about the origins of civilization, Nietzsche posits that:

> The noble caste was in the beginning always the barbarian caste: its predominance did not initially lie in its physical strength, but rather in its mental strength. They were the more *whole* people (which, on every level, also means "the more whole animals").[58]

The struggle, the *agon*, between civilization and culture, then, concerns the, by turns, hindrance or establishment of "the more whole animal." We purchase civilization's value at the cost of an *"animal taming of the human being,"* the terrible added price of which is an enervating "intolerance of the most spirited and boldest natures" (think: Hermodor). I should mention here that the Proto-Indo-European root meaning of "civilization" is "to lie down, to lie asleep."[59]

What might this duality mean in real terms? I mentioned earlier that I find it helpful to run the ideas that I encounter in philosophy through real-life instances. Although it risks oversimplifying the issue, not doing so risks keeping the idea an empty abstraction. I encourage the reader to do a thought experiment using a scenario familiar to them. I will take as my example a university classroom.

---

56 *NF*–1888, 16[10].
57 *Online Etymological Dictionary*, https://www.etymonline.com. Accessed July 8, 2023.
58 *Beyond Good and Evil*, 257.
59 See *Online Etymological Dictionary, s.v.,* *kei- (1), https://www.etymonline.com. Accessed July 8, 2023.

Culture (nature, the animal, the body) is present in the classroom if *life* is present in the classroom. Life, again, is the insatiable, dark, driving, self-desiring power that courses through each participant's body. Life is the Dionysian chaos that knows nothing of measure or morality. How might students and professor speak and behave *out of life*? They would, in the first instance, *be* alive; they would be animated and alert. The classroom would be bristling with energy and possibility. The body's active animal life would percolate up to their minds and speech, charging their mutual relations with "original response." That is Robert Frost's term from his depiction of a decidedly Nietzschean scene. In the poem "The Most of It," a person feels himself isolated and alone because he exists in an echo chamber of his own making.

He thought he kept the universe alone;
For all the voice in answer he could wake
Was but the mocking echo of his own
From some tree-hidden cliff across the lake.
Some morning from the boulder-broken beach
He would cry out on life, that what it wants
Is not its own love back in copy speech,
But counter-love, original response.
And nothing ever came of what he cried
Unless it was the embodiment that crashed
In the cliff's talus on the other side,
And then in the far distant water splashed,
But after a time allowed for it to swim,
Instead of proving human when it neared
And someone else additional to him,
As a great buck it powerfully appeared,
Pushing the crumpled water up ahead,
And landed pouring like a waterfall,
And stumbled through the rocks with horny tread,
And forced the underbrush—and that was all.

Every teacher knows this kind of dull, uncommitted rote response from students. *Life, nature, the body, the animal* demand something wholly different. But "nothing ever came of what he cried" because of the deadening effect of civilization on people. What comes back is predictable, formulaic, "copy speech." Not so in a classroom brimming with *life*. There, an animal vibrancy and rawness endures. In Frost's poem, nature does respond to the alienated human who has ears to hear. It responds as an "embodiment" from "the other side," and as a wild being.

In the terms of our thought experiment, what might the actions of the final four lines signify? In my experiment, they speak to the unleashing of human-animal nature in the classroom. They signify the unpredictability, urgency, provocation, stimulation, and so on, that emerges when civilization is held in check. Speaking of civilization, we must ask: and what about the absence of measure and morality? Well, one approach is to consider that animals *are* measured and modest. Unlike "the cruelest animals,"[60] humans, who *unnecessarily* slaughter trillions of human and nonhuman sentient beings annually, nonhuman animals rarely kill outside of necessity. Another approach is to consider that measure and morality are precisely civilizational strategies for curbing nature. They are not, in other words, natural, inevitable, or eternal categories. As that consideration suggests, a third approach is to note that civilization itself, for better or for worse, acts as a regulator of culture.

And how might we imagine civilization (society, the human, the individual) as a presence in the classroom? The most obvious way is through the presence of that which "lies in all languages about good and evil,"[61] the state. "The state" is shorthand for the norms, ethics and morals, rules, and laws dictated by society. In our thought experiment, it is the aspect of the educational civilization, or institution, that lays down the rules and norms that govern classroom life. It is the lecture; the grades; the assignments; the breaking down of the student's "performance" into percentages; the professor's standing at the front of the classroom; the professor's domination of discussions; the atmosphere of emotional discomfort and verbal silencing. Clearly, in this thought experiment, an immediate result of civilization is to hold culture in check. Culture demands of education that the classroom remain a "free, meandering brook." Civilization forces that natural brook

---

60 *Thus Spoke Zarathustra*, "The Convalescent." For animal slaughter alone, see the "Animal Kill Clock," https://animalclock.org. When aquatic deaths are included, the number is over a trillion overall. For humans, there are numerous specific databases that calculate annual deaths from warfare, murder by firearms and knives, domestic and elder violence fatalities, climate-related fatalities, environmentally-caused cancers, and so on. A reliable general source is "Our World in Data," https://ourworldindata.org/grapher/number-of-deaths-per-year. Accessed July 17, 2023.

61 *Thus Spoke Zarathustra*, "The New Idol."

into a "straight-cut ditch."[62] The overly civil classroom is one where uniformity, conformity, predictability, order, even stultification, reign.

A decisive issue for Nietzsche concerning these abyssally antagonistic formations is the manner and extent to which they *remain* antagonistic. What happens to, say, the passion of anger, when it meets the ethic of politeness? Is the passion repressed? Is the ethic circumvented? In the next section, we will look at specific examples from Nietzsche's work. First, I can intimate the answer. It involves "the ever-increasing spiritualization and 'deification' of cruelty, which pervades the entire history of higher culture."[63] But what, exactly, does this mean for us?

REPRESENTATIVE TYPES

Nietzsche is an incisive, often devastating, critic of our modern world. Yet he also offers his reader a host of highly positive, if necessarily suggestive, conceptions. In particular, for our purposes in this chapter, he serves up an impressive array of human-animal *types*. We can consider these types as rough exemplars of how we might be, how we might live, in our world. As always with Nietzsche, however, a firm caveat is in order before we proceed.

I began this book with the claim that Nietzsche's animating passion throughout his career as a thinker is how to create a better world for ourselves. Unlike the "improvers of humankind," whom he despises for their hypocrisy, misplaced optimism, and facile "solutions," Nietzsche does not *tell us* how that world should be. At an even more basic level, and despite his prodigious acuity as both a psychologist and an anthropologist, he most certainly does not tell us how we should be. Yes, he insists that we must recall ourselves as *homo natura*. But this recollection is a bare minimum if we are ever to overcome our current configuration of the sick human toward something healthier. Indeed, let us clear the air once and for all of the very conceit that Nietzsche intends to play the role of an improver of humankind.

Let us consider how extremely naive it is to say "humans *should* be such and such!" Reality shows us a delightful wealth of types, the

---

62 Henry David Thoreau asked: "What does education often do? It makes a straight-cut ditch of a free, meandering brook." *Journal, 1850–1851*, https://www.gutenberg.org/cache/epub/59031/pg59031-images.html.
63 *On the Genealogy of Morals*, 2.6.

luxuriance of an extravagant play of forms and changes: and some miserable moralistic deadbeat says "no! humans should be *other* than they are.".…He even knows how humans should be, this sanctimonious ass. He draws an image of himself on the wall and says *ecce homo— behold man!*[64]

Nietzsche is expressing the utter futility of prescribing and legislating human *being*. It is futile, he says, because "human being" names not *a* type but rather a lush, sumptuous multifariousness of ever-mutating forms perpetually adapting to ever-mutating environmental circumstances. This mutable diversity is, moreover, not the postulate of an abstract theory but an empirically verifiable state of affairs. Would we ever desire such uniformity in either the plant or animal worlds? Of course not. That would be a disaster. Nietzsche, recall, wants to retranslate and transplant[65] the human back into nature. That means he wants us to recognize that we humans exist *on a continuum with* plants and animals. So the answer to our question, *what to do*, must also fall within this continuum. Finally, we can glimpse another reason for Nietzsche's being so disdainful of our gurus and priests. It is because they, as improvers of humankind, believe that they are gazing into the depths of what is human when, in fact, they are merely beholding an idealized image of themselves. So this is our task and our caveat:

I am not concerned with the problem of what should replace humanity in the order of being (—the human is an endpoint—): rather, which type of human we should *cultivate*, we *should want*, as a being of higher value, more worthy of life, more certain of a future.[66]

Do we share Nietzsche's belief that "We have to be lifted up," as Zarathustra did the human-fish? If so, must we, too, not ask: "and who are they who lift us?"[67] I will now present several Nietzschean types. *Are* these the types of people we should want in our midst, should want to…*become*?

---

64 *Twilight of the Idols*, "Morality as Counter-Nature," 6.
65 Nietzsche's term is *zurückübersetzen*, which, with some poetic license, can mean "transplant."
66 *The Antichrist*, 1.3. On "cultivate" for *züchten*, see "Overcoming" footnote 139.
67 *Untimely Meditations*, "Schopenhauer as Educator," 5.

THE HUMAN ANIMAL

We begin our exploration of Nietzschean types by clarifying a point about our being animal. Although the human is literally an animal, it is also obviously a quite unusual animal. All primates, of course, differ from one another in ways both minuscule and massive. But humans differ from nonhuman animals in one profound manner in particular. Nietzsche characterizes this distinction in an early essay:

> Truly, it is a harsh punishment thus to live as an animal, laden with hunger and desire yet incapable of any kind of insight into the nature of this life, and there is no heavier fate than that of the beast of prey [...] to hang on to life so blindly and madly without knowing any higher worth beyond that fate.[68]

According to this passage, what sets the human animal apart from the non-human animal is its ability (i) to reflect on its existence and (ii) to ascribe meaning to its existence. I think we can posit an implicit third ability here, namely, that of imagining a future for its existence. Risking an exaggeration, I suggest that we can reduce Nietzsche's entire body of work to these three concerns. Now, given the human's capacity for the life-enhancing *lie*, a capacity, as we have seen, that is endemic to our very capacity for reflection—we can fashion a tale about the deeper significance of this state of affairs:

> If the whole of nature presses towards the human, it thereby gives us to understand that the human is necessary for its redemption from the curse of animal life, and that, in the human, existence holds up a mirror to itself in whose reflection life appears no longer senseless, but rather in its metaphysical significance.[69]

Given what we know of Nietzsche's attitude toward both metaphysics and teleology, we should read the "if" in that sentence as loaded to the max. Yet this speculation should also serve as a reminder that Nietzsche does not repudiate the project of meaning-making per se. In fact, the creation of new meanings and values for ourselves is precisely what will save us from irretrievably inundation in the torrent of nihilism.

---

68 *Untimely Meditations,* "Schopenhauer as Educator," 5.
69 *Untimely Meditations,* "Schopenhauer as Educator," 5.

None of this is to say that human animals are in any way *superior* to nonhuman animals. As we have seen, Nietzsche believes that just the opposite is often the case. A seemingly advanced cognitive capacity, such as reflection, can at any given instant turn out to be enfeebling rather than enhancing. In one of his last writings, Nietzsche clarifies his position on this matter.

> We have relearned. We have become more modest in all respects. We no longer derive the human from "spirit," from "deity." We have placed the human back among the animals. We consider the human to be the strongest animal because it is the most cunning: one consequence of this is its intellectuality. On the other hand, we defend ourselves against a certain vanity that would like to be loudly heard again here: as if the human were the great ulterior objective of animal development. The human is absolutely not the crown of creation; every being is, next to the human, on the same level of perfection…And in claiming this we are claiming still too much: the human is, relatively speaking, the most thwarted animal, the sickest, the one that has strayed most dangerously from its instincts—of course, for all of this, also the most interesting![70]

Early in his career, Nietzsche spoke of "those real *people, who are no longer animal.*"[71] Does this statement not mitigate against everything I have been saying? The great Nietzsche translator and interpreter Walter Kaufmann boldly claimed that "Nietzsche himself never renounced his early theories but only tried to strengthen them."[72] Knowing what we aspiring perfect readers now know of Nietzsche's thought, might we read the statement as one concerning transformation rather than repudiation, overcoming rather than negation? The *real* human is, at least, no longer the kind of animal who is unable to reflect on life or to imagine a future. Indeed, many humans—the "last mortals," for example—remain *such* animals. Yet exploring the difference that Nietzsche is asking us to consider, the question becomes: "where does the animal end, where does the human begin?"[73]

---

70 *The Antichrist*, 14.
71 *Untimely Meditations*, "Schopenhauer as Educator," 5.
72 Walter Kaufmann, *Nietzsche: Psychologist, Philosopher, Antichrist* (Princeton: Princeton University Press, 2013 [1950]), 175.
73 *Untimely Meditations*, "Schopenhauer as Educator," 5.

THE ARTIST

In the first sentence of the first paragraph of his first book, *The Birth of Tragedy* (published 1872), Nietzsche commences what will become a long, complicated relationship to art and artists:

> We will have gained much for the discipline of aesthetics once we arrive at, not merely the logical intuition, but the immediate certainty of vision, that the continued development of art is bound up in the duality of the *Apollonian* and the *Dionysian*.[74]

This passage represents Nietzsche's early view of art—in particular, the tragic theater—as the fusion of life's dark, abyssal, destructive Dionysian elements and its joyous, bright, and creative Apollonian elements. In this case, art, in particular the tragic arts, allowed the viewer to confront the dark features of existence without succumbing to them. Art, then, had an overall positive value for the individual and society. Emerging from his affection for Schopenhauer and Wagner, however, Nietzsche would soon swing fairly far in the other direction. In *Human, All Too Human* (1878), for instance, he equates art—in particular, orchestral music—with two of his most despised formations, Christianity and metaphysical philosophy. Like the priest and the metaphysician, the artist engages in the "narcotization of human suffering."[75] The degenerate result is that art enables us to "reinterpret an evil as a good" (like the slave moralist) or "awaken pleasure in pain" (like the decadent ascetic). With *The Gay Science* (1882) a few years later, however, Nietzsche comes to a maturer—and more generalizable—view of art and the artist. Indeed, we can call this later view a *more Nietzschean* view because it encompasses those earlier views while also looking farther, deeper, and otherwise. Art, in this view, permits a fuller experience of being human. Similar to, but far less grand than, the earlier Dionysian/Apollonian distinction, Nietzsche says that art, as "the cult of the untrue," enables us to avoid the catastrophic consequences of honesty and science, namely, "disgust and suicide." (Recall that "The falseness of a judgment is, for us, no objection to that judgment...The question is to what extent the judgment is life-fostering."[76]) In allowing us to view our lives as "an aesthetic phenomenon," art

---

74 *The Birth of Tragedy*, 1.1.
75 *Human, All Too Human*, 108.
76 *Beyond Good and Evil*, 4.

becomes a "countervailing power" to brute reality. Art, in short, gives us a more complete, more accepting, view of ourselves.

> We must occasionally rest from ourselves by looking down at ourselves from an aesthetic distance, by laughing *at* ourselves or crying *over* ourselves; we must discover the *hero* and also the *fool* who abide in our passion for knowledge; we must be joyous for our foolishness from time to time if we are to remain joyous for our wisdom! And precisely because we are ultimately heavy and serious people and more severe than others, nothing does us so much good as to don *dunce's caps*: we need them ourselves—we need boisterous, floating, dancing, mocking, childish, and blessed art in order not to forfeit that *freedom over things* which our ideal demands of us.[77]

Let's shift our focus from *art* to *the artist*. What is this figure "the artist," and what can we learn from it? More importantly, what is it about this figure that is being *recommended* to you? One way to think about each of the types is as a *drive*. In that sense, in the preceding passage "artist" designates not a per-sonified producer of paintings or operas but rather a potential *drive* within us, a proclivity that impels us toward creative understanding. The artist in us is, for instance, that drive to worship in "the cult of the untrue." It does so, however, not to conjure shadowy chimeras to assist us in evading life's truths. Rather, it does so to assist us in not being *engulfed* by life's truths. And so the artist is the drive to live with eyes wide open, to see the world as it is and ourselves as we are. As *creator*, the artist's task persists throughout our lives. Most important among its creative tasks is to retain the *freedom over things*. If the artist drive is not strong in us, the unflinching severity of honesty and of science—or, indeed, of herd mentality—will result in our forfeiture of this freedom to craft, mold, transform, and revalue *things*.

I think of Nietzsche's types as drives that have become manifest as char-acter traits. In a few passages, Nietzsche comes close to being prescriptive regarding the type of *person* who manifests the artist drive. For example, he speaks of "an artist, as I love artists, modest in their needs: they actually want only two things, bread and art."[78] Nietzsche himself was, of course, extraor-dinarily modest. Like the artist he loves, his possessions basically consisted only of what was required to make his art. He lived in small, cheap, rented rooms; he could fit all of his belongings in a couple of trunks; his income

---

77 *The Gay Science*, 107.
78 *Twilight of the Idols*, "Epigrams and Arrows," 17.

barely covered subsistence; his clothes were clean but worn, and so on. He endured all of this precisely in order to *create*. In this, he was practicing a way of life that fuses his figure *the artist* with that of *the philosopher*. As we will see later, the Nietzschean type, *philosopher*, values creativity and experimentation over rationality and finality. When we come to that figure, I will present the remainder of the above passage. But I want to mention here that the passage ends by saying: "And as long as you are still somehow ashamed of yourself, you do not yet belong to us!" Become an "artist," literally or figuratively, and the endless shaming strategies of modern society—of your family and friend groups, of the trillion-dollar weight, beauty, age, image industries—will have little to no hold on you. The cultural and civilizational ramifications of the artist's way of being are even more important for Nietzsche than the individual consequences. In a world full of uncreative Philistines, herd-people locked into the ruts of borrowed being, the artist reveals to the Last mortals a way of living life *otherwise*.

> Artists alone hate this casual adoption of borrowed manners and protruding opinions, and reveal the secret, the bad conscience of everyone, the principle that every person is a unique miracle. Artists dare to show us that each person, down to every twitch of his muscles, is himself alone. And more still, that in this strict consistency of his uniqueness he is beautiful and worthy of regard, is new and incredible like every work of nature, and by no means boring.[79]

The question for us perfect readers is: what does all of this mean, in real terms, for *us*? More specifically, how might we nourish the drive of the artist and manifest it in our daily lives?

THE FREE SPIRIT

I was a teenager when I first came across "free spirit" in Nietzsche. I still recall it because I was so taken aback. "Free spirit" was a term that was lingering from the fading counterculture of the 1960s. Every self-respecting hippie was a "free spirit," and many young "freaks" in the 1970s still found the idea attractive. But, wait, I thought, those free-spirited hippies were so *soft*, and Nietzsche was imploring us to "become hard!"[80] Was he

---

79 *Untimely Meditations*, "Schopenhauer as Educator," 3.1.
80 *Thus Spoke Zarathustra*, "On Old and New Tablets," 29.

recommending that we live like hippies? Was Nietzsche just another starry-eyed Romantic after all? *The free spirit*—what a lame idea!

It turns out that twentieth-century American counterculture shares the bulk of its DNA with nineteenth-century German counterculture. Indeed, substantial evidence can be marshaled in favor of a German origin to hippie culture itself. Several young acolytes of the "Life-Reform Movement" *(Lebensreformbewegung)* made their way to California in the early twentieth century. Styling themselves "Nature Boys," they lived in log cabins, practiced vegetarianism and yoga, strummed guitars, danced naked in the night, and slowly spread the spirit to disaffected young Californians.[81]

It also turns out that young Nietzsche himself felt an affinity to the free-spirited ideals of the German Life-Reform Movement. The spirit of the movement that would eventually be known by that name ("Life-Reform Movement" was not coined until the end of the century) was already swirling in numerous clubs, societies, associations, and even friend groups from the mid-eighteenth century. At the time that Nietzsche began writing a book subtitled *A Book for Free Spirits* (1878), his own friend group was headed by the feminist author Malwida von Meysenbug. She later wrote of her dream at this time to "establish a kind of mission-house to lead young adults of both sexes to a free development of the noblest intellectual life, so that they could then go out into the world to scatter the seeds of a new, intellectualized culture."[82] Nietzsche was enthusiastic about the project and offered to serve as a teacher. Their search for a site reflects the return to nature, antimodernist, and communal education impulses of the movement as a whole.

> We were already looking for a suitable location in magnificent Sorrento, amid blissful nature, far from narrow urban confines. We had found several spacious grottoes, down below by the beach…We thought them to be very suitable for us to hold our classes there on hot summer days, since in general all this studying was supposed to be more a mutual learning in the manner of the Peripatetics and generally more on a Greek model rather than on a modern one.

Nietzsche's enthusiasm for this project is consistent with the advice he offers the youth in "Schopenhauer as Educator." The topic of that advice is

---

81 See Gordon Kennedy and Kody Ryan, "Hippie Roots & the Perennial Subculture," https://web.archive.org/web/20100924180439/http://hippy.com/modules.php?name=News&file=article&sid=243. Accessed July 21, 2023.
82 Gilman, *Conversations with Nietzsche*, 84.

precisely the topic of this chapter—becoming who one is—and constitutes
a kind of blueprint for the *free spirit*. Nietzsche is addressing the perennial
question "How do we find ourselves? How can one know oneself?"

> The young soul looks back on its life with the question: what have
> you truly loved so far, what has lifted up your soul, what has domi-
> nated it and, at the same time, made it happy? Set up these admired
> objects before you, and perhaps, through their nature and their effects,
> they will yield to you a law, the foundational law of your actual self.
> Compare these objects, see how each supplements the other, extends
> it, surpasses it, transfigures it, how they create a stepladder on which
> you have so far climbed up to yourself. For, your true being lies not
> deep within you but immeasurably high above you, or at least over that
> which you habitually call your "I."[83]

At its most basic, becoming who you are requires reaching for fuller participation in that which all evidence seems to point to as *you*. Note that
Nietzsche avoids the "true self lies within" cliché. His spatial image here
of "high above" *(hoch über)* instead prefigures the perpetual *overcoming*
(überwinden) that characterizes the *overhuman (Übermensch)*. As joyous as
this "follow your bliss" approach may sound, Nietzsche makes it clear that
it is difficult. To youth still in the midst of their education, he warns that
their very schooling perverts and hardens the soul's natural inclination to
bend toward what makes it happy. Modern education is pulling out every
stop to ensure that the student becomes the very antithesis of a free spirit,
namely, a "bound spirit," a person who is habitually "swept away by the
despicable money economy…so that one quickly becomes a money-earn-
er."[84] In fact, *habituation* is the knot in the fetter. In a passage titled *Origin
of faith*, Nietzsche says: "The bound spirit takes a position not on the basis
of reasons, but rather on the basis of habit."[85] A person is a Christian not
because he engages in a prolonged study of all religions and eventually
arrives at the discernment that Christianity is true. A person is certainly not
a Christian because he has gained insight into the depths of the cosmos,
thus compelling that conclusion. A person is a Christian—or a Buddhist or a
liberal or a meateater, ad infinitum—for one reason only: he has unquestion-
ingly accepted the ideology of a community. What the bound spirit is bound

---

83 *Untimely Meditations*, "Schopenhauer as Educator," 1.
84 *Untimely Meditations*, "David Strauss, the Confessor and the Writer," 1.
85 *Human, All Too Human*, 226.

up in, then, is faith, ritual, and habit. By contrast, Nietzsche's free spirit is one who *resists* precisely these forces: "We call that person a free spirit who thinks differently from what we would expect on the basis of that person's place of origin, environment, class and office, or on the basis of dominant contemporary views."[86] None of this means that the free spirit is necessarily closer to the truth in any given matter than is the bound spirit. It does mean, however, that the free spirit is one who demands reasons where the bound spirit rests on faith. The larger consequence of this difference is where the risks and difficulties of being a free spirit arise. For the consequence is that "the free spirit…has released himself from what is conventional."[87]

With that image, the free spirit comes into clearer view. It is a person who stands apart: "That person is the exception; bound spirits are the rule."[88] His or her relation to accepted conventions is one of an outsider, a nomad, a stranger, a heretic. Free spirits are compelled to this position because they are "'the conscientious ones' or 'the penitents of the spirit' or 'the unbound ones' or 'the great seeking ones.'"[89] What might it mean that *such* qualities have the effect of setting a person apart from their community? It brings to mind the feminist notion of the "killjoy" referred to earlier,[90] as well as to Dr. Martin Luther King, Jr.'s plea for people "of goodwill all over the nation to be maladjusted." King's maladjustment logic is similar to Nietzsche's free spirit rationale: we must cultivate it "until the good society is a reality." King continues in a manner that, I believe, Nietzsche would endorse.

I never intend to adjust myself to the evils of segregation and discrimination. I never intend to become adjusted to religious bigotry. I never intend to adjust myself to economic conditions that will take necessities from the many to give luxuries to the few. I never intend to become adjusted to the madness of militarism, and the self-defeating effects of physical violence. And I think now it has come for men all over the nation and all over the world to be maladjusted to all of these things. For it may well be that the salvation of our world lies in the hands of the maladjusted.[91]

86 *Human, All Too Human*, 225.
87 *Human, All Too Human*, 225.
88 *Human, All Too Human*, 225.
89 *Thus Spoke Zarathustra*, "The Song of Melancholy," 2.
90 See Ahmed, *The Promise of Happiness*.
91 Dr. Martin Luther King, Jr., "The American Dream"; speech held on July 4, 1965, https://www.americanrhetoric.com/speeches/mlkihaveadream.htm. Accessed April 7, 2024.

In taking this stand, free spirits risk almost certain castigation from the community. People will insist that their free-spiritedness stems from virtually any trait *but* conscientious reason-seeking.

[Bound spirits] reproach [free spirits] saying that their free principles have their origin either in their yearning to stand out or even in free actions, that is, in actions that can be seen as being incompatible with bound morality. Sometimes, people also say that this or that principle can be derived from eccentricity or mental hysteria.[92]

Reader, ask yourself: do I feel this spirit moving in me? Do I feel the urge to "*become free*," to "take possession of [myself] again"?[93] Recall how we are employing Nietzsche's typology: "the free spirit" first manifests as a psychological or physiological drive, impulse, longing, and so on, and then, through nourishment, forms into a consistent character trait. Consider, too, that once you manifest your free-spiritedness, you cannot control the reactions of the bound spirits who surround you. It is not a happy condition. Like the later Existentialists, who would in fact claim him, Nietzsche likens the condition to that of *nausea*. If you are among those "conscientious ones" who call themselves "free spirits," Zarathustra speaks thus:

All of you who suffer *from heavy nausea* as I do, all of you for whom the old God has died and no new God yet lies swathed in the cradle—to all of you, my evil spirit and magic devil is beholden.[94]

Who among us is really prepared to embrace Nietzsche's magic devil? Nietzsche is always playing the long game. As for the free spirits in his midst, he says that there "were none," that he "*invented*" them whenever he "needed their company...to remain in good spirits in the midst of bad things (illness, isolation, alienation, acedia,[95] idleness), as courageous com-

---

92 *Human, All Too Human*, 225.
93 *Ecce Homo*, "Human, All Too Human," 1.
94 *Thus Spoke Zarathustra*, "The Song of Melancholy," 2.
95 This is a very interesting word choice. Originally a Greek word indicating carelessness or heedlessness due to indifference, *acedia* was adapted by early Christian monastics and dubbed "the noonday demon." John Cassian (360–435) described the condition of the afflicted monk as follows: "The fifth or sixth hour brings him such bodily weariness and longing for food that he seems to himself worn out and wearied as if with a long journey, or some very heavy work, or as if he had put off taking food during a fast of two or three days. He looks about anxiously this way and that, and sighs that none of the brethren come to see him, and often goes in and out of his cell, and frequently gazes up at the sun, as if it was too

panions and specters with whom one chats and laughs whenever ones feels like chatting and laughing."[96] As we saw previously regarding Malwida von Meysenbug's project, Nietzsche was, in fact, surrounded by actual free spirits as he was writing these words. So what might he mean when he says he invented them? Nietzsche being Nietzsche, I read it as meaning that no "free spirit" truly lived up to the name. Certainly, he detected the disqualifying failings of those in his midst—Paul Rée, Lou Salomé, Malwida von Meysenbug herself, and the long parade of *Freigeister* who passed through her villa during this period. Yet Nietzsche understood the *spirit*, and so could keep alive, if only in his imagination, the hypothesis that "such free spirits *could* one day come."

That our Europe will have among its sons of tomorrow and the day after tomorrow such lively and daring fellows, real and palpable and not merely, as in my case, as shades and a hermit's shadow play. I want to doubt that least of all. I already see them coming, slowly, slowly; and perhaps I will do something to accelerate their coming if I describe in advance under which circumstances I *see* them coming into being, on which paths I *see* them coming?

And when they do come, they will have all the markings of "the new philosopher."

THE NEW PHILOSOPHER

Bound spirits are those of a *conventional faith*. Free spirits are those of a *different faith*. In what does that difference consist? In the section on democracy, we saw the negative aspect of this difference. "We who are of a different faith," Nietzsche said there, commit a breach of one of the taboos of Western social-political thought. It concerns an idea that was emerging in Nietzsche's day and has become a sacred cow in our own. Our new faith, namely, compels us to reject the assumption that *liberal democracy* represents the pinnacle of enlightened governance and final goal of human community. For we who are of a different faith have seen with our own eyes what liberal democracy has wrought. How can we *not* "view the democratic movement not merely

---

slow in setting, and so a kind of unreasonable confusion of mind takes possession of him like some foul darkness." *The Institutes,* Book Ten, "On the Spirit of Accidie" (chapter four).
96 Until otherwise noted, *Human, All Too Human*, Preface, 2.

as a decayed form of political organization but rather as a decayed, that is to say, diminutive, form of the human, as the human's mediocritization and degradation of worth"? This is not an endorsement of illiberal democracy or of any other political form. It is an opening to further thought about the matter. So, Nietzsche, being an exemplary critical thinker—namely, one who also provides *affirmative* material for further thought—then poses the necessary question: "to where must we reach with our hopes?" We have seen his answer already—toward the free spirit. Here, Nietzsche casts that somewhat spectral figure—suggested by the very term, free *spirit*—into one of unquestionable historical concreteness.

> To where must we reach with our hopes? Toward *new philosophers*, there is no choice. Toward spirits, strong and original enough to give impetus to opposite evaluations, and to transvalue, to invert "eternal values"; toward advance envoys, toward people of the future who in the present fasten to themselves the pressures and knots that force onto *new* tracks the will of millennia…It is the image of such leaders that hovers before *our* eyes—may I say it out loud, you free spirits?[97]

The task of the new philosopher lies at the very heart of Nietzsche's thought: a revaluation of values. Consistent with every other drive-type we have looked at so far, the new philosopher is someone who has experienced the "sensitive pain" of observing once extraordinary people lose their way and become shadows of their former exemplary selves. Out of this pain, the new philosopher develops "the rare eye for the overall danger that 'the human' *degenerates* itself." The new philosopher is someone who recognizes that our individual and collective self-destruction is a "disaster that lies buried in the idiotic innocence and blind confidence of 'modern ideas' and even more so in the whole Christian-European morality." On the constructive side, this same rare eye can "grasp with a single glance what kind of *human might yet be cultivated*, through a favorable accumulation and intensification of energies and tasks." New philosophers are exceedingly careful and practiced observers of human communities (families, friend groups, the workplace, society as a whole). The new philosophers "know, with all the knowledge of their conscience, how the human is still unexhausted for the greatest possibilities, and how often already the type 'human' has confronted mystifying decisions and new paths." Any reader who still views Nietzsche as a merely

---

97 And all following quotes unless noted, *Beyond Good and Evil*, 203.

or mainly destructive thinker must read that extraordinarily affirmative statement with some surprise. For although the new philosopher "knows a kind
of nausea like no other person," he or she knows "perhaps also a new *task*!"
Whatever else it might be, the new philosophizing is something that is *done*.

An assumption is at work here that, I imagine, will cause some readers
to balk. All of the new philosopher's recognitions and actions assume "the
monstrous contingency that up to now has played its game in relation to
humanity's future." This "game" of *chance*, of existential randomness and
natural chaos, could not be any more real, more present, thus more obvious
to those with the "rare eyes" to see. Yet this assumption stands in direct
contrast to the faith of bound spirits. For Nietzsche insists that this is "a
game in which no hand, not even a finger, of God plays!" Yet this godless
view is an essential, nonnegotiable requirement for setting out for new seas.

> Indeed, we philosophers and "free spirits," when we hear the news that
> the "old god is dead," feel as if a new dawn has shone on us; our heart
> then overflows with gratitude, amazement, premonition, expectation—
> at long last the horizon appears free to us again, even if it should not
> be bright; at long last our ships may venture out again, venture out to
> face any danger; every daring of the discoverer is permitted again; the
> sea, *our* sea, lies open again; perhaps there has never yet been such an
> "open sea!"[98]

When Nietzsche adds that we set out toward the horizon "even if it should
not be bright," he is indicating a further assumption that is held by the new
philosopher. In the space once filled by our superabundant God, a shadow
now spreads. For those few whose "*suspicion* in the eyes is strong and
subtle enough for this spectacle, it seems as if a certain sun has set, a certain
ancient and profound trust has turned into doubt." Unlike the improvers of
humankind, with their quick fixes and easy solutions, the new philosopher
is clear-eyed about one fact: "A long period of abundant and consequential
demolition, destruction, decline, and upheaval now stands before us."

How might we understand the new philosopher as a *drive*? I tend to think
of it as that urge to start afresh. How much mental, emotional, physical clut-
ter have we accumulated over the years? How much of this accumulation
truly serves our present journey, much less enhances it? Does not a truly
fresh start require us to set out with new assumptions? From where will we

---

98 And following two paragraphs, *The Gay Science*, 343.

derive these new assumptions, these new *values*? Most importantly, what must we do, now, while we can? Such urgent considerations, such *impulses*, belong to the new philosopher. They extend well beyond mere personal or psychological consideration and into the social, political, cultural, and civilization spheres. Discerning the interconnectedness of the part and the whole, the type "new philosopher" cannot give thought to the renewal of the person without giving thought to the renewal of society, and vice versa. This implies a massive task, one that "lies beyond the comprehension of many." And so, a sense of impossibility burrows into the impulse of the new philosopher. This sense is compounded by a premonition: a creeping sensation that at the heart of our darkening catastrophe lies the worm of…

THE IMMORALIST

…"our entire European morality."

And so we are in need of "the immoralist." Of all the types Nietzsche sketches in his work, only Zarathustra is as personal to him as this figure. With great pride, he declares himself to be an immoralist. Why would he do so? The ears of his contemporaries would have bristled at the very term. In hyper-moralistic Victorian Europe, an "immoral" person was one prone to transgressions of etiquette and decorum to the point of the vilest depravity. The immoral person was *anathema*, "a thing cursed," a social pariah who violated sacred norms of propriety, purity, and of goodness itself. The immoralist's relation to the human body, to sexuality, to gender norms, to respectable dress and grooming, to God and the church, to the family, to authority, and beyond, meant that he or she was nothing short of "a thing devoted to evil."[99] So, again, why would Nietzsche outright *declare* himself such a person?

One answer is that it was a provocation, similar to titling his book *The Antichrist* (another profoundly goading term). Unquestionably, Nietzsche means to provoke. So maybe that's part of the explanation. I can certainly picture Nietzsche, sitting at his wooden desk overlooking the icy mountains of Sils Maria, getting an emotional kick with every jotting of *immoralist!* But provocation is far less important for Nietzsche than stating the "very disagreeable truths" that his incisive "critique of modernity" yield.[100]

---

99 For these two definitions of "anathema," see *The Online Etymological Dictionary*, https://www.etymonline.com/word/anathema. Accessed August 11, 2023.
100 *Ecce Homo*, "Genealogy of Morality" and *Ecce Homo*, "Beyond Good and Evil," 2.

Another answer is that Nietzsche meant only that he was against the morality of his day. Around the time of his birth, people were beginning to undergo what historian Harold Perkin calls "the Moral Revolution." Perkin describes its manifestation in England as:

that profound change in national character which accompanied the Industrial Revolution. Between 1780 and 1850 the English ceased to be one of the most aggressive, brutal, rowdy, outspoken, riotous, cruel and bloodthirsty nations in the world and became one of the most inhibited, polite, orderly, tender-minded, prudish and hypocritical.[101]

In his 1887 book, *On the Genealogy of Morals*, Nietzsche offers his own analysis of the same phenomenon. He sees it as a shift away from "the instinct of cruelty" toward "*ressentiment*." Cruelty, in Perkin's language, is aggressive, brutal, rowdy. For Nietzsche, this instinct is "one of the oldest and most irrefutable substrata of culture." Resentment or *ressentiment* is polite, orderly, tender-minded. It is "a countermovement in its very essence, a mighty revolt against the domination of *noble* values." The impelling force of this shift occurs when "the instinct of cruelty turns back on itself once it becomes impossible to discharge itself externally." This turn initially occurred with the victory of Christianity over paganism two millennia ago and spread throughout the world along with the religious institution. The ultimate result of the turn is "our entire European morality." Nietzsche the psychologist sees morality at work in our very notion of *conscience*. While the devout view conscience as "the voice of God in the person,"[102] the psychologist understands it to be the gutted, suffocated voice of repressed cruelty perversely twisted into morality.[103] So Nietzsche's emphasis on Christianity's role in the development of "our entire European morality" could indeed be interpreted as evidence that his immoralist stance is limited to *that* version of morality. Similarly, he tells us that his term *immoralist* contains two negations.

---

101 Harold Perkin, *The Origins of Modern English Society* (London: Routledge, 1969), 280.

102 *Ecce Homo*, "Genealogy of Morality."

103 So many examples from history support Nietzsche's contention. Think of the ways in which the following formations teetered on the seesaw of Ultra Good and Ultra Evil: the Puritans, the Crusades, the Inquisition, the 395, 216 American Christians who collectively enslaved 3.9 million people as Nietzsche was writing his book on morality and cruelty. See Angela McMillian, "Slavery in America," *Library of Congress*. https://guides.loc.gov/slavery-in-america. Accessed April 8, 2024.

I negate first a type of person, one who until now has been considered the highest, *the good, the benevolent, the charitable*; then I negate a type of morality that in its repute and authority has come to mean morality in itself—the morality of decadence, or more clearly, *Christian* morality.[104]

A third possibility is that Nietzsche wants us to become immoralists only in relation to moral *idealism*, but to be moralists in relation to moral *naturalism*. By the former term I mean to capture three kinds of *idealisms*: systems of morality that (i) base their principles on reason alone; (ii) aim for the optimal society; and (iii) universalize personal feelings. People who may have been on Nietzsche's mind are: (i) Plato and Immanuel Kant; (ii) John Stuart Mill and Jeremy Bentham; (iii) everybody! Concerning the latter, we have already seen that Nietzsche considers philosophy to be run through with the autobiography (and digestive system) of the person doing the philosophizing. Regarding morality, specifically, he says that whenever we hear a moral principle being promoted, we might ask, "what does such a contention tell us about the person who makes it?" This question is followed by a remarkable typology of moral systems: "There are moralities that are meant to justify their author before others; other moralities are meant to calm him and make him satisfied with himself; with others the author wants to hammer and mortify himself on the cross; with others he desires to take revenge, with others conceal himself, with others transfigure himself and establish himself high up and far away." Such moralizers often "want to exert their power and creative whimsy over humanity." In any case, for the moral idealist, morality is nothing but *"a sign language of the affects."*[105] Reason deludes itself that it is gleaning universal principles when, in fact, it is doing the bidding of quite localized bodily drives, compulsions, impulses, urges, needs. Moral concepts derived from rationality are wholly incapable of capturing the ramifications of "that dark, driving, insatiable self-desiring force" that we call life, concerning good and evil and how we should act in the world. It is difficult to communicate just how much Nietzsche despised idealism. This passage from a letter he wrote to Malwida von Meysenbug might help.

I handle idealism as an instinct that has become untruthfulness, as a *wanting*-not-to-see reality at all costs: *every* sentence of my writings is

---

104 *Ecce Homo*, "Why I Am A Destiny," 4.
105 *Beyond Good and Evil*, 187.

saturated with *contempt* for idealism. There has been no worse fate for humanity to date than *this* intellectual squalidness; we have devalued the worth of all reality so that we may *lie about* an "ideal world."[106]

What about the alternative to idealism—moral *naturalism*? After all, Nietzsche titled a section of *Beyond Good and Evil* "On the Natural History of Morality." A natural historical approach entails a study of how morality has *lived* within its environment over time. The preceding typology is an example of a natural historical observation. Like his later "genealogical" approach to morality, a natural history contains an implicit refutation of idealism at the outset. For, unlike rationally (ideally) derived universal principles, *natural* and *history* imply mutation over time and place. Up to now, Nietzsche argues, the ostensible scientist-philosophers of morality have done an "amateurish, clumsy, and heavy-handed"[107] job of studying their object. One reason for this poor job is that moral thinkers are myopic. Even if they were employing the methods of natural history, their vision has thus far been limited to the morality of their "environment, class, church, spirit of the times, climate, and corner of the world." How could such (ideal) universal claims be made from such a limited sample? Nietzsche says it is "precisely because they have been poorly informed and even lacking curiosity concerning different peoples, ages, and past times." Because of their myopia, "our moral philosophers…have never come face to face with the actual problems of morality—which only emerge through a comparison of *many* moralities." Once you begin comparing the moralities of different cultures, you discover that moral principles have no fixed meaning. This is true for moral categories such as good and evil, right and wrong, as well as for moral dicta such as "always tell the truth," "do not kill," or indeed Kant's famous "Act only according to that maxim whereby you can at the same time will that it should become a universal law." Our moral philosophers typically resolve the problem of relativism by arguing from the values derived from their own "environment, class, church." And around and around we go.

So it is beginning to look like the reason for the poor job made of studying morality has something to do with the fact that, when observed in its lived environment, "the moral" becomes a woefully slippery concept. What about the second reason that I mentioned? Can we salvage hope for a future "natural science of morals" by correcting the current practitioners' clumsy error? No, we cannot. On the contrary, it leads us into a refutation of the very

---

106 *BVN*–1888, 1135.
107 And following quotes, *Beyond Good and Evil*, 186.

category "the moral." The fatal error made by moral thinkers, Nietzsche argues, is that they *assume* its very existence: "every philosopher has up to now believed to have established a foundation for morality; morality itself, however, was taken as a 'given.'" From the perspective of "nature, as it is, in all of its profligate and indifferent magnificence,"[108] nothing like "morality" is necessary, and so no such thing as morality is ever to be found. This is not to say that morality has no reality or force in the human world. It obviously does. But so does Santa Claus. Nietzsche's point is that by not recognizing that morality is something altogether different from what we make it out to be, we are exacerbating our diminution and delaying our *task*. This is not the way of the artist, the free spirit, the new philosopher, much less of the *immoralist*.

Darkly and dangerously, a fourth possibility now comes into focus. It is the most drastic possibility: Nietzsche is against *all* morality, against morality per se. Much more importantly, he believes that the future of humanity depends on you and I and many others becoming immoralists as well. Can that be? What would being a literal immoralist even entail? And to where is the *drive to immorality* directing us?

Nietzsche expands on the term in several passages. For instance, at the beginning of his book for free spirits, he refers to himself as an "old immoralist," someone who "speaks un-morally, extra-morally, 'beyond good and evil.'"[109] Thinking and speaking outside of the very framework of morality, the immoralist can view more clearly the workings of the human heart and mind, and far beyond. What makes this possible is that the immoralist—indeed, like nature itself—no longer takes into consideration the "utility of the herd."[110] As our moral philosophers taught us earlier, this merely amounts to "good *faith* in the prevailing morality."[111] That is, in rough terms, whatever preserves the community status quo is *good;* whatever threatens it is *bad,* or indeed *evil.* Clearly, even at such a rudimentary level, such moralistic valuation is problematic. We have already seen how enslavement has served the utility of the status quo from the beginning of civilization to the present day. We can take the example further. The "runaway" enslaved person was *evil* incarnate, a fugitive animal operating outside of the just norms of propriety, the law, and the state. But the people who cooperated to hold that person in brutal captivity were *goodness* in the flesh. They were the pillars

---

108 *Beyond Good and Evil*, 188.
109 *Human, All Too Human*, Preface, 1.
110 *Beyond Good and Evil*, 201.
111 *Beyond Good and Evil*, 186.

of the righteous community—the pious preachers, the doctors and lawyers, the virtuous wives and mothers. What is "morality," asks Nietzsche, but an "instrument of the common welfare," as one of countless "herd maxims" has it?[112] Yes, then as today, of course, "one 'knows' what is good and evil."[113] Right?

When Nietzsche adds "up to now," he is announcing the advent of "the first *immoralist*," namely, himself.[114] His very way of speaking or thinking is meant to serve as an example of *how to be an immoralist*. Indeed, in many respects, so is his very life, with its solitude, integrity, humor, courage, and more, as we will see later. At a minimum, being an immoralist indicates that, unlike everyone else, Nietzsche does *not* believe he has "established a foundation for morality" or that morality is to be "taken as a 'given.'" What else does being an immoralist entail?

I have extended the discussion in this section because I feel it represents a particularly treacherous curve in our journey. So many imagined readers' objections to immoralism ring in my ears. I believe that this may be why numerous Nietzsche scholars have endeavored to show that, when all is said and done, Nietzsche remains committed to *some version* of morality. It is as if we cannot conceive of someone being anything but the most abhorrent deviant *unless* he subscribes to *some form* of morality—and, preferably, to *our* morality. Nietzsche is aware of this looming opprobrium and so emphatically declares: "I am no moral monster."[115] He justifies his bracketing of "morality" by placing it within his project as a whole, namely, "the seeking of all that is strange and questionable in existence, of all which has hitherto been banned by morality." This entire book is intended as an accompaniment of Nietzsche in his "wandering in that which is *forbidden*," and thus, like him, aims to "learn to consider the causes, out of which until now have come moralizing and idealizing, to be very different from what may be desired."[116] Let's complete this stretch of our journey, then, with a remarkably affirmative passage that only an *immoralist* could love.

> Whoever persists in dealing with [a moral problem] and so *learns* how to question, will undergo what I have undergone—a tremendous new perspective opens up to him, a possibility seizes him like vertigo, every

---

112 *Beyond Good and Evil*, 199.
113 *Beyond Good and Evil*, 202.
114 *Ecce Homo*, "The Untimely Ones," 2.
115 *Ecce Homo*, Preface, 2.
116 *Ecce Homo*, Preface, 3.

type of mistrust, suspicion, fear, leaps forward, the belief in morality, in all of morality, falters—finally, a *new demand* rings out. Let us say it out loud, this new demand: a *critique* of moral value is required of us, *the value of these values is itself first to be placed in question*—and this requires knowledge of the conditions and circumstances out of which these values have grown, under which they have developed and shifted (morality as consequence, as symptom, as mask, as foolishness, as sickness, as misunderstanding; but also morality as cause, as medicine, as stimulant, as inhibition, as poison), as knowledge such as has not yet been available or desired.[117]

Nietzsche then doubles down on his earlier observation that not a single one of us has ever even considered the possibility that morality might be something other than the absolute "given" that it and its acolytes present it as. Neither have we doubted for an instant that we know what good and evil are or that the "good person" is better than the "evil person." And then Nietzsche asks a severe question:

Really? And what if the reverse were true? Really? What if inherent in the "good" were a symptom of decline, likewise a danger, a seduction, a poison, a narcotic, through which the present, perhaps, were living *at the expense of the future*? Perhaps [living] more comfortably, less dangerously, but at the same time in a more lowly style, meaner?... So that precisely morality would be to blame if the entirely feasible *highest power and splendor* of the type "human" were never attained? So that precisely morality were the danger of dangers?[118]

THE *ÜBERMENSCH*

The *Übermensch* is Nietzsche's most famous figure. In the specific form preached by Zarathustra, it is also his exemplar extraordinaire. I think that anyone who reads Nietzsche broadly[119] will come away with the sense that he was exceptionally proud of his creation. He speaks, for instance, of the

---

117 *Geneology of Morals,* Preface, 6.
118 *On the Genealogy of Morals*, Preface, 6.
119 By "broadly," I mean reading the correspondence, notebooks, and fragments along with all of the authorized manuscripts and published works.

Übermensch as taught by his "son," Zarathustra.[120] And he insists that the 1883 work in which the *Übermensch* so prominently figures, *Thus Spoke Zarathustra*, "stands completely on its own."[121] Conceived "6000 feet above humanity and time," not even a Goethe, Shakespeare, or Dante "would know how to breathe for an instant in this tremendous passion and height." Out of this rarefied atmosphere emerges the *Übermensch* as "the *highest type of all beings.*" Yet, in the end, it is still but another "type," available to those of us with lungs to scale such heights.[122]

While Nietzsche's *Übermensch* figure is his most famous and his most exalted, it is also his most ridiculous. As Nietzsche would want us to believe, however, this is through no fault of his own (but is it?). With the arrival of Nietzsche's colossal postsanity fame in the early 1890s, the *Übermensch*, too, blasted onto the cultural scene, high and low. George Bernard Shaw's 1903 play *Man and Superman* is an interesting example in that it mixes these two levels. For instance, owing its very title to Nietzsche (the "Epistle Dedicatory" section of the printed play mentions our Immoralist five times), Shaw's *Übermensch* is very much a Darwinian figure, evolving from mere "man" to "superman." As we will see, nothing could be further from Nietzsche's conception; but given the amount of space that evolutionary theory occupied in the intellectual and artistic circles of his day, Shaw can be excused for this stumble. To his credit, Shaw's male protagonist, the anarchist-leaning John Tanner, certainly *aspires* to genuine *Übermensch* qualities, such as superior intellect, subtle cunning, transgression of moral codes, and being a promulgator of self-determined values. Even more to Shaw's credit is the fact that, as far as I can make out, it is the female protagonist of *Man and Superman*, Anne Whitefield, who actually *embodies* these traits.[123] Be that as it may, inexcusable and unfortunate is Shaw's popularization of

---

120 Nietzsche refers to Zarathustra as his son in several letters; for example: *BVN*–1883, 421 (letter to his friend Marie Baumgartner) and *BVN*–1883, 431 (letter to his friend Franz Overbeck). In *Thus Spoke Zarathustra*, "On the Tarantulas," Zarathustra himself says: "What the father keeps silent, the son brings to speech; and I often found the son to be the father's secret laid bare."

121 *Ecce Homo*, "Thus Spoke Zarathustra," 6.

122 *Ecce Homo*, "Thus Spoke Zarathustra," 1 and 6, respectively.

123 Indeed, Margaret Sanger (1879–1966) the American women's rights activist, believed that Nietzsche had, in fact, created the conditions for a new Super*woman*. Against the constricting morality and suffocating repression that defined the lives of women, Nietzsche's *Übermensch*, she was convinced, encouraged women to seek out "life in its fullness and all that is high, beautiful, and daring" and to understand that "the individual is the original source and constituent of all value." Quoted in Ratner-Rosenhagen, *American Nietzsche*, 115.

the translation "superman."[124] Again, as far as I can determine, "superman" was Shaw's own translation from the German. For, the first translation of the work into English, Alexander Tille's *Thus Spake Zarathustra*, appeared before Shaw's play, in 1896, and had "beyond-man" for *Übermensch*. And we don't get "superman" until Thomas Common's translation in 1909, several years after Shaw's play. It is likely that Common's choice was in part taking advantage of the popularity of *Man and Superman*. In any case, it is with the "superman" motif that the *Übermensch* slides into low culture. I have not found any evidence that Jerry Siegel and Joe Shuster, the Cleveland teenagers who created the superhero "Superman" in 1933, had any knowledge of Nietzsche's *Übermensch* (nor of Shaw's play). Yet the two figures, *Übermensch* and Superman, quickly became enmeshed in the popular imagination. Hollywood gave us the former in many conflicting yet compelling guises: as aggressive advocate of social Darwinism; as degenerate; gangster; genius; as Dionysian libertine; and as frivolous free spirit.[125] The cumulative image was of the *Übermensch* as part egoist, part sociopath, and part savior superhero. The depraved culmination of this mishmash was the grotesque murder of fourteen-year-old Bobby Franks by Nathan Leopold and Richard Loeb, who, as we saw earlier, "thought they were Nietzschean supermen."[126] This unsightly *Übermensch* is now a popular internet figure, often confused with Nietzsche (who is often confused with Zarathustra) himself. Just witness the memes of a pumped-up, bare-chested, ripped Nietzsche on steroids screaming, "WHAT DOES NOT KILL US MAKES US STRONGER!!!" To top it all off, always on the lookout for cultural representations of all things Nietzsche, I started to listen to a podcast recently that began: "The incel Zarathustra went forth from his cave…" (I didn't get much further.) For readers unfamiliar with the term "incel," it is a combination of "involuntary" and "celibate." Self-proclaimed incels form a subculture of almost exclusively young, white, heterosexual males who, for various reasons, find themselves incapable of forming intimate relationships with women. Thus excluded from the circuit of dating, romance, relationships, sex, and marriage, incels are presented in social media as being pathetic, misogynist, self-loathing—and dangerous. Several mass shootings in the United States

---

124 I hereby decree that *Übermensch*, like kindergarten, gesundheit, doppelganger, blitz, hamburger, rucksack, Volkswagen, fest, kitsch, schadenfreude, wanderlust, spiel, kaputt, angst, and so on and so forth, be granted admission to the English language. Any possible translation pales—*pales!*—before *Übermensch*, particularly given that magnificent umlaut.

125 See Matthew Rukgaber, *Nietzsche in Hollywood: Images of the Übermensch in Early American Cinema* (New York: State University of New York Press, 2022).

126 Ratner-Rosenhagen, *American Nietzsche*), 145.

have been perpetuated by self-identified incels.[127] According to the *Incels Wiki*, by the way, Nietzsche himself was a "protocel," an incel "prior to the incelosphere age."[128]

Why am I telling you all of this? I am doing so to clear the air, for some readers, and as an inoculation, for others. I have lost track of how many otherwise thoughtful and well-informed people I know who dismiss Nietzsche out of hand because of his public image. They are embarrassed for Zarathustra and sickened by what they view as the über-macho, über-corny *Übermensch.* And, to be fair, Friedrich *I am not a man I am dynamite* Nietzsche is not entirely free of fault here. Like so many stereotypes and caricatures, there is a grain of truth to the image. The prophet of the *Übermensch, Zarathustra,* is as often as not an overdrawn figure. Take, for instance, "Light am I: oh, that I were night!/But this is my loneliness that I am engirded with light/Ah, that I were dark and nocturnal!/How I wanted to suck the breasts of light!"[129] After reviewing (in *Ecce Homo)* several dozen of these lines of Zarathustra talking to himself before sunrise, Nietzsche informs the reader that "Such as this has never before been put to verse, never been felt, never been *suffered*; thus suffers a god, a Dionysus."[130] Expressed like this, the idea sounds ridiculous to our ears. But—and this is the question driving this book like a battering ram—does that make it *unworthy* of further consideration; indeed, does that make it *untrue*?

Nietzsche, in fact, invented neither the term nor the conception of the *Übermensch.* As a scholar of ancient Greece, he almost certainly would have been aware of its usage in the work of the satirist, Lucian of Samosata (125–200).[131] In fact, in a section titled "What I Owe the Ancients," Nietzsche

---

127 See, for instance, Maya Yang, "'Incels' are a rising threat in the US, Secret Service report finds," *The Guardian.* https://www.theguardian.com/us-news/2022/mar/16/involuntary-celibates-incels-threat-us-secret-service. Accessed April 7, 2024.

128 "Friedrich Nietzsche." *Incels Wiki,* https://incels.wiki/w/Friedrich_Nietzsche. Accessed August 6, 2023.

129 *Ecce Homo,* "Thus Spoke Zarathustra," 7.

130 *Ecce Homo,* "Thus Spoke Zarathustra," 8.

131 I count eight references to Lucian in letters, one in a notebook fragment, and one in *Human, All Too Human* ("A Wanderer and his Shadow," 107). Nietzsche could well have come across the concept of the *Übermensch* in a wide range of near contemporary sources, most likely in Goethe's *Faust,* but also in Herder, Novalis, and Heine. For these references, see *Grimm Wörterbuch, s.v., Übermensch,* https://woerterbuchnetz.de/?sigle=DWB#1. In German, the term appears in religious commentaries on scripture, in philosophical texts, and in literary fiction, drama, and poetry. In general usage, it concerns "the attribution of extraordinary qualities or abilities that raise the thus stylized people above the everyday mass of people." See Georg Hartmann, *"Übermensch,"* in: C. Auffarth, *et. al.* (eds.) *Metzler Lexikon Religion* (J. B. Metzler: Stuttgart, 2005). Finally, as an admirer of Ralph Waldo Emerson, Nietzsche would have likely encountered his essay "The Over-soul." Like Zarathustra, this

mentions that he admires "satura Menippea," the very style of satire in which Lucian wrote of a figure called the *hyperanthropos*.[132] *Übermensch* is, of course, a direct German translation of this Greek term: *hyper*/über = over, above, beyond, across, exceeding; and *anthropos*/Mensch = man, human. Significantly, both Lucian and Nietzsche insinuate a counterintuitive twist to this prefix of traversal: *under, down*. In Lucian's *The Downward Journey*, the poor cobbler Micyllus mocks a wealthy tyrant who, in life, he says, "appeared to me a superman *(hyperanthropos)*" because of his physical stature, wealth, and "majestic gait, who carried his head high and dazzled all he met." Even superhuman tyrants, alas, must one day engage in a going-under. And in so doing, in *going under*, their true worth is revealed. Micyllus continues: "But when he was dead [and enroute to Hades], not only did he cut an utterly ridiculous figure in my eyes on being stripped of his pomp, but I laughed at myself even more than at him because I had marveled at such a worthless creature, inferring his happiness from the savour of his kitchen."[133] Zarathustra likewise goes under. But because his going-under is integral to his—and to *our*—overcoming, it is an altogether different affair. Living alone in his mountain cave for ten years, Zarathustra accumulated an excess of wisdom, like bees accumulate excess honey. Addressing the morning sun, he says that he feels himself in need of outstretched hands in which to place his overabundance.

> I want to bestow and dispense, until the wise among the people once again rejoice in their foolishness, and the poor, in their wealth.
>
> To that end, I must descend into the deep: as you [the sun] do in the

---

figure is "The Supreme Critic on the errors of the past and the present, and the only prophet of that which must be."

132 *Twilight of the Idols*, "What I Owe the Ancients," 2. In part, his admiration must have been based on the fact that "Menippean satire" attacked conceptual ideas and mental attitudes rather than the individuals who held them. Furthermore, in texts such as *Lover of Lies* and *The Sorcerer's Apprentice*, Lucian wrote in an often mocking style ridiculing believers in the supernatural. He was even less kind to public figures. Nietzsche would have found in him an ally and perhaps even a model of sorts.

133 The Loeb Classical Library 14, *Lucian,* translated by A. M. Harmon, (Cambridge, MA: Harvard University Press, 1913), 35 (the Greek is on page 34). On Micyllus's comment about the kitchen and for a full discussion of the connection between our two terms, see Babette Babich, "Nietzsche's Zarathustra and Parodic Style: On Lucian's *Hyperanthropos* and Nietzsche's *Übermensch*" (*Diogenes,* 2013). *Articles and Chapters in Academic Book Collections*, 56. https://fordham.bepress.com/phil_babich/56. Accessed August 7, 2023. Babich makes a compelling argument that the connection to Lucian reveals Nietzsche's satirical intent in *Thus Spoke Zarathustra*. Micyllus's kitchen remark is but one example. Babich compares it to "The Evening Meal," where we read that "With Zarathustra, to be sure, even a king may be a cook."

evening, when you go behind the sea and once more bring light to the underworld, you overabundant star.

Like you, I must *go under*, as people call it, to those to whom I wish to descend.

So, bless me then, you calm eye that can also see an all-too-great happiness without envy!

Bless the cup that wants to overflow so that water flows golden out of it and carries over the land the reflection of your delight!

Look! This cup wants to become empty again, and Zarathustra wants to become human again.

—Thus began Zarathustra's going-under.[134]

The final word of that passage is the noun *Untergang*. This can also mean *decline, ruin, destruction, downfall, loss*. In the case of a "last mortal," a *letzter Mensch* (more later), such as the tyrant is, that is exactly what going under turns out to be. But not only for a tyrant. *Anyone* who merely plays the prescripted role dictated by the values of their milieu goes under in this sense. For most, then, going under entails *negation*—loss, diminishment. Stripped of pomp and pretense, the sham *hyperanthropos* is revealed to be but an empty shade. In the case of a person engaged in perpetual overcoming, however, going under is a vital feature of realizing the "great health"[135] that is the *Übermensch*. It is also an act of radical *affirmation*, one that takes nature itself as its model. Late in his journey, Zarathustra determines to go down once again to where the people are. He does so in order to give them his "richest gift." Unlike the diminished going under of "'good' people," "'modern' people," pompous tyrants, and "other nihilists,"[136] the aspiring *Übermensch's* descension entails abundance.

I learned this from the sun, the Overabundant One, when it goes down: it pours gold into the sea out of its inexhaustible wealth —

—so that the poorest fisherman may yet row with *golden* oars! I saw this once, and, watching, could not stop my tears.——

Zarathustra wants to go under like the sun; now, he sits here and waits, old broken tablets strewn about him, and new ones, too—half-written.[137]

---

134 *Thus Spoke Zarathustra*, "Zarathustra's Preface," 1.
135 *On the Genealogy of Morals*, 2.24.
136 *Ecce Homo*, "Why I Write Such Good Books," 1.
137 *Thus Spoke Zarathustra*, "Of Old and New Tablets," 3.

Those old tablets in whose midst Zarathustra sits contain, of course, the (broken) moral law that has served us until now. The new ones are only half-written because Zarathustra/Nietzsche only initiates the task and the journey. It is up to the artists, free spirits, new philosophers, immoralists, in short, *Übermenschen,* to carry it further. And this, I believe, is the single most, absolute concern driving Nietzsche's thought: how to *cultivate* the type of people to realize our greatest promise as a species. The concept of cultivation is crucial here. The promising *individual* appears now and then, here and there, seemingly randomly and coincidentally. That is not enough. A bedrock assumption of Nietzsche's is that for humanity to have a future, we must *change*—that is, what counts as a *human being* must change. And this change involves the cultivation of a new type.

> The problem that I am posing here is not what will replace humanity in the succession of beings (—the human is an *end*—): rather, which type of person we should *cultivate*, we should *want,* as the one of higher value, more worthy of life, more certain of a future.
>
> This person of higher value has been among us often enough: but as a fluke, as an exception, never as *wanted.* In fact, *that person* has always been the most feared, indeed, has up to now, practically been Fear *itself*—and out of that fear the opposite type has been wanted, cultivated, *achieved*: the domesticated pet, the herd animal, the sick animal called the human being—the Christian.[138]

Such talk about people "of higher value" rightfully makes us nervous. Given the history of the recent twentieth century alone, it seems to be a noxious concept *prima facie*—immediately, obviously, and on the very face of it. Add to this talk related notions as "more worthy of life" and "Fear *itself*" and, intentionally or not, Nietzsche is once again forcing his perfect reader to slow down. What are our options here? At one extreme, we can assume that such talk is proof that the Nazis got Nietzsche right and that he provided them with fodder for their murderous racial policies.[139] At another extreme,

---

138 *The Antichrist*, 3.
139 His word choice might be seen as further damning evidence. For he uses *züchten*, which I translated as "cultivate." The German term also means "breed," as in animal and plant husbandry. And Nietzsche does seem to have some sense of this notion in mind as well. The problem, of course, is that such talk of breeding sounds dangerously close to twentieth-century eugenics. I will simply put the question to the reader: is it possible that such a dangerous correspondence might only seem to be the case *in retrospect*? For consideration, here is Nietzsche's own definition, from his notebooks: "Breeding, as I understand it, is a

we can explain it all away as Nietzschean bluster and provocation. Many points of possibility, however, exist between these two untenable extremes. By the time we reach the end of this book, I hope to have convinced the reader that something altogether different—and much more *interesting*— could well be the case. For instance, the key to a fairer understanding of this particular passage lies, I think, in the clause "more certain of a future." As I have said repeatedly, Nietzsche's driving concern is *our future as a species.* A person of "higher value" read back from "more certain of a future," just acknowledges that value is always relative and that *certain* types will better serve the aspiration. We could also experiment with understanding "more worthy of life" in conjunction with Nietzsche's usage of "life alone, that dark, driving, insatiable self-desiring power."[140] Speaking of experiments, I again encourage the reader to give thought to how these three comparatives might apply to, say, your workplace or community.

Let us continue looking at some of the assumptions at work in Nietzsche's conception of the *Übermensch.* In a repudiation of the then-emerging trope of "modern progress" as well as of popular conceptions of Darwin's theory of species development, Nietzsche posits that real instances of the *Übermensch* have appeared. He also makes it clear that these instances have not been limited to Europe or to Europeans.

Humanity does not represent a development for the better or stronger or higher in the sense in which it is believed today. "Progress" is just a modern idea, that is, an erroneous idea. Today's European is, in his worth, far below the European of the Renaissance; further development is simply not, out of some sort of necessity, elevation, increase, strengthening.

In another sense, there is continuous success of individual cases, in the most diverse places of the world and from the most diverse cultures, through which a *higher* type has indeed manifested: a type that, in relation to the totality of humanity, is a kind of *Übermensch.*

means of storing up the tremendous forces of mankind so that the generations can build upon the work of their forefathers—not only outwardly, but inwardly, organically growing out of them and becoming something stronger." It is a rough, vague, inconclusive notion, this breeding; and perhaps that is why Nietzsche "abandoned the title *Zucht* and *Züchtung* as soon as he had written it down." There is evidence that he *knew* the danger of the concept. With the likes of his brother-in-law, the antisemitic Bernhard Förster (1843–1889), and other proto-Nazis on the prowl, how could he *not*? For those two quotes and a further discussion of Nietzsche's use of *züchten*, see Walter Kaufmann, *Nietzsche: Psychologist, Philosopher, Antichrist* (Princeton: Princeton University Press, 2013 [1950]), 304–306.

140 *Untimely Meditations,* "The Use and Abuse of History for Life," section 3.

Such flukes of great success have always been possible, and perhaps will always be possible. And even entire races, tribes, peoples, can, under the right conditions, score such a *success*. [141]

As I understand it, becoming an *Übermensch* is not the rare, almost messianic achievement that many interpreters make it out to be. Nietzsche insists that it is the goal for all of humanity. In the spirit of a Zen koan, he writes in his notebook:

> Human existence is uncanny and perpetually without meaning…
> Why does this person live? Why does that person die?
> No one can know, for there is no Why therein…
> I want to teach people the meaning of their existence: and that meaning is the *Übermensch*.[142]

A meaning that has no meaning. A Whyless Why. A bridge without end.[143] Indeed, placed within the frame of perpetual *becoming*, we all engage in *Übermensch*-like modes of being continually. That is, we are constantly "overcoming" what we previously were. Even a virtuoso pianist strives continually to improve. In fact, Nietzsche presents this idea as an integral feature of existence, a "law of life": "All great things bring about their own destruction through an act of self-cancellation: thus the law of life will have it, the law of the necessity of 'self-overcoming' is the nature of life."[144] Nietzsche calls such continual overcoming "great health." Of course, many of us do not do so. But not to do so is to stagnate into automaticity, or, in Nietzschean terms, into sickness, decadence, and passive nihilism. Some of us do just that, of course. Some of us merely strive for the status quo. Some of us are the antithesis of the *Übermensch,* namely, the *letzter Mensch,* "the last mortal." Who is this person?

   As we saw, after ten years alone in his mountain hut, Zarathustra desired to go under in order to speak with the people of the village. He had become weary of keeping his wisdom to himself and desired to give it away, like bees do their honey. When he arrives in the marketplace, the people have all gathered to watch a tightrope artist. Zarathustra takes his position and speaks. All eyes on him—because they think he is the tightrope artist!—he

---

141 *The Antichrist*, 4.
142 *NF*–1882, 5[28].
143 *Thus Spoke Zarathustra*, "Of Old and New Tablets," 3.
144 *On the Genealogy of Morals*, 3.27.

sums up his wisdom in a single word: *"I teach you the Übermensch."*[145] He then presents his major premise, followed by a challenge: "The human is something to be overcome. What have you done to overcome it?" With his next utterance, Zarathustra overturns two thousand years of Western history, and commences a cataclysmic shift from transcendence to immanence.

> The *Übermensch* is the meaning of the earth. Let your will say: *may* the *Übermensch* be the meaning of the earth!
>
> I beseech you, my friends, *remain true to the earth* and do not believe those who speak to you of supernatural hope! They are mixers of poison, whether or not they know it.
>
> Despisers of life they are, dying and themselves poisoned, of whom the earth is weary: so let them pass on!
>
> Once, to sin against God was the greatest sin, but God died, and with him died these sinners. To sin against the earth is now the most terrible sin, and to esteem the entrails of the unknowable higher than the meaning of the earth!

The immanence wherein is found—indeed, that *is*—the *Übermensch,* descends deeper still, into our very bodies. Simultaneously, Nietzsche renounces the idealist and religious pretenses of soul-talk.

> Once, the soul looked contemptuously at the body: and, at that time, this contempt was the highest—the soul wanted the body emaciated, ghastly, and starved. In this way, the soul thought it could slip away from the body and from the earth.
>
> Oh, this soul itself was still emaciated, ghastly, and starved: and cruelty was the lust of this soul!
>
> But you, too, my friends, tell me: what does your body proclaim about your soul? Is your soul not poverty and squalor and a pathetic contentment?

The poverty of the soul is the result of its being, until the advent of Zarathustra/Nietzsche, the locus of supposed goodness and morality. It is the "Christian" soul that is meager. It is an anorexic soul and ever-vigilant self-conscious controller of what may or may not be consumed. Such a soul becomes emaciated *because* it denies itself life's abundance. But it must

---

145 Until noted, all following citations are from *Thus Spoke Zarathustra*, "Zarathustra's Preface," 3–5.

not do so. Zarathustra tells the crowd that he "loves the soul that is filled to the brim, so that it forgets itself, and all things fill it: thus will all things become the soul's going under." If only the crowd could realize this point, the rest would follow. And what is this point: it is that the very basis of our current collective life is "poverty and squalor and a pathetic contentment." Similarly to the Buddha, who taught the counterintuitive notion that the path to awakening begins when the practitioner feels a *disenchantment (nibbidā)* with the status quo that amounts to *disgust*,[146] Zarathustra tells the crowd that what is required to commence the (endless) journey to the self-overcoming is "contempt." In fact, Nietzsche's several usages of one of the Buddha's most important tropes for *nirvana*, "the other shore," makes me wonder if this is an intentional reference. In a statement that combines the two points, Zarathustra proclaims: "I love the great despisers, for they are the great venerators and arrows of longing for the other shore."

Why is it necessary to become a "great despiser"? The reason is the same for both the Buddha and Zarathustra: until we do so, nothing will change. This "until" may seem drastic. But such disaffection is arguably a near ubiquitous theme in the literature of self-transformation from around the world. Another common theme is the role of introspection. In line with this theme, Zarathustra tells the crowd that once they look into their souls, they will surely come to despise them. And once they come to despise their souls, they will surely come to see that their happiness, their powers of reason, their virtue, their uprightness, and their pity toward others are all but "poverty and squalor and a pathetic contentment." Nietzsche is, of course, referring to the "diminution and leveling" of people that he witnesses all around him, to a descent "into what is thinner, more good-natured, more clever, more comfortable, more mediocre, more indifferent."[147] Yet, as bad as it is, if these same people would but look with open eyes turned inward, a bolt of blinding insight might flash—"lightning to lick them with its tongue." He assures the people that this devastating flash is the "madness with which you will be inoculated." Their turning away is only "madness," of course, in the eyes of the very world toward which they have become disgusted. And so it carries with it an "inoculation" against *caring* too much about the world's response. Finally, with this crackling crescendo, Zarathustra concludes: "Behold, I

---

146 See the Pali Dictionary entry, *s.v., nibbidā*: "disenchantment; aversion; disgust; weariness." With the arising of *nibbidā*, the mind and heart begin to turn away from the desires and objects and values that drive this world of perpetual pain. As with Nietzsche, higher values are then possible. See *The Wisdom Library*, https://www.wisdomlib.org/definition/nibbida. Accessed April 3, 2024.

147 *On the Genealogy of Morals*, 1.12.

teach you the *Übermensch*: the one who is this lightning, the one who is this madness!"

Because the German word *Mensch* is a masculine noun, a literal translation would have "he" for "the one who." For this and other reasons, many interpreters treat the *Übermensch* as a singular (male) individual, even as a kind of messiah figure. Given Nietzsche's disdain for the "sanctimonious asses" who style themselves "'improvers' of humankind,"[148] as well as his preoccupation with clearing the ground for a general *type* indexed as "*Übermensch*," I encourage readers to consider *themselves* as being addressed here. This approach comports much better, too, with another interpretative move I have been encouraging the reader to make throughout this chapter, namely, to see each of these types as *potential internal drives*. After all, psychologist Nietzsche understands a type to originate in a prerational drive (urge, disposition, instinct, motivation). So, in this reading, Zarathustra has now offered the crowd the honey of his wisdom, as follows: *Look around you and into your hearts and you will surely discover "poverty and squalor and a pathetic contentment" with the way things are. Do so, and you will ignite the Übermensch in you. Then, for better or for worse, you will step with others onto the interminable bridge of self-overcoming; and if you all do so, the world just might have a future that we find worthy.* In other words, this is the Good News for our post-God era. Wonderful!

So how does the crowd respond to this extraordinary message of radical possibility for personal and social change?

They laugh.

> "There they stand," Zarathustra said to his heart, "there they laugh; they don't understand me; I am not the mouth for these ears. Must one first smash their ears for them so that they learn to hear with their eyes? Must one make a racket like a bass drum and preachers of repentance do? Or do they believe only a stammerer?"

Zarathustra reasons that they must be a proud people to stand there thus mockingly. And so he tries another tactic. He will preach to them the *opposite* of the *Übermensch*. He will preach to them of the "last mortal." This is the figure that they will become (or remain) if they reject the *Übermensch*. Zarathustra feels certain of winning them over, for the "last mortal" is such

---

148 *Twilight of the Idols*, "The 'Improvers' of Humankind."

a shameful, pathetic figure. He will tell them about "the most contemptible of people: "the last mortal."

It is time that the people set their goal. It is time that the people plant the seed of their highest hope.

The soil is yet fertile enough for that. But this soil will one day become poor and tame, and no high tree will be able to grow out of it.

Beware! The time will come when the people no longer shoot the arrow of their longing beyond the human, and the strings of their bow will forget how to whirr!

I tell you: one must still have chaos in oneself to give birth to a dancing star. I tell you: you still have chaos in you.

Beware! The time is coming when the people will no longer give birth to a star. Beware! The time of the most contemptible of people is coming, of those who do not even hold themselves in contempt.

Look! I am showing you *the last mortal*.

"What is love? What is creation? What is desire? What is a star?"— thus asks the last mortal, and blinks.

The earth then becomes small, and on it hops the last mortal, who makes all things small. Their race is indelible, like the flea; the last mortal lives the longest.

"We have invented happiness"—say the last mortals, and they blink.

They have left the regions where life was hard: for one needs warmth. One still loves the neighbors and rubs against them: for one needs warmth.

To become sick and to have mistrust counts as sinful to them: one treads carefully. A fool that still stumbles over stones or people!

A little poison occasionally: that makes for pleasant dreams. And a lot of poison in the end, for a pleasant death.

One still works, for work is entertainment. But one is careful that the entertainment does not attack them.

No one becomes poor or rich: both are too onerous. Who still wants to govern? Who to obey? Both are too onerous.

No shepherd and a single herd! Everyone wants the same thing, everyone is the same: whoever feels differently goes voluntarily into the madhouse.

"Erstwhile, the entire world was insane"—say the finest among them, and they blink…

"We have invented happiness"—say the last mortals, and they blink.

Having clearly revealed the ridiculousness of the last mortals, Zarathustra awaits the response of the crowd. We should not be surprised.

> "Give us this last mortal, oh Zarathustra," they cried, "help us to become these last mortals! And we will give you the *Übermensch*." And all the people cheered and clicked their tongues…But Zarathustra became sad and said to his heart…"And now they gaze at me and laugh: and, laughing, they hate me still. There is ice in their laughter."

Zarathustra/Nietzsche is not alone in believing that our decadent, life-denying, narcotized, nihilistic culture is a direct result of the "hopelessly mediocre and insipid people" who perpetuate it with their acquiescence. The simultaneous decay of traditional ways of life and rise of the bourgeoisie to positions of political and economic power in the nineteenth century was the cause of much hand-wringing among people from the working class to the intelligentsia. The interconnected rise of urbanization, industrialization, commercialization, and individualization, it was believed, could not possibly bode well for the future. Indeed, Nietzsche's "torrent of nihilism" trope seems hardly overwrought in light of the pervasive sense that unprecedented forms of personal anxiety, social dissolution, and global violence were swelling up. (Edvard Munch's famous 1893 painting *The Scream* captures the angst of the period.) What might be done to redirect this torrent? The *Übermensch* is, of course, one answer to this question. But in a metaphor that has become all too real, Zarathustra warns that our soil will soon be too depleted to produce "higher trees." Nietzsche, recall, is convinced that "to keep from destroying ourselves" during this late, nihilistic stage of Western culture, we must act with urgency. As Zarathustra's characterization of the last mortals suggests, however, this seems unlikely.

Interestingly, given Nietzsche's disdain for the two movements, the uncanny sense that "we suffer from *human beings*"[149] has much in common with the antiestablishment, countercultural criticism coming out of European Bohemian and anarchist circles of the day. The former sought alternatives to what they perceived as suffocating restrictions on personal freedom and artistic expression. The latter, often at the cost of life and limb, fought robustly to change what they perceived as unacceptable social monstrosities, such as rampant child labor, treacherous working conditions, poverty wages, lack of a social net of any kind, and so much more. In terms of, respectively,

---

149 *On the Genealogy of Morals,* 1.11. Emphasis added; the emphasis is on *suffer* in the original.

lifestyle and social policy, the Bohemians and anarchists actually offered many solutions. Nietzsche, of course, rejected these solutions as "decadent" and ultimately self-defeating.[150] In its place, and as an integral feature of his own social criticism, Nietzsche articulates a robust, indeed a profound, affirmationism. We will complete this discussion of the *Übermensch* with a glance at Nietzsche's central concepts of affirmation: the eternal return, *amor fati*, and great health.

Zarathustra, the prophet of the *Übermensch*, is also the teacher of the eternal return.[151] Nietzsche first announces the idea, however, in an earlier book, *The Gay Science*. (Interestingly, the passage announcing the eternal return is followed by one titled *Incipit tragoedia* [the tragedy begins], which gives us our first glimpse of Zarathustra descending from his mountain.) The passage is titled *"Das grösste Schwergewicht."* That last word means both "heavy weight" and "emphasis." I think the double meaning is in play. The passage contains a thought experiment whose consequences will initially feel like a heavy weight on the mind and emotions of the experimenter. Thus, the experiment entails a cataclysmic shift in the gravitational *(Schwerkraft)* pull of one's life. In that sense, the experiment also entails a radically new orientation, or *emphasis*, on how we view and indeed live our lives.

---

150 Echoing the speech of the bourgeois press that he so despised, Nietzsche speaks of "the increasingly furious howls, the increasingly undisguised teeth-gnashing of the anarchist dogs who now ramble through the alleyways of European culture" (*Beyond Good and Evil*, 202). Still, the anarchists adored *him*. No less a formidable figure than "Red Queen" Emma Goldman (1869–1940) insisted, loudly, that "Nietzsche was an anarchist." She has a point. Consider that Nietzsche and the anarchists shared a nauseating hatred of: the state and its capitalism, nationalism, colonialism, antisemitism, and racism; the vapid, obedience-oriented education system; the hivemind of "the herd"; the cruelty and inhumanity of labor; the cheapness and mindlessness of mass consumerism. Likewise, they shared a desire for the *Übermensch*, the human being who sloughs off Christian morality, dissolves the inner slave, becomes a master, and lives beyond good and evil. Here is Goldman on Nietzsche: "In Vienna one could hear interesting lectures on modern German prose and poetry. One could read the works of the young iconoclasts in art and letters, the most daring among them being Nietzsche. The magic of his language, the beauty of his vision, carried me to undreamed-of heights. I longed to devour every line of his writings…I had to do my reading at the expense of much-needed sleep; but what was physical strain in view of my raptures over Nietzsche? The fire of his soul, the rhythm of his song, made life richer, fuller, and more wonderful for me…Nietzsche was not a social theorist but a poet, a rebel and innovator. His aristocracy was neither of birth nor of purse; it was of the spirit. In that respect Nietzsche was an anarchist, and all true anarchists were aristocrats." In a snippet that could have occurred yesterday (and will, I am afraid, occur countless times yet) Goldman hears someone criticize Nietzsche. "'But you haven't read Nietzsche!' I objected heatedly; 'how can you talk about him?'" See Emma Goldman, *Living My Life* (New York: Knopf, 1931), *Anarchist Library*, https://theanarchistlibrary.org/library/emma-goldman-living-my-life. Accessed August 17, 2023.

151 *Thus Spoke Zarathustra*, "The Convalescent," 2.

The greatest weight. What if, one day or night, in your loneliest solitude, a demon were to creep up to you and say: "This life, as you have lived it in the past and live it now, you must once more and for countless times live again; and nothing new will occur, rather every pain and every joy and every thought and sigh and every unutterably small detail and large event of your life must return to you, and everything in the same sequence and order—and even this spider and this moonlight between the trees, and even this moment and I myself. The eternal hourglass of being will forever be turned over—and you along with it, speck of dust!"—Would you not throw yourself down and gnash your teeth and curse the demon who spoke thus? Or have you ever experienced a sublime moment when you would answer: "You are a god, and never have I heard anything more divine!" If ever you should be overcome by such a thought, it would transform you, just as you are, and perhaps crush you. The question concerning everything and everyone—"Do you want this once again and for countless more times?"—will lie on your actions like the heaviest weight! Or how good must you become with yourself and life in order *to require* nothing more than this eternal confirmation and sealing?[152]

The heaviness of this message is made even heavier by the fact that it is delivered by a *demon*, an infernal tempter and persuader of evil, and heavier again when this demon finds us utterly alone in the loneliest, most vulnerable, of our moments. As heavy as this passage is, however, Nietzsche places it in *The Gay Science*, a book that is "Yes-saying, deep, but bright and kindhearted…to the highest degree."[153] That description applies as well to *Dawn*, he says. Clearly, these two cheerfully titled books mean to provide ways of genuine affirmation, of averting the blight of passive nihilism by learning to say *yes* to life. Central to Nietzsche's solution is to engage in the thought experiment of "eternal confirmation and sealing." You do so until you are utterly transformed—or crushed, which might amount to the same thing. As far as what this means in real terms, I think the passage is straightforward. We are confronted by decisions large and small every day of our lives. Generally speaking, what factors are typically in play in your decision? Money? Relationships? Job? Family? Convenience? Contentment? Whatever the case may be, the eternal return strategy has you place the *emphasis*—the *Schwergewicht*—on whether or not your decision is one you

---

152 *The Gay Science*, 341.
153 *Ecce Homo*, "The Gay Science."

would be willing to repeat for all eternity. The complications, implications, and intricacies of this approach are obviously too much to dive into here. But recall that it is a *thought experiment*, something *done* to catalyze an outcome, and to observe its effect. At a minimum, the eternal return might challenge you simply to give thought to what your life would be like, how full and fulfilled it would be, if you honestly *could* seal it with "this eternal confirmation."

The language and imagery that attends the eternal return evokes religion. The idea even has its own *Genesis*, surrounding it with a nimbus of revelation. Nietzsche was walking through the woods in the mountains of the Swiss village of Sils Maria, when he came to the lake of Silvaplana. It was there, next to "a powerful towering pyramidal rock" that he experienced the momentous flash: "The thought of the eternal return, this highest formula of yes-saying that can possibly be attained, occurred in August, 1881: it was jotted down on a piece of paper with the note: '6,000 feet beyond humanity and time.'"[154] In the oldest sense of "religion," that is exactly what the eternal return is: it is an *oath* of sorts; it is *conduct indicating reverence*; it is *conscientiousness*; it is, most of all, *going through again, repeatedly.*[155] Of course, from the perspective of its contemporary usage, it may be better to speak of the eternal return as evoking *antireligion*. For it is turned wholly toward "this spider and this moonlight between the trees"—toward *this* world, *this* life, indeed, toward *just this* action in *just this* instant of existence. The eternal return is thus a teaching of radical immanence as opposed to religion's omnipresent otherworldly transcendence.

Nonetheless, drawing on certain of Nietzsche's notes that can fairly be characterized as metaphysical speculations, some interpreters have understood the eternal return to be a cosmological theory. Nietzsche, for sure, is not coy about the fact that, in positing the concept, he is trading in the same goods as Heraclitus, Hinduism, Buddhism, Plato and Aristotle, Pythagoras, and the Stoics.[156] For example, when Zarathustra seems to be dying, those most natural of beings, the animals who surround him, implore him to hang on. In so doing, they invoke his teaching of eternal return.

---

154 *Ecce Homo*, "Thus Spoke Zarathustra," 1.
155 See *Online Etymological Dictionary*, *s.v.* religion, https://www.etymonline.com/word/Religion. Accessed August 19, 2023.
156 See, for example, *Ecce Homo*, "The Birth of Tragedy," 3: "The teaching of 'the eternal return,' that is, of the unconditional and infinitely repeated circle of all things—this teaching of Zarathustra's could also have been taught by Heraclitus. At least, the Stoics, who inherited nearly all of their basic conceptions from Heraclitus, have traces of it."

"Oh, Zarathustra," said the animals, "to those who think as we do, all things themselves dance: they approach us and reach out their hand and laugh and flee—and then return.

Everything passes, everything returns. The wheel of being turns eternally. Everything dies, everything blossoms again. The year of being loops eternally.

Everything breaks, everything is repaired again. The same house of being builds itself eternally. Everything comes apart, everything greets again. The ring of being remains eternally loyal to itself.

In every instant being begins. Around every Here the ball rolls There. The middle is everywhere. Crooked is the path of eternity."

Zarathustra, failing and forgetful, becomes nauseated and shudders at the very thought of which the animals speak. But the animals quiet him, and remind him of what his very teachings would have him say.

You would say without trembling, rather respiring out of bliss: for a heavy weight and stuffiness would have been taken from you, the most patient!—"Now I die and disappear, and in an instant will I become a nothing. Souls are just as mortal as the body.

But the knot of causes in which I am entwined will return—they will create me anew! I myself belong to the causes of the eternal return.

I will come again, together with this sun, with this earth, with this eagle, with this snake *not* to a new life or to a better life or to a similar life:

—I will eternally return to this exact same life, in matters large and small, so that I can again teach the eternal return of all things —

—so that I can again speak the word about the great midday of the earth and humanity, so that I can again announce the *Übermensch* to humanity."[157]

Nietzsche is also surely aware of the theories of the physicists of his day who argue some version of cyclical recurrence. In a section of his notebooks titled *The New World-Conception*, and subtitled, *The Eternal Return*, our psychologist-philosopher has become a provocative physicist.

If the universe *may* be thought of as a determinate magnitude of energy and as a determinate quantity of energy centers—and every other

---

157 *Thus Spoke Zarathustra*, "The Convalescent," 2.

conception remains indeterminate and consequently *unusable*—it follows that it has to undergo a calculable number of combinations in the great dice throw of its being. In an infinity of time, every possible combination would at some point be attained; more still, the combination would be attained an infinite number of times. And since, between each "combination" and its next "return," all possible combinations must have elapsed, and each of these combinations conditions the entire sequence of combinations in the same order, a circle of absolutely identical sequences would thus be demonstrated: the universe as a cycle that has already infinitely repeated itself and that plays its game *in infinitum.*[158]

Nietzsche was clearly fascinated by the age-old image of the eternal circle. And he obviously meditated intently on the corresponding notions that he found in the religious literature that so attracted and repelled him. His notes contain many ruminations along the lines of the above passage. We saw that Nietzsche was fascinated by the possibility of translating the human back into nature. As these ruminations on cyclical existence show, and beyond, he was equally fascinated by the prospect of translating spirit back into matter. That is, the question for him is not, or at least not always, how to get rid of some pernicious idea, such as "another world" or a transcorporeal soul, but rather how to render it useful to our existence in *this* world.

Having said all of this, I want to emphasize that the passage from the notebooks is just that: a *note*. Nietzsche is doing what he asks his perfect readers to do: *experiment with thought.* Some of us could, of course, feel inclined to take the eternal return literally, as a true fact of cosmic existence. Nietzsche would probably expect as much. Indeed, the rhetorical intensity pervading his body of work is in large part due to the often intransigent human longing for supernatural, "spiritual," solutions to mortality. If, however, we do take the idea as literal, then we have to negate all the rest of Nietzsche's work. The decisive point, however, is this: Even if eternal return were demonstrably factual, that fact would not interest Nietzsche. What interests him is the *as if* axiomatic nature of the thought experiment. What interests him is the result of the experiment on our *affect*. The point is to *feel* the power of *yes-saying* rising in us. This is exactly what is happening in the passage where the animals remind Zarathustra to apply his teaching of the eternal

---

158 *NF*–1888, 14[188]. For a very interesting article introducing Nietzsche to physicists, see Juliano C. S. Neves, "Nietzsche for Physicists," *Philosophia Scientiæ*, Vol. 23, No. 1 (2019), 185–201.

return in order to stop his own slide into passive nihilism. Act in a manner, they implore him, that "seals" your actions with "eternal confirmation." Doing so, you will come to love your fate.

The "seal" of the eternal return is the imprimatur of *amor fati*, the love of one's fate. With the *Übermensch* in his sights, Nietzsche proclaims, "my formula for greatness in a person is *amor fati*." He then explains that phrase to mean that "one wants nothing to be otherwise than as it is, not forwards, not backwards, not for all eternity." With the mention of "necessity," he next places an interesting condition on the notion: "Not merely to endure what is necessary, even less to conceal it—all idealism is dishonesty in the face of that which is necessary." Finally, he reveals the pith of his prescription for facing our fate: "*love* it."[159]

Before we join hands with Nietzsche and celebrate our love of fate, let's ask some hard questions. What, for example, would it mean for an impoverished person or an entire oppressed group to "want nothing to be otherwise"? Is *amor fati* just a strategy for adjusting your attitude to a hostile world? Is it just a form of sad resignation, indeed, of passive nihilism itself? The idea is not uncommon, particularly among conservative thinkers. Its basic form currently is this: the world's troubles are intractable, but you *can* change your thinking. The idea also appears to hover near the tyranny of positivity, the noxious notion whereby one's fate is determined by one's attitude. It is really a double tyranny: to thrive in life, you *must* exhibit positivity at all times; fail to do so, and bad things will *inevitably* come your way. Finally, why does Nietzsche use "fate," a word that means "that which is ordained, destiny…that which must be"?[160]

I think the key to sorting out these quite legitimate concerns lies in the statement "all idealism is dishonesty in the face of that which is necessary." We have had several occasions to hear Nietzsche express his disdain for idealism. Just to jog the reader's memory, "Plato is a coward in the face of reality—thus, he takes refuge in the ideal."[161] The love of our fate demands that we reject the idealist's compulsion to *conceal* what is necessary. And what is necessary? The body is necessary, and with it, the body's functions, pain, aging, limitations, and so on; but the idealist conceals all of this with the belief in an "immortal soul." The natural world is necessary, and with it, nature's capriciousness, disasters, brutality, relentless cycle of blossom and

---

159 *Ecce Homo*, "Why I Am So Clever," 10.
160 See *Online Etymological Dictionary*, *s.v.* fate, https://www.etymonline.com/search?q=fate. Accessed August 20, 2023.
161 *Twilight of the Idols*, "What I Owe the Ancients," 2.

decay, birth and death, and so on; but the idealist conceals all of this with an image of healing, harmonious nature as a "plantation of God, where a decorum and sanctity reign, a perennial festival."[162] And an abiding theme for Nietzsche, of course, is that the amorality of the real is necessary; but the idealist conceals it with morality. The idealist's accoutrements may enable some of us to *endure* what is necessary but not without a refusal squarely to face necessity that borders on the pathological. The love of our fate—as that which is *necessary*—demands that we reject such "dishonesty."

What about the other danger, that *amor fati* leads to passivity? If you love your fate, no matter how badly it is unfolding, what incentive would you have to change anything? Once again, *amor fati* appears to graft easily onto passive nihilism. I can only ask the following question to anyone who reads Nietzsche: surely, you must feel the passion with which he does *not* want us merely to accept so much of the world as it is (think: current morality, culture, politics, work, democracy, capitalism, education, music, and the arts, indeed, even our conception of what it is to be a human being at all). Let us consult a witness. Perhaps Nietzsche's most trustworthy reader in this regard is someone who also happens to have been one of the fiercest advocates for personal and social change in his lifetime. I am referring to the anarchist Emma Goldman, who, as we have seen, loved and praised and promoted Nietzsche precisely for his unrelenting advocacy for *deep* change. By "fate," then, Nietzsche means that which is *intransitive*, that which is the case regardless of human desires, dreams, hopes, and conceptions. The transitive, by contrast, is that which *is* dependent on the ever-mutating conceptions embedded in human-constructed ideologies. Nietzsche's work can be characterized as an unflinching effort to distinguish the one from the other, both individually and collectively. Only then, he believes, can we determine a better course of action. To "love that which is necessary—*amor fati*"[163] is thus a no-nonsense, clear-eyed stance in the face of reality. Its ultimate result, though, is an affirmation that is purified in the crucible of an honest heart.

For the new year. I am still alive, I am still thinking: I must continue to live for I must continue to think. *Sum, ergo cogito: cogito, ergo sum.* On this day, everyone allows themselves to express their wishes and their dearest thoughts: well, I, too, want to say what I wish from myself

---

162 Ralph Waldo Emerson, "Nature," https://emersoncentral.com/texts/nature-addresses-lectures/nature2/chapter1-nature. Accessed August 20, 2023.
163 *NF*–1881, 15[20].

today and which thought first passed through my heart this year—which thought should be my foundation, security, and sweetness for the rest of my life! I want always to learn more, to see the necessity of things as beauty—thus will I be one of those people who make things beautiful. *Amor fati*: from this moment on, may it be my love! I do not want to fight a war against the ugly. I do not want to accuse, I do not even want to accuse the accuser. *Looking away* will be my sole negation! And all in all and on the whole: someday this is all I want to be.[164]

This poignant New Year's resolution is all the more touching when we consider Nietzsche's lifelong struggles with his health. Suffering as he did from chronic insomnia, migraines, near blindness, war-related nightmares, and nausea, not to mention his perpetual loneliness and sense of social alienation, Nietzsche's yes-saying borders on the incredible. His affirmationism is not a case of merely willing himself to be so or of assuming an attitude. On the contrary, it lies on the other side of a profoundly perilous and consequently journey. As I have tried to show throughout this book, this journey is initially in thought. We experiment in thinking about the matters that impact us without the guardrails of received morality. We learn to think, in short, beyond good and evil. Already, thinking and speaking and questioning in this manner makes us suspect to the mass of people. Over time, thinking like this permeates our affective life and our new, self-determined values. Finally, it becomes *what we are* and thus coextensive with our moment to moment being in the world.

Like so much in Nietzsche, this alchemical transmutation of a base object (morality, value, the human) into a higher one (immorality, transvaluation, the *Übermensch)* occurs through a *traversal*, a passing through, an *undergoing*, a *going-under*. Similarly, if we are to achieve a genuine *amor fati*, we need a new conception of "health." Nietzsche himself could not attain what the world counts as health. But, in his own act of overcoming, he was able to conceive of, and to a great extent to realize, a more profound type of health than the norm. He calls this new standard *"the great health."*

The great health. We new ones, nameless ones, hard to understand ones, we who are born too early for a still unproved future—we require, for a new purpose, a new means, namely a new health, one that is stronger craftier rawer bolder more convivial than all types of health that

164 *The Gay Science*, 276.

have existed until now. Whoever's soul has thirsted to experience the
entire range of values and desires, and to have sailed to all coasts of
this ideal "inland sea" (Mediterranean), who wants to know from the
adventures of their own experiences, how it feels to be a conqueror
and discoverer of ideals, similarly, how it feels to be an artist, a saint,
a lawgiver, a sage, a scholar, a devotee, a soothsayer, a God-hermit
as of old; for that person, one matter above all is necessary, *the great
health*—a health that one does not merely have, but rather also perpetually acquires, and must acquire because one constantly gives it away,
must give it away!…And now, after we have long been underway like
this, we argonauts of the ideal, braver, perhaps, than is prudent, and
often enough shipwrecked and suffering damage, but, as I said, healthier than others would like to grant us, dangerously healthy, always
healthy yet again—it seems to us, as if as a reward, we have before
us a still undiscovered country whose boundaries no one has yet seen,
a beyond from all previously existing lands and corners of the ideal,
a world so abundant in that which is beautiful, strange, questionable,
terrible, and divine that our curiosity as well as our thirst for possession
are out of control—oh, that nothing more could sate us! How could we,
after beholding such vistas and with such a ravenous appetite in our
conscience for knowledge, still be satisfied with *contemporary people*?
Bad enough: it is, however, unavoidable that we look on their worthi-
est goals and hopes with a badly maintained seriousness, or perhaps
no longer even look on. A different ideal passes before us, a strange,
seductive, dangerous ideal, of which we have no desire to convince
anyone because we do not so easily concede anyone *the right to it*:
the ideal of a spirit that naîvely, that is to say, unintentionally, and in a
spirit of overflowing plentitude and potency plays with everything that
until now was considered holy, good, untouchable, divine; a spirit for
whom the highest, on which the people justly place their measure of
value, would already mean as much as danger, decline, diminishment,
or, at least, recovery, blindness, a temporary self-forgetting; the ideal of
a human-overhuman [*menschlich-übermenschlichen*] being-well and
wanting-to-be-well that often enough seems *inhuman* [*unmenschlich*],
for example, when it stands next to all of the earthly seriousness here-
tofore, next to every solemnity in gesture, word, tone, look, morality,
and task, as their most embodied involuntary parody—and with that,
despite all of that, *the great seriousness* first arises, the real question

mark will be placed for the first time, the destiny of the soul turns, the clock ticks forward, the tragedy *begins*…[165]

As befits a New Year's meditation, this passage is precisely that: *a passage*. It represents a liminal space between the old and the new. As such, it is also an esoteric hail. Only "we" can discern its import. The question Nietzsche implicitly puts to you, the reader, is whether you are willing to undergo the transmutation of the "we." This day marks a liminal passage from the old to the new. It marks a starkly divided pathway. "We" know too well the path of the old, the named, the old goal, the small health. The path of the initiated leads to the new, the nameless, the hard to understand, to a still unproved future, to an utterly new goal. It leads to a new health, to the great health. Do we consent? Yes? Happy New Life! The tragedy begins.

---

165 *The Gay Science*, 382.

VIRTUE

W HY TRAGEDY? NIETZSCHE'S SENSE OF THE TRAGIC IS DERIVED FROM CLAS- sical, or "Attic," drama. In ancient Greek theater, a tragedy is the story of a protagonist who, through social position or personal quality, is exalted above the norm. Yet, through a combination of a character flaw and intractable external circumstances, the protagonist is ultimately thrust into irredeemable failure. So are we aspiring perfect readers doomed to failure? Something about the tragic wholeness sought by Nietzsche's collective "we" certainly suggests a lifelong struggle. The *agon* we are inciting has both internal and external repercussions. For it involves the perpetual antagonism of the Apollonian and the Dionysian. For Nietzsche, at least, it is this dual drive that defines our struggle.

> These two different drives run parallel to one another, mostly in open antagonism, and incite one another to perpetually new, more power- ful births in order to perpetuate within themselves the struggle of that object which the common word "art" only superficially reconciles; until, finally, through a metaphysically miraculous act of Hellenic "will," they appear paired, and through this pairing finally create the equally Dionysian and Apollonian artwork of Attic tragedy.[1]

Later in this chapter, Nietzsche offers an example of a "reconciliation," a wholeness, that he wants us to see as something other than failure. But, as always, we should amble slowly toward that example. Let's give further thought to the tragedy that we have begun. Let us do so by observing a scene. We are in Athens, 450 B.C.E. A person is walking down a cobblestone path- way, "under majestic Ionic colonnades." He casts his curious gaze upward, into the brilliant blue sky—

> toward a horizon that is cut off by pure and noble lines; beside him, in luminous marble, are reflections of his transfigured form; all around

---

1 *The Birth of Tragedy*, 1.

him are solemnly striding or gently moving people with harmoniously sounding voices and rhythmically expansive gestures—ensconced within this continuous influx of beauty, would this man not be compelled to raise his hand to Apollo and cry out: "Blessed people of Hellas!"

Let's continue watching.

An old man stands nearby and observes the person's exuberant display. Is he not being too hasty in his unbridled enthusiasm? Is the beauty not causing him to overlook one particular matter of great importance? The old man looks at him with the "sublime eyes of Aeschylus," the father of dramatic tragedy, and, approaching him, says:

> But say this, too, you wondrous stranger: how much must this people have suffered to be able to become so beautiful! But now, follow me to the tragedy, and sacrifice with me in the temple of both gods!

To conclude this book, I present six qualities that Nietzsche considers essential for the journey: curiosity, honesty, courage, pathos of distance, solitude, and humor.[2] I am not sure how best to characterize these qualities. Although we colloquially refer to them as traits, they are not strictly traits at all, at least not in the sense of *necessarily* inborn personal qualities or innate dispositions. For we can catalyze, cultivate, and develop each one. Neither are they "values," in the sense of beliefs that motivate a person. They might be *valued*, and they certainly enable us to undertake the great Nietzschean task of *revaluing all values*, but there is something about the willed nature of a value that misses the point here. I also think that calling them "virtues" is problematic. Scholars, in fact, often classify Nietzsche's thought as "virtue ethics," so my view needs some explanation. First, Nietzsche is obviously

---

2 With the exception of *honesty*, this grouping was inspired by Mark Alfano, *Nietzsche's Moral Philosophy* (Cambridge: Cambridge University Press, 2019). Alfano arrives at the list of drives through a (still) novel digital humanities methodology. He explains this approach as follows: "I map the prevalence and interconnections among the main topics and theses of Nietzsche's philosophical writings as they develop over time. Along the way, I compare this map with the composite map produced by other scholars" (3). Highly intriguing questions emerge: "How accurate and informative is this composite map? If every scrap and trace of Nietzsche's writings were to disappear instantaneously, could we construct his philosophy from the secondary literature?" The answer is that scholars "have generally done a poor job" of treating the themes that a digital humanities approach, at least, shows to have preoccupied Nietzsche the most throughout his life. The scholars and Nietzsche fans' favorite, "the will to power," it turns out, is not one of them.

wary of the very notion. "Virtue" hews too closely to "morality." Like it, virtue limits us, reins us in, stifles, and stultifies. For example, he says that the free spirit cultivates honesty, but warns:

> Let us beware that our honesty does not become our vanity, our finery and pomp, our limit, our stupidity! Every virtue tends toward stupidity, and every stupidity, toward virtue; "stupid to the point of saintliness," as they say in Russia—let us beware that, through our honesty, we do not ultimately become saints and bores. Is life not a hundred times too short—to be bored in it?[3]

This passage occurs in a section titled "Our Virtue." The section opens with a signal that Nietzsche's relationship to the concept is fraught: "Our virtues?" Okay, he says, maybe we can still claim virtues for ourselves, but not in the "innocent and straightforward" manner of our forebears. "*If* we are to have virtues," he says, we are presumably to have only those which have "learned best to be compatible with our most secret and cordial tendencies, with our hottest needs."[4] For Nietzsche, a virtue, like a moral principle, is just so much "posturing." It smacks of the ballerina's *attitude*.[5] Any characteristic that we might dub a "virtue" would be better off being forgotten altogether: "Blessed are the forgetful, for they will also be 'done with' their stupidities." What happens when, say, my curiosity, is no longer on display *as* a "virtue," indeed, is no longer a part of my social identity or even of my conscious self-understanding but rather has become deeply integrated into my very way of being? Can we speak of a "forgotten" curiosity, and so on, as a *behavioral disposition*? Nietzsche, I think, would even take it a step further and say that we are dealing with *drives* here. Whether or not Nietzsche offers a coherent "drive psychology," as some scholars claim, he certainly employs the concept as an explanatory concept throughout his work. We can get a rough read on what he generally means by the term from the following note.

> Animals follow their drives and affects: we are animals. Do we do something else? Perhaps it is a mere illusion that we follow morality? In truth, do we follow the drives, and morality is just the sign language

---

3 *Beyond Good and Evil*, 227.
4 *Beyond Good and Evil*, 214.
5 *Beyond Good and Evil*, 216. Nietzsche's word is *Attitüde*.

of our drives? What is "duty," "right," "good," the "law"—which life-drives correspond to these abstract signs?[6]

Nietzsche considers himself the first psychologist-philosopher precisely because he alone is not "stuck on moral prejudices and fears," he alone has "dared to descend into the depths" and to understand that the "morphology and *developmental theory of the will to power*" lay right there, in the amoral depths of the drive.[7] Our will to power is our urge to self-actualization. The drive thus aims to "discharge"[8] in a manner that serves to fortify and increase the expression of our power. Another way of saying all of this is that when our drives are "healthy," in the sense that we have seen Nietzsche use that term, we *become who we are.*

Obviously, the concept of the drive is very complex, and I imagine that I have stimulated more questions than I can address here. My point is to encourage the reader to consider that *curiosity, honesty, courage, pathos of distance, solitude,* and *humor* are part of the "morphology" of the *Übermensch.* We can acquire these qualities or traits and cultivate them to the degree of habituation. That is, as with the fluency with which we come to speak our native language, we eventually forget them altogether. This image actually suggests a final way of thinking about them. Bringing together several of the themes just touched on, Nietzsche asks, "What is happiness?" and answers, "the feeling that power is *growing*, that resistance is being overcome." He then underscores his point by refuting what he assumes most of his readers to hold: happiness is "*not* contentment, but power; *not* peace, but war; *not* virtue, but virtuosity (virtue in the Renaissance style of *virtù*, morality-free Virtue—that is, pure excellence or ability)."[9] The German word that I am rendering as "virtuosity" is *Tüchtigkeit*: competency, capability, proficiency. As far as I can make out, it is etymologically related to *Tugend*, virtue, through the verb *taugen*: to be fit, qualified, capable.[10] Virtue, in either of the two contexts that Nietzsche recommends, the Greek elsewhere and the Renaissance here, carries none of the moralizing sense of "virtue." It could not, in fact, be any more distant from the otherworldly

---

6 *NF*–1883, 7[76].

7 *Beyond Good and Evil*, 23.

8 *Dawn*, 119, for instance.

9 *The Antichrist*, 2. Please remember that Nietzsche's "power" does not involve the domination of others, but mastery over oneself (as *will to power*); and that his "war" involves not gunpowder, but *agon*.

10 *Deutsches Wörterbuch von Jacob Grimm und Wilhelm Grimm, s.v.* Tugend, https://woerterbuchnetz.de/?sigle=DWB#1. Accessed August 25, 2023.

heights of morality. It has to do with nothing less than the "salvation of humanity," but in the way that *food*, rather than God, does. Nietzsche says that his concern is "the question of *nutrition*" and elaborates this statement as "nourishment…in order to achieve your maximum of strength, of *virtù* in the Renaissance style of morality-free virtue."[11] It is helpful to think of each of the six qualities as a "virtuosity." That term best captures the multiple senses of "virtue" that, I believe, Nietzsche intends: self-mastery, excellence, potency, character, flourishing. It is also crucial to bear in mind that, as the connection to nutrition indicates, these virtues are wholly a matter for each *individual* and cannot be universalized.

Before we look at each term, Nietzsche's comment on Johann Wolfgang von Goethe (1749–1832) will shed a good deal of light on the nature of the matter at hand. In short, the comment concerns the realization of a generalized *type*. Nietzsche expressed unequivocal admiration for Goethe.[12] It is not Goethe's voluminous poetry, literature, drama, scientific theories, and statesmanship that Nietzsche singles out; it is his very person. As such, the comment points to an *exemplar*, to a person who shows us *what is possible*.

> *Goethe.* Not a German event, rather a European one: a superb effort to overcome the eighteenth century through a return to nature, through an ascent to the naturalness of the Renaissance, a type of self-overcoming on the part of this century.—He carried the Renaissance's strongest instincts within himself: sensitivity, the idolatry of nature, the anti-historical, the idealistic, the unreal, and the revolutionary (the latter is only a form of the unreal). As an aid, he took history, natural science, antiquity, as well as Spinoza, and especially practical activity; he surrounded himself with numerous closed horizons; he did not detach himself from life, he placed himself within it; he was not despondent and took as much as possible on himself, above himself, within himself. What he wanted was *totality*; he fought the division between reason, sensuality, feeling, and will (as was preached in the most abhorrent scholasticism by *Kant*, the very antipode of Goethe); he disciplined himself to wholeness, *he created himself*…In the midst of a delusion-minded age, Goethe was a convinced realist: he said Yes to everything that was akin to him in this—he had no greater experience

---

11 *Ecce Homo*, "Why I Am So Clever," 1.
12 I count over 600 mentions of Goethe in the *Collected Works*.

than that *ens realissimum* [most real being] named Napoleon.[13] Goethe conceived of a strong, highly educated person, skillful in corporality, self-contained, reverent toward oneself, a person who dares to indulge himself or herself with the entire extent of nature's wealth, who is strong enough for this freedom; a person of tolerance, not out of weakness, but of strength because he still knows how to use to his advantage that which would destroy the average nature; the person to whom nothing more is forbidden, unless it is *weakness*, whether called vice or virtue…Such a *freed* spirit stands in the midst of all with a joyful and trusting fatalism, in the *belief* that only the individual is objectionable, that in the whole everything is redeemed and affirmed—*he no longer negates*…Such a belief, however, is the highest of all possible beliefs: I have baptized it in the name of *Dionysus*.[14]

Nietzsche believes that we who live in an increasingly fragmenting, atomizing, individualizing world might want to carefully consider this example of a *whole* person. Goethe himself wrote that "man can achieve so much through the appropriate use of his individual abilities…But he can only accomplish the unique, the wholly unexpected, if all of his qualities unite within him and work together as one."[15] This is an image of wholeness as *integrity*—collectedness, self-containment, and also as soundness and being principled. Of course, not every such self-unified person is worthy of emulation. Imagine,

---

13 On Goethe's account of meeting Napoleon in 1808, the latter famously exclaimed, "*voilà un homme!*"—now there's a man!—on first laying eyes on him. Napoleon repeated the phrase as Goethe was leaving the room after their hour-long conversation. (See *Letters of Goethe*, edited by Edward Bell [London: George Bell & Sons, 1884], lxxxvi). Perhaps Nietzsche had read of Goethe's report to his publisher of his conversation with Napoleon: "Nothing higher and more gratifying could happen to me in my whole life," Goethe said. (See Ben Hutchinson, review of Rüdiger Safranski's *Voilà un Homme! Goethe: Life as a Work of Art*, at the *Literary Review*, https://literaryreview.co.uk/voila-un-homme. Accessed August 27, 2023.) Goethe certainly was taken with the French emperor, telling Eckermann: "Napoleon was the man! Always enlightened, always clear and decided, and endowed with sufficient energy to carry into effect whatever he considered advantageous and necessary. His life was the stride of a demi-god, from battle to battle, and from victory to victory. It might well be said of him, that he was found in a state of continual enlightenment. On this account, his destiny was more brilliant than any the world had seen before him, or perhaps will ever see after him." (See Johann Peter Eckermann and Frédéric Jacob Soret, *Conversations of Goethe with Eckermann and Soret*, translated by John Oxenford, Vol. II (London: George Bell & Sons, 1850), 40. Finally, Nietzsche uses the opportunity to attack yet again one of his favorite targets: "'*Voilà un homme!*'—that meant: 'Now that is a *man*! And I had expected a mere German.'" (*Beyond Good and Evil*, 209.)
14 *Twilight of the Idols*, ""Raids of an Untimely Man," 49.
15 *Goethe: The Collected Works*, vol. 3, "Winckelmann and His Age," 100f.

for instance, the extraordinary force of nature that "that most real being named Napoleon" must have been. Born into the social, ethnic, and political periphery of France, feeling himself a perpetual outsider, treated with little respect, Napoleon went on to effect change in Europe and beyond that is felt to this day. Yes, millions and millions of soldiers, civilians, and animals died gruesome deaths in the process. Yes, his armies unleashed untold destruction and committed inhuman atrocities along the way to world domination. But we must ask our all-too-Nietzschean question once again: does that make him any less impressive? When all is said and done, Nietzsche certainly does not recommend a person like Napoleon. He describes him as "Napoleon, this synthesis of *inhuman* [*unmensch*] and *overhuman* [*Übermensch*]."[16] In fact, he says more or less the same thing about every one of his "predators" that most of us feel queasy about (Niccolò Machiavelli, Cesar Borgia, Alcibiades, Julius Caesar, Friedrich II, the blonde beasts). As always, Nietzsche knows (intends?) that he will likely offend with his provocations; but for him, making his point outweighs regard for the reader's sensitivity: "Those to whom I confided that they should sooner look even for a Cesare Borgia than for a Parsifal, could not believe their ears."[17] They could not believe their ears because they were accustomed to hearing sung the praises of men with weak impulses and checked drives like Parsifal, indeed, of "virtuous" men overcome with *ressentiment*. Neither could they (we) stomach the thought that the Borgias of the world were anything but *pure inhumans*. In any case, it might put some of us at ease to know that Nietzsche finds a crucial fault with these figurative and literal blonde beasts: they are devoid of "creative self-restraint."[18] In the end, they lack wholeness. Hence, for Nietzsche, it will always be a Goethe over a Borgia.

Let us now turn to the six "morality-free virtues." I present them as interrelated drives that build on one another. I think the case can be made that Nietzsche would see them as drives; that they are sequential, however, is my invention. I present them as I do to demonstrate how the individual drives might be understood as an interconnecting whole. Indeed, Nietzsche uses a pregnant alchemical metaphor that might suggest such an approach. Portraying the expert or scholar, he presents an image of an "enmeshed network of very different drives and impulses, an absolute impure metal."[19]

---

16 *On the Genealogy of Morals*, 2.16.
17 *Ecce Homo*, "Why I Write Such Good Books," 1.
18 *Untimely Meditations*, "Schopenhauer as Educator," 3.
19 *Untimely Meditations*, "Schopenhauer as Educator," 6.

As in chemistry, a key feature to success is thus proper *integration* of the elements.

However we reckon these six *virtùs*, they just might help to move us along on our own journey from *unmensch* to *Übermensch* and even, who knows, to *becoming who we are.*

CURIOSITY

It all begins with curiosity. This is how it is done: "First and foremost, take a strong and increasingly heightened curiosity, one that seeks adventures of knowledge, the incessantly stimulating force of the new and rare in contrast to the old and boring."[20] Indeed, the German term, *Neugier*, suggests a lust *(Gier)* for the new *(neu)* bordering on the immoderate. The term I translate as "force" *(Gewalt)* can also mean "violence." *Gier* was, in fact, the biblical translation of Latin *cupiditas* (avarice), one of the seven deadly sins.[21] Interestingly, Nietzsche also has in mind essential qualities that English *curiosity* brings out, for instance: careful attention to detail; avidity; choosiness; diligence; desire to see or learn what is rare, strange, or unknown. Finally, the connection of the word to *care* via Latin *cura* is central to Nietzsche's conception of curiosity.[22]

So why does it all begin with curiosity? Until this *"drive to knowledge"*[23] begins to swell in us, we are content with marching along with the herd. When it erupts, our tragedy begins. That inescapable burst of curiosity heralds the birth of our intellectual conscience. It augurs our exit from a condition that Nietzsche considers "despicable," namely, "to stand in the midst of this *rerum concordia discors* [discordant harmony of things] and the whole wonderful uncertainty and ambiguity of existence *without questioning*, without trembling with the longing and rapture of questioning."[24] To possess Nietzschean curiosity is to be irreversibly slammed by *the rapture of questioning.* This catalyzes in "us" (Nietzsche's esoteric community) a "new passion."

---

20 *Untimely Meditations*, "Schopenhauer as Educator," 6.
21 See *Deutsches Wörterbuch von Jacob Grimm und Wilhelm Grimm*, *s.v.* Gier, https://woerterbuchnetz.de/?sigle=DWB#3. Accessed September 4, 2023.
22 See *Online Etymological Dictionary*, *s.v.* curiosity, https://www.etymonline.com/search?q=curiosity. Accessed September 3, 2023.
23 *Dawn*, 429.
24 *The Gay Science*, 2.

The new passion. Why do we fear and hate a possible regression to barbarism? Because it would make people unhappier than they are? Oh, no! Barbarians of all times have been happier than we are: let us not deceive ourselves about that!—It is rather that our *drive to knowledge* is too strong for us to be able still to value happiness without knowledge or the happiness of a strong, firm madness; it pains us even to imagine such conditions! The restlessness of discovery and conjecture has become as enticing and indispensable to us as *unhappy* love is to the lover: which the lover would for no price exchange for a state of indifference.—Yes, perhaps we, too, are unhappy lovers! Knowledge has transformed within us into a passion that is daunted by no sacrifice and in principle fears nothing but its own extinguishment; we sincerely believe that all of humanity, under the compulsion and suffering of *this* passion, must consider itself more elevated and comforted than before, when it had not yet overcome the envy of the coarser contentment, which [envy] follows from barbarism. Perhaps humanity will even be destroyed by this passion for knowledge!—this thought, too, has no effect on us! Did Christianity ever shy away from a similar thought? Are love and death not siblings? Yes, we hate barbarism—we all prefer the demise of humankind to the decline of knowledge! And finally: if humanity is not destroyed by a *passion*, it will be destroyed by a *weakness*: which does one prefer? That is the main question. Do we want humanity's end to be in fire and light, or in sand.[25]

Is Nietzsche suggesting a direct line from curiosity to an apocalyptic conflagration? As always, a central truth turns slowly in his hyperbolic image. Curiosity generates illumination where the dull grit of "strong, firm delusion" has prevailed. The accumulated effect of such light is the destruction of the world that arises out of that delusion—belief by belief, delusion by delusion. For curiosity directs its fire at all "crude answers."

I am too curious, too *questionable*, too high-spirited to be pleased with crude answers. "God" is a crude answer, an indelicacy committed against us thinkers—in principle, it is only a crude prohibition directed at us: you must not think![26]

---

25 *Dawn*, 429.
26 *Ecce Homo*, "Why I Am So Clever," 1.

That same passage begins with an allusion to the kinds of questions we should and should not give over to curiosity, as well as to how a matter unfurls in curiosity's light. He says, for example, "By no means do I know atheism as a result, and even less as an event: it is understood by me instinctually." Nietzsche did not arrive at his insight that "God is dead" through the severe methods of logical deduction. Neither is atheism a personal or historical occurrence, one that "happens" to some people or epochs but not others. Nietzsche's atheism, his insight into the death of God, is "instinctual" because it ensues from a sustained questioning catalyzed by an insatiable curiosity about why we are as we are. It is also the pressing, existential nature of the issue at hand that drives the questioning into the level of the instinctual. All of this explains, too, why Nietzsche is interested in "psychological questions in general." The "truth" of God or atheism is uninteresting to him. What *is* interesting is how the very idea of "God" (or of "atheism") *functions*, as both a personal and social force, what it enables and determines, what it disables and forecloses. Nietzsche mentions a peculiar "scruple," attending him since youth, that provides for him a basic criterion for what counts as a question: "my curiosity as well as my suspicion had to come to a stop at times at the question of where good and evil actually *originate*." His interest in psychological questions, Nietzsche tells us, "soon transformed my problem into another one." He specifies in a manner that we might consider programmatic for the Nietzschean project in general:

> under what conditions did people contrive these value judgements good and evil? and *what value do these judgements themselves possess*? Have they thus far impeded or fostered human thriving? Are they a sign of crisis, of impoverishment, of degeneration of life? Or the other way around, do they reveal in themselves the fullness, the strength, the will of life, its courage, its confidence, its future?[27]

Nietzsche's "scruple," finally, explains his sustained interest in questions of morality and psychology. It also provides a fundamental rule for curiosity: "I have never contemplated questions that are none—I have not wasted myself."[28] In short, he does *not* ask "boring" questions and *does* ask "interesting" ones. What is a boring question? Virtually every one thus far posed by philosophy and theology—questions concerning logic, the thing-in-itself, the principles of identity and noncontradiction, the transcendental Forms,

---

27 *On the Genealogy of Morals*, Preface, 3.
28 *Ecce Homo*, "Why I Am So Clever," 1.

the Good; God, redemption, sin, the immortality of the soul, the beyond. What is an interesting question? To ears unaccustomed to Nietzsche, the answer will sound flip. A question, for example, that he finds "much more interesting" than those above is one on which nothing less than the "'salvation of humanity'" depends: "the question of *nutrition*." Nietzsche means this literally, figuratively, and *personally*. He asks: "how do precisely *you* feed yourself to attain your maximum of strength, of *virtù* in the Renaissance style, of morality-free virtue?"[29]

Finally, when it all starts to feel too heavy, let us recall our ultimate destination and say, along with our guide, *Yes*!

The allure of everything problematic, the joy of X is, however, too great in more intellectual, more spiritualized people, such that this joy does not repeatedly crash like a bright glow over all crises of the problematic, over all the dangers of uncertainty, even over the jealousy of the lover. We know a new happiness.[30]

HONESTY

Honesty is the one "virtue we free spirits cannot get away from."[31] It is nothing less than the bedrock of the Nietzschean experiment's cardinal practice: *intellectual conscience*. Without honesty, the experiment shrivels into yet another farcical self-help project (and we know what Nietzsche thinks about the improvers of humanity!). Nietzsche encourages us "not to acknowledge anything as being great that is not connected with *honesty against itself*."[32] Honesty must keep a check on "honesty"—it must be careful not to lapse into something lesser, such as rationalization (concerning oneself) or malice (concerning others).

Honesty, in our Nietzschean experiment, is relentless. It is not a quality that makes our lives any *easier*. We should not be surprised if "one day our honesty becomes weary and sighs and stretches its limbs and finds that we are too hard, and prefers to have us be lighter, gentler, like a pleasant vice." The honesty that the Immoralist presents us with is *hard*. The contract that we signed with the Human Mutual Agreement Society stipulates that we *just*

---

29 *Ecce Homo*, "Why I Am So Clever," 1.
30 *The Gay Science*, Preface, 3.
31 And following quotes unless otherwise noted, *Beyond Good and Evil*, 227.
32 *NF*–1880, 7[53].

be nice, that we *pretend not to notice,* that we *just get along.* Nonetheless, hard we remain. This is not, however, the kind of hardness depicted in the caricature of the muscular Nietzsche memes. In an account of the type of hardness that he is proposing to us, Nietzsche employs the ironic tone that he uses when he suspects his readers will likely balk at his recommendation. Let us send as aid to Honesty, he advises:

> whatever devilry we have in us—our disgust of the clumsy and the approximate, our *nitimur in vetitum,*[33] our adventurous courage, our shrewd and spoiled curiosity, our most subtle disguised spiritualized will to power and world-overcoming that covetously rambles and raves over all empires of the future—let us come to the aid of our "God" with all of our "devils"!

The honesty that Nietzsche has in mind entails the unleashing of a quality into thought and into interpersonal relationships (as we will see shortly) that transgresses the accepted norms of society. In being honest, we are making things difficult for ourselves.

> It is likely that because of [our honesty] people will misjudge us and take us for someone we are not: who cares! People will say "their honesty"—that is their devilry and nothing else! Who cares! And even if they were right! Have not all gods up to now been such demons rebaptized and made holy? And what do we ultimately know of ourselves? And what do we know what the spirit that leads us wants to be *called*? (It is a matter of names.) And what do we know of how many spirits we shelter?

We do not know these things because we have been living far too long on the world's side of that "who cares!" What, then, is it, exactly, about honesty that propels us to the other side? Nietzsche does give a name to this spirit that leads us there. I have been calling it *honesty.* The German name is *Redlichkeit.* That name requires that we say more about the spirit it shelters.

---

33 "We strive for the *forbidden.*" From Ovid's *Amores,* III.4:17: "We always strive for what is forbidden: want what is denied/so the sick man longs for the water he's refused." In *Ecce Homo,* Nietzsche uses the phrase in a manner that sheds light on his intended meaning: "I do not refute ideals; I simple put gloves on in their presence…Nitimur in *vetitum*: under the sign of this saying, my philosophy will one day be victorious, for, until now, only one thing has in principle been forbidden: the truth" ("Preface," 3).

Philosopher Vanessa Lemm translates *Redlichkeit* as "probity."[34] Taking a closer look at "probity" will shed a good deal of light on Nietzsche's meaning. Its etymological root is in Latin *probitatem*: "uprightness, honesty," from Latin *probus* "worthy, good." What I find most interesting about the word is its active quality: "*tried* virtue or integrity, strict honesty."[35] For a quality to be *tried* it must be *enacted*. Trying is something *done*, hence the additional meanings "tested, proven." The German noun *Probe* actually contains all of these senses: test, rehearsal, trial, proof. Nietzsche's *honesty* is thus not a mere internal potential: it is an active, externalized charge of far-reaching consequences. As Lemm argues, probity is "lived and embodied truth where the return to nature is oriented towards the future and enables a transvaluation of all values including a transvaluation of human nature."[36] That is, it is through *Redlichkeit* that we see things anew, more *naturally*, beyond the good and evil constructed by the world.

Another crucial feature of Nietzschean honesty is the aspect of *speech*. Embedded within the noun *Redlichkeit* is the verb *reden*, to speak. Honesty is thus manifested through *speaking the truth*—both to ourselves and to others. Lemm and others see in this aspect the influence of the pre-Socratic Cynics on Nietzsche's conception of honesty. Indeed, Nietzsche writes this charged comment in his notebook:

> I am thinking about the first night of Diogenes: all ancient philosophy was directed toward the simplicity of life, and taught a certain lack of need, the most important medicine against all thought of social upheaval. In this regard, a few philosophical vegetarians have done more for humanity than all recent philosophers; and as long as philosophers are incapable of mustering the courage to seek an entirely different way of life and to show through their example, they are worthless.[37]

---

34 See Vanessa Lemm, *Homo Natura: Nietzsche, Philosophical Anthropology, and Biopolitics* (Edinburgh: Edinburgh University Press, 2020). This book and Lemm's *Nietzsche's Animal Philosophy: Culture, Politics, and the Animality of the Human Being* (New York: Fordham University Press, 2009) have been central to my understanding of the far-reaching ramifications of "the animal" in Nietzsche. Likewise, her thesis on the influence of the Cynics on Nietzsche has been highly illuminating for me. She states: "The intimate connection between nature and liberation that the Cynics intuited may have inspired Nietzsche's vision of the philosopher as a *homo natura*" (*Homo Natura*, 37).

35 See *Online Etymological Dictionary, s.v.,* probity, https://www.etymonline.com. Accessed August 31, 2023. Emphasis on "tried" added.

36 Lemm, *Homo Natura*, 31.

37 *NF*–1873, 31[10].

Diogenes (412–323 B.C.E.) is, of course, the Cynic Diogenes of Sinope, the notorious practitioner of the "dog-like" (Greek: *kynicos*) form of philosophy. Contemporaries of the Cynics called them "dogs" with the intent to shame them. But *shame* is not something that concerns a Cynic. And they saw in dogs honorable beings. As a consequence, the Cynics thought the term quite apt and wore it with pride. Like dogs, they shamelessly did everything in public—lived, slept, sought food, had sex, defecated, and urinated. They did not do so in order to shock the public or because they were sociopaths. As Diogenes puts it, "Other dogs bite their enemies, I bite my friends to save them."[38] Save them from what? From suffocating social constraints, from the burden of status, from the fetter of materialism, from the hypocrisy of morality, from the oppression of fabricated need. In a sense, Diogenes ultimately sought to save his friends from the socially inflicted shame of being a *homo sapiens* primate. Everyone urinates. But having been taught to feel shame in this most basic of needs, we hide the act from others. The site of a Cynic urinating in public, their reasoning goes, just might wake you up to the fact that civilization is brutal artifice. By prohibiting public urination, we have enhanced "public health," the reasoning continues, but at what cost to an even greater health? Might there be an element of sickness in our shame before nature? If such reasoning catalyzes in you some insight, the Cynic reasoning continues, you just might find yourself on the path to *eudaimonia*, a flourishing of life permeated by mental clarity. The idea of flourishing while living in a large barrel and possessing nothing more than a thin old cloak, a crooked wooden staff, and a cup,[39] as Diogenes did, must seem utterly preposterous. But the fundamental assumption of the Cynics was that only a contentment that is in agreement with nature can enable genuine flourishing.

The manner in which Diogenes "bit" his friends is significant for our understanding of Nietzsche's conception of honesty. He bit them with *parrhesia*. As far as I can determine, Nietzsche nowhere uses this Greek term; nonetheless, Lemm persuasively argues that *Redlichkeit* is Nietzsche's intended term for *parrhesia*. In short, *parrhesia* involves *speaking frankly and fearlessly*. It was a cornerstone of Athenian democracy, and its absence in the *polis* equaled tyranny. The reader has certainly observed that Nietzsche's

---

38 George Converse Fisk, *Lucilius and Horace: A Study in the Classical Theory of Imitation* (Madison: University of Wisconsin Press, 1920), 279.

39 Diogenes used his cup for drinking. A famous story goes that one day he saw a boy drinking water from a stream by cupping his hands. Realizing the superfluity of his cup, Diogenes threw it away.

very writing attests to his desire for truthful expression. In fact, in case you have not already noticed, he wants you to know that with his books "you attain here and there the highest that can be attained on earth: Cynicism."[40] Cultivating the Cynic drive for honesty, we might have what we need to exit the dead end of civilizational morality and finally create *new* values.

> We should also be *able* to stand *above* morality: and not merely to stand with the anxious stiffness of a person who fears slipping and falling at any moment, but rather to float and play above it! To this end, how could we dispose of art or of the fool?—And as long as you are still somehow ashamed of yourself, you do not yet belong to us![41]

It would be very difficult to find a greater example of an unashamed (yet self-aware and sane) person than Diogenes of Sinope. And this is why Nietzsche was contemplating Diogenes's first night. Considering it more closely, we can glimpse honesty toward oneself in practice. The reference is to the first night that Diogenes spent as a practicing Cynic. His father had been a banker. Diogenes did not take to the streets of Athens out of poverty. He freely chose to do so out of conviction. Still, that first night presented a challenge to him that threw his entire project into question. As he was cozying up with his ragged blanket in his large barrel on the edge of the *agora*, the public marketplace, Diogenes overheard the drinking and singing and laughter and general revelry pouring out of the city's open windows. This caused him to fall "into a train of thought likely to turn him from his purpose and shake his resolution." Why, he asked himself, had he taken on "a toilsome and unusual kind of life" without *having* to do so and thus sitting there "debarred of all the good things"?

> At that moment, however, a mouse stole up and began to munch some of the crumbs of his barley-cake, and he plucked up his courage and said to himself, in a railing and chiding fashion, "What say you, Diogenes? Do your leavings give this mouse a sumptuous meal, while you, the gentleman, wail and lament because you are not getting drunk yonder and reclining on soft and luxurious couches?" Whenever such depressions of mind are not frequent, and the mind when they take place quickly recovers from them, after having put them to flight as

---

40 *Ecce Homo*, "Why I Write Such Great Books," 3.
41 *The Gay Science*, 107.

it were, and when such annoyance and distraction is easily got rid of, then one may consider one's progress in virtue as a certainty.[42]

Like Diogenes, we are not driven to the choices Nietzsche presents to us by *necessity*. There is comfort and protection in the collective. There is pleasure and joy, too. We can get along perfectly well without honesty and all the rest. So why bother? Is it worth the considerable trouble? There is only one way to find out. But it will take courage.

COURAGE

Recall Nietzsche's assessment that "Plato is a coward in the face of reality—thus, he takes refuge in the ideal."[43] This comment gives us a clue as to what Nietzsche takes courage to be. It is, in the first instance, an *intellectual* and *affective* virtue. To *face* reality by *not* taking refuge in the ideal happens in our minds and feelings. Beliefs rooted in "the ideal" also have tremendous ramifications for bodily *action*. The "ideal," as we have seen, involves contrived beliefs about other worlds (like heaven), nonexistent entities (like the soul), transcendental realities (like Plato's forms or Kant's thing-in-itself), and so on. In the same passage where he criticizes Plato, Nietzsche praises the Greek historian Thucydides (c. 460–400 B.C.E.) for having such courage. Thucydides, says Nietzsche, is a cure for the "morality- and idealism-fraud of the Socratic school."

> Thucydides is the great sum, the last manifestation of that strong, strict, hard factuality that lay in the older Hellenistic instinct. *Courage* is what distinguishes such natures as Plato and Thucydides: Plato is a coward—consequently, he takes refuge in the ideal—Thucydides has control of *himself*, consequently he has control of things.[44]

"Thucydides," says Nietzsche, "is the type that stands nearest to me."[45] Thucydides is known for his clear-eyed, hard-nosed, no-nonsense approach

---

42 In Plutarch, *De virtute morali*, 9.5, https://www.gutenberg.org/files/23639/23639-h/23639-h.htm. Accessed August 31, 2023.
43 *Twilight of the Idols*, "What I Owe the Ancients," 2.
44 *NF*–1888, 24[1]
45 *NF*–1880, 6[383]. See also *Dawn*, 168 for a description of what Nietzsche "loves about Thucydides" and why he "honors him higher than Plato." I get the sense that Nietzsche sees much of himself in Thucydides. For example, both the philosopher and the Greek historian

to history writing. Unlike his predecessors and contemporaries, the gods played no explanatory role in his analysis of human affairs. To what, then, should we ascribe historical causality? *To humans!* insisted Thucydides. Not fate, destiny, or divinity, but human behaviors, values, beliefs, desires, fears, self-interest, and so forth, are what drive history. In other words, to put it in contemporary terms, Thucydides was a historical and political *realist*. Nietzsche sums all of this up in a note: "Historian (struggle against the mythical)—Thucydides."[46]

At the end of the passage, Nietzsche offers us a suggestive account of the cardinal feature of such a courageous nature: it is to "have possession of oneself, and consequently to have possession of things." Recall Nietzsche's earlier admonishment "not to forfeit that *freedom over things* which our ideal demands of us."[47]

To possess the drive of *courage* together with the drive that compels us to *honesty* means, in short, that we will continually find that we have wandered away from "the herd." In matters of values, views, thought, speech, aspirations, relations, and more, we will, almost as a matter of course, given the nature of the two drives, take an independent path. It is taking this path that enables our "freedom over things." This is a good place for a thought experiment. Imagine what it would take to be independent in a consequential matter where the majority are against you. The easy way is just to go along— after all, you do not *have* to take an opposing stand. But what if principally *honesty* and *courage* are driving you to act? If the following passage is as autobiographical as it seems to me, Nietzsche must have felt his independence of mind and behavior as a socially treacherous compulsion.

> Independence is for the very few: it is the prerogative of the strong. And whoever attempts it, even with the best right to do so, but without *having* to do so, proves that they are likely not only strong but also daring to the point of exuberance. They enter into a labyrinth, they increase a thousandfold the dangers that life already brings with it; not the least of which is that no one sees with their own eyes how and where they go astray, become isolated, and are ripped to pieces by some cave minotaur of conscience. Assuming that such people are

---

have a broad appreciation for all types of people; they assume that everyone possesses a "quantum of *good sense*" and seeks to discover it, and so on.

46 *NF*–1874, 32[3]. For Thucydides, I consulted Christine Lee and Neville Morley (eds.), *A Handbook to the Reception of Thucydides* (New York: John Wiley & Sons, Ltd., 2015).

47 *The Gay Science*, 107.

destroyed, it happens so far away from the comprehension of others that they can neither feel it nor sympathize with it.—and they [the few] cannot go back! neither can they return to the pity of the people![48]

The image of precariously making our way through a labyrinth on our way to independence is severe enough. Nietzsche goes further and places within this mazelike architectural structure the Minotaur of Crete. Being a ferocious half bull-half man, the minotaur is rendered an apt figure for Nietzsche's "the people" and "others." Manifesting honesty together with courage, you will find yourself in a nomad sphere of uncertain passageways; and around every corner difficulties lie in wait. The only way out of the labyrinth is to find your way through it. And "the others" will lose their inclination to assist your way back. No wonder that the labyrinth is an ancient symbol for perilous transformation.

PATHOS OF DISTANCE

The combined drives of *curiosity, honesty,* and *courage* catalyze the painful realization that we *cannot run with the herd.* Just as we found ourselves in the labyrinth, we now find ourselves with an aversion to the majority, to the mass, the status quo, the conventional, the mainstream: we resign our membership in the Human Mutual Agreement Society. A drive grows in strength that facilitates our labyrinthine journey. This drive is the *pathos of distance.* Again, this drive is not attended by worldly joy. Not immediately, anyway. Ultimately, each of us aspiring perfect readers is, like Zarathustra, "an enemy of the spirit of gravity"[49] and so may well find joy in our knowledge. But a labyrinth has no shortcuts. As a phenomenon of *pathos*, the *pathos of distance* carries within it a charge of grief, sorrow, and pain. We saw this earlier when we considered Nietzsche's statement that what we call "equality" is itself "unequal and laughably superficial."[50] It may be a lovely notion, this liberal democratic equality, but it never lands squarely among actual people. As a policy and a way forward, it is thus a dead end. As we have seen on numerous occasions, Nietzsche wants us to take *difference*

---

48 *Beyond Good and Evil*, 29.
49 *Thus Spoke Zarathustra*, "On the Spirit of Gravity," 1. Like English "gravity," which suggests "graveness," from Latin *gravis*, "heavy, ponderous, burdensome, the German word, *Schwere*, can also mean heaviness, severity, weighty. See *Online Etymological Dictionary, s.v.,* grave, https://www.etymonline.com. Accessed September 2, 2023.
50 *Beyond Good and Evil*, 44.

seriously. Without it, *agon* is shackled and, along with it, revaluation and transformation. If, as Nietzsche implores us, we are to value multiplicity of all kinds, then we cannot avoid yielding to the "order of priority" or rank among people that the *pathos of distance* demands.

I said that it is aversion that propels us from our place in the collective. What is it, more specifically, that causes us to turn away from the herd? When Nietzsche announces that "*nausea* toward people is my danger,"[51] he is showing us a double-edged sword. Nausea toward others is a danger because it can cause us to fall into an inescapable hole of resigned nihilism. No-saying and destruction are necessary, but only as *conditions* for Yes-saying.[52] Given that we are dealing with Nietzsche, "danger" can also be understood ironically, in the sense of being a danger to the status quo. In that case, nausea catalyzes the cultivation of the *Übermensch*. Zarathustra predicts that the hour of contempt will prove to be the most important of our lives.

> Truly, the human is a dirty stream. One must be a sea to absorb a dirty stream without becoming unclean.
>
> See, I teach you the *Übermensch*: that one is this sea; your great contempt can go under in that one.
>
> What is the greatest event that you can ever experience? It is the hour of great contempt. The hour in which even your own happiness turns to nausea, and your reason and your virtue, too.[53]

I wonder how many readers feel aversion not to *the human*, as Zarathustra/ Nietzsche recommends, but to the very suggestion that *the human is a dirty stream*? The image works well with *pathos of distance* because we are all repelled by dirt and filth. And, being so repelled, we can get a better perspective on crucial matters, including whether there is value in the proposition that *the human is a dirty stream*. What might "dirty" mean here? Again, think of colleagues, friends, family members, politicians, historical figures, neighbors—might the notion not have *something* to it? Contempt and nausea create distance, which in turn creates perspective. In yet another fecund image, Nietzsche says that "the devil has the widest perspective on God, which is why he keeps so far away from him—the devil, that is to say, as

---

51 *Ecce Homo*, "Why I Am A Destiny," 6.
52 *Ecce Homo*, "Why I Am A Destiny," 4.
53 *Thus Spoke Zarathustra*, "Zarathustra's Preface," 3.

the oldest friend of knowledge."[54] Like the devil, Zarathustra, high up in his mountain cave, gained the perspective that made him "the first psychologist of the good—consequently—a friend of the evil."[55] Might we, too, see more from the "evil" perspective, one that is not contaminated by the status quo?

A person or group of people are not subject to the *pathos of distance* because of any readily identifiable trait, such as race, ethnicity, or gender: "At first, moral feeling developed in relation to people (high status at the fore!) and only later was it transferred to actions and character traits. The *pathos of distance* is at the very heart of that feeling."[56] The reader should have a sense by now of what it is we are being asked to consider as contemptible in society (the state, capitalism, socialism, newspapers, popular opinion, nationalism, patriotism, democracy, utilitarianism, the education system) and in other people and ourselves (cultural philistinism, herd mentality, mediocrity, asceticism, pity, faith). The question for our philosopher of the stomach is whether any of these terms induce *nausea* in us.

The *pathos of distance* is a complicated drive. It is an instance of what Nietzsche calls "cases where nausea mixes with enchantment."[57] Although he makes that statement in a slightly different context, the characterization applies to the *pathos of distance.* Our curiosity about why things are as they are and not otherwise is sparked by an enchantment with the world. The world catches and holds our attention. It fascinates us. We become curious. Human psychology, the question of *why* people think and act as they do becomes a kind of irritant. Such issues are like Ludwig Wittgenstein's buzzing fly in the bottle—they hold us rapt *and* are irritating. We want to let the fly out of the bottle and have peace. To this end, in the Nietzschean experiment, we become particularly attentive to *morality*. What is it, exactly, that makes *this* "good" and *that* "bad" or even "evil"? Morality, that largely unspoken code of right and wrong, seems to permeate all aspects of our lives: the social, psychological, emotional, political, economic, and more. We know this, moreover, because we observe it. And it is precisely through observing it that a certain disgust sets in. It is not through cool, rational analysis that we begin to feel ourselves distant from others. Contrary to Nietzsche's reputation, it is also not through a feeling of superiority, arrogance, or elitism. Like one of Nietzsche's blinding migraines or debilitating stomachaches, this *pathos* is a dis-ease. And just like the nausea that accompanies severe

---

54 *Beyond Good and Evil*, 129.
55 *Ecce Homo*, "Why I Am A Destiny," 5.
56 *NF*–1885, 1[7].
57 *Beyond Good and Evil*, 26.

physical ailments, *pathos of distance* attends to our insight into the world—into our realizations about human motivation, language use and misuse, social ideology, power dynamics, and so on—drastically complicating our ability to engage socially. And so, the drive to the *pathos of distance* will induce the drive to *solitude*.

SOLITUDE

The drive to solitude has physical, emotional, and strategic aims all at once. It is the means by which we are "released" from our incessant requirement to adapt to the ways of society. By physically stepping away from others, we disentangle ourselves emotionally from the very norms that manipulate our social lives. Thus released, we can better discern the matters that catalyzed our *pathos of distance*. This assumes, of course, that we aim to be "knowers, in the grand and exceptional sense" that Nietzsche has in mind. Such an aspiring knower cannot help but mix nausea with enchantment. Somewhat paradoxically, perhaps, neither can such a seeker of knowledge *of* the world avoid retreating *from* the world.

> Every choice person instinctively seeks his citadel and privacy where he is *released* from the masses, the many, the majority, where he may forget the norm "human," as its exception…Whoever does not occasionally shimmer in all the colors of distress, green and gray with nausea, tedium, pity, gloominess, loneliness, is certainly not a person of higher taste. If we suppose, however, that he does not take all of these burdens and dislikes voluntarily on himself, he evades them perpetually and, as I said, hides himself quietly and proudly in his citadel, well, then one thing is certain: he is not made for, is not bound for, knowledge. For, as a person who is made for knowledge, he would have to say to himself one day, "may the devil take my good taste! but the norm is more interesting than the exception, than me, the exception!"—and he would go *down*, and especially "inside."[58]

Removed from society, we are *released, liberated, saved, rescued,* in a word, *redeemed* from "the many" and their herdlike obedience to "the norm 'human.'" These terms are meanings of Nietzsche's word: *erlöst*.

---

58 *Beyond Good and Evil*, 26.

How are we redeemed? By retreating into our citadel and privacy we may repurchase (Latin: *redimere*) ourselves from society. Only once we have recovered ourselves by purchase can we deliver ourselves from the spiritual death that is blind participation in the world.[59] Nietzsche's understanding of solitude thus brings to mind two ancient senses. The first sense comes from the Skeptic Pyrrho (365–275 B.C.E.). Nietzsche considers Pyrrho to be an example of philosophical "decadence," like Socrates, as well as "a Greek Buddhist."[60] Such language typically spells criticism for Nietzsche. But perhaps "Buddhist" in this instance merely marks a contemplative tendency. For Nietzsche's "citadel and privacy" has elements in common with the Skeptic's *epochē*. Like Nietzsche's perspectivism, the Skeptic's *epochē* involves a suspension of, check on, or pause in judgment by means of setting propositions, viewpoints, conclusions, and so on, in opposition to one another. The term even has a musical connotation that would have thrilled Nietzsche: a moment of vibration.[61] From several remarks in Nietzsche's notebooks, I sense an ambivalence toward Pyrrho and the Skeptics in general. He asks, for instance, "what *inspires* the *Skeptics*?" and then offers an equivocal answer: "a hatred of the dogmatists—or a need for calm, a weariness, as with Pyrrho."[62] How is this answer equivocal? First, Nietzsche himself is nothing if not hostile to the dogmatists. However, second, he usually equates weariness with passive nihilism. And yet, third, he himself possesses *and* is wary of the need for calm. Indeed, one of his most abiding criticisms is that ascetic calm is an escape from the bodily, mental, and emotional energies that precisely constitute *life*. Undeniably, however, Nietzschean solitude is not without its own version of asceticism.

All of the sciences, the natural as well as the *unnatural*—as I call the self-critique of knowledge—is today aimed at dissuading humanity

---

59 See *Online Etymological Dictionary*, *s.v.*, redeem, https://www.etymonline.com. Accessed September 11, 2023, and *Deutsches Wörterbuch von Jacob Grimm und Wilhelm Grimm*, *s.v.*, erlösen, https://www.woerterbuchnetz.de/DWB. Accessed September 11, 2023.
60 *NF*–1888, 15[5] and *NF*–1888, 14[85]. Nietzsche's seemingly critical statements belie a certain affinity for Pyrrho. With a grain of salt, could not the following statement be said of Nietzsche himself? "Pyrrho, the mildest and most patient person who ever lived among the Greeks, a Buddhist although Greek, a Buddha himself, was thrown out of control only once, by whom?—by his sister, with whom he lived: she was a midwife. Since then, philosophers have feared the sister the most—the sister! Sister! sounds so terrible!—*and* in front of the midwife! (Origin of celibacy)." *NF*–1888, 14[162].
61 See *A Greek-English Lexicon*, *s.v.*, ἐποχή, https://www.perseus.tufts.edu/hopper/text?doc=Perseus%3Atext%3A1999.04.0057%3Aentry%3De%29poxh%2F. Accessed September 11, 2023.
62 *NF*–1888, 15[58].

from its previous self-regard, as if it had been nothing but a bizarre self-conceit; one might even say that therein science has its own pride, its own austere form of Stoic *ataraxia*, this hard-won *self-contempt* of humanity as their last, most serious claim to maintain regard for themselves (rightly so, indeed: for the one who feels contempt is still one who "has not forgotten how to respect.") Does this actually *work against* the ascetic ideal?[63]

It does *not* work against the *Nietzschean* ascetic ideal. Nietzsche's seekers of knowledge must first traverse self-contempt before reaching genuine self-regard. They must come to see through the "norm 'human.'" In the first instance, they do this by working in "citadel and privacy," like scientists in their labs, removed from the demands of the world. This is the *epochē*. A certain peace ensues from forfeiting the game of human self-regard. For Nietzsche, the Stoic goal of *ataraxia*, tranquility born of equanimity, is achieved through a forfeiture not of dogma, in general, as with the classical Stoics, but of the particular dogma of the "norm 'human.'" Nietzsche, of course, recognizes that he and his seekers of knowledge engage in a form of ascetic practice. Crucially, however, for him the "ascetic ideal"[64] is not that of traditional contemplative practitioners, namely, silencing the passions, negating the needs of the body, purifying the self, and rejecting the ways of the world. Rather, it is aimed specifically at creating the conditions for practicing the "self-critique of knowledge" and its overall aim: self-overcoming and cultural renewal.

All this talk of asceticism brings to mind the second of Nietzsche's resonances with ancient views of solitude, namely, solitude as a means to *purgation, illumination,* and *unification.* I am referring to the path to perfection devised by the Neoplatonic mystical theologian known as Dionysius the Pseudo-Areopagite (flourished c. 500).[65] I hasten to add that Nietzsche nowhere mentions this path per se, so I do not want to press this point too far. However, the three elements do seem to be present in Nietzsche's conception of solitude. In short, the sequence in Nietzsche goes as follows. *Purgation.* It is only once we come to solitude, to our "citadel and privacy," that we can properly engage the practice of the "unnatural" science of "the self-critique

---

63 *On the Genealogy of Morals*, 3.25.

64 The third essay of *On the Genealogy of Morals* is titled, "What is the Meaning of Ascetic Ideals."

65 Nietzsche does mention Dionysius, albeit in one of the shortest notes in all of the *Nachlass*, which reads in its entirety: "Plato and Dionysius." *NF*–1871, 16[45]. The Neoplatonic monk, Dionysius, should not be confused with the Greek god, Dionysus.

of knowledge." It is through this practice that we purge ourselves of the "norm 'human'" and of all that that purgation entails—release from: morality, herd mentality, transcendental illusion, the need for other worlds, ascetic denial of the emotions and body, the stunting of the human and the taming of the human-animal, and so on. *Illumination.* Our "intellectual conscience" develops. We become inveterate *skeptics*, at least in the fundamental sense of ruthlessly *investigating* matters of importance.[66] We come "to stand in the midst of this *rerum concordia discors* [discordant harmony of things] and the whole wonderful uncertainty and ambiguity of existence" with questioning, trembling with "the longing and rapture of questioning."[67] *Unification.* Thus, attaining a certain *ataraxia*, or tranquility in the midst of the "monster of energy"[68] that is the world, we "want always to learn more, to see the necessity of things as beauty" and so become "one of those people who make things beautiful," declaring along with Nietzsche "*amor fati*: from this moment on, may it be my love!" And "all in all and on the whole," we become one who says *Yes!*[69] To say Yes! is to unify with the world.

It is absolutely crucial to understand that solitude for Nietzsche is not an escape from the world. Nietzsche's affirmation, his Yes-saying, does not entail aloof acquiescence to the way things are. To do so would be to engage in passive nihilism. Solitude is the means to remedy the fact that "the *vita contemplativa*…time for thinking and calmness in thinking is missing" from our lives, together with its lamentable consequence that "no one considers dissenting views anymore: one is content merely to hate them."[70] Such work absolutely *requires* robust engagement in the world. In fact, only someone who can say, "The norm [of humanity] is always more interesting to me than the exception" is "in knowledge far advanced and belongs to the initiated."[71] This is not to say that the initiated then jumps joyously back into the fray of the *vita practica*, the practical life, once she has gained the secret knowledge. The balance between solitude and the world is delicate. To that end, I leave the reader with the following passages for contemplation.

---

66 The primary meanings of the Greek term *skepsis* are "investigation" and "examination." The secondary meanings of "doubt" and "hesitation" develop only with the philosophical school. See σκέψις, https://en.wiktionary.org/wiki/%CF%83%CE%BA%CE%AD%CF%88%CE%B9%CF%82. Accessed September 13, 2023.
67 *The Gay Science*, 1.2.
68 *The Gay Science*, 354.
69 *The Gay Science*, 276.
70 *Human, All Too Human*, 282.
71 *Dawn*, 442.

Do not renounce! To renounce the world without knowing it, as a nun does—that engenders a fruitless, perhaps melancholy solitude. This has nothing in common with the solitude of the thinker's *vita contempla-tiva*: if the thinker *chooses* solitude, he will definitely renounce nothing; rather, to him it would be renunciation, melancholy, and downfall if he had to persevere in the *vita practica*: he foregoes the *vita practica* because he knows it, because he knows himself. Therefore, he dives into *his* water, and thus attains *his* cheerfulness.[72]

Why that which is most near to us becomes increasingly distant. The more we think about everything that has been or will be, the paler becomes everything that is right now. If we live with the dead, and in their dying die with them, then what to us are "neighbors"? We become lonelier—and indeed *because* the whole flood of humanity roars around us. The blaze in us, which belongs to all of humanity, increases constantly—and *that is why* we gaze at that which surrounds us as if it had become more indifferent and shadowy. But our cold gaze *insults.*[73]

The wanderer in the mountains to himself. There are clear signs that you have gone forward and climbed higher: it is now freer and the views are more promising around you than as before, the air blows cooler on you, yet milder, too—you have given up the foolishness that confuses mildness with warmth—your gait has become livelier and more stable; courage and prudence have become entwined—for all of these reasons, your path may now be more lonely and in any case more dangerous than your earlier one, though certainly not to the degree that those believe who watch you, the wanderer, stride the mountains from the misty valley.[74]

SENSE OF HUMOR

Nietzsche is obviously a *very* serious writer. It may be less obvious that he is also a very funny one. There is literally enough comical material in Nietzsche to source a show of philosophical stand-up. Read the following,

---

72 *Dawn*, 440. Interestingly, the German term for "renounce" *(entsagen)* means to "dis-say" or "un-say."
73 *Dawn*, 441.
74 *Human, All Too Human*, "Assorted Opinions and Sayings," 237.

for instance, with the voice of your favorite comedian in mind (for some reason, I hear Sarah Silverman's delivery):

> The most godless utterance emanated from a god himself. The utterance: "There is but one God. You shall have no other gods beside me."—Speaking so, an old wrath-bearded god forgot himself in his jealousy.—And at this utterance, all of the gods laughed and shook on their thrones…And this is how the old gods come to an end, and, truly, a good, joyous god-end it was! For they met their death by—*laughing!*[75]

A bit clunky, sure, but "for those with ears to hear," pretty funny. Here are a few more. Drumroll, please!

> Okay, maybe I'm jealous of Stendhal. After all, he stole my atheism joke: "God's only excuse is that he doesn't exist."[76]

> Humility has its limits. Many people have needed the humility that says: "I believe because it is absurd," sacrificing their reason. But no one, as far as I know, has taken the one step further to the humility that says: "I believe because *I* am absurd."[77]

> *Truth.* No one dies these days from deadly truths anymore: there are too many antidotes.[78]

> Hey, all respect to nannies: but isn't it about time that philosophy be done with the faith of nannies?…Speaking of nannies: Oh Voltaire! Oh humanity! Oh nonsense! "Truth" and the search for truth has something to it; but when a human is all too human about it—"He seeks the truth only to do good"—I bet he finds nothing![79]

---

75 *Thus Spoke Zarathustra*, "On the Apostates," 2. I have taken a few small liberties with the translations here and there. For an excellent collection, see Laurence Lampert, "Nietzsche's Best Jokes," *Nietzsche's Futures*, edited by John Lippitt (London: Palgrave Macmillan, 1999), 65–81.

76 *Ecce Homo*, "Why I Am So Clever," 3.

77 *Dawn*, 417.

78 *Human, All Too Human*, 516.

79 *Beyond Good and Evil*, 34 and 35.

> People ask me when I travel abroad: "Are there German philosophers? Are there German poets? Are there any *good* German books? I blush.[80]

And, finally, a reprise:

> The most gentle and proper man may, if he has a large mustache, sit in its shade, as it were, and feel at ease. Passersby will see him as the *accessory* of a large mustache, and say: a militaristic, cantankerous, potentially violent character—and treat him accordingly.[81]

Nietzsche's books are chock full of humor in numerous forms: parody, slapstick, satire, spoof, farce, wordplay, clever irony, self-deprecation, other-deprecation, hyperbole, bombastic braggadocio, ventriloquism, even dark and gallows. Readers of *Ecce Homo* have reported their annoyance at Nietzsche's bombast, even ascribing his over-the-top approach in that book—"Why I Am So Wise," "Why I Write Such Great Books," and so on—to evidence of his insanity. I read that book over several sessions with a group of people, and *I* can report that it was one of the most mirth-filled times of my life. *Ecce Homo* is funny! It is also profoundly poignant, philosophically sophisticated, and rich in intellectual gems. Like most of Nietzsche's work, *Ecce Homo* is, in short, a literary masterpiece. And humor is a vital aspect of its virtuosic style. No small part of Nietzsche's accomplishment is his rhetorical efficacy; and here, too, humor features centrally. Nietzsche is in superb company in this regard. Think of dark, brooding, existentially profound Samuel Beckett and his self-described "tragicomedy": "Birth was the death of him"; "We are all born mad. Some remain so"; "Nothing is funnier than unhappiness." Think of nightmarish, hallucinatory, absurdist Franz Kafka, whose close friend, Max Brod, "talked of how Kafka found humor in his dark works, especially the chilling *The Trial*, which he thought a hoot, laughing so hard while reading the first chapter aloud, that he repeatedly had to stop to collect himself."[82] Even the almost pathologically *unfunny* Ludwig Wittgenstein reportedly said that "a serious and good philosophical work could be written that would consist entirely of *jokes*." He said this "without being facetious," of course.[83]

---

80 *Twilight of the Idols*, "What the Germans Lack," 1
81 *Daybreak*, "Daybreak, Book IV, Section 381.
82 See Kate Connolly, "Kafka's Jovial Side Revealed," *The Guardian*, https://www.theguardian.com/books/booksblog/2008/jul/03/post26. Accessed September 14, 2023.
83 See Tim Madigan, "Philosophy and Humor," *Philosophy Now*, https://philosophynow.org/issues/25/Philosophy_and_Humor. Accessed September 14, 2023.

Obviously, something serious is at work in such humor. In short, Nietzsche has a penchant for "mixing serious things with jokes, jokes with serious things."[84] Take, for example, the time when Zarathustra was staying in a (humorously named) town called "Colorful Cow." People recommended that he should go hear a certain wise teacher who lived there. This teacher's entire wisdom consisted in virtue and...*sleep*. When Zarathustra arrived, many young people were gathered around the master's feet. Sitting on his teaching chair, thus spoke the wise man:

> Honor and abashment toward sleep! That is the first thing! And stay away from all who sleep poorly and awaken at night! [...]

> No small art is sleep: to that end, it is necessary to keep awake all day.

> Ten times a day must you overcome yourself: that makes for good tiredness and is opium for the soul.

> Sleep taps on my eyes: they become heavy. Sleep caresses my mouth: it remains open. Verily, on soft soles it comes to me, this dearest of thieves, and steals my thoughts: dully I stand there, like this teaching chair.

> But not for long do I so stand: there, already I am lying down.

When Zarathustra heard this teaching, he began to laugh to himself. The thought occurred to him: "This wise man is a fool. I do think, however, that he knows a lot about sleeping...Blessed are the sleepy, for they shall soon nod off."[85]

One of the funny things about this passage is that the Guru of Sleep sounds an awful lot like Zarathustra himself. And I would not be surprised if the chronically sleep-deprived Nietzsche did not come to similar conclusions as the Guru of Sleep himself. Nietzsche is, of course, fully aware of these similarities. The passage thus has a self-deprecating element to it, one that *should* alert the reader to the dangers of Zarathustra's (and Nietzsche's) own gurulike tendencies. When Zarathustra (and Nietzsche) starts straying into "improvers of humanity" territory, it is best to start laughing at him as just

---

84 Babich, "Nietzsche's Zarathustra and Parodic Style," 59. Babich is quoting Erasmus on Lucian.
85 *Thus Spoke Zarathustra*, "On the Professorships of Virtue."

another of those "sanctimonious asses."[86] The same goes for us. The path to the *Übermensch* is strewn with perilous pitfalls of ridiculousness regarding our egos. Humor helps us to lighten up.

> I would only believe in a god who knew how to dance.
> And when I beheld my devil, I saw him serious, rigorous, profound, solemn: he was the spirit of gravity—through him all things fall.
> One kills not by wrath but by laughter. Come now, let us kill the spirit of gravity!…
> Now I am light, now do I fly, now do I see myself beneath myself, now does a god dance through me.
> Thus spoke Zarathustra.[87]

Nietzsche asks us to take on the "Olympic vice," and, like the gods, become capable of a "*golden* laughter."

> I would even permit myself an order of priority among the philosophers, each according to the rank of their laughter—up to those who are capable of *golden* laughter. And, supposing that gods philosophize, which conclusion has already urged itself on me—I would not doubt that they thereby know how to laugh in an overhuman [*übermenschliche*] and new way—and at the cost of all serious matters! Gods are inclined to mockery: it seems that they cannot even refrain from laughing during sacred rituals.[88]

Finally, what better way to end our journey through Nietzschean thinking than with a redeeming comment, one *from another perspective*, about a person he constantly derides as a repellent buffoon: Socrates.

> And what, honestly, did he do his entire life long but to laugh at the bumbling incompetence of his noble Athenians, people of instinct like all noble people, who could never give sufficient information about the reasons for their actions? In the end, however, in silence and in secrecy, he also laughed at himself.[89]

---

86 *Twilight of the Idols*, "The 'Improvers' of Humankind."
87 *Thus Spoke Zarathustra*, "On Reading and Writing."
88 *Beyond Good and Evil*, 294.
89 *Beyond Good and Evil*, 191.

I would like to bring *Nietzsche NOW!* to a close by suggesting that a sense of humor is a Nietzschean "morality-free virtue." Even more importantly, I ask the reader to consider that a sense of humor is a necessary *drive* in the work that is the Nietzschean experiment of perpetual self-overcoming. Doing this work, this logic of interconnected virtue-drives goes, you will find more and more humor in the entire massive "monster of energy," in this "brazen magnitude of energy"[90] that is the All, including in yourself. But the laughter serves crucial and necessary ends, such as taking oneself somewhat less seriously than our sincere self-regard recommends; looking at world events from a vastly more extensive vantage point than our narrow self-interest wants to allow; finding more value in other people, nature, and animals than our current ideologies of individual atomization permit. Nietzsche's central concepts of the eternal return and *amor fati*—of acceptance of our lives to the extent that we would do it all over again, just as before—might appear to collapse under the spirit of gravity; for these ideas are nothing if not *heavy*. But what if they were tinged with humor? Might we learn to *dance* with such ideas? Might we surprise ourselves by hearing *Yes! Yes! to life* leaping out of our mouths?

---

90 *NF*–1885, 38[12].

BIBLIOGRAPHY

PRIMARY SOURCES

Abbreviations

BVN = Briefe von Nietzsche [Letters from Nietzsche]
NF = Nachgelassene Fragmente [Posthumous Fragments]
NS = Nachgelassene Schriften [Posthumous Writings]

Nietzsche's Works

I used the *Digitale Kritische Gesamtausgabe von Nietzsches Werken und Briefen* [Digital Critical Edition of Nietzsche's Collected Works and Letters]: http://doc. nietzschesource.org/de/ekgwb. All translations are mine and from this source unless otherwise noted. For readers seeking English editions, the texts that I have referred to are given in the *Gesamtausgabe* as follows:

Beyond Good and Evil: Prelude to a Philosophy of the Future
Dawn: Thoughts on the Prejudices of Morality
Ecce Homo: How to Become What One Is
Human, All Too Human: A Book for Free Spirits
On the Genealogy of Morality: A Polemic
The Antichrist: A Curse on Christendom
The Birth of Tragedy: Or, Hellenism and Pessimism
The Gay Science: ("la gaya scienza")
Thus Spoke Zarathustra: A Book for All and None
Twilight of the Idols: Or, How to Philosophize with a Hammer
On the Pathos of Truth
On Truth and Lies in an Extramoral Sense
Untimely Meditations
   David Strauss: The Confessor and the Writer
   Schopenhauer as Educator
   The Use and Abuse of History for Life
We Philologists

Additional Original Sources

Hymnus an das Leben [Hymn to Life]. Musical composition by Friedrich Nietzsche. YouTube. Accessed August 13, 2022. https://www.youtube.com/watch?v=aOfNaVnFmU8.

The Nietzsche Channel. "Homer's Wettkampf" [Homer's Contest]. Accessed November 5, 2022. http://www.thenietzschechannel.com/works-unpub/five/hcg.htm.

The Nietzsche Channel. "Lectures." Accessed July 17, 2022. http://www.thenietzschechannel.com/lectures/lectures.htm.

The Nietzsche Channel. "Rückblick auf meine zwei Leipziger Jahre" [A Look Back at My Two Years in Leipzig]. Accessed July 17, 2022. http://www.thenietzschechannel.com/works-unpub/youth/1868-rolg.htm.

SECONDARY SOURCES

Abbey, Edward. *One Life at a Time, Please.* New York: Henry Holt and Company, 1978.

Ahmed, Sara. *The Promise of Happiness.* Durham: Duke University Press, 2010.

Alfano, Mark. *Nietzsche's Moral Philosophy.* Cambridge: Cambridge University Press, 2019.

Althusser, Louis. *Lenin and Philosophy and Other Essays.* Translated by Ben Brewster. New York: Monthly Review Press, 2001 [1971].

Anderson, Nate. *In Emergency, Break Glass: What Nietzsche Can Teach Us About Joyful Living in a Tech-Saturated World.* New York: W. W. Norton and Company, 2021.

Animal Kill Clock. 2024. Accessed July 12, 2022. https://animalclock.org.

"AOC's 'Squad' Blasted as 'Marxist Cabal Who Hate the US,' Book Claims." *The Sun.* June 21, 2021. Accessed June 9, 2022. https://www.thesun.co.uk/news/15349099/alexandria-ocasio-cortez-squadmarxist-cabal-new-book.

Aristotle. *Metaphysics.* Accessed January 19, 2023. https://www.csus.edu/indiv/m/merlinos/arimetaiv.html.

Aristotle. *Metaphysics.* Translated with an introduction and commentary by Stephan Makin. Oxford: Clarendon Press, 2006.

Armstrong, John. *Love, Life, Goethe: Lessons of the Imagination from the Great German Poet.* New York: Farrar, Straus and Giroux, 2006.

Avicenna. *The Metaphysics of Healing.* Translated by Michael E. Marmura. Provo: Brigham Young University Press, 2005.

Baatz, Simon. *For the Thrill of It: Leopold, Loeb, and the Murder that Shocked Jazz Age Chicago.* New York: Harper Perennial, 2009.

Babich, Babette. "Nietzsche's Zarathustra and Parodic Style: On Lucian's *Hyperanthropos* and Nietzsche's *Übermensch.*" *Articles and Chapters in*

Academic Book Collections, 56. Accessed August 7, 2023. https://fordham.bepress.com/phil_babich/56.

Baer, Ulrich, "Note on the Translation." *Beyond Good and Evil*. Translated by Ulrich Baer. New York: Warbler Press, 2021.

Beattie, James. "An Essay on the Nature and Immutability of Truth in Opposition to Sophistry and Scepticism" (1778).

Bell, Edward. *Letters of Goethe*. London: George Bell & Sons, 1884.

"Billionaires Are $2.2 Trillion Richer Since 2017 Trump-GOP Tax Law." 2023. Americans for Tax Fairness. September 28, 2023. Accessed June 26, 2022. https://americansfortaxfairness.org/billionaires.

Blaxland, Beth. "Humans are Apes—Great Apes." Australian Museum. August 26, 2022. Accessed April 7, 2024. https://australian.museum/learn/science/human-evolution/humans-are-apes-great-apes.

Blow, Charles. "The War On Wokeness." *The New York Times,* November 10, 2021.

Bodle, Andy. "How New Words Are Born." *The Guardian*. February 4, 2016. Accessed June 26, 2022. https://www.theguardian.com/media/mind-your-language/2016/feb/04/english-neologisms-new-words.

Brobjer, Thomas H. "Nietzsche's Forgotten Book: The Index to *Rheinisches Museum für Philologie*." *New Nietzsche Studies* 4 (2000): 157–161.

Brobjer, Thomas H. "Nietzsche's Reading About Eastern Philosophy." *Journal of Nietzsche Studies,* no. 28 (Autumn 2004): 3–35.

Brobjer, Thomas H. *Nietzsche's Philosophical Context: An Intellectual Biography*. Champaign: University of Illinois Press, 2008.

Brooks, David. "This is How Wokeness Ends." *The New York Times*. Accessed June 9, 2022. https://www.nytimes.com/2021/05/13/opinion/this-is-how-wokeness-ends.html.

Brown, Wendy. "Wounded Attachments." *Political Theory,* vol. 21, no. 3 (August 1993): 390–410.

Brownlee, Dana. "Exhibit A Bill Maher: Why White People Should Stop Using The Term 'Woke'…Immediately." *Forbes*. Accessed June 21, 2022. https://www.forbes.com/sites/danabrownlee/2021/04/19/why-white-people-should-stop-using-the-term-wokeimmediately/?sh=6ba39b717779.

Bruno, Giordano. *The Expulsion of the Triumphant Beast*. Accessed January 2, 2023. https://www.abrahamicstudyhall.org/2021/11/05/the-expulsion-of-the-triumphant-beast-giordano-bruno.

Burnham, Douglass. *The Nietzsche Dictionary*. London: Bloomsbury Academic, 2015.

Calaor, Jesa Marie. *Allure*. January 10, 2023. Accessed January 18, 2023. https://www.allure.com/story/gwen-stefani-japanese-harajuku-lovers-interview.

Chamberlain, Leslie. *Nietzsche in Turin: And Intimate Biography*. New York: Picador Books, 1996.

Chomsky, Noam. *The Common Good*. Berkeley: Odonian Press, 1998.

CNN Freedom Project. "How Much Does A Slave Cost?" January 5, 2017. Accessed

April 7, 2024. https://edition.cnn.com/videos/world/2017/01/05/freedom-project-slave-cost.cnn.

"Combahee River Collective Statement." Accessed March 10, 2023. https://combaheerivercollective.weebly.com/the-combahee-river-collective-statement.html.

"Conformity, Compliance, and Obedience." *Pressbooks.* Accessed March 17, 2023. https://opentext.wsu.edu/psych105nusbaum/chapter/conformity-compliance-and-obedience.

Connolly, Kate. "Kafka's Jovial Side Revealed." *The Guardian.* July 3, 2008. Accessed September 14, 2023. https://www.theguardian.com/books/booksblog/2008/jul/03/post26.

Connolly, Peter, and Hazel Dodge. *The Ancient City.* Oxford: Oxford University Press, 2001.

Cowboy State Daily. September 15, 2022. Accessed January 11, 2023. https://cowboystatedaily.com/2022/09/15/pronouns-controversy-teachers-will-not-get-prosecuted-in-sweetwater-county-for-misgendering-students.

Cowper, William. "Retirement." (1779). *Wikisource.* Accessed April 8, 2024. https://en.wikisource.org/wiki/Retirement_(Cowper).

Cristy, Rachel. "Commanders and Scientific Labourers: Nietzsche on the Relationship between Philosophy and Science." *Proceedings of the Aristotelian Society,* vol. 122, issue 2 (July 2022): 97–118.

Crowley, Matthew. "What Does It Mean To Be Woke." *Politifact.* Accessed March 8, 2023. https://www.politifact.com/article/2023/mar/07/what-does-it-mean-to-be-woke.

Dawkins, Richard. *The Selfish Gene.* Oxford: Oxford University Press, 1976.

Del Caro, Adrian. "Nietzsche, Sacher-Masoch, and the Whip." *German Studies Review,* vol. 21, no. 2 (May, 1998): 241–261.

"Democracy Under Siege." *Freedom House.* 2021. Accessed September 13, 2022. https://freedomhouse.org/report/freedomworld/2021/democracy-under-siege.

Derrida, Jacques. *Spurs: Nietzsche's Styles.* Translated by Barbara Harlow. Chicago: University of Chicago Press, 1979.

Deutsches Wörterbuch von Jacob Grimm und Wilhelm Grimm. https://www.woerterbuchnetz.de/DWB.

"Divided America." *The Associated Press.* June 6, 2016. Accessed December 19, 2022. https://www.ap.org/media-center/press-releases/2016/divided-america-series-to-explore-tensions-underlying-campaign.

Dreher, Rod. "Why are Conservatives in Despair? *The American Conservative.* 2021. Accessed June 9, 2022. https://www.theamericanconservative.com/dreher/why-are-conservatives-in-despair.

Eckermann, Johann Peter, and Frédéric Jacob Soret. *Conversations of Goethe with Eckermann and Soret.* Translated by John Oxenford. London: George Bell & Sons, 1850.

Eco, Umberto. *Six Walks in the Fictional Woods.* Cambridge: Harvard University Press, 1994.

Ehrenreich, Barbara. *Bright-Sided: How the Relentless Promotion of Positive Thinking Has Undermined America.* New York: Metropolitan Books, 2009.

Emerson, Ralph Waldo. *Representative Men.* "Plato; Or, The Philosopher." Emerson Central. Accessed August 9, 2022. https://emersoncentral.com/texts/representative-men/plato-or-the-philosopher.

Emerson, Ralph Waldo. "Nature." Emerson Central. Accessed August 20, 2023. https://emersoncentral.com/texts/nature-addresseslectures/nature2/chapter1-nature.

Enloe, Chris. "AOC attacks members of her own party." *Blaze Media.* June 6, 2022. Accessed June 26, 2022. https://www.theblaze.com/news/alexandria-ocasio-cortez-rant-democrats-latinx.

Equidem. "The Legacy of Qatar FIFA World Cup." Accessed April 7, 2024. https://www.equidem.org/blogs/the-legacy-of-qatar-fifa-world-cup-2022.

Fisk, George Converse. *Lucilius and Horace: A Study in the Classical Theory of Imitation.* Madison: University of Wisconsin Press, 1920.

Fisher, Mark. *Capitalist Realism: Is There No Alternative?* Winchester: Zero Books, 2009.

Förster-Nietzsche, Elizabeth. *The Life of Nietzsche*, vol. 2. Translated by Paul V. Cohn. New York: Sturgis and Walton Company, 1915.

"Friedrich Nietzsche." *Incels Wiki.* Accessed August 9, 2023. https://incels.wiki/w/Friedrich_Nietzsche.

Frost, Robert. "The Most of It." internetPoem. Accessed July 17, 2022. https://internetpoem.com/robert-frost/the-most-of-it-poem.

Gagnon, Jean-Paul. "2, 234 Descriptors of Democracy: An Update to Democracy's Ontological Pluralism." *Democratic Theory*, no. 5, vol. 1. 2018: 92–113.

Gerhardt, Volker. "Nachwort." *Zur Genealogie der Moral.* Stuttgart: Philipp Reclam GmbH & Co., 2020.

Gildersleeve, Basil. "Friedrich Ritschl." *The American Journal of Philology*, vol. 5, no. 3 (1884): 340–341.

Gilman, Sander L., ed. *Conversations with Nietzsche: A Life in the Words of His Contemporaries.* Translated by David G. Parent. Oxford: Oxford University Press, 1987.

Global Language Monitor, The. 2022. Accessed June 26, 2022. https://language-monitor.com.

Global Slavery Index. Accessed December 31, 2022. https://www.globalslaveryindex.org/2018/findings/global-findings.

"Global State of Democracy Report 2021." Accessed November 1, 2022. https://www.idea.int/gsod.

Goldberg, Michelle. "The Right's Obsession with Wokeness is a Sign of Weakness." *The New York Times*, Opinion, March 10, 2023.

Goldman, Emma. *Living My Life.* The Anarchist Library. 2019. Accessed August 17, 2023. https://theanarchistlibrary.org/library/emma-goldman-living-my-life.

Günther, Karl-Heinz. 1988. "Profiles of Educators: Wilhelm von Humboldt

(1767–1835).” *Prospects,* vol. 18: 127–136. Accessed July 15, 2022. https://doi. org/10.1007/BF02192965.

“Gwen Stefani Sparks Outrage with Shocking Announcement: ‘I am Japanese.’” *MSN.* Accessed January 11, 2023. https://www.msn.com/en-us/news/world/ gwen-stefani-sparks-outrage-withshocking-announcement-i-am-japanese/ ar-AA16roSx.

Harriot, Michael. “Weaponizing ‘Woke’: A Brief History of White Definitions.” *The Root.* 2021. Accessed June 9, 2022. https://www.theroot.com/ weaponizing-woke-an-brief-history-of-whitedefinitions-1848031729.

Hartmann, Georg. “*Übermensch.*” In C. Auffarth, *et. al.* eds. *Metzler Lexikon Religion.* J. B. Metzler: Stuttgart, 2005.

Hartmann, Micah. “Does Slavery Exists in America Today?” *The Exodus Road.* October 12, 2018. Accessed December 31, 2022. https://theexodusroad.com/ does-slavery-exist-in-america-today.

Hellie, Richard. “Slavery.” *Encyclopedia Britannica.* 2018. Accessed December 31, 2022. https://www.britannica.com/topic/slavery-sociology.

Hemelsoet, D., K. Hemelsoet, and D. Devreese. “The neurological illness of Friedrich Nietzsche,” *Acta Neurologica Belgica,* vol. 108, no. 1 (2008): 9–16. Accessed August 9, 2022. https://pubmed.ncbi.nlm.nih.gov/18575181.

Heraclitus. “Fragments of Heraclitus.” *Wikisource.* Accessed November 5, 2022. https://en.wikisource.org/wiki/Fragments_of_Heraclitus#Fragment_121.

Hess, Amanda. “Earning the ‘Woke’ Badge,” *The New York Times.* April 19, 2016. Accessed June 9, 2022. https://www.nytimes.com/2016/04/24/magazine/earn-ing-the-woke-badge.html.

Higgins, Kathleen. “The Whip Recalled.” *Journal of Nietzsche Studies,* no. 12 (Autumn 1996): 1–18.

Hodal, Kate. “One in 200 People Is a Slave. Why?” *The Guardian.* February 25, 2019. Accessed December 31, 2022. https://www.theguardian.com/news/2019/ feb/25/modern-slavery-trafficking-persons-one-in-200.

“How Millennials Get News.” American Press Institute. March 16, 2015. Accessed June 9, 2022. https://www.americanpressinstitute.org/publications/reports/ surveyresearch/millennials-news.

Hunt, Peter. “Slavery.” *The Cambridge World History,* vol. 4. “A World with States, Empires and Networks 1200 BCE–900 CE.” Cambridge: Cambridge University Press, 2015: 76–100.

Illing, Sean. “Wokeness is a Problem and We All Know It.” *Vox.* April 17, 2021. Accessed June 8, 2022. https://www.vox.com/22338417/ james-carvilledemocratic-party-biden-100-days.

Jones, Ernest. *The Life and Work of Sigmund Freud,* vol. 2. New York: Basic Books, 1955.

Janz, C. P. *Friedrich Nietzsche: Biographie,* 3 vols. Munich and Vienna: Carl Hanser Verlag, 1978.

Jardina, Ashley. *White Identity Politics.* Cambridge: Cambridge University Press, 2019.

Kant, Immanuel. *Kritik der reinen Vernunft*. Internet Archive. Leipzig: F. Meiner. 1919. Accessed April 13, 2023. https://archive.org/details/kritikderreinenv19kant/mode/2up.

Karson, Michael. "The Psychology of 'Wokeism.'" *Psychology Today*. August 9, 2021. Accessed June 27, 2022. https://www.psychologytoday.com/us/blog/feeling-our-way/202108/the-psychology-wokeism.

Kaufmann, Eric. *Whiteshift: Populism, Immigration, and the Future of White Majorities*. New York: Abrams Press, 2019.

Kaufmann, Walter. *Nietzsche: Psychologist, Philosopher, Antichrist*. Princeton: Princeton University Press, 2013 [1950].

Kaufmann, Walter. *The Portable Nietzsche*. London: Penguin Books, 1984 [1954].

Kaufmann, Walter. *Basic Writings of Nietzsche*. New York: The Modern Library, 2000 [1967].

King, Martin Luther, Jr. "The American Dream." Accessed April 7, 2024. https://www.americanrhetoric.com/speeches/mlkihaveadream.htm.

Koberg, Kelsey. "The Woke Mob is Everywhere." *Fox News*. July 23, 2021. Accessed June 8, 2022. https://www.foxnews.com/media/the-woke-mob-is-everywhere-heres-where-it-came-from-and-victor-davis-hansons-solution-for-stopping-it.

Kogan, Terry S. "Sex Separation: The Cure-All for Victorian Social Anxiety." In Harvey Molotch and Laura Norén, *Toilet: Public Restrooms and the Politics of Sharing*. New York: New York University Press, 2010: 145–154.

Lampert, Laurence. "Nietzsche's Best Jokes." In *Nietzsche's Futures*. Edited by John Lippitt, 65–81. London: Palgrave Macmillan, 1999.

Lee, Christine, and Neville Morley, eds. *A Handbook to the Reception of Thucydides*. New York. John Wiley & Sons, Ltd., 2015.

Lemm, Vanessa. *Nietzsche's Animal Philosophy: Culture, Politics, and the Animality of the Human Being*. New York: Fordham University Press, 2009.

Lemm, Vanessa. *Homo Natura: Nietzsche, Philosophical Anthropology, and Biopolitics*. Edinburgh: Edinburgh University Press, 2020.

Lemm, Vanessa. "Nietzsche: Truth, Embodiment and Consciousness." Institute of Philosophy and Technology. YouTube. Accessed April 13, 2023. https://www.youtube.com/watch?v=p7QQDJfDN64&t=2441s.

LeTourneau, Nancy. "Republicans are the Party of the Wealthy Elite." *Washington Monthly*. October 22, 2019. Accessed June 26, 2022. https://washingtonmonthly.com/2019/10/22/republicans-are-the-party-of-the-wealthy-elite-2.

Lucian. Translated by A. M. Harmon. Loeb Classical Library 14. Cambridge, MA: Harvard University Press, 1913.

Madigan, Tim. "Philosophy and Humor." *Philosophy Now*. Accessed September 14, 2023. https://philosophynow.org/issues/25/Philosophy_and_Humor.

Mainländer, Philipp. *Die Philosophie der Erlösung*. Erster Band. Berlin, 1876. Internet Archive. Accessed April 16, 2023. https://archive.org/details/mainlander-philipp-philosophie-der-erlosungband-1/mode/2up.

Marchand, Suzanne L. *Down from Olympus: Archaeology and Philhellenism in*

Germany, 1750–1970. Princeton: Princeton University Press, 1996.

McMillian, Angela. "Slavery in America." Library of Congress. Accessed April 8, 2024. https://guides.loc.gov/slavery-in-america.

Media Bias/Fact Check. Accessed July 27, 2022. https://mediabiasfactcheck.com.

"Modern Slavery: The True Cost of Cobalt Mining." *Human Trafficking Search.* Accessed January 2, 2023. https://humantraffickingsearch.org/resource/modern-slavery-the-true-cost-of-cobalt-mining.

Muldoon, Ryan. *Social Contract Theory for a Diverse World: Beyond Tolerance.* New York: Routledge, 2016.

Myers, Fraser. "Meet the Anti-Woke Left," *Spiked.* Accessed June 9, 2022. https://www.spiked-online.com/2019/07/04/meet-the-anti-woke-left.

"My Truth." *Urban Dictionary.* 2020. Accessed June 26, 2022. https://www.urban-dictionary.com/define.php?term=My%20Truth.

Neves, Juliano C. S. "Nietzsche for Physicists." *Philosophia Scientiæ,* 23–1 (2019): 185–201.

"New Woke CIA Ad." *BreakThrough News.* May 5, 2021. Accessed June 9, 2022. https://www.breakthroughnews.org/post/new-woke-cia-ad.

Nicholson, Rebecca. "Poor Little Snowflake." *The Guardian.* Accessed October 23, 2023. https://www.theguardian.com/science/2016/nov/28/snowflake-insult-disdain-young-people.

"Nibbidā." *The Wisdom Library.* August 10, 2008. Accessed August 12, 2023. https://www.wisdomlib.org/definition/nibbida.

"Nietzsche und das Archiv Seiner Schwester. Kritiken Und Rezensionen: Walter Benjamin." Accessed October 13, 2023. https://www.textlog.de/benjamin/kritik/nietzsche-archiv-schwester.

"No Preferred Racial Term Among Most Black, Hispanic Adults." *Gallup.* August 4, 2021. Accessed June 26, 2022. https://news.gallup.com/poll/353000/no-pre-ferred-racial-term-among-black-hispanic-adults.aspx.

Online Etymological Dictionary. https://www.etymonline.com.

Oppel, Frances Nesbitt. *Nietzsche and Gender: Beyond Man and Woman.* Charlottesville: University of Virginia Press, 2005.

Our World in Data. Accessed July 17, 2023. https://ourworldindata.org/grapher/number-of-deathsper-year.

Parkhurst, William A. B. "Does Nietzsche Have a 'Nachlass'?" *Nietzsche-Studien* 49 (2020): 216–257.

Perkin, Harold. *The Origins of Modern English Society.* London: Routledge, 1969.

Pierce, Charles P. "The Real Cost of the I-phone in Your Pocket." *Esquire.* October 7, 2016. Accessed January 2, 2023. https://www.esquire.com/news-politics/politics/news/a49363/cobalt-miners-congo-smartphones.

Plato. *Plato in Twelve Volumes*, vol. 1. Translated by Harold North Fowler. Cambridge: Harvard University Press, 1966.

Plutarch. *De virtute morali,* 9.5. Project Gutenberg. 2007. Accessed August 31, 2023. https://www.gutenberg.org/files/23639/23639-h/23639-h.htm.

Prideaux, Sue. *I Am Dynamite!: A Life of Friedrich Nietzsche.* New York: Tim Duggan Books, 2018.

"Prison Inmates Are Fighting California's Fires, But Are Often Denied Firefighting Jobs After Their Release." *CNN.* Accessed December 31, 2022. https://www.cnn.com/2019/10/31/us/prison-inmates-fightcalifornia-fires-trnd/index.html.

Prison Policy Initiative. Accessed December 31, 2022. https://www.prisonpolicy.org/blog/2017/04/10/wages.

"Prisoners in 2021." *Bureau of Justice Statistics.* Accessed December 31, 2022. https://bjs.ojp.gov/library/publications/prisoners-2021-statistical-tables.

"Qatar World Cup of Shame." 2016. Amnesty International. March 31, 2016. Accessed January 2, 2023. https://www.amnesty.org/en/latest/campaigns/2016/03/qatar-world-cup-of-shame.

Ratner-Rosenhagen, Jennifer. *American Nietzsche: A History of an Icon and His Ideas.* Chicago: University of Chicago Press, 2012.

Ravitz, Jessica. "Why Do Americans Love the Dalai Lama?" *CNN.* Accessed January 9, 2023. https://www.cnn.com/2010/LIVING/02/22/americans.love.dalai.lama/index.html.

Retta, Mary. "How to Radicalize Your Parents." *Vice.* February 4, 2021. Accessed June 10, 2022. https://www.vice.com/en/article/n7v53z/howto-radicalize-your-parents-prison-abolition-anti-capitalism.

Reuters. Accessed November 3, 2022. https://www.reuters.com/graphics/USA-ELECTION/SENATE-FUNDRAISING/yxmvjeyjkpr/.

Rheinisches Museum für Philologie. Accessed July 17, 2022. https://rhm.phil-fak.uni-koeln.de/en/inhaltsverzeichnisse/rhm-1860-1869.

Ringer, Fritz K. "Higher Education in Germany in the Nineteenth Century." *Journal of Contemporary History*, vol. 2, no. 3, "Education and Social Structure" (1967): 123–138.

Rosenblatt, Kalhan. *NBC News.* Accessed January 18, 2023. https://www.nbcnews.com/news/asian-america/gwenstefani-says-japanese-response-cultural-appropriation-charges-rcna65203.

Ruehl, Martin A. "In Defence of Slavery: Nietzsche's Dangerous Thinking." *Independent.* Accessed December 30, 2022. https://www.independent.co.uk/news/long_reads/nietzsche-ideas-superman-slaverynihilism-adolf-hitler-nazi-racism-white-supremacy-fascism-a8138396.html.

Rukgaber, Matthew. *Nietzsche in Hollywood: Images of the Übermensch in Early American Cinema.* New York: State University of New York Press, 2022.

Safranski, Rüdiger. *Nietzsche: A Philosophical Biography.* New York: W. W. Norton and Company, 2003.

Shearer, Elisa. "More than eight-in-ten Americans get news from digital devices." Pew Research Center. January 12, 2021. Accessed April 7, 2024. https://www.pewresearch.org/short-reads/2021/01/12/more-than-eight-in-ten-americans-get-news-from-digital-devices.

Sherer, Michael. "Battle of the Bathroom." *Time.* May 19, 2016. Accessed January

11, 2023. https://time.com/4341419/battle-of-thebathroom.

Smith, Terrance. 2020. "Timeline: Voter Suppression in the US from the Civil War to Today." *ABC News.* August 20, 2020. Accessed November 1, 2022. https://abcnews.go.com/Politics/timeline-voter-suppression-us-civil-war-today/story?id=72248473.

Springer, Kimberly. *Living for the Revolution: Black Feminist Organizations, 1968–1980.* Durham: Duke University Press, 2005.

"The Meaning of 'Wokeness,' Explained." *The Elm.* April 2021. Accessed May 24, 2002." https://blog.washcoll.edu/wordpress/theelm/2020/10/the-meaning-of-wokeness-explained.

"The Use of 'LatinX' by Hispanic Voters." *Politico.* Accessed June 26, 2022. https://www.politico.com/f/?id=0000017d-81be-dee4-a5ff-efbe74ec0000.

Thoreau, Henry David. *Journal, 1850–1851. Project Gutenberg.* Accessed July 17, 2022. https://www.gutenberg.org/cache/epub/59031/pg59031-images.html.

Tuncel, Yunus. "Nietzsche's Aphoristic Style: The Art of Concise and Polemical Writing." *The Agonist*, vol. IX, nos. I and II (Fall 2015–Spring 2016). Accessed June 1, 2022. http://www.nietzschecircle.com/Nietzsche_and_La_Rochefoucauld_Yunus.html.

Ulatowski, Joseph. "Folk-Theoretic Foundations of Truth Theory." In *Commonsense Pluralism about Truth.* New York: Palgrave Macmillan, 2017. Accessed April 13, 2023. https://doi.org/10.1007/978-3-319-69465-8_1.

Vasquez, Everett. "What Is Identity Politics? Definition and Effects." *Polling Place Photo Project.* September 9, 2020. Accessed January 17, 2023. https://polling-placephotoproject.org/what-is-identity-politics-definition-and-effects.

Voices of Democracy: The U.S. Oratory Project. Accessed April 12, 2023. https://voicesofdemocracy.umd.edu/clarence-darrow-plea-for-leopold-and-loeb-22-23-and-25-august-1924-speech-text.

"Voter Turnout." *FairVote.* Accessed November 1, 2022. https://fairvote.org/resources/voter-turnout.

Wai, Jonathan, and Kaja Perina. "Expertise in Journalism: Factors Shaping a Cognitive and Culturally Elite Profession." *Journal of Expertise.* Accessed June 27, 2022. https://www.journalofexpertise.org/articles/volume1_issue1/JoE_2018_1_1_Wai_Perina.html.

Walker, Mason. "Nearly a quarter of Americans get news from podcasts." Pew Research Center. February 15, 2022. Accessed April 7, 2024. https://www.pewresearch.org/short-reads/2022/02/15/nearly-a-quarter-of-americans-get-news-from-podcasts.

Wanshel, Elyse. "Gwen Stefani Says, 'I'm Japanese' to an Asian Reporter." *Huffington Post.* January 10, 2023. Accessed January 11, 2023. https://www.huffpost.com/entry/gwen-stefani-japanese-allure-interview_n_63bddbe8e4b0d6724fc82241.

Weisberg, Jacob. "Elite Nonsense." *Slate.* October 2, 2010. Accessed June 27, 2022. https://slate.com/news-and-politics/2010/10/the-right-s-favorite-scare-word-is-elitism-what-does-it-mean.html.

Well, C. "How Many Smartphones in the World." *Uniwa*. March 17, 2022. Accessed January 2, 2023. https://www.cwelltech.com/how-many-smartphones-in-the-world.

Westmoreland, John. "Modern Slavery Finds Its Roots in Capitalism." *Counterfire*. Accessed January 2, 2023. https://www.counterfire.org/article/modern-slavery-finds-its-roots-in-capitalism.

"Why Do People Believe in Conspiracy Theories?" PsychCentral. May 28, 2021. Accessed February 12, 2023. https://psychcentral.com/blog/conspiracy-theories-why-people-believe.

Wilamowitz-Moellendorff, Ulrich von. "Zukunftsphilologie! Eine Erwidrung auf Friedrich Nietzsches *Geburt der Tragödie*. Berlin: Gebrüder Borntraeger, 1872.

Wittgenstein, Ludwig. *Tractatus Logico-Philosophicus,* 1921. Accessed January 27, 2023. https://www.wittgensteinproject.org/w/index.php/Tractatus_Logico-Philosophicus_(English).

Yang, Maya. "'Incels' are a rising threat in the US, Secret Service report finds." *The Guardian*. March 16, 2022. Accessed April 7, 2024. https://www.theguardian.com/us-news/2022/mar/16/involuntary-celibates-incels-threat-us-secret-service

Young, Julian. *Friedrich Nietzsche: A Philosophical Biography*. Cambridge: Cambridge University Press, 2010.

Young, Julian. "Nietzsche and Women." *The Oxford Handbook of Nietzsche*. Edited by John Richardson and Ken Gemes. Oxford: Oxford University Press, 2013.

Zanotti, Emily. "NY Dems are Redrawing Congressional Districts." *The Daily Wire*. January 1, 2020. Accessed June 8, 2022. https://www.dailywire.com/news/new-york-dems-are-redrawing-congressional-districts-and-it-could-put-alexandria-ocasio-cortez-out-of-a-job.

Žižek, Slavoj. "A Plea For Leninist Intolerance." *Critical Inquiry*, vol. 28, no. 2 (2002): 542–544.

ACKNOWLEDGMENTS

THE IDEA FOR THIS BOOK AROSE IN A CONVERSATION WITH MARY BAHR, THE publisher and editor-in-chief of Warbler Press. In passing, Mary mentioned some heated culture war issue. Having just read some Nietzsche, I said *Oh, Nietzsche would have something interesting to say about that.* Nietzsche? Really? Hmm. It is not an exaggeration to say that at that very moment, the spirit of *Nietzsche NOW!* was discharged into the world. So, my deep gratitude to Mary for being the provocative coconspirator in bookwriting that she has been for me.

Nietzsche appreciated a "fine feeling for nuances," a quality possessed in abundance by Hannes Schumacher, who painstakingly read through my translations and made many invaluable improvements.

As I was writing the book, I had the pleasure of reading and discussing Nietzsche with a unique group of Hyperboreans in biweekly sessions of a group called "Microdosing Nietzsche," at Incite Seminars. The members of this group helped me to hear the interlacing layers of Nietzsche's rich compositions—seriousness harmonizing with playfulness, bluntness with subtlety, profundity with humor, compassion with tough love, and so much more. Thank you all!

Conversations about my work with my daughters, Alexandra and Mia, give me hope that the next generation will bring boldness, critical intelligence, and care into our precarious future. Finally, I could not do my work at all without the encouragement, support, and loving generosity of my wife, Friederike Baer. For that, I could not be more grateful.

ABOUT THE AUTHOR

GLENN WALLIS holds a Ph.D. in Buddhist Studies from Harvard University's Department of Sanskrit and Indian Studies. Prior to that, he studied at the renowned Institute for Indology and Buddhist Studies at the University of Göttingen, Germany. Wallis has published widely on various aspects of Buddhism. His books include *A Critique of Western Buddhism: Ruins of the Buddhist Real; Cruel Theory\Sublime Practice: Toward a Revaluation of Buddhism; Buddhavacana: A Pali Reader; Basic Teachings of the Buddha; The Dhammapada: Verses on the Way; Mediating the Power of Buddhas: Ritual in the Mañjuśrīmūlakalpa,* and *Non Buddhist Mysticism: Performing Irreducible and Primitive Presence.* He has also published with Warbler Press *How to Fix Education: A Handbook for Direct Action* and *An Anarchist's Manifesto.*

Wallis taught in the religion departments of Brown University, Bowdoin College, and the University of Georgia. In 2006, he gave up tenure to initiate an innovative meditation program at the newly formed Won Institute of Graduate Studies, near Philadelphia. The program trained professionals (teachers, psychologists, nurses, social workers, etc.) to incorporate meditation programs into their work. It emphasized the interconnected necessity for individual and collective solutions to social ills.

In 2011, Wallis founded the groundbreaking blog *Speculative Non-Buddhism* (speculativenonbuddhism.com), which one critic considers "the most strikingly original, penetrating, and provocative writing about Buddhism on the web." To date, the blog has published over 120 long-form critical essays. Its notorious comment section houses over 7,000 comments. With views approaching one million, this influential blog has been written about in several scholarly books and articles and on numerous online sites.

Currently, Wallis codirects Incite Seminars (inciteseminars.com), the counterinstitutional educational cooperative he founded in Philadelphia in 2016. As its tagline, "rigorous & rebellious learning," indicates, Incite Seminars offers spirited public courses on topics relevant to its aim of upsetting the status quo toward a better world for all sentient beings.

www.ingramcontent.com/pod-product-compliance
Lightning Source LLC
Chambersburg PA
CBHW021353090426
42742CB00009B/833